Elizabeth D. Capaldi Phillips
(1945-2017)

We had to call her Betty, in spite of her high powered academic credentials testified to by an endless sequence of publications, a litany of presentations, honors, and awards. She came to every task, whether research, academic administration, student success, publication, institutional organization, university budgets and finance, or institutional advocacy with focus and intensity leavened by charm, imagination, and humor. Betty worked harder than any of us. She wore us out with her enthusiasm and commitment to getting things right. And she inspired us with her unshakable belief that whatever needed doing could be done if we just worked harder, collected the data better, analyzed the information we had more thoroughly, and most importantly, did something useful and significant to move the university forward. .

In looking back over an exemplary person's life we can never capture it fully whether we recall favorite anecdotes or critical accomplishments. Sometimes, though, it helps to divide up an extraordinary lifetime of achievement into categories, for Betty provided us with what it would have taken at least three ordinary academics to achieve. As we look at each one separately, we need always remember, that Betty pursued all of them simultaneously at the highest level of performance.

Her academic life rests on the foundation of innovative, deep, scientific research in cognitive psychology. We, who encountered Betty along the way, quickly learned that this research involved complex experiments of such significance that the NSF and NIMH provided continuous support for over 35 years and the results of this work appeared in an endless series of scientific articles in specialized journals. The associations of her scientific peers found Betty's work of such importance and her commitment to the profession so significant that they elected her to leadership roles including the presidency of their various organizations such as the American Psychological Society. And her achievements in experimental psychology provided the context and substance of her collaboration on a long running multi-author textbook in the field, now in its fourth edition, and her forthcoming book based on her long career of research in the field on *The Psychology of Eating* (Routledge).

A second simultaneous career evolved from the respect she inspired in her university colleagues, whether first as Head of the Department of Psychological Sciences at Purdue University and then through her leadership of the Institutional Research Office and subsequently Provost at the University of Florida. But it didn't stop there. The remarkable achievements in university administration, the innovative programs for student success begun at Florida and further developed at Arizona State University, the exceptional commitment to the development of university research seen in the dramatic expansion of funded investigations and research institutes and centers at UF, at the University at Buffalo and the SUNY system, and then in the expansion of the Arizona State University research portfolio, all testify to her ability to create, identify, support, inspire, energize, and, yes, drive high performance initiatives in a wide range of academic disciplines. Her commitment to university research prompted her sustaining work on the annual *Top American Research Universities* report since its first edition in 2000. Students recognized her commitment to their academic success awarding her elected membership in the *Friends of Students Hall of Fame* and her selection by Student Government for the *C. Arthur Sandeen Improving the Quality of Life Award*, both at the University of Florida.

But as if these two were not enough, Betty's colleagues discovered early her third gift of explaining complicated things to different audiences. Group after group, organization after organization, inundated her with invitations from academic, scientific, and public groups to lecture, talk, and consult on topics ranging from the science of eating to the best systems for managing university budgets to the process of enhancing productivity and quality in complex university settings. She could explain anything to anyone in a fashion that captured the essence of the subject and the importance of the issues with a style that held the audience's interest and inspired their understanding. Legislators, donors, faculty, administrators, students, trustees, and general audiences all fell under her magic explanatory spell.

When we try to capture this remarkable individual's life and work we can only hope to provoke the memories of her friends, colleagues, collaborators, and beneficiaries. But perhaps a fine token of her remarkable talents can be found in a recent initiative: *Eating Psychology with Betty,* a TV production sponsored on PBS by Arizona State University. In thirteen full episodes from March to October 2016, Betty took a lifetime of scientific research, writing, and teaching on nutrition, eating, and obesity, and applied it to how we should think about food, diet, and cooking. Here, in these thirteen episodes, we can see her expertise, her charm, and her skillful ability to capture both research-validated substance and human interest and engagement. As always, as she works with her colleagues on the show, we can see so clearly that she knows whereof she speaks, and we recognize that we should do what, in her graceful engaging way, she tells us we should do.

All of us who had the opportunity to participate in one or another aspect of Betty's world know that we were provided a unique privilege, and for that she will remain always in our memories.

The Advisory Board and Staff of The Center for Measuring University Performance
Arizona State University and the University of Massachusetts Amherst
September 23, 2017

Table of Contents

INTRODUCTION

This edition of the *Top American Research Universities* follows the format and structure of previous reports and includes an introductory essay and an extensive display of tables that illustrate the measures we have followed for many years. As is our practice, we also include a discussion of data issues and adjustments required to maintain reasonable comparability across the years of this project. The Center for Measuring University Performance (MUP) also maintains the data that underlie and extend the materials included in this printed report at the MUP website [http://mup.asu.edu].

As most of our readers know, this project has enjoyed strong support from multiple institutions from its beginning at the University of Florida and the University of Florida Foundation in 2000 and continuing with additional assistance over the years from the University at Buffalo, Arizona State University, and the University of Massachusetts Amherst and we appreciate their continuing commitment to our work.

However, it is with great sadness that we report the passing of Mr. Lewis M. Schott (1922-2017) who was our initial benefactor, and a constant and enthusiastic friend, throughout the years. A celebration of his life as a major supporter of many projects and programs at the University of Florida and elsewhere included the comment that "for all the institutional significance of his contributions to the university's work and activities, Lewis was inspired by people, individuals who needed his help and whose work he appreciated. For all his stellar accomplishments, and a resume that leaves us in awe, Lewis was a wonderful friend, wise as an advisor, and steadfast in his beliefs." [http://jvlone.com/schott.pdf]

The Center for Measuring University Performance Staff

American Research Universities in an Era of Change: 2006-2015

John V. Lombardi and Diane D. Craig

Who Are We?

Over the years that we have measured various aspects of America's most competitive research universities, we have sought to identify the elements that characterize these institutions within the larger context of the higher education industry. Measuring colleges and universities is no easy task, as the endless surveys and ranking schemes demonstrate when they attempt to pinpoint the features that distinguish one institution from another. The task is complicated by the difficulty of describing the structure of the higher education business, reflected in the imprecision of the words we use. We speak of colleges and universities as if these words identify institutions belonging to a reasonably well defined universe when the terms cover a wide range of significantly different institutions designed to impart some element of knowledge or skill to some subset of the population.

We generally expect that colleges and universities are places that engage young people who have recently completed the equivalent of 12 years of schooling, but we also include older individuals whose life experience encourages them to acquire additional information or skills. We sometimes talk about higher education as being a process in which individuals learn how to become proficient at some skill or profession. We expect higher education to transfer important values and standards, we think higher education should serve as a vehicle to enhance equity and social justice, and we expect the industry that accomplishes this to be of high quality, inexpensive, efficient, effective, and inclusive.

Our students are often clearer about college and university, and simply refer to the institutions that make up this industry as schools. They say "Where did you go to school?" When they mean "What institution of higher education did you attend?" or "Where did you earn your degree or certificate?" This simplification clarifies what the institutions do by recognizing that the fundamental functions of all these places are instructional. Instruction provides the common link among most of the institutions that make up America's higher education system.

Almost all efforts to provide a clear taxonomy of American higher education fail to achieve precision because the range of institutional variation around common types is wide. We have what we call four-year colleges, institutions that

provide programs leading to a baccalaureate degree. We take some comfort in this designation even as we know that an elite private college with a large endowment, small classes, primarily residential and well-qualified students, highly trained and credentialed permanent professors, and elegant facilities is not operated in the same fashion as a small rural state college campus with modest facilities, predominantly commuter students, many under-prepared students, significant numbers of part-time adjunct faculty with basic credentials, and fragile budgets. We know that small private colleges with enrollment below 1,500 and minimal endowments operate on the thinnest of margins and live from year to year with the possibility of fiscal failure and extinction while large state flagships and prestigious private research universities may face financial challenges but never contemplate bankruptcy.[1]

As a rough indication of the scale of American higher education, the National Center for Educational Statistics (NCES) reports the existence of some 4,583 degree granting institutions (a number that understates the total number of separate institutions since branch campuses are sometimes reported with the main campus). Of these, 3,004 are four-year campuses and 1,579 are two-year.

Although this gives a general notion of scale, it is useful to further separate the institutions by control or ownership: public or private. About a third of all institutions (1,620) are public, and of these publics 710 are four-year and 910 are two-year. The other two-thirds (2,963) are private, and of these some 1,701 are nonprofit and 1,262 are for-profit. Among the nonprofit private institutions, 94% are four-year (1,594) while among the for-profit institutions, 55% are four-year (700). In conversations about higher education we often find that many observers do not fully recognize that four year nonprofit privates outnumber public institutions by more than two to one.

This landscape is further complicated by the distribution of students among the various types of institutions. In Fall 2015 there were some 20 million students in degree-granting colleges and universities. Of those 15.6 million (or 73 percent) were in public institutions and 4.1 million in nonprofit private colleges and universities. However, the subdivisions and categories used by NCES are many. For example, in the group of public institutions, in an admirable effort to create a detailed taxonomy of higher education institutions, NCES provides information within the following categories:[2]

Research university, very high
Research university, high
Doctoral/research university
Master's
Baccalaureate
Special-focus
            Arts, music, or design
            Business and management
            Engineering and other technology-related
            Law
            Medical schools and centers
            Other health professions
            Tribal colleges
2-year
            High transfer institutions
            Mixed transfer/career and technical institutions
            High career and technical institutions
Special-focus 2-year
            Health professions
            Tribal colleges
            Other programs

This short summary provides a glimpse into the complexity and diversity of higher education institutions and contexts in the US and helps explain the difficulty in generalizing about "American higher education."[3]

The Operation of America's Higher Education Industry

All of these institutions, whatever their variety and complexity, share a commitment to schooling, providing training that meets a broad but nonetheless mostly standardized set of expectations, established and enforced by the accreditation process that certifies them eligible for federal financial support. We define the schooling through the designation of various levels of student accomplishment recognized by the award of degrees: Bachelors, Masters, and Doctoral degrees, but with a complex nomenclature that specifies various subcategories within these degrees: Bachelors of science or arts, Masters of business administration or public health, Doctors of philosophy or education.

While all this variety offers endless opportunity to those who participate in these schools, the complexity also reflects the competitive needs of the higher education industry. Colleges and universities constitute a highly competitive marketplace that sells relatively standardized services to a wide range of customers. Although the rhetoric of education imagines an enterprise that seeks a common benefit for society through the preparation of citizens capable of contributing to a prosperous community, American schooling has always been a process for training occupationally successful individuals to play significant roles in society. The nation at large surely benefits from the trained people schooled in colleges and universities, but the participants engage these institutions in search of the personal benefits that result from their educational work. Even when we look at society's gains from education, they are not the result of preparing people with the best attitudes and values but from the necessity of preparing productive citizens whose schooling makes them effective at producing and delivering the goods and services that drive the American economy.[4]

The institutions that make up the higher education industry offer a wide range of elegant explanations of mission and purpose, but their behavior recognizes that their first priority is to attract sufficient business to generate the revenue needed to survive. Once survival is ensured, the institutions then compete to expand their reach and enhance their resources. This behavior can look much like the commercial behavior of other American business enterprises that expand to capture additional revenue, increase economies of scale, and generate higher value to their owners. However, colleges and universities (and here we speak of the nonprofit sector) have no stockholders. Their owners, whether the citizens of a state for public or trustees for private universities, do not operate to generate a profit for owners nor do the owners receive any significant direct personal benefit from the success of the institutions. Instead, the colleges and universities optimize a different set of characteristics.

Most colleges and universities compete to acquire within their institutional domains the highest level and the largest amount of quality possible. Some institutions focus on acquiring the highest quality student body, some seek the greatest research presence and the most qualified and competitive faculty, some compete to acquire quality in every institutional aspect. In almost every case the goal is to enhance the institution's capabilities and quality.[5]

The schools then sell the opportunity to participate in the enterprise to many customers. They sell students the chance to be part of the high quality campus intellectual and social life, they sell industry the opportunity to acquire the highest quality graduates, they sell the government the opportunity to invest in the production of research results that can enhance the national economy, and they sell donors the opportunity to associate with the best as they give money to further the institutional competition for quality.[6]

Although a common notion imagines that universities take in students, process them in some fashion, and graduate them, creating a product that then goes into the American employment marketplace, this is not exactly how it works. Instead, the schools create an enterprise that sells students and parents the opportunity to participate and take away some individual value from that participation. In this view schools are more like orchestras or opera companies than commercial enterprises. An orchestra's primary goal is to accumulate the musicians and other personnel who have the highest quality possible and then sell the opportunity for others to experience this quality through concerts and other performances. The transaction is surely financial, but a nonprofit orchestra does not generate revenue for its owners, and those who pay to experience a quality concert seek no tangible element but only the personal and individual value they derive from an encounter with a quality performance.

In this model the transaction requires no exchange of product but only an individual purchaser's right to enjoy and benefit personally from the quality displayed. A key characteristic here is that the value to the consumer is individually determined. Not all members of a concert audience will take away the same benefit from the same performance. Some, with extensive musical backgrounds and perhaps talent, will understand and take away a complex and sophisticated understanding of the performance, the artists' talents, the significance of the conductor's choices, and the context of the composers' creativity. Some, will simply enjoy the music. Others, may decide they do not need this experience, and leave at intermission. While everyone in the audience has the same opportunity, and participates in the same experience of the performance, the benefit achieved by each attendee will vary significantly.

This rather abstract conversation offers some insight into the nature of America's higher education industry and helps explain the behavior of these institutions. Indeed, while perhaps something of an exaggeration, it is not too far off to say that the vast majority of accredited not-for-profit higher education institutions in America (of whatever size or characteristics) provide a reasonable undergraduate education. We know this not because we have excellent well established quality tools to measure the efficacy of a higher education institution but because the graduates of these places, of widely varying characteristics, generally become adults who perform well with good to exceptional lifetime records. Every college has a roster of distinguished graduates whose accomplishments the institution celebrates with the implied notion that these stellar achievements rest on the schooling provided at an earlier time. The data also show that having participated in any college and especially acquiring any post-secondary credential produces higher lifetime earnings than a high school credential alone.

Because the educational content of colleges are more or less academically equivalent, the key element for many is the opportunity to associate with and participate in a high quality environment rather than the guarantee that one environment or another will provide better schooling. Students compete to enter elite colleges to participate with other elite students in elite contexts, not because the elite school can guarantee that the chemistry they learn will be different from or better than the chemistry available at a nearby regional public campus. Indeed, what the customers seek is access to the quality elements assembled inside the college or university. Were it otherwise, the institutions would promote the rigor of their coursework, the challenge of achieving graduation, the competitive skills acquired measured against standardized external metrics, and not the context and experience of attending the college.[7]

Innovation, Change, and Competition

Over the years, the nation has argued about the roles, functions, styles, and values of colleges and universities. In the effort to adjust to the ever-changing international marketplace and the restructuring of enterprises in response to a highly technology-driven post industrial world, universities have modified a number of their operational practices to accommodate these external changes. Many of these modifications reflect the rapid introduction and spread of technology. Of all the technologies that often seem to overwhelm past practices, communication is one of the most significant for colleges and universities.

This is because schooling is mostly about communication between students and teachers, among research personnel, and between university people and others outside the university. Translating the new technologies to match and enhance the schooling styles and expectations of students and teachers and reconfiguring colleges to effectively use new technologies has provided endless examples of innovation and experimentation. Yet the traditional structure of classroom and teacher, assignment and testing, projects and laboratories remains the predominant modality for schooling in spite of the dramatic spread of computer-mediated distance education and the tremendous interest in MOOCs.[8]

The issue here of course is the distinction between the transmission of information and the participation of students. Information has always been available as demonstrated by the long-term commitment to public libraries in almost every American community. The electronic innovations brought by the Internet and the ubiquity of relatively affordable computing devices has expanded and facilitated the availability of information. But information is not schooling, for schooling requires a selection of a subset of information and the packaging of that information with a variety of tool skills that permit its effective use. Availability of information is much less valuable than the skills that make information useful. Providing skills is more complicated than providing information, and as a result, colleges and universities have changed less rapidly in recent decades than other industries that rely on information and technology.

This communication expansion has, nonetheless, had multiple consequences for colleges in the techniques and styles of instruction and in the organization and operation of the institutions. One of the most significantly visible consequences has been the dramatic redefinition of the role and function of university and college libraries. Once places for books and the quiet pursuit of information, libraries have dramatically reduced their on-site book inventories and transformed their physical facilities into student-focused educational support operations. Learning commons, where students gather individually or in groups to work on projects and engage with electronic resources, are now common features on almost every campus. The libraries no longer seek the largest physical collections but instead subscribe to electronic databases of scholarly and other materials, relegating their previous, often extensive, book collections to remote storage. Librarians become experts in technology and information search and retrieval, they assist students in completing course work and faculty in using electronic resources for research. They struggle with the redefinition of their functions and purpose as it changes from custodian of core institutional information resources to facilitator of access to remotely maintained data and materials essential to university work.

The quality of libraries is no longer determined by the total size of a physical collection but by the adequacy of subscription access to current, remotely stored, information resources available to all. The prestige element of a library now tends to rely on the existence of unique physical resources in special collections of the institution. Of course, even here, the library with a special unique collection may well find the means to digitize it and provide it to the world, thereby reducing the uniqueness of the institution's physical resource. The library is a bell weather of the ability of higher education institutions to adapt to the opportunities of technological change without fundamentally changing the underlying academic structure of teaching and research.[9]

If we were to rely only on what appears in the media about colleges and universities we might come to believe that the industry is in great crisis, that dramatic change is in the offing or well underway, and that the institutions we know today will be radically different tomorrow. Some of this comes from the financial difficulties experienced by all of higher education throughout the early years of the 21st century, felt most severely during the economic downturn of 2008, and followed by the slow recovery since. Public universities and colleges saw a significant decline in state funding that has recovered some but not fully in the post-2008 years. Public institutions substituted tuition dollars for state funding to some extent but not enough to recover the lost public support. They also aggressively recruited out-of-state students and international students who paid higher prices and received smaller discounts. Private institutions reliant on endowment returns, suffered significant losses in the economic recession and also raised tuition although they had been adjusting tuition upward as a normal process throughout the years.[10]

Yet as nominal college prices rose, both public and private institutions found it necessary to expand traditional price discounting to acquire sufficient students to sustain their scale and operations. Something on the order of 80% of all students receive some type of tuition discount from their institutions with the overall discount rate for private institutions reaching 50% or more. All institutions expanded fund raising operations and launched significant to magnificent campaigns to raise funds for operations, capital, and schol-

arships. With all the national interest in college and university sticker prices, however, few focused on the fact that the net revenue from tuition and fees almost never covers the cost of the educational experience provided. Instead, institutions draw on endowment, annual giving, and state subsidies to cover the expense.[11]

Institutions also instituted new programs to increase revenue. Small private colleges, as well as most universities, expanded masters degree and certificate programs, both online and residential, tailored to specific occupational specialties. These programs, because they are designed to enhance the earning power of their graduates, do not generally discount tuition and are profitable compared to standard bachelors degree programs that generally require a subsidy. Most institutions also expanded their online educational initiatives to capture student constituencies outside the traditional group of 18-24 year olds. These new customers are often adult learners, returning working students who need to complete a degree, or professionals seeking an all online degree or certificate. Such students may not require a tuition discount, and the programs, if operated at scale, can be significant revenue earners. Institutions also developed collaborations with for-profit enterprises to leverage commercial efficiencies on behalf of university or college operations.[12] All of this innovation can give a sense of great change, but perhaps the visibility is more dramatic than the fundamental change it reflects.[13]

As an example, in most of the innovative revenue-generating activities, one of the key values provided is not the content (which in most cases is generic: algebra is algebra, accounting rules are standard) but the institutional brand attached to the content. MOOCs become significant when endorsed by Harvard and MIT; for-profit educational service providers are made legitimate when accredited or covered by the brand of Purdue University. This tells us that the core competitive issues for colleges and universities remain much the same, even if expressed through new modalities enabled by technological and pedagogical innovations. Would a MOOC sponsored by a small rural state university campus have the same viability as one sponsored by MIT, even if the curriculum and programs were identical? Would Kaplan have made a deal with a little known private college rather than Purdue? Probably not.[14]

As a result, the primary driver of college and university prestige and reputation remains the acquisition of internal quality (faculty, students, facilities, research accomplishments, sports teams, student life amenities, and other highly visible internal assets). This constant pursuit of internal quality explains the relative stability of the general higher education marketplace, and especially the persistence of institutional success (as reflected in our core measure of annual federal science and engineering research expenditures) among the top research universities.

To be sure, some universities decline or rise as measured by one or another indicator. Among public research universities, for example, the change in state funding has been dramatic, but in spite of the reductions, other indicators of university performance do not appear to have been significantly impacted. This is because these institutions identified the resources needed to buffer short term changes, buy the time required to readjust expenditures and redesign program delivery methods, and the opportunity to invest in new revenue enhancing activities. Much the same is true of private research universities that have traditionally had large endowments and effective programs of annual giving. Absent a tradition of significant public tax based support, private universities have always been better prepared for changes in the economy. They move quickly to adjust, delaying large projects, readjusting expenditures, eliminating programs, and otherwise dealing directly with both the income and expenses of their operations. They too innovate and redesign programs and instructional modalities, but rarely undermine the core design based on the acquisition of internal quality.

For example, among the 125 public research universities we study (defined in the Appendix), the median contribution of state appropriations to total revenue (including investment income) between 2006 and 2015, after often steep reductions followed by partial recovery, declined by 5.7 percent. The experience of public institutions over this decade varied widely as different states pursued different policies in adjusting to declines in state revenue and increases in requirements for high priority state services. As the table below indicates, the largest percent reduction in state appropriations as a percentage of university revenues reached 21% while the largest percent increase over the decade reached almost 6%. In dollar terms, the top increase in state appropriations produced a $215 million increase while the largest reduction was $179 million. This helps illustrate the difficulty of generalizing about individual institutional experiences from aggregate data.

In looking at the state contribution to institutional revenue, it is important to recognize that even if a state increased its dollar contribution to a university's revenue, the percentage of state funding within a university's overall revenue may nonetheless have declined because the institution raised tuition and fees or generated funds from many other sources that increased revenue even more. As a result, an increase in state appropriations may represent a smaller percent of a large total institutional revenue. For example, with the median net change in state contribution to institutional revenue declining by 5.7 percent, the institutions nonetheless experienced a median increase in state appropriations from 2006 to 2015 of about $6.8 million. As the table above illustrates, the median change in net tuition and fee dollars as a portion of total revenue for the 125 institutions reached 6.5 percent or $124 million.

The most successful public research universities show a somewhat different profile. Between 2006 and 2015, the top 10 public universities, measured by 2015 federal research expenditures, saw the state contribution to their revenue drop by a median of 4.7 percent. However, like other universities, these institutions identified a range of income sources beyond state dollars so that state revenue contribution as a percentage of total revenue declined even as the median state contribution in dollar terms increased by about $2 million. Of course, in the worst case among these top ten, the reduction in the state percentage contribution to revenue also reflected a net loss of state funds over the 2006-2015 period of $55 million. Among these top 10, all increased their tuition's share of the total budget over the past decade. While the median change in percentage of net tuition and fee dollars was somewhat lower than their public counterparts at 4 percent, the median increase of $250 million was much greater.

In our work, one of the more useful indicators of research university performance has always been the annual federal research expenditures. Although changes in state support of public research universities over the decade 2006-2015 caused considerable institutional stress, required many readjustments in university operations that affect employment, restructured services, prompted outsourcing, encouraged the development of new programs and the elimination of others, the research mission of most of these institutions remained strong. The median increase in federal research

Top Public Research Universities: Change from 2006 to 2015 in State Funding, Tuition, Students, and Research

Public Research Institutions by Federal Research Expenditures	Net Change in % of State Appropriations	Net Change in State Approp $ (000s)	Net Change in % of Tuition & Fees	Net Change in Tuition & Fees (000s)	Percent Change in Fall Enrollment	Net Change in Fall Enrollment	Percent Change in Federal Research	Net Change in Federal Research $ (000s)
Top 125 Public Research Institutions								
Median	-5.7%	$6,764	6.5%	$124,380	12.1%	2,504	20.8%	$10,512
Maximum Increase	5.9%	$215,140	22.3%	$720,556	98.2%	18,867	708.7%	$290,312
Max Decrease/Min Increase	-21.1%	-$179,132	-16.9%	-$1,864	-16.6%	-4,921	-58.3%	-$35,741
Top 10 Public Research Institutions								
Median	-4.7%	$2,191	4.0%	$250,186	7.9%	3,106	31.1%	$143,652
Maximum Increase	-1.8%	$184,734	10.0%	$720,556	39.6%	7,098	112.6%	$290,312
Max Decrease/Min Increase	-12.1%	-$55,001	2.1%	$140,772	0.6%	276	-0.2%	-$1,102

expenditures among these 125 reaches 21% or an increase of $10.5 million. Among the top 10 research performers the median increase was 31% or about $144 million. As we have identified over the years in these annual reports, the success of America's public research universities in the federal research competition has been remarkably stable with most of the same institutions continuing their success over the decades. Indeed, even in the difficult times reflected in the 2006-2015 data, the best predictor of the growth in annual federal research expenditures of these institutions is the amount of research expenditures in 2015 (a correlation of .80).

The experience of 49 private research universities over this decade follows much the same pattern as observed among the 125 public institutions, although net tuition and fee dollar increases were slightly higher in the public sector, no doubt reflecting the tuition and fee adjustments made by private institutions over many previous years without the need to adjust to substantial changes in state appropriations. In addition, private institutions showed median increases in federal research dollars that somewhat exceeded those of their public counterparts. However, given the wide range of research performance among these top institutions, both public and private, clear distinctions are difficult to draw. As is the case with public institutions, the best predictor of the change in federal research expenditures between 2006 and 2015 is the amount of federal research expenditures in 2015.

If these high powered, prestigious public and private institutions appear to have managed the transition across the 2008 recession reasonably well, a counter example appears at the other end of the higher education industry among small private colleges with enrollments around 1,500 or less. These institutions are vulnerable to all the forces that challenge higher education. Deferred maintenance, declining college age populations, lower transfer rates from community colleges, higher percentages of tuition discounting to acquire sufficient student numbers to survive, and of course constant competition from public institutions with lower tuition and support from the remaining state subsidies. Between 2005 and 2015, 44 private nonprofit four-year institutions ceased operation. Of these 28 disappeared in the first five years and 16 additional in the second five years.

These institutional failures have attracted significant attention in the higher education press and lend some substance to the notion that American higher education is in a major existential crisis. However, while 44 institutions are a significant number, especially for their alumni, current students, and employees, they represent only 3 percent of institutions in this category and by the time of their failure often had very small remaining enrollment. Although not the topic of this paper, it should be noted that 122 for-profit two-year institutions also failed in the same ten-year period. As a related development, some state systems dealt with small campuses that fell below some reasonable level of survival by combining institutions or institutional

Top Private Research Universities: Change from 2006 to 2015 in Tuition, Students, and Research

Private Research Institutions by Federal Research Expenditures	Net Change in % of Tuition & Fees	Net Change in Tuition & Fees (000s)	Percent Change in Fall Enrollment	Net Change in Fall Enrollment	Percent Change in Federal Research	Net Change in Federal Research $ (000s)
Top 49 Private Research Institutions						
Median	6.5%	$121,053	11.8%	1,243	19.5%	$18,002
Maximum Increase	18.5%	$409,012	67.8%	10,012	152.6%	$681,540
Max Decrease/Min Increase	-3.8%	$5,370	-30.6%	-3,471	-48.9%	-$17,840
Top 10 Private Research Institutions						
Median	1.5%	$184,961	12.8%	1,972	26.5%	$120,950
Maximum Increase	6.5%	$622,934	30.0%	10,012	52.1%	$681,540
Max Decrease/Min Increase	-3.0%	$54,303	-4.3%	-767	2.2%	$10,288

Note: As is often the case in measuring federal research expenditures, the Johns Hopkins University totals distort some indicators. The maximum increase in the table above would be $144.1M rather than $681.5M if we exclude Johns Hopkins.

As an additional recognition of the adjustments made by both public and private research universities in our group, we can observe that almost all institutions, public or private, increased enrollment (all credit earning enrollment) during this period. While the increase reached about the same percentage for the median institution in both groups, the public institutions, increased by just over twice as many students, reflecting the larger student bodies involved. It seems likely that these increases reflect not only strategic pursuit of greater scale but also revenue, for both public and private institutions the median increase in enrollment was accompanied by higher net tuition revenue.

management without necessarily eliminating the physical places.[15]

The Constant of Change

The challenge of capturing the changes currently underway in American higher education is to recognize the significance of many trends while at the same time understanding the flexibility and adaptability of this educational industry. Change is a constant of American higher education, and the institutions are remarkably skillful at adopting and absorbing the effects of changes in the external environment without damaging continuing operations or substantially modifying the competitive structure of the business.

Each generation of students, faculty, staff, administrators, legislators, and citizens imagines that the changes of their time represent a critical moment that may force America's colleges and universities to become dramatically different in some fundamental way. And yet, crisis after crisis, the higher education enterprise slowly absorbs the changes that become necessary. Institutions readjust their operations to accommodate destructive pressures on one side and capture emerging opportunities on the other.

To be sure, the universities of today are different in many ways than they were in the 1970s or 1980s. But they still fundamentally operate on much the same basis, compete for the same elements of quality that continue to determine success and reputation, and engage in a constant and endless pursuit of the money that permits them to buy the essential elements of quality. Many of the trends apparent in the past decade or so will continue. Public university state funding will remain a challenge as the many other demands on tax dollars will continue to crowd out higher education needs. Moreover, we anticipate significant differences by state and by institution that make reliable overall predictions about the higher education industry based on aggregate data much less useful for understanding the circumstances of individual institutions.

Those states with growing populations in the 18-24 year-old category will likely see increased state revenue related to enrollment. Moreover, as states introduce various mechanisms of performance-based funding, generally indexed to graduation rates, employment success, or similar measures, the elite public institutions will fare significantly better than others in their states because the elite institutions already have high graduation rates and their graduates already find good employment or significant graduate educational opportunities. This is a function of institutional selectivity which ensures that well-prepared entering students produce successful graduates. Those institutions with less selective admissions struggle to overcome whatever educational deficits some students may have and find it much more difficult to meet high graduation and employment metrics. They also have many students with financial challenges who may take longer to graduate or drop out to take jobs. Institutions, both public and private, in states with declining populations will find recruitment and retention of students much more difficult.[16]

The marketplace of 18-24 year-olds appears to have leveled out primarily as a result of stagnant population growth and the already high level of participation in college, making enrollment growth difficult for less selective institutions. This development places increasing pressure on small

public institutions and marginally funded private colleges without the name brand, extensive program options, and resources of more competitive institutions. We can expect these institutions to introduce post-baccalaureate certificate and degree programs and invest in various online education products to allow them to reach more distant audiences and adult and other under-served populations. Whether these strategies will succeed remains to be seen as these marketplaces are increasingly being served by large public institutions and other perhaps better funded providers.[17]

As is always the case in American higher education, the best institutions (those with the highest levels of internal quality and thus prestige), whether public or private and whether four year undergraduate colleges or major research universities will continue to prosper, modifying, innovating, and readjusting their programs and activities to take advantage of changes in the economy, in the technologies available for higher education, and in the competitive marketplace for sustaining and renewing institutional quality. Others, less well endowed, less well funded from public sources, challenged to maintain student quality and numbers, and reaching a limit on the net tuition they can collect, will struggle. They have already seen significant changes in curricular structure, in the balance between part-time contingent and tenure or tenure-track faculty, and in the engagement with various systems of technology enabled instruction.

If we were to predict the future structure of American higher education, it does not take much insight to imagine that the separation between elite, semi-elite, generic, and struggling institutions will grow greater. The demographic pressures, the financial challenges, the advent of technology enhanced national competition will all provide an increasing advantage to the elite, the selective, and the well funded. Some number of small colleges will continue to fail, although it is hard to predict the scale of this change. While the elite continue to prosper, mid-range comprehensive universities will experience the greatest change as their faculty continue the trend towards majority part-time and contingent instructors, their programs become increasingly occupationally focused, and they seek combinations, collaborations, and mergers to enhance their scale and competitive position. Some innovations and transformations will be dramatic such as the creation of the Purdue-Kaplan institution, some will be prosaic such as the increased outsourcing of college and university administrative and operational functions.

Yet throughout, the long-standing trends of American higher education are likely to prevail: continuing readjustments to respond to external expectations, opportunities, and constraints performed against the constant background of the intense competition for internal quality.

1 For a clear view of the process that produced our current post second-ary system see the definitive treatment in Arthur M. Cohen and Carrie B. Kisker, *The Shaping of American Higher Education: Emergence and Growth of the Contemporary System*, (2nd Edition, San Francisco: Jossey-Bass, 2010)

2 *National Center for Education Statistics*, Washington DC, 2016. [https://nces.ed.gov/programs/digest/current_tables.asp]

3 *The Carnegie Classification of Institutions of Higher Education*, Bloomington IN, 2016 [http://carnegieclassifications.iu.edu/index.php]

4 The commentary and analysis of the value of higher education to soci-ety and individuals is extensive. The following represent but a selection from this conversation. Joseph G. Altonji and Seth D. Zimmerman. "The Costs of and Net Returns to College Major," *NBER Working Paper Series* #23029, National Bureau of Economic Research, January 2017; Richard Vedder and Justin Strehle. "The Diminishing Returns of a College Degree. In the Mid-1970s, Far Less than 1% of Taxi Drivers Were Graduates. By 2010 More than 15% Were," *The Wall Street Jour-nal*, June 4, 2017; Gareth Williams, "Higher Education: Public Good or Private Commodity?" *London Review of Education* (14:1, 2016); Arthur M. Cohen, Carrie B. Kisker, and Florence B. Brower. "The Economy Does Not Depend on Higher Education," *The Chronicle of Higher Education*, October 28, 2013; Robert G. Valletta, "Recent Flattening in the Higher Education Wage Premium: Polarization, Skill Downgrading, or Both?" *NBER Working Paper Series* #22935, National Bureau of Economic Research, December 2016; Anthony P. Carnevale, Tamara Jayasundera, and Artem Gulish. *America's Divided Recovery: College Haves and Have-Nots*. Washington, DC.: George-town University, Center on Education and the Workforce, 2016; Roger A. Kaufman, *Mega Planning: Practical Tools for Organizational Success*, Thousand Oaks, CA: Sage Publications, 2000.

5 For a collection of work on the topic of research competition see the publications listed on the website of The Center for Measuring Univer-sity Performance, 2001-2015 [https://mup.asu.edu/Publications].

6 For an example of the institutional perspective on college quality see *The Ideal College Experience, Two Centuries in the Making* [https://www.indiana.edu/about]; *About UC Santa Barbara* [http://www.ucsb.edu/pop]; *Pomona College* [https://www.pomona.edu/about]; *The Johns Hopkins University: About Us* [https://www.jhu.edu/about/]. For alumni achievement see for example *Columbia College Toady, Alumni in the News*, June 19, 2017 [https://www.college.columbia.edu/cct/latest/alumni-news] or M*ontana State University Collegian*, 2016 [http://www.msuaf.org/s/1584/index.aspx?sid=1584&gid=1&pgid= 1432]. These examples can be duplicated for almost every college and university in America.

7 *Arizona State University: Prospective Students*, 2017 [http://www.msuaf.org/s/1584/index.aspx] *University of Chicago Admissions, Academics*, 2017 [https://collegeadmissions.uchicago.edu/academics]. For a view of the undergraduate academic programs see for example *Berkeley, Academic Guide, 2017-18* [http://guide.berkeley.edu/undergraduate/education/#collegerequire-mentstext]; Some colleges cater to student preferences through open curricula with many options although nonetheless provide structured majors *Amherst College Open Curriculum and Majors, 2017* [https://www.amherst.edu/academiclife/open-curriculum] and [https://www.amherst.edu/academiclife/departments]. The websites of every college and university offer similar perspectives on academic opportunities.

8 As a clear example of the need to connect online courses to name brand institutional quality see the EdX site at [https://www.edx.org/] or the *Coursera* site at {https://www.coursera.org]. A useful positive view of MOOC programs is available through Educause, Massive Open Online Course (MOOC). Blumenstyk, Goldie. "Same Time, Many Locations: Online Education Goes Back to Its Origins," *The Chronicle of Higher Education*, June 14, 2016. A valuable literature review is in George Veletsianos and Peter Shepherdson, "A Systematic Analysis and Syn-thesis of the Empirical MOOC Literature Published in 2013–2015," *International Review of Research in Open and Distributed Learning* (17:2, 2016).

9 For a clear picture of the challenges electronic technology has brought to university libraries see the articles in the peer reviewed journal *portal: Libraries and the Academy*, The Johns Hopkins University Press, 2001-.

10 For an overview of state higher education finance see *SHEF: FY 2016 State Higher Education Finance*, State Higher Education Executive Officers Association, Boulder, CO: 2017.

11 Seltzer, Rick. "Private Colleges and Universities Increase Tuition Discounting Again in 2016-17," *Inside Higher Ed*, May 15, 2017; The *2016 NACUBO Tuition Discounting Study*, National Association of College and University Business Officers, 2017.

12 For an example of the proliferation of occupationally related graduate programs see the website for Baypath University, a small private insti-tution in Longmeadow, Massachusetts. The site lists over 50 certificate, masters, or doctoral programs with specific occupational focus [http://www.baypath.edu/academics/graduate-programs]

13 University outsourcing of services has been a long standing trend in-cluding such activities as food services and bookstores. Many institu-tions contract with private developers for student housing and other infrastructure projects, Technology services in particular have become key avenues for outside providers as is summarized in Jacqueline Bichsel, "IT Service Delivery in Higher Education: Current Methods and Future Directions," *Educause 2015* [https://library.educause.edu/~/media/files/library/2015/5/ers1501a.pdf ?la=en]. Institutions also outsource online academic services Marc Parry "Outsourced Ed: Colleges Hire Companies to Build Their Online Courses," *The Chronicle of Higher Education*, July 18, 2010 [http://www.chronicle.com/article/Outsourced-Ed-Colleges-Hire/66309]. A cursory search for university public-private partner-ships will produce many project examples.

14 In addition to the items cited above see Goldie Blumenstyk, "Purdue's Purchase of Kaplan Is a Big Bet--and a Sign of the Times," *The Chron-icle of Higher Education*, April 28, 2017; Paul Fain, "Purdue Acquires Kaplan University to Create a new Public, Online University under Purdue Brand," *Inside Higher Ed*, April 28, 2017; Robert Shireman, "There's a Reason the Purdue-Kaplan Deal Sounds Too Good to Be True," *The Chronicle of Higher Education*, April 30, 2017.

15 U.S. Department of Education, National Center for Education Statis-tics, IPEDS Fall 2000 through Fall 2014, Institutional Characteristics Component. (Table was prepared July 2016.) The challenges of sus-taining small private colleges have been a topic for at least the last fifteen years. John L. Pulley, "How Eckerd's 52 Trustees Failed to See Two-Thirds of Its Endowment Disappear," *The Chronicle of Higher Education*, August 18, 2000. James M. O'Neill, "Survival 101: Small Private Colleges on The Financial Brink," *The Philadelphia Inquirer*, 2001; Martin Van Der Werf, "Mount Senario's Final Act," *The Chroni-cle of Higher Education*, June 14, 2002; Kent John Chabotar, "What About the Rest of Us? Small Colleges in Financial Crisis," *Change*, (July-August 2010); Mark Keierleber, "Financially Strapped Colleges Grow More Vulnerable as Economic Recovery Lags," *The Chronicle of Higher Education*, March 24, 2014; Lawrence Biemiller, "Survival at Stake In the Aftermath of the Recession, Small Colleges Adapt to a New Market," T*he Chronicle of Higher Education*, March 2, 2015; Kellie Woodhouse, "Enrollment Declines Drove Closure of Marian Court College," *Inside Higher Ed*, June 18, 2015; Rick Seltzer, "Vermont Pushes to Combine Public Colleges' Administrations," *Inside Higher Education*, July 27, 2016, and the *University System of Georgia Board of Regents Approves Proposals to Consolidate Institutions*, 2017 [http://www.usg.edu/news/release/board_of_ regents_approves_proposals_to_consolidate_institutions]

16 For an example of the differential impact of performance-based funding models see the results for the State University System of Florida, *Performance Funding Model* at [http://www.flbog.edu/board/office/budget/performance_funding.php].

17 For an interesting presentation on the impact of changing population composition on college enrollment see Luke Juday, "The Demograph-ics of Declining College Enrollment," *Stat Chat, Demographics Research Group*, University of Virginia, October 2. 2014. NCES in "The Condition of Education, Undergraduate Enrollment" (May 2017) provides projections that anticipate flat to gradually rising enrollments nationwide through 2026 [https://nces.ed.gov/programs/coe/indicator_cha.asp]. A short-term view of enrollment changes is available from the *National Student Clearinghouse*, "Current Term Enrollment Estimates – Spring 2017", Research Center, May 23, 2017 [https://nscresearchcenter.org/ currenttermenrollmentestimate-spring2017/].

APPENDIX

The appendices list the institutions studied and their change between 2006 and 2015 on four key variables: percentage of state appropriations in budget, percentage of net tuition and fees, fall enrollment (undergraduate and graduate), and federal research expenditures. The 174 institutions (125 public and 49 private) included in this study are those that ranked in the top 200 on federal research expenditures between 2006 and 2015. We then excluded those with missing data that could not be reasonably estimated and standalone medical or specialized institutions.

Some universities changed how they report over the ten-year period and we had to combine campuses to make the data comparable. While we prefer to maintain the single campus approach as found in our annual Top American Research University tables for this exercise we felt it was important to leave these institutions in the analysis given their high research performance over the years and the dominance, among most campuses, of the main campus. The combined data are reflected in the institution's name

and include Penn State, Rutgers, Texas A&M, Tennessee, Connecticut, Kansas, and Mississippi. Though we attempt to account for any reporting changes, we recognize there may be others missed as IPEDS data definitions change and how those definitions are interpreted may vary over time within an institution and between institutions.

Finance variables used:

IPEDS Finance GASB - Publics

- F1B01 Net tuition and fees
- F1B11 State appropriations
- F1B25 Total revenue

IPEDS Finance FASB - Privates and a few publics

- F2D0 Net tuition and fees
- F2D03 State appropriations
- F2D18 Total revenue (2006)
- F2D16 Total revenue (2015)

Table A-1. Top Public Research Universities: Change from 2006 to 2015 in State Funding, Tuition, Students, and Research

2015 Federal Research ($000)*	Institution	Net Change % of State Approp	Net Change in State Approp $ ($000)	Net Change in % of Tuition & Fees	Net Change in Tuition & Fees (000s)	Percent Change in Fall Enrollment	Net Change in Fall Enrollment	Percent Change in Federal Research	Net Change in Federal Research $ ($000)
851,573	University of Washington - Seattle	-4.5%	-$55,001	8.0%	$577,605	14.9%	5,884	30.9%	$201,179
728,712	University of Michigan - Ann Arbor	-1.8%	-$23,729	3.4%	$399,415	9.1%	3,626	28.8%	$162,973
601,184	University of California - San Diego	-5.4%	$28,967	2.8%	$308,320	25.4%	6,659	29.6%	$137,377
577,574	Univ. of North Carolina - Chapel Hill	-4.9%	$39,116	3.7%	$199,123	4.9%	1,367	75.4%	$248,359
554,658	University of Pittsburgh - Pittsburgh	-2.9%	-$27,646	10.0%	$232,892	6.7%	1,789	31.3%	$132,342
548,063	Georgia Institute of Technology	-12.1%	-$6,746	8.3%	$212,442	39.6%	7,098	112.6%	$290,312
512,206	Penn. State University, all campuses	-4.0%	-$38,176	4.2%	$720,556	3.4%	2,586	39.5%	$144,991
506,910	University of Wisconsin - Madison	-2.5%	$28,758	2.8%	$140,772	4.1%	1,688	3.1%	$15,100
482,771	Univ. of California - Los Angeles	-8.3%	$184,734	9.9%	$267,481	14.5%	5,297	-0.2%	-$1,102
468,482	University of Minnesota - Twin Cities	-5.9%	$11,128	2.1%	$209,092	0.6%	276	43.6%	$142,312
406,941	Ohio State University - Columbus	-4.0%	-$2,894	0.8%	$308,865	13.2%	6,845	28.8%	$91,027
342,042	University of California - Berkeley	-14.6%	-$111,563	8.6%	$437,675	12.6%	4,269	30.7%	$80,324
341,828	University of Colorado - Boulder**			-0.4%	$210,142	4.4%	1,391	52.8%	$118,162
333,413	Rutgers, all campuses + UMDNJ	-8.3%	-$179,132	9.9%	$414,218	21.9%	12,119	23.3%	$63,034
332,079	University of Maryland - College Park	1.7%	$137,583	2.7%	$144,219	8.7%	3,038	58.3%	$122,315
331,388	University of Texas - Austin	-2.1%	$16,870	1.9%	$135,962	2.5%	1,253	21.3%	$58,241
330,479	Univ. of Illinois - Urbana-Champaign	-6.7%	-$21,662	6.0%	$359,013	7.3%	3,104	24.9%	$65,834
325,008	University of Alabama - Birmingham	-3.6%	$5,119	2.7%	$95,317	10.7%	1,772	10.9%	$32,046
322,919	University of California - Davis	-8.0%	-$34,637	2.1%	$241,105	18.8%	5,558	30.1%	$74,729
291,714	Texas A&M University + Hlth Sci. Ctr.	-6.6%	$151,222	3.5%	$302,363	36.7%	17,121	20.8%	$50,258
281,317	University of Florida	-10.7%	$42,217	4.7%	$223,315	-0.5%	-267	13.3%	$32,995
270,311	University of Utah	-4.3%	$38,321	1.1%	$161,576	3.5%	1,081	54.6%	$95,423
266,147	University of Colorado - Denver**			1.7%	$124,380	17.4%	3,509	20.3%	$44,933

* Indiana U., IUPUI, and U. Oklahoma 2015 Federal Research is based on preliminary estimate.
** The methods used by Colorado to fund state appropriations changed, which made comparisons unreliable so we did not include those data.

Appendix A-1. Top Public Research Universities: Change from 2006 to 2015 in State Funding, Tuition, Students, and Research (cont.)

2015 Federal Research ($000)*	Institution	Net Change % of State Approp	Net Change in State Approp $ ($000)	Net Change in % of Tuition & Fees	Net Change in Tuition & Fees (000s)	Percent Change in Fall Enrollment	Net Change in Fall Enrollment	Percent Change in Federal Research	Net Change in Federal Research $ ($000)
265,878	University of Arizona	-14.8%	-$84,147	12.2%	$361,270	15.7%	5,790	-11.8%	-$35,741
256,228	Michigan State University	-9.5%	-$83,341	11.1%	$424,227	11.0%	5,018	51.5%	$87,112
250,457	University of Cincinnati - Cincinnati	-0.4%	$19,281	16.3%	$209,177	27.2%	7,715	24.1%	$48,715
223,730	University of Iowa	-7.5%	-$54,480	1.8%	$181,320	7.0%	2,028	3.3%	$7,209
213,685	Colorado State University	0.2%	$2,355	7.3%	$177,724	10.8%	2,978	17.0%	$31,037
209,005	Purdue University - West Lafayette	-3.6%	$23,569	8.0%	$260,487	-0.3%	-137	32.8%	$51,567
199,818	University of Hawaii - Manoa	-5.7%	-$1,419	7.8%	$93,749	-7.3%	-1,492	-1.3%	-$2,601
196,215	University of South Florida - Tampa	-8.4%	-$4,848	7.0%	$119,217	-3.6%	-1,569	27.6%	$42,478
196,058	North Carolina State University	-4.6%	$81,588	5.9%	$135,034	9.3%	2,885	49.4%	$64,796
192,930	University of Illinois - Chicago	-5.5%	-$33,231	2.6%	$160,155	17.9%	4,404	-5.4%	-$10,945
191,080	Virginia Polytechnic Inst. and St. U.	-8.7%	$3,264	6.5%	$196,885	14.7%	4,193	59.2%	$71,086
186,890	Arizona State University	-15.5%	-$30,526	18.4%	$671,600	25.9%	18,867	70.1%	$76,997
186,676	University of Virginia	-2.3%	-$8,364	3.4%	$222,972	-0.8%	-185	-8.4%	-$17,102
174,146	University at Buffalo	-6.5%	$29,920	8.3%	$116,623	7.1%	1,973	13.7%	$20,994
170,622	University of California - Irvine	-4.0%	$31,836	6.0%	$263,196	22.2%	5,606	0.4%	$639
151,619	Univ. of New Mexico - Albuquerque	-5.2%	$37,107	0.1%	$48,819	6.1%	1,564	18.5%	$23,712
150,625	Oregon State University	-11.0%	$15,299	1.5%	$160,389	52.8%	10,224	29.2%	$34,039
145,829	Indiana U. - Purdue U - Indianapolis	-1.9%	$18,322	5.7%	$110,244	1.2%	341	42.4%	$43,448
145,097	University of Kentucky	-7.2%	-$34,682	2.4%	$155,669	12.7%	3,345	-4.1%	-$6,141
140,964	Univ. of Tennessee - Knoxville + HSC	-4.4%	-$85,375	8.1%	$90,649	-3.7%	-1,056	7.9%	$10,274
135,349	Univ. of Connecticut + Health Center	-2.3%	$215,140	0.6%	$138,145	11.0%	3,143	8.4%	$10,512
133,569	Florida State University	-7.1%	$30,130	8.8%	$137,281	2.1%	857	21.0%	$23,211
128,374	University of Kansas + Medical Ctr.	-3.9%	-$7,576	5.8%	$104,668	-5.8%	-1,664	11.1%	$12,852
127,825	University of Georgia	-13.0%	-$18,653	9.6%	$217,674	6.4%	2,171	38.0%	$35,173
123,665	Virginia Commonwealth University	-8.2%	$10,685	7.6%	$157,044	2.4%	729	26.7%	$26,089
121,627	Washington State Univ. - Pullman	-11.6%	-$30,939	9.5%	$159,219	25.5%	6,031	49.6%	$40,303
119,945	Temple University	-4.8%	-$41,098	3.1%	$323,277	12.2%	4,142	135.6%	$69,041
119,811	Utah State University	-2.6%	$44,108	9.0%	$78,887	98.2%	14,178	24.5%	$23,569
115,031	Stony Brook University	-5.6%	$80,324	3.2%	$122,333	12.2%	2,750	1.8%	$2,058
114,596	Univ. of California - Santa Barbara	-7.6%	-$2,566	11.1%	$170,569	11.5%	2,415	7.9%	$8,427
113,443	Iowa State University	-8.5%	$4,783	7.6%	$163,619	40.3%	10,252	8.5%	$8,890
109,258	University of Delaware	-3.6%	-$2,411	14.0%	$195,333	12.1%	2,472	37.2%	$29,618
108,221	Wayne State University	-6.5%	-$25,867	9.2%	$101,747	-15.4%	-4,921	-8.3%	-$9,821
102,852	University of Missouri - Columbia	-4.1%	-$1,677	3.8%	$156,730	25.7%	7,240	1.1%	$1,120
97,206	Univ. of Massachusetts - Amherst	-6.0%	$48,329	4.8%	$145,288	14.4%	3,676	40.5%	$28,030
94,763	University of Nebraska - Lincoln	-4.9%	$53,109	4.9%	$101,640	14.3%	3,154	17.4%	$14,032
91,249	University of California - Santa Cruz	-2.2%	$48,939	7.9%	$118,725	16.3%	2,504	37.4%	$24,859
84,723	Univ. of South Carolina - Columbia	-11.6%	-$44,317	7.6%	$176,375	23.1%	6,334	-5.1%	-$4,571
83,733	University of Vermont	-1.5%	$3,514	8.8%	$112,164	8.0%	945	1.5%	$1,214
83,106	Univ. of New Hampshire - Durham	-3.5%	-$6,549	8.4%	$76,002	3.7%	540	-3.8%	-$3,310
82,276	Louisiana State Univ. - Baton Rouge	-14.0%	-$67,544	7.5%	$143,195	5.3%	1,599	3.9%	$3,115
81,788	University of Central Florida	-9.1%	$56,990	10.2%	$167,078	35.0%	16,307	115.4%	$43,814
79,181	Mississippi State University	-2.0%	$34,690	6.7%	$67,415	28.8%	4,667	-15.8%	-$14,892
78,985	University of Alaska - Fairbanks	4.8%	$64,918	1.5%	$16,168	3.6%	298	-19.7%	-$19,345
78,824	University at Albany	4.8%	$36,955	6.0%	$35,963	-1.5%	-256	-24.1%	-$25,011
78,524	Indiana University - Bloomington	-7.1%	-$11,752	12.3%	$341,044	26.8%	10,267	15.0%	$10,270
78,253	New Mexico State Univ. - Las Cruces	2.2%	$19,100	4.6%	$23,945	-5.6%	-925	-23.2%	-$23,596
67,293	Florida International University	-6.9%	$56,368	12.6%	$176,134	31.0%	11,785	46.6%	$21,399
66,632	Kansas State University	-13.9%	-$4,758	3.3%	$106,547	4.3%	1,005	26.6%	$13,983
66,608	West Virginia University	-7.8%	$14,494	6.1%	$174,391	6.1%	1,661	4.5%	$2,844
66,564	University of Alabama - Huntsville	0.8%	$705	13.8%	$26,117	10.9%	775	49.1%	$21,928

Appendix A-1. Top Public Research Universities: Change from 2006 to 2015 in State Funding, Tuition, Students, and Research (cont.)

2015 Federal Research ($000)*	Institution	Net Change % of State Approp	Net Change in State Approp $ ($000)	Net Change in % of Tuition & Fees	Net Change in Tuition & Fees (000s)	Percent Change in Fall Enrollment	Net Change in Fall Enrollment	Percent Change in Federal Research	Net Change in Federal Research $ ($000)
66,100	University of Louisville	-10.8%	-$26,178	4.7%	$99,478	2.5%	509	-6.2%	-$4,381
62,827	Montana State University - Bozeman	0.7%	$21,267	8.1%	$58,004	26.4%	3,184	-16.6%	-$12,535
62,642	University of California - Riverside	-2.3%	$76,916	10.1%	$163,982	26.7%	4,510	8.0%	$4,619
61,085	University of Rhode Island	-9.2%	-$13,266	6.0%	$84,896	10.3%	1,551	30.3%	$14,187
60,230	University of Oklahoma - Norman	-4.0%	$18,186	9.3%	$142,460	5.8%	1,505	23.8%	$11,581
58,797	Univ. of Mississippi + Medical Center	-6.1%	$70,347	3.1%	$140,845	38.0%	6,394	-13.2%	-$8,920
56,448	University of Oregon	-6.6%	-$9,065	5.8%	$186,480	18.1%	3,684	21.2%	$9,865
54,516	University of Houston - University Park	-6.2%	$6,764	8.2%	$160,594	24.4%	8,370	41.4%	$15,957
54,113	George Mason University	-10.9%	$4,799	6.6%	$171,698	13.5%	4,040	50.7%	$18,202
50,554	New Jersey Institute of Technology	-10.2%	$9,800	7.6%	$63,997	38.0%	3,116	42.4%	$15,065
49,977	University of Nevada - Reno	-8.6%	-$37,401	9.4%	$58,901	25.4%	4,235	-22.5%	-$14,499
49,591	University of Idaho	-5.3%	-$541	7.5%	$37,432	-3.1%	-367	5.5%	$2,573
47,939	Auburn University	-10.8%	$238	9.0%	$176,069	15.9%	3,740	5.3%	$2,399
47,591	Univ. of Maryland - Baltimore County	0.4%	$37,645	2.7%	$42,819	17.3%	2,041	6.2%	$2,761
47,232	University of Wyoming	-0.9%	$86,013	0.7%	$22,633	-4.2%	-555	82.8%	$21,388
45,292	Clemson University	-9.4%	-$28,333	11.3%	$149,981	31.1%	5,389	-19.5%	-$10,976
43,526	San Diego State University	-15.6%	-$36,222	10.9%	$93,454	2.4%	813	23.1%	$8,175
41,721	Cleveland State University	-5.6%	$1,040	7.0%	$49,938	14.2%	2,108	708.7%	$36,562
40,334	University of Texas - El Paso	-0.1%	$23,892	6.3%	$46,339	17.9%	3,555	108.6%	$21,003
38,498	Oklahoma State University - Stillwater	-6.3%	$23,962	7.9%	$114,551	10.4%	2,431	1.5%	$555
37,900	City University of NY - City College	-12.7%	$41,561	-4.4%	$18,346	19.9%	2,623	77.0%	$16,492
37,457	University of North Dakota	0.3%	$44,204	-4.6%	$37,998	16.5%	2,117	-3.6%	-$1,391
36,843	Georgia State University	-18.3%	-$7,091	4.4%	$116,157	22.7%	5,923	47.6%	$11,875
35,037	North Dakota State University	0.9%	$48,869	3.0%	$51,163	18.4%	2,258	-22.9%	-$10,381
35,033	University of Maine - Orono	-3.4%	$374	7.4%	$33,124	-7.4%	-875	-15.4%	-$6,361
33,617	University of Montana - Missoula	3.9%	$24,981	-0.7%	$19,653	-6.3%	-881	1.7%	$578
33,578	Colorado School of Mines**			11.0%	$73,400	39.0%	1,697	63.5%	$13,035
33,486	University of Arkansas - Fayetteville	-6.2%	$32,509	7.8%	$105,684	49.3%	8,828	4.9%	$1,560
31,250	San Jose State University	-21.1%	-$22,576	10.0%	$98,914	10.7%	3,169	34.7%	$8,053
30,776	University of Texas - Dallas	-6.9%	$28,842	15.3%	$166,920	69.1%	10,031	54.2%	$10,822
28,998	University of Massachusetts - Lowell	-15.6%	$15,368	6.8%	$95,302	61.0%	6,840	54.7%	$10,257
28,581	Michigan Technological University	-10.0%	-$1,870	9.4%	$42,441	10.3%	672	52.4%	$9,824
28,488	South Dakota State University	-11.4%	$6,967	4.5%	$43,074	11.3%	1,273	122.8%	$15,700
28,029	University of Alabama - Tuscaloosa	-9.9%	$292	22.3%	$317,297	55.6%	13,260	22.7%	$5,182
27,857	Old Dominion University	-9.0%	$29,624	6.4%	$74,972	14.1%	3,047	1.3%	$351
27,722	College of William and Mary	-5.2%	$14,990	7.2%	$86,571	10.1%	775	-4.8%	-$1,399
26,970	University of Nevada - Las Vegas	-6.1%	-$20,295	9.7%	$68,740	2.5%	688	-36.9%	-$15,802
26,858	University of Texas - Arlington	-10.0%	$15,788	7.8%	$124,205	69.1%	17,163	41.3%	$7,852
26,814	Wright State University - Dayton	-2.6%	-$6,406	11.1%	$42,751	6.1%	982	19.5%	$4,384
26,700	Florida A&M University	0.7%	$1,184	2.4%	$6,699	-16.6%	-1,979	7.2%	$1,798
26,428	University of Toledo	-9.6%	$30,939	-16.9%	$65,816	5.2%	1,003	59.8%	$9,894
25,458	Texas Tech University	-13.0%	$30,315	-9.2%	$117,263	28.1%	7,863	14.3%	$3,180
24,710	University of Southern Mississippi	-0.4%	$8,523	6.0%	$27,505	-1.5%	-226	-28.5%	-$9,867
24,222	University of Wisconsin - Milwaukee	-1.7%	$35,857	-1.0%	$59,943	-5.6%	-1,583	52.7%	$8,355
23,389	Portland State University	-10.4%	$5,150	-11.2%	$66,605	13.3%	3,234	24.4%	$4,592
23,108	University of Texas - San Antonio	-1.2%	$28,289	6.2%	$73,965	1.4%	408	14.0%	$2,831
19,975	New Mexico Inst. of Mining and Tech.	5.9%	$11,293	3.5%	$5,800	17.3%	317	-58.3%	-$27,926
18,449	Jackson State University	-0.3%	$4,098	4.3%	$11,812	18.7%	1,546	-40.1%	-$12,334
18,177	University of Puerto Rico - Rio Piedras	4.6%	$57,183	-1.4%	-$1,864	-13.7%	-2,621	7.7%	$1,296
17,306	Missouri Univ. of Science and Tech.	-3.7%	$6,318	17.5%	$48,522	51.7%	3,028	-22.6%	-$5,045
9,286	South Dakota Sch. of Mines and Tech.	-7.9%	$4,355	8.3%	$13,353	52.1%	1,106	-5.6%	-$548

Table A-2. Top Private Research Universities:
Change from 2006 to 2015 in Tuition, Students, and Research

2015 Federal Research ($000)*	Institution	Net Change in % of Tuition & Fees	Net Change in Tuition & Fees (000s)	Percent Change in Fall Enrollment	Net Change in Fall Enrollment	Percent Change in Federal Research	Net Change in Federal Research $ ($000)
1,988,993	Johns Hopkins University	0.8%	$216,439	15.1%	2,978	52.1%	$681,540
645,633	Stanford University	-3.0%	$118,448	-4.3%	-767	19.5%	$105,564
597,791	University of Pennsylvania	-0.6%	$246,123	4.8%	1,133	24.9%	$119,018
577,833	Columbia University	6.5%	$421,656	25.9%	5,769	28.1%	$126,646
558,566	Duke University	1.3%	$153,482	19.5%	2,611	34.8%	$144,147
530,382	Harvard University	5.7%	$257,853	15.0%	3,874	31.5%	$126,924
486,650	Massachusetts Institute of Technology	1.7%	$132,651	10.5%	1,078	2.2%	$10,288
471,381	Yale University	1.2%	$54,303	8.5%	970	35.3%	$122,881
424,723	Washington University in St. Louis	2.4%	$133,123	10.0%	1,333	4.0%	$16,321
408,105	University of Southern California	1.7%	$622,934	30.0%	10,012	22.4%	$74,727
390,701	Vanderbilt University	-0.1%	$84,038	8.3%	960	30.1%	$90,278
385,868	Northwestern University	4.4%	$171,971	17.1%	3,169	54.4%	$135,888
346,534	Emory University	0.9%	$121,957	11.8%	1,450	29.4%	$78,640
326,691	New York University	-3.8%	$626,083	22.4%	9,157	72.6%	$137,415
307,960	Case Western Reserve University	9.6%	$94,472	18.2%	1,748	0.3%	$980
302,781	Cornell University	9.6%	$181,140	11.5%	2,265	19.5%	$49,504
291,397	University of Chicago	2.0%	$129,660	7.9%	1,128	15.0%	$37,926
269,156	California Institute of Technology	0.7%	$17,200	8.1%	169	8.3%	$20,565
261,023	University of Rochester	1.8%	$128,000	25.5%	2,259	-6.2%	-$17,376
256,562	Boston University	12.6%	$335,446	1.9%	584	7.5%	$18,002
214,976	University of Miami	-2.9%	$175,224	7.4%	1,155	42.9%	$64,568
187,259	Carnegie Mellon University	8.1%	$209,296	29.6%	2,964	1.0%	$1,870
180,791	Yeshiva University	9.0%	$17,498	-0.3%	-17	17.6%	$27,006
157,867	Princeton University	-0.1%	$19,309	14.9%	1,053	34.0%	$40,022
148,084	Wake Forest University	6.5%	$106,284	16.3%	1,098	6.1%	$8,535
145,807	Dartmouth College	4.8%	$74,094	10.4%	597	3.8%	$5,377
135,667	George Washington University	4.2%	$212,927	6.9%	1,681	80.4%	$60,458
127,886	Brown University	13.1%	$117,584	16.4%	1,333	31.9%	$30,964
120,181	Tufts University	15.9%	$121,053	15.6%	1,499	25.2%	$24,217
87,268	Georgetown University	4.4%	$211,006	30.5%	4,311	-5.4%	-$5,000
84,143	Tulane University	8.4%	$142,088	22.0%	2,248	0.1%	$91
82,615	University of Notre Dame	1.8%	$82,088	5.9%	689	48.3%	$26,905
78,379	Northeastern University	12.6%	$409,012	-14.8%	-3,471	117.3%	$42,308
74,548	University of Dayton	8.7%	$83,098	7.1%	747	31.3%	$17,769
73,817	Rice University	12.5%	$76,873	33.7%	1,695	37.0%	$19,937
67,226	Drexel University	13.9%	$330,766	28.9%	5,735	-1.9%	-$1,273
59,417	Rensselaer Polytechnic Institute	11.1%	$78,840	4.5%	302	33.0%	$14,727
46,764	Brandeis University	14.5%	$60,625	8.3%	439	13.5%	$5,580
38,051	Howard University	7.1%	$48,003	-7.1%	-769	8.8%	$3,092
27,380	Loyola University Chicago	14.1%	$138,428	8.2%	1,243	7.7%	$1,960
27,343	Saint Louis University - St. Louis	8.9%	$73,344	14.4%	2,150	-39.5%	-$17,840
26,769	Syracuse University	17.3%	$198,823	14.2%	2,707	5.8%	$1,470
25,743	Worcester Polytechnic Institute	17.1%	$83,737	67.8%	2,655	152.6%	$15,550
25,479	Illinois Institute of Technology	15.7%	$77,519	15.5%	1,045	33.3%	$6,358
25,054	Stevens Institute of Technology	12.8%	$75,970	31.7%	1,530	11.3%	$2,553
21,082	Loma Linda University	14.8%	$67,968	15.7%	609	-26.8%	-$7,706
20,680	Lehigh University	18.5%	$60,762	2.9%	196	13.3%	$2,432
17,409	Boston College	5.8%	$115,145	-2.1%	-307	-5.1%	-$935
14,609	Hampton University	5.5%	$5,370	-30.6%	-1,883	-48.9%	-$13,965

*Cornell's 2015 Federal Research is based on preliminary estimate.

Part I – The Top American Research Universities

The Center for Measuring University Performance determines the Top American Research Universities by their rank on nine different measures: Total Research, Federal Research, Endowment Assets, Annual Giving, National Academy Members, Faculty Awards, Doctorates Granted, Postdoctoral Appointees, and SAT scores. (The Source Notes section of this study provides detailed information on each of the nine indicators.) The tables group research institutions according to how many times they rank in the top 25 on each of these nine measures. The top category includes those universities that rank in the top 25 on all nine indicators. The bottom category includes universities with only one of the nine measures ranked in the top 25. Within these groups, institutions are then sorted by how many times they rank between 26 and 50 on the nine performance variables, with ties listed alphabetically. A similar methodology produces a second set of institutions—those ranked 26 through 50 on the same nine measures.

For the purpose of this study, *The Center for Measuring University Performance* includes only those institutions that had at least $40 million in federal research expenditures in fiscal year 2014. This is the same dollar cutoff used since the 2008 report. There were 160 institutions who met our criteria, 112 public and 48 private.

The first two tables list each institution with the most current data available for each measure and its corresponding national rank (i.e., rank among all institutions regardless of whether they are privately or publicly controlled). The third through sixth tables provide the same nine data measures but with the groupings determined by the control rank (i.e., rank among all private or all public institutions). Institutions ranking in the top 25 on at least one measure are included in the tables with the (1-25) identifier, while those ranking 26 through 50 are found in the tables labeled with the (26-50) header. Many research universities rank highly both nationally and among their public or private peers, and therefore appear in more than one table.

- **The Top American Research Universities (1-25)** identifies the 49 institutions (25 private, 24 public) that rank in the top 25 nationally on at least one of the nine measures.

- **The Top American Research Universities (26-50)** identifies the 27 institutions (8 private, 19 public) that rank 26 through 50 nationally on at least one of the nine measures.

- **The Top Private Research Universities (1-25)** identifies the 32 private institutions that rank in the top 25 among all private universities on at least one of the nine measures.

- **The Top Private Research Universities (26-50)** identifies the 6 private institutions that rank 26 through 50 among their private counterparts on at least one of the nine measures.

- **The Top Public Research Universities (1-25)** identifies the 41 public institutions that rank in the top 25 among all public universities on at least one of the nine measures.

- **The Top Public Research Universities (26-50)** identifies the 31 public institutions that rank 26 through 50 among their public counterparts on at least one of the nine measures.

- **The Top Medical and Specialized Research Universities** tables identify the institutions that have at least one measure that ranks in the top 50 nationally or among their private and public counterparts.

Data found in these tables may not always match the figures published by the original source. *The Center for Measuring University Performance* makes adjustments, when necessary, to ensure that the data reflect the activity at a single campus rather than that of a multiple-campus institution or state university system. When data are missing from the original source, *The Center for Measuring University Performance* may substitute another figure, if available. A full discussion of this subject, and the various adjustments or substitutions made to the original data, is in the Data Notes section of this report.

The Center for Measuring University Performance presents these tables, along with prior years' top universities, in Microsoft Excel spreadsheets on its website [http://mup.asu.edu].

Top American Research Universities (1-25)		Number of Measures in Top 25 Nationally	Number of Measures in Top 26-50 Nationally	Research				Private	
Institutions in Order of Top 25 Score, then Top 26-50 Score, then Alphabetically				2014 Total Research x $1000	2014 National Rank	2014 Federal Research x $1000	2014 National Rank	2015 Endowment Assets x $1000	2015 National Rank
Private	Columbia University	9	0	844,766	13	591,523	8	9,639,065	11
Private	Harvard University	9	0	875,964	11	554,944	11	36,448,817	1
Private	Massachusetts Institute of Technology	9	0	815,008	15	480,991	16	13,474,743	5
Private	Stanford University	9	0	912,244	10	608,342	4	22,222,957	4
Private	University of Pennsylvania	9	0	792,314	17	606,115	5	10,133,569	8
Private	Duke University	8	1	1,031,404	6	556,847	10	7,296,545	14
Public	University of Michigan - Ann Arbor	8	1	1,279,603	2	733,779	3	9,952,113	9
Private	Yale University	8	1	764,002	18	475,585	17	25,572,100	2
Public	University of California - Berkeley	7	2	708,485	22	309,305	33	4,045,451	23
Public	University of California - Los Angeles	7	1	920,183	9	458,157	19	3,493,903	27
Public	University of Washington - Seattle	7	1	1,091,135	3	849,713	2	3,076,226	30
Public	University of Wisconsin - Madison	7	1	984,830	7	522,251	13	2,792,622	33
Private	Johns Hopkins University	6	3	2,227,536	1	1,936,953	1	3,412,617	28
Private	Northwestern University	6	3	621,504	30	385,888	24	10,193,037	7
Private	University of Southern California	6	3	650,506	27	421,887	20	4,709,511	20
Public	University of Minnesota - Twin Cities	6	2	850,880	12	483,542	15	3,297,460	29
Public	Ohio State University - Columbus	5	3	752,836	19	416,177	21	3,633,887	24
Private	University of Chicago	5	3	378,322	56	276,237	43	7,549,710	13
Public	University of California - San Diego	5	2	1,060,207	5	597,270	7	951,367	92
Private	Cornell University	4	5	580,936	32	299,320	36	4,760,560	19
Public	Univ. of North Carolina - Chapel Hill	4	4	955,601	8	601,933	6	2,988,806	32
Public	University of Texas - Austin	4	4	526,173	35	313,955	32	10,507,795	6
Private	Washington University in St. Louis	4	4	646,756	28	410,115	22	6,818,748	15
Public	University of Pittsburgh - Pittsburgh	4	3	835,838	14	565,409	9	3,588,775	25
Private	Vanderbilt University	4	3	659,418	25	408,743	23	4,133,542	22
Private	Princeton University	4	2	287,730	78	163,805	72	22,723,473	3
Private	New York University	3	5	490,614	40	314,712	31	3,576,180	26
Public	Pennsylvania State Univ. - Univ. Park	3	5	702,912	23	461,896	18	1,854,222	46
Public	Texas A&M University - College Station	3	5	735,273	20	266,877	45	9,856,983	10
Public	University of Florida	3	4	652,341	26	279,920	40	1,555,703	58
Public	Univ. of Illinois - Urbana-Champaign	3	4	598,531	31	336,172	26	1,530,658	59
Public	University of California - Davis	3	3	699,689	24	327,697	30	1,013,936	87
Private	University of Notre Dame	3	1	160,461	113	79,192	119	8,566,952	12
Private	Emory University	2	6	551,556	34	329,254	27	6,684,305	16
Private	California Institute of Technology	2	5	358,137	59	276,447	42	2,198,887	39
Public	Georgia Institute of Technology	2	5	720,248	21	510,422	14	1,858,977	45
Public	Rutgers University - New Brunswick	2	3	627,076	29	355,116	25	710,802	130
Private	Dartmouth College	2	1	204,360	96	145,080	76	4,663,491	21
Private	Rice University	2	1	136,419	124	73,782	124	5,557,479	18
Public	Arizona State University	2	0	380,581	55	186,126	65	643,188	143
Public	Purdue University - West Lafayette	1	5	502,457	37	227,857	53	2,397,902	35
Public	University of Maryland - College Park	1	5	472,235	42	328,828	28	482,628	173
Public	Michigan State University	1	4	492,501	39	247,970	49	2,673,652	34
Public	University of Colorado - Boulder	1	4	362,882	58	302,877	34	598,355	152
Public	University of Virginia	1	4	337,732	64	192,907	63	6,180,515	17
Private	Brown University	1	3	291,917	76	125,005	84	3,073,349	31
Private	Carnegie Mellon University	1	2	250,497	82	198,247	61	1,739,474	52
Private	Tufts University	1	0	156,411	115	115,046	91	1,593,019	57
Public	University of California - Santa Barbara	1	0	225,614	89	119,816	86	265,930	260

Support		Faculty				Advanced Training				Undergraduate	
2015 Annual Giving x $1000	2015 National Rank	2015 National Academy Members	2015 National Rank	2015 Faculty Awards	2015 National Rank	2015 Doctorates Granted	2015 National Rank	2014 Post Docs	2014 National Rank	2014 Median SAT	2014 National Rank
552,682	6	134	6	34	8	564	24	1,274	6	1480	8
1,045,872	2	371	1	84	1	745	9	5,761	1	1505	3
439,404	16	268	3	41	5	606	20	1,516	4	1495	6
1,625,036	1	320	2	56	2	688	13	2,048	2	1475	10
517,198	9	117	8	30	12	566	23	919	13	1455	18
472,008	11	66	19	30	12	485	35	656	23	1460	13
394,310	18	108	13	42	4	882	2	1,238	7	1390	38
440,807	14	114	11	30	12	426	45	1,201	8	1505	3
366,116	20	230	4	45	3	826	6	1,148	10	1370	46
473,205	10	101	14	29	19	774	7	1,088	11	1325	66
447,021	12	115	10	39	6	687	14	1,184	9	1230	137
330,454	23	77	16	30	12	857	3	767	16	1280	97
582,675	5	97	15	33	9	535	27	1,715	3	1435	26
536,831	8	43	28	33	9	438	39	708	18	1475	10
653,025	3	50	25	30	12	685	16	480	37	1380	43
344,303	22	41	29	35	7	725	11	679	19	1260	107
359,798	21	32	35	17	38	832	4	629	28	1300	82
443,792	13	69	17	25	23	392	48	583	32	1518	2
171,059	46	117	8	29	19	505	32	1,338	5	1310	79
434,465	17	62	20	30	12	487	34	466	39	1420	28
301,177	25	38	33	19	33	519	30	802	15	1320	70
310,212	24	69	17	19	33	899	1	370	49	1290	94
246,714	29	46	26	29	19	292	70	625	29	1460	13
124,602	65	32	35	13	49	438	39	659	22	1270	103
121,909	69	36	34	15	42	340	59	634	27	1460	13
549,840	7	120	7	22	26	371	51	464	41	1500	5
439,662	15	59	21	27	22	438	39	596	30	1345	59
155,658	50	27	43	19	33	673	17	365	50	1190	184
255,179	26	27	43	14	45	740	10	386	48	1195	179
215,580	33	25	48	23	24	754	8	644	25	1265	104
177,235	40	56	22	30	12	829	5	525	35	1300	82
185,840	38	45	27	12	54	553	25	765	17	1205	164
379,869	19	4	111	14	45	244	83	171	96	1460	13
228,034	31	32	35	19	33	264	78	674	20	1370	46
161,929	47	112	12	16	40	182	110	552	34	1550	1
119,118	73	31	38	21	27	526	29	217	80	1400	35
127,846	63	39	31	20	29	597	21	345	54	1215	157
218,832	32	15	62	6	98	85	192	222	78	1455	18
122,186	67	25	48	6	98	176	113	206	84	1470	12
130,775	61	22	55	23	24	687	14	253	68	1145	273
172,219	44	27	43	19	33	717	12	358	51	1205	164
122,694	66	26	46	20	29	654	18	437	46	1315	77
131,499	60	13	65	11	58	577	22	450	43	1170	215
151,553	52	30	41	21	27	434	43	879	14	1220	143
233,218	30	24	50	15	42	366	52	447	44	1355	56
187,754	37	22	55	20	29	215	94	244	71	1440	23
139,563	57	39	31	13	49	333	62	215	81	1440	23
62,131	118	11	70	6	98	116	153	194	88	1440	23
63,413	116	56	22	12	54	349	56	285	64	1235	133

Top American Research Universities (26-50)		Research				Private	
Institutions in Order of Top 26-50 Score, then Alphabetically		Number of Measures in Top 26-50 Nationally	2014 Total Research x $1000	2014 National Rank	2014 Federal Research x $1000	2014 National Rank	2015 Endowment Assets x $1000	2015 National Rank
Public	University of Arizona	6	575,864	33	286,595	38	767,940	118
Private	Boston University	4	353,850	60	254,285	48	1,644,117	53
Public	University of Utah	4	476,017	41	284,125	39	1,023,004	86
Private	Case Western Reserve University	3	417,436	49	328,548	29	1,775,999	51
Public	Indiana University - Bloomington	3	172,380	106	80,109	117	960,625	91
Public	North Carolina State University	3	440,392	44	177,722	70	983,979	89
Public	University of California - Irvine	3	322,315	65	180,431	69	512,904	166
Public	University of Iowa	3	436,852	45	234,122	52	1,263,043	67
Private	University of Rochester	3	347,161	61	265,686	46	2,050,199	43
Private	George Washington University	2	213,334	92	139,148	82	1,616,357	56
Private	Georgetown University	2	162,983	112	99,567	103	1,528,869	60
Private	Northeastern University	2	111,779	137	77,401	120	729,400	125
Public	University of Alabama - Birmingham	2	421,475	48	276,112	44	388,405	205
Public	University of Colorado - Denver	2	401,230	51	277,209	41	491,942	171
Public	University of South Florida - Tampa	2	436,578	46	205,155	57	417,415	196
Public	Virginia Polytechnic Institute and State University	2	502,486	36	198,092	62	817,759	107
Public	Florida International University	1	107,487	140	68,946	126	178,750	340
Public	Florida State University	1	231,390	87	140,995	79	605,275	150
Private	Rensselaer Polytechnic Institute	1	104,844	143	58,940	136	676,546	136
Public	University of Cincinnati - Cincinnati	1	399,571	52	243,705	51	1,195,899	71
Public	University of Georgia	1	313,445	70	122,145	85	1,004,987	88
Public	University of Kansas - Lawrence	1	169,884	108	88,725	111	1,170,313	73
Public	University of Massachusetts - Amherst	1	183,210	99	102,682	101	303,984	238
Private	University of Miami	1	342,852	62	202,818	58	887,329	97
Public	University of Missouri - Columbia	1	233,613	86	102,784	100	857,471	101
Public	University of Nebraska - Lincoln	1	254,879	81	93,190	106	906,156	95
Public	University of Oklahoma - Norman	1	120,322	134	53,223	145	1,066,117	82

Support		Faculty				Advanced Training				Undergraduate	
2015 Annual Giving x $1000	2015 National Rank	2015 National Academy Members	2015 National Rank	2015 Faculty Awards	2015 National Rank	2015 Doctorates Granted	2015 National Rank	2014 Post Docs	2014 National Rank	2014 Median SAT	2014 National Rank
190,184	36	31	38	9	76	528	28	451	42		
140,393	56	20	58	16	40	484	36	444	45	1300	82
126,244	64	23	54	10	67	384	50	429	47	1130	286
132,826	58	20	58	11	58	197	101	190	90	1370	46
211,471	34	8	84	15	42	538	26	144	108	1175	213
119,150	72	20	58	11	58	512	31	473	38	1245	114
66,617	114	31	38	20	29	390	49	315	57	1160	240
159,532	48	22	55	10	67	453	38	355	53	1170	215
108,217	80	24	50	12	54	267	77	222	78		
248,030	28	12	68	14	45	222	91	94	133	1295	93
172,452	43	9	77	4	127	114	154	127	116	1420	28
59,857	122	3	119	14	45	157	121	117	122	1420	28
76,612	106	8	84	0	473	170	115	228	75	1110	347
171,102	45	14	63	5	110	103	168	267	66	1050	560
59,903	121	8	84	13	49	321	67	300	61	1160	240
86,391	99	13	65	10	67	488	33	226	76	1215	157
23,312	212	1	163	13	49	189	108	64	146	1080	475
68,634	112	7	92	9	76	424	46	211	83	1240	118
38,364	164	7	92	5	110	164	119	82	137	1395	37
119,700	71	8	84	10	67	213	96	466	39	1170	215
104,108	84	6	99	6	98	467	37	231	74	1235	133
176,704	42	5	104	11	58	365	53	154	103	1150	252
35,327	170	7	92	17	38	268	76	153	104	1215	157
193,809	35	11	70	7	90	208	98	198	87	1320	70
108,689	79	9	77	9	76	435	42	184	93	1170	215
177,321	39	3	119	3	144	325	65	201	85	1150	252
252,475	27	1	163	9	76	218	93	145	107	1190	184

Top Private Research Universities (1-25)				Research				Private	
Institutions in Order of Top 25 Score, then Top 26-50 Score, then Alphabetically		Number of Measures in Top 25 Control	Number of Measures in Top 26-50 Control	2014 Total Research x $1000	2014 Control Rank	2014 Federal Research x $1000	2014 Control Rank	2015 Endowment Assets x $1000	2015 Control Rank
Private	Columbia University	9	0	844,766	5	591,523	4	9,639,065	8
Private	Duke University	9	0	1,031,404	2	556,847	5	7,296,545	11
Private	Harvard University	9	0	875,964	4	554,944	6	36,448,817	1
Private	Massachusetts Institute of Technology	9	0	815,008	6	480,991	7	13,474,743	5
Private	Northwestern University	9	0	621,504	12	385,888	12	10,193,037	6
Private	Stanford University	9	0	912,244	3	608,342	2	22,222,957	4
Private	University of Chicago	9	0	378,322	20	276,237	20	7,549,710	10
Private	University of Pennsylvania	9	0	792,314	7	606,115	3	10,133,569	7
Private	Washington University in St. Louis	9	0	646,756	11	410,115	10	6,818,748	12
Private	Yale University	9	0	764,002	8	475,585	8	25,572,100	2
Private	California Institute of Technology	8	1	358,137	21	276,447	19	2,198,887	25
Private	Cornell University	8	1	580,936	13	299,320	17	4,760,560	15
Private	Emory University	8	1	551,556	14	329,254	13	6,684,305	13
Private	Johns Hopkins University	8	1	2,227,536	1	1,936,953	1	3,412,617	20
Private	University of Southern California	8	1	650,506	10	421,887	9	4,709,511	16
Private	Vanderbilt University	8	1	659,418	9	408,743	11	4,133,542	18
Private	New York University	8	0	490,614	16	314,712	15	3,576,180	19
Private	Princeton University	7	2	287,730	29	163,805	28	22,723,473	3
Private	Carnegie Mellon University	5	4	250,497	30	198,247	25	1,739,474	35
Private	University of Notre Dame	5	4	160,461	37	79,192	39	8,566,952	9
Private	Boston University	5	3	353,850	22	254,285	23	1,644,117	36
Private	University of Rochester	5	3	347,161	23	265,686	21	2,050,199	28
Private	Brown University	4	5	291,917	28	125,005	33	3,073,349	21
Private	Rice University	3	6	136,419	40	73,782	42	5,557,479	14
Private	Dartmouth College	3	5	204,360	33	145,080	30	4,663,491	17
Private	George Washington University	3	5	213,334	32	139,148	32	1,616,357	37
Private	University of Miami	3	4	342,852	24	202,818	24	887,329	61
Private	Case Western Reserve University	2	7	417,436	18	328,548	14	1,775,999	34
Private	Georgetown University	1	8	162,983	36	99,567	36	1,528,869	39
Private	Tufts University	1	8	156,411	38	115,046	34	1,593,019	38
Private	Northeastern University	1	7	111,779	43	77,401	40	729,400	80
Private	Yeshiva University	1	5	306,826	26	186,885	26	1,061,440	56

Support		Faculty				Advanced Training				Undergraduate	
2015 Annual Giving x $1000	2015 Control Rank	2015 National Academy Members	2015 Control Rank	2015 Faculty Awards	2015 Control Rank	2015 Doctorates Granted	2015 Control Rank	2014 Post Docs	2014 Control Rank	2014 Median SAT	2014 Control Rank
552,682	5	134	4	34	4	564	7	1,274	5	1480	8
472,008	9	66	11	30	7	485	10	656	11	1460	13
1,045,872	2	371	1	84	1	745	1	5,761	1	1505	3
439,404	13	268	3	41	3	606	5	1,516	4	1495	6
536,831	7	43	17	33	5	438	12	708	8	1475	10
1,625,036	1	320	2	56	2	688	2	2,048	2	1475	10
443,792	10	69	10	25	14	392	16	583	17	1518	2
517,198	8	117	6	30	7	566	6	919	7	1455	18
246,714	17	46	16	29	12	292	20	625	14	1460	13
440,807	11	114	7	30	7	426	15	1,201	6	1505	3
161,929	23	112	8	16	18	182	32	552	18	1550	1
434,465	14	62	12	30	7	487	9	466	21	1420	28
228,034	18	32	20	19	17	264	22	674	9	1370	44
582,675	4	97	9	33	5	535	8	1,715	3	1435	26
653,025	3	50	15	30	7	685	3	480	20	1380	41
121,909	31	36	19	15	20	340	18	634	13	1460	13
439,662	12	59	13	27	13	438	12	596	15	1345	54
549,840	6	120	5	22	15	371	17	464	22	1500	5
139,563	27	39	18	13	24	333	19	215	30	1440	23
379,869	15	4	44	14	21	244	23	171	36	1460	13
140,393	26	20	28	16	18	484	11	444	23	1300	71
108,217	34	24	24	12	25	267	21	222	28		
187,754	21	22	27	20	16	215	26	244	27	1440	23
122,186	30	25	23	6	33	176	33	206	31	1470	12
218,832	19	15	31	6	33	85	65	222	28	1455	18
248,030	16	12	33	14	21	222	25	94	47	1295	80
193,809	20	11	34	7	31	208	28	198	32	1320	62
132,826	28	20	28	11	26	197	30	190	34	1370	44
172,452	22	9	37	4	45	114	48	127	40	1420	28
62,131	43	11	34	6	33	116	47	194	33	1440	23
59,857	46	3	47	14	21	157	35	117	43	1420	28
59,420	47	13	32	5	39	96	59	303	25	1240	90

Top Private Research Universities (26-50)		Number of Measures in Top 26-50 Control	Research				Private	
Institutions in Order of Top 26-50 Score, then Alphabetically			2014 Total Research x $1000	2014 Control Rank	2014 Federal Research x $1000	2014 Control Rank	2015 Endowment Assets x $1000	2015 Control Rank
Private	Tulane University	8	148,784	39	94,287	37	1,220,464	45
Private	Brandeis University	7	67,048	48	45,800	47	915,087	59
Private	Drexel University	7	124,464	41	75,557	41	668,386	89
Private	Rensselaer Polytechnic Institute	7	104,844	44	58,940	44	676,546	88
Private	Wake Forest University	6	176,380	35	153,069	29	1,167,400	49
Private	University of Dayton	2	83,409	45	63,881	43	500,407	104

Support		Faculty				Advanced Training				Undergraduate	
2015 Annual Giving x $1000	2015 Control Rank	2015 National Academy Members	2015 Control Rank	2015 Faculty Awards	2015 Control Rank	2015 Doctorates Granted	2015 Control Rank	2014 Post Docs	2014 Control Rank	2014 Median SAT	2014 Control Rank
88,422	39	1	64	4	45	123	45	124	41	1360	50
60,196	45	11	34	9	29	100	55	102	45	1365	47
88,916	38	7	39	5	39	213	27	74	49	1200	122
38,364	68	7	39	5	39	164	34	82	48	1395	36
99,763	35	7	39	3	53	53	89	152	39		
28,219	84	0	86	0	189	34	110	10	82	1205	116

Top Public Research Universities (1-25)		Number of Measures in Top 25 Control	Number of Measures in Top 26-50 Control	Research				Private	
Institutions in Order of Top 25 Score, then Top 26-50 Score, then Alphabetically				2014 Total Research x $1000	2014 Control Rank	2014 Federal Research x $1000	2014 Control Rank	2015 Endowment Assets x $1000	2015 Control Rank
Public	Ohio State University - Columbus	9	0	752,836	11	416,177	12	3,633,887	6
Public	University of California - Berkeley	9	0	708,485	14	309,305	18	4,045,451	5
Public	University of California - Los Angeles	9	0	920,183	7	458,157	11	3,493,903	8
Public	Univ. of Illinois - Urbana-Champaign	9	0	598,531	19	336,172	14	1,530,658	21
Public	University of Michigan - Ann Arbor	9	0	1,279,603	1	733,779	2	9,952,113	2
Public	University of Minnesota - Twin Cities	9	0	850,880	8	483,542	9	3,297,460	9
Public	Univ. of North Carolina - Chapel Hill	9	0	955,601	6	601,933	3	2,988,806	11
Public	University of Wisconsin - Madison	9	0	984,830	5	522,251	7	2,792,622	12
Public	University of California - San Diego	8	1	1,060,207	4	597,270	4	951,367	34
Public	University of Florida	8	1	652,341	17	279,920	22	1,555,703	20
Public	University of Texas - Austin	8	1	526,173	21	313,955	17	10,507,795	1
Public	University of Washington - Seattle	8	1	1,091,135	2	849,713	1	3,076,226	10
Public	Texas A&M University - College Station	8	0	735,273	12	266,877	25	9,856,983	3
Public	Georgia Institute of Technology	7	1	720,248	13	510,422	8	1,858,977	16
Public	Purdue University - West Lafayette	6	3	502,457	23	227,857	30	2,397,902	14
Public	University of California - Davis	6	3	699,689	16	327,697	16	1,013,936	30
Public	University of Pittsburgh - Pittsburgh	6	3	835,838	9	565,409	5	3,588,775	7
Public	Pennsylvania State Univ. - Univ. Park	6	2	702,912	15	461,896	10	1,854,222	17
Public	University of Arizona	6	2	575,864	20	286,595	20	767,940	44
Public	University of Maryland - College Park	6	2	472,235	26	328,828	15	482,628	68
Public	Rutgers University - New Brunswick	5	4	627,076	18	355,116	13	710,802	47
Public	University of Virginia	5	4	337,732	40	192,907	38	6,180,515	4
Public	Michigan State University	4	4	492,501	24	247,970	26	2,673,652	13
Public	University of Colorado - Boulder	4	4	362,882	38	302,877	19	598,355	57
Public	University of Utah	3	5	476,017	25	284,125	21	1,023,004	29
Public	Indiana University - Bloomington	3	2	172,380	71	80,109	79	960,625	33
Public	North Carolina State University	2	7	440,392	27	177,722	44	983,979	32
Public	University of Iowa	2	6	436,852	28	234,122	29	1,263,043	23
Public	Virginia Polytechnic Inst. and St. Univ.	2	6	502,486	22	198,092	37	817,759	41
Public	Arizona State University	2	5	380,581	36	186,126	39	643,188	51
Public	University of Cincinnati - Cincinnati	2	5	399,571	34	243,705	28	1,195,899	25
Public	University of California - Irvine	2	4	322,315	41	180,431	43	512,904	63
Public	University of Colorado - Denver	2	3	401,230	33	277,209	23	491,942	66
Public	University of California - Santa Barbara	1	4	225,614	59	119,816	53	265,930	104
Public	University of Alabama - Birmingham	1	3	421,475	31	276,112	24	388,405	83
Public	University of Kansas - Lawrence	1	3	169,884	73	88,725	74	1,170,313	26
Public	University of Nebraska - Lincoln	1	2	254,879	52	93,190	69	906,156	36
Public	University of Oklahoma - Norman	1	2	120,322	93	53,223	99	1,066,117	28
Public	University of Delaware	1	1	169,641	74	111,933	61	1,341,373	22
Public	University of Massachusetts - Amherst	1	1	183,210	65	102,682	66	303,984	96
Public	Virginia Commonwealth University	1	1	177,540	69	119,507	54	1,638,147	18

Support		Faculty				Advanced Training				Undergraduate	
2015 Annual Giving x $1000	2015 Control Rank	2015 National Academy Members	2015 Control Rank	2015 Faculty Awards	2015 Control Rank	2015 Doctorates Granted	2015 Control Rank	2014 Post Docs	2014 Control Rank	2014 Median SAT	2014 Control Rank
359,798	6	32	16	17	21	832	4	629	15	1300	12
366,116	5	230	1	45	1	826	6	1,148	4	1370	3
473,205	2	101	6	29	8	774	7	1,088	5	1325	8
177,235	19	56	9	30	6	829	5	525	17	1300	12
394,310	4	108	5	42	2	882	2	1,238	2	1390	2
344,303	7	41	12	35	4	725	10	679	11	1260	23
301,177	10	38	15	19	17	519	22	802	8	1320	9
330,454	8	77	7	30	6	857	3	767	9	1280	17
171,059	24	117	3	29	8	505	24	1,338	1	1310	11
215,580	14	25	26	23	10	754	8	644	13	1265	22
310,212	9	69	8	19	17	899	1	370	26	1290	14
447,021	3	115	4	39	3	687	12	1,184	3	1230	36
255,179	11	27	22	14	25	740	9	386	25	1195	53
119,118	42	31	18	21	12	526	21	217	51	1400	1
172,219	22	27	22	19	17	717	11	358	28	1205	49
185,840	17	45	11	12	30	553	18	765	10	1205	49
124,602	36	32	16	13	26	438	28	659	12	1270	21
155,658	26	27	22	19	17	673	14	365	27	1190	56
190,184	16	31	18	9	48	528	20	451	20		
122,694	37	26	25	20	14	654	15	437	23	1315	10
127,846	34	39	14	20	14	597	16	345	31	1215	43
233,218	13	24	27	15	23	366	35	447	22	1355	5
131,499	31	13	34	11	33	577	17	450	21	1170	66
151,553	27	30	21	21	12	434	30	879	7	1220	38
126,244	35	23	28	10	40	384	34	429	24	1130	98
211,471	15	8	47	15	23	538	19	144	69	1175	65
119,150	41	20	31	11	33	512	23	473	18	1245	27
159,532	25	22	29	10	40	453	27	355	30	1170	66
86,391	60	13	34	10	40	488	25	226	49	1215	43
130,775	32	22	29	23	10	687	12	253	42	1145	92
119,700	40	8	47	10	40	213	70	466	19	1170	66
66,617	72	31	18	20	14	390	33	315	33	1160	73
171,102	23	14	32	5	72	103	114	267	40	1050	192
63,413	74	56	9	12	30	349	39	285	38	1235	33
76,612	65	8	47	0	285	170	82	228	48	1110	115
176,704	21	5	62	11	33	365	36	154	66	1150	80
177,321	18	3	73	3	92	325	46	201	54	1150	80
252,475	12	1	100	9	48	218	68	145	68	1190	56
44,896	89	7	54	9	48	237	64	166	63	1190	56
35,327	99	7	54	17	21	268	56	153	67	1215	43
67,256	71	6	58	6	66	282	53	249	43	1105	132

Top Public Research Universities (26-50)		Number of Measures in Top 26-50 Control	Research				Private	
Institutions in Order of Top 26-50 Score, then Alphabetically			2014 Total Research x $1000	2014 Control Rank	2014 Federal Research x $1000	2014 Control Rank	2015 Endowment Assets x $1000	2015 Control Rank
Public	Iowa State University	6	297,293	48	115,285	57	786,205	43
Public	University of Georgia	6	313,445	45	122,145	52	1,004,987	31
Public	University of Kentucky	6	322,313	42	140,450	50	1,142,722	27
Public	University of South Florida - Tampa	6	436,578	29	205,155	34	417,415	80
Public	Colorado State University - Fort Collins	5	300,572	47	206,958	33	281,355	99
Public	Indiana University-Purdue University - Indianapolis	5	316,650	44	142,589	48	825,184	40
Public	Stony Brook University	5	210,301	62	111,386	62	247,397	108
Public	University at Buffalo	5	370,083	37	185,144	40	619,296	54
Public	University of Illinois - Chicago	5	339,644	39	201,646	36	302,121	97
Public	University of Missouri - Columbia	5	233,613	56	102,784	65	857,471	38
Public	Florida State University	4	231,390	57	140,995	49	605,275	56
Public	University of Hawaii - Manoa	4	319,818	43	202,574	35	280,210	101
Public	University of Houston - University Park	4	122,163	92	55,574	94	707,437	48
Public	University of Oregon	4	77,655	114	62,824	90	719,111	46
Public	University of South Carolina - Columbia	4	181,363	66	87,844	75	625,186	53
Public	Washington State University - Pullman	4	287,942	49	112,568	60	885,777	37
Public	Louisiana State University - Baton Rouge	3	282,462	50	93,584	68	427,852	78
Public	University of Connecticut - Storrs	3	142,332	82	80,317	77	279,699	102
Public	University of Tennessee - Knoxville	3	170,471	72	106,778	63	608,873	55
Public	Auburn University	2	140,110	83	49,739	103	641,993	52
Public	Clemson University	2	116,871	94	44,673	108	648,611	50
Public	University of New Mexico - Albuquerque	2	221,817	60	151,082	46	403,670	81
Public	Florida International University	1	107,487	97	68,946	84	178,750	133
Public	Oregon State University	1	229,456	58	143,815	47	505,369	65
Public	Temple University	1	206,556	63	118,892	55	386,230	84
Public	University of Alabama - Huntsville	1	85,994	107	73,913	82	65,978	224
Public	University of California - Riverside	1	128,506	89	56,327	93	185,335	131
Public	University of California - Santa Cruz	1	147,536	80	89,206	73	164,331	141
Public	University of Louisville	1	163,199	76	63,258	89	844,288	39
Public	University of Maryland - Baltimore County	1	64,329	123	46,993	106	75,752	198
Public	West Virginia University	1	156,946	77	67,450	85	533,599	60

Support		Faculty				Advanced Training				Undergraduate	
2015 Annual Giving x $1000	2015 Control Rank	2015 National Academy Members	2015 Control Rank	2015 Faculty Awards	2015 Control Rank	2015 Doctorates Granted	2015 Control Rank	2014 Post Docs	2014 Control Rank	2014 Median SAT	2014 Control Rank
105,512	49	8	47	6	66	336	42	331	32	1150	80
104,108	50	6	58	6	66	467	26	231	47	1235	33
118,190	43	3	73	10	40	295	50	155	65	1150	80
59,903	76	8	47	13	26	321	48	300	36	1160	73
41,342	92	9	41	11	33	251	59	297	37	1130	98
121,989	38	6	58	3	92	69	143	249	43	1000	320
86,687	59	14	32	10	40	347	40	224	50	1250	26
30,565	105	8	47	6	66	342	41	301	35	1150	80
62,590	75	6	58	11	33	314	49	238	46	1130	98
108,689	46	9	41	9	48	435	29	184	59	1170	66
68,634	70	7	54	9	48	424	31	211	53	1240	29
90,650	56	10	37	4	83	239	63	243	45	1085	161
95,602	55	9	41	4	83	326	45	258	41	1145	92
145,109	29	9	41	11	33	199	71	85	89	1110	115
113,506	44	1	100	9	48	358	37	144	69	1210	47
106,370	47	9	41	7	60	281	54	169	61	1030	237
130,763	33	3	73	5	72	331	44	141	73	1170	66
40,751	94	1	100	9	48	323	47	121	78	1240	29
119,749	39	5	62	8	56	353	38	143	71	1205	49
106,353	48	1	100	3	92	257	58	40	121	1220	38
81,861	63	2	87	3	92	237	64	65	95	1245	27
68,992	68	5	62	10	40	222	67	139	75	1050	192
23,312	110	1	100	13	26	189	77	64	97	1080	166
99,318	52	5	62	5	72	215	69	201	54	1105	132
58,792	77	4	68	10	40	197	72	192	56	1120	111
2,032	348	0	136	2	115	33	181	19	151	1220	38
16,985	133	8	47	7	60	272	55	141	73	1130	98
24,831	109	10	37	8	56	151	88	120	79	1130	98
86,309	61	2	87	5	72	170	82	97	85	1150	80
7,663	212	0	136	2	115	100	116	63	98	1210	47
110,384	45	2	87	8	56	183	78	67	94	1090	144

Top Medical and Specialized Research Universities				Research				Private	
Institutions in Order of Top 25 Score, then Top 26-50 Score, then Alphabetically		Number of Measures in Top 25 National	Number of Measures in Top 26-50 National	2014 Total Research x $1000	2014 National Rank	2014 Federal Research x $1000	2014 National Rank	2015 Endowment Assets x $1000	2015 National Rank
Public	University of California - San Francisco	6	1	1,084,031	4	544,697	12	2,124,970	41
Private	Icahn School of Medicine at Mount Sinai	1	2	463,429	43	300,667	35	717,372	129
Private	Scripps Research Institute	1	2	386,231	54	292,268	37		
Public	Univ. of Texas MD Anderson Cancer Ctr.	1	2	794,980	16	158,986	73	1,200,742	70
Private	Rockefeller University	1	1	316,368	69	81,820	114	1,987,027	44
Private	Baylor College of Medicine	0	4	496,314	38	264,641	47	1,095,326	80
Public	Univ. of Texas SW Medical Ctr. - Dallas	0	4	434,627	47	185,137	67	1,620,501	55
Private	Weill Cornell Medical College	0	2	293,791	75	139,514	81	1,276,986	66
Public	Oregon Health & Science University	0	1	313,112	71	246,050	50	571,341	153

Top Private Medical and Specialized Research Universities				Research				Private	
Institutions in Order of Top 25 Score, then Top 26-50 Score, then Alphabetically		Number of Measures in Top 25 Control	Number of Measures in Top 26-50 Control	2014 Total Research x $1000	2014 Control Rank	2014 Federal Research x $1000	2014 Control Rank	2015 Endowment Assets x $1000	2015 Control Rank
Private	Baylor College of Medicine	4	3	496,314	15	264,641	22	1,095,326	53
Private	Scripps Research Institute	4	1	386,231	19	292,268	18		
Private	Weill Cornell Medical College	3	4	293,791	27	139,514	31	1,276,986	44
Private	Icahn School of Medicine at Mount Sinai	3	3	463,429	17	300,667	16	717,372	83
Private	Rockefeller University	2	4	316,368	25	81,820	38	1,987,027	29
Private	Cold Spring Harbor Laboratory	0	4	76,733	47	41,845	48		
Private	Medical College of Wisconsin	0	4	199,713	34	111,241	35	778,315	73
Private	Thomas Jefferson University	0	4	118,378	42	54,676	45	437,750	114
Private	Woods Hole Oceanographic Institution	0	4	220,016	31	177,616	27		
Private	Rush University	0	2	80,551	46	53,501	46	555,610	98

Top Public Medical and Specialized Research Universities				Research				Private	
Institutions in Order of Top 25 Score, then Top 26-50 Score, then Alphabetically		Number of Measures in Top 25 Control	Number of Measures in Top 26-50 Control	2014 Total Research x $1000	2014 Control Rank	2014 Federal Research x $1000	2014 Control Rank	2015 Endowment Assets x $1000	2015 Control Rank
Public	University of California - San Francisco	7	0	1,084,031	3	544,697	6	2,124,970	15
Public	Univ. of Texas MD Anderson Cancer Ctr.	4	2	794,980	10	158,986	45	1,200,742	24
Public	Univ. of Texas SW Medical Ctr. - Dallas	3	4	434,627	30	185,137	41	1,620,501	19
Public	Oregon Health & Science University	0	5	313,112	46	246,050	27	571,341	58
Public	University of Maryland - Baltimore	0	4	390,682	35	220,700	31	256,008	105
Public	Univ. of Mass Med. Sch. - Worcester	0	3	241,869	54	183,582	42	194,251	127
Public	Uniformed Services Univ. of the HS	0	1	262,489	51	213,389	32		

Support		Faculty				Advanced Training			
2015 Annual Giving x $1000	2015 National Rank	2015 National Academy Members	2015 National Rank	2015 Faculty Awards	2015 National Rank	2015 Doctorates Granted	2015 National Rank	2014 Post Docs	2014 National Rank
608,580	4	135	5	31	11	130	139	1,051	12
109,733	78	17	61	6	98	28	320	670	21
		26	46	8	85			648	24
176,908	41	12	68	3	144			640	26
18,562	262	51	24	7	90	28	320	298	62
61,656	119	24	50	6	98	111	157	594	31
149,243	53	40	30	13	49	88	186	571	33
156,176	49	28	42	10	67	68	220	322	56
141,018	55	10	73	8	85	43	268	270	65

Support		Faculty				Advanced Training			
2015 Annual Giving x $1000	2015 Control Rank	2015 National Academy Members	2015 Control Rank	2015 Faculty Awards	2015 Control Rank	2015 Doctorates Granted	2015 Control Rank	2014 Post Docs	2014 Control Rank
61,656	44	24	24	6	33	111	50	594	16
		26	22	8	30			648	12
156,176	24	28	21	10	28	68	74	322	24
109,733	33	17	30	6	33	28	127	670	10
18,562	133	51	14	7	31	28	127	298	26
		5	43	2	115	0	335	153	38
20,907	112	3	47	0	189	26	134	175	35
38,809	67	4	44	1	97	21	143	119	42
		3	47	1	97			97	46
3,689	402	2	56	0	189	17	162	33	57

Support		Faculty				Advanced Training			
2015 Annual Giving x $1000	2015 Control Rank	2015 National Academy Members	2015 Control Rank	2015 Faculty Awards	2015 Control Rank	2015 Doctorates Granted	2015 Control Rank	2014 Post Docs	2014 Control Rank
608,580	1	135	2	31	5	130	98	1,051	6
176,908	20	12	36	3	92			640	14
149,243	28	40	13	13	26	88	124	571	16
141,018	30	10	37	8	56	43	171	270	39
69,153	67	9	41	3	92	81	132	358	28
8,328	204	7	54	12	30	61	152	315	33
		4	68	2	115			36	127

Part II – The Center for Measuring University Performance – *Research Universities*

The Center for Measuring University Performance's research universities consist of academic institutions that had more than $40 million in federal research expenditures in fiscal year 2014. In the following tables, institutions are listed alphabetically with the most current data available on each measure and their rank on each measure for each year. *The Center for Measuring University Performance* provides both the national rank (rank among all universities) and the control rank (rank within private or public universities). We include five years of data for each measure, which correspond to the same data years used in each of the five prior *The Top American Research Universities* reports. In addition to the nine performance variables presented in Part I tables, these tables also include other institutional characteristics related to student enrollment, medical schools, land grant status, ownership, research focus, and National Merit and Achievement Scholars. The Source Notes section of this report provides detailed information on each data element. Tables in this section include the following:

- **Total Research Expenditures** (2010-2014)

- **Federal Research Expenditures** (2010-2014)

- **Research by Major Discipline** (2014)

- **Endowment Assets** (2011-2015)

- **Annual Giving** (2011-2015)

- **National Academy Membership** (2011-2015)

- **Faculty Awards** (2011-2015)

- **Doctorates Awarded** (2011-2015)

- **Postdoctoral Appointees** (2010-2014)

- **SAT Scores** (2010-2014)

- **National Merit and Achievement Scholars** (2011-2015)

- **Change: Research** presents trend data on total, federal, and non-federal research (2005 and 2014) in constant dollars.

- **Change: Private Support and Doctorates** provides trend data on endowment assets (2006 and 2015) and annual giving (2006 and 2015) in constant dollars, and doctorates awarded (2006 and 2015).

- **Change: Students** includes trend data on median SAT scores (2005 and 2014), National Merit and Achievement Scholars (2006 and 2015), and student headcount enrollment (2005 and 2014).

- **Institutional Characteristics** includes state location, highest degree offered, medical school and land grant status, federal research focus (summary of federal research by discipline), and total student enrollment.

- **Student Characteristics** provides headcount enrollment data broken out by level (i.e., undergraduate and graduate), part-time enrollment by level, and degrees awarded.

- *The Center for Measuring University Performance* measures presents the number of times a university ranks in the top 25 (or 26-50) on the nine quality measures in this year's report as compared to the past five years (i.e., 2011-2016 reports).

Data found in these tables may not always match the figures published by the original source. *The Center for Measuring University Performance* makes adjustments, when necessary, to ensure that the data reflect the activity at a single campus rather than that of a multiple-campus institution or state university system. When data are missing from the original source, *The Center for Measuring University Performance* may substitute another figure, if available. A full discussion of this subject, and the various adjustments or substitutions made to the original data, is in the Data Notes section of this report.

The prior years' data or ranks may differ slightly from our last report due to revised figures or estimates from the data source or institution.

The Center for Measuring University Performance's website [http://mup.asu.edu] provides these same tables in Microsoft Excel spreadsheets for ease of analysis. In addition to the over-$40-million group, the online tables contain data on all institutions reporting any federal research in the past five years.

Total Research

	Institutions with Over $40 Million in Federal Research, Alphabetically	2014 Total Research x $1000	2014 National Rank	2014 Control Rank	2013 Total Research x $1000	2013 National Rank	2013 Control Rank
Public	Arizona State University	380,581	55	36	367,277	59	38
Public	Auburn University	140,110	122	83	143,545	120	81
Public	Augusta University	64,116	173	125	64,033	176	128
Private	Baylor College of Medicine	496,314	38	15	508,799	35	14
Private	Boston University	353,850	60	22	359,312	61	22
Private	Brandeis University	67,048	168	48	69,398	168	48
Private	Brown University	291,917	76	28	222,945	89	30
Private	California Institute of Technology	358,137	59	21	333,548	64	24
Private	Carnegie Mellon University	250,497	82	30	270,898	77	28
Private	Case Western Reserve University	417,436	49	18	422,041	47	18
Public	Clemson University	116,871	136	94	116,138	133	92
Public	Cleveland State University	61,291	175	127	67,137	174	126
Private	Cold Spring Harbor Laboratory	76,733	162	47	78,236	161	47
Public	Colorado State Univ. - Fort Collins	300,572	73	47	303,461	71	47
Private	Columbia University	844,766	13	5	845,847	13	5
Private	Cornell University	580,936	32	13	556,288	32	12
Private	Dartmouth College	204,360	96	33	198,995	95	32
Private	Drexel University	124,464	132	41	118,754	132	41
Private	Duke University	1,031,404	6	2	987,393	7	2
Private	Emory University	551,556	34	14	493,734	36	15
Public	Florida International University	107,487	140	97	92,463	147	105
Public	Florida State University	231,390	87	57	224,425	87	58
Public	George Mason University	85,493	152	108	82,849	155	111
Private	George Washington University	213,334	92	32	192,152	98	34
Private	Georgetown University	162,983	112	36	170,503	109	36
Public	Georgia Institute of Technology	720,248	21	13	726,377	20	12
Private	Harvard University	875,964	11	4	910,569	10	3
Private	Icahn School of Med. at Mount Sinai	463,429	43	17	428,654	45	17
Public	Indiana University - Bloomington	172,380	106	71	173,464	107	72
Public	Indiana U. - Purdue U. - Indianapolis	316,650	68	44	325,562	68	44
Public	Iowa State University	297,293	74	48	259,320	79	50
Private	Johns Hopkins University	2,227,536	1	1	2,149,770	1	1
Public	Kansas State University	178,304	101	67	177,525	103	68
Public	Louisiana State Univ. - Baton Rouge	282,462	79	50	276,748	74	48
Private	Massachusetts Inst. of Technology	815,008	15	6	833,884	15	6
Private	Medical College of Wisconsin	199,713	98	34	201,237	94	31
Public	Medical University of South Carolina	242,594	83	53	245,451	81	52
Public	Michigan State University	492,501	39	24	479,145	40	25
Public	Mississippi State University	200,251	97	64	197,359	97	64
Public	Montana State University - Bozeman	104,646	144	100	103,144	140	98
Public	Naval Postgraduate School	91,400	149	105	89,616	150	107
Public	New Jersey Institute of Technology	94,371	147	103	97,088	142	100
Public	New Mexico State Univ. - Las Cruces	129,124	128	88	136,254	122	83
Private	New York University	490,614	40	16	435,095	43	16
Public	North Carolina State University	440,392	44	27	413,524	49	31
Private	Northeastern University	111,779	137	43	111,134	138	42
Private	Northwestern University	621,504	30	12	612,009	29	10
Public	Ohio State University - Columbus	752,836	19	11	743,321	18	10
Public	Oregon Health & Science University	313,112	71	46	307,134	70	46

2012 Total Research x $1000	2012 National Rank	2012 Control Rank	2011 Total Research x $1000	2011 National Rank	2011 Control Rank	2010 Total Research x $1000	2010 National Rank	2010 Control Rank
344,611	62	39	323,567	65	42	296,458	67	43
130,222	125	86	161,785	109	73	143,874	117	79
70,526	169	122	73,486	166	119	72,015	167	120
474,700	36	14	466,061	38	15	447,874	37	15
330,247	66	24	348,593	60	23	344,687	58	22
69,489	170	48	71,638	168	48	67,672	169	48
234,906	86	30	223,455	85	30	201,116	93	30
374,075	57	22	374,636	53	21	359,245	52	21
254,992	79	29	240,956	81	29	221,376	85	29
430,246	43	16	428,206	43	17	417,805	42	17
110,493	137	96	135,681	121	83	144,562	116	78
60,481	182	134	55,044	191	142	33,857	219	165
84,072	152	45	95,984	146	43			
335,336	65	42	321,130	67	43	291,621	68	44
847,809	11	4	841,173	12	5	770,888	12	5
507,012	34	13	514,843	35	14	486,150	33	13
195,251	97	34	210,274	93	32	193,608	94	31
112,390	135	41	109,729	137	40	115,458	130	39
1,004,759	7	2	1,018,241	5	2	980,514	4	2
474,537	37	15	522,900	32	13	498,309	31	12
83,639	154	109	97,804	144	102	92,250	147	105
208,005	93	62	216,869	90	60	208,834	89	60
79,913	160	114	80,284	161	115	77,966	158	114
187,652	98	35	189,427	100	35	189,113	98	34
171,829	105	36	164,301	106	36	155,538	106	36
683,894	23	15	650,588	25	17	611,226	24	16
753,973	16	7	623,116	26	9	561,703	28	10
400,680	51	19	363,091	59	22	370,666	51	20
151,240	117	79	160,038	111	75	156,996	105	70
308,101	69	45	314,004	69	45	290,490	69	45
252,675	80	51	261,016	77	50	243,890	77	50
2,092,999	1	1	2,135,547	1	1	1,997,252	1	1
169,863	106	70	163,494	107	71	154,888	107	71
279,019	75	48	281,221	72	47	280,432	71	47
770,367	15	6	693,714	18	7	646,222	21	7
209,040	92	31	215,358	91	31	191,816	97	33
236,586	83	54	213,346	92	61	224,632	83	55
471,620	38	23	423,766	45	27	399,358	45	27
222,320	88	58	217,793	88	58	223,032	84	56
113,235	134	94	114,244	134	95	124,227	126	88
124,531	129	90	95,153	147	104	96,067	143	101
91,407	149	105	89,250	151	108	81,240	157	113
135,214	123	84	137,301	120	82	146,364	115	77
425,043	45	17	402,327	50	19	343,762	59	23
400,046	52	33	374,446	54	33	357,802	53	32
102,911	140	42	81,230	158	46	74,998	163	46
602,451	28	10	595,202	28	10	554,228	29	11
720,082	17	10	794,023	14	9	719,574	15	10
305,360	70	46	334,324	63	40	314,990	63	40

Total Research

	Institutions with Over $40 Million in Federal Research, Alphabetically	2014 Total Research x $1000	2014 National Rank	2014 Control Rank	2013 Total Research x $1000	2013 National Rank	2013 Control Rank
Public	Oregon State University	229,456	88	58	231,342	85	56
Public	Penn State Univ. - Hershey Med. Ctr.	82,793	155	110	82,501	156	112
Public	Pennsylvania State Univ. - Univ. Park	702,912	23	15	742,510	19	11
Private	Princeton University	287,730	78	29	264,998	78	29
Public	Purdue University - West Lafayette	502,457	37	23	528,564	34	21
Private	Rensselaer Polytechnic Institute	104,844	143	44	92,365	148	43
Private	Rice University	136,419	124	40	128,621	129	40
Private	Rockefeller University	316,368	69	25	298,474	72	25
Private	Rush University	80,551	159	46	81,770	158	46
Public	Rutgers University - New Brunswick	627,076	29	18	474,192	41	26
Public	San Diego State University	77,474	161	115	69,338	169	121
Private	Scripps Research Institute	386,231	54	19	399,899	53	19
Private	Stanford University	912,244	10	3	900,547	11	4
Public	Stony Brook University	210,301	94	62	224,030	88	59
Public	Temple University	206,556	95	63	207,190	93	63
Public	Texas A&M Univ. - College Station	735,273	20	12	708,528	24	16
Private	Thomas Jefferson University	118,378	135	42	89,273	151	44
Private	Tufts University	156,411	115	38	154,694	116	38
Private	Tulane University	148,784	117	39	151,314	117	39
Public	Uniformed Services Univ. of the HS	262,489	80	51	164,232	111	75
Public	University at Albany	129,434	127	87	135,879	123	84
Public	University at Buffalo	370,083	57	37	371,387	57	36
Public	University of Alabama - Birmingham	421,475	48	31	434,882	44	28
Public	University of Alabama - Huntsville	85,994	151	107	96,932	143	101
Public	University of Alaska - Fairbanks	152,352	116	78	118,907	131	91
Public	University of Arizona	575,864	33	20	616,487	28	19
Public	Univ. of Arkansas for Med. Sciences	131,438	125	85	133,677	126	87
Public	University of California - Berkeley	708,485	22	14	690,299	25	17
Public	University of California - Davis	699,689	24	16	715,870	23	15
Public	University of California - Irvine	322,315	65	41	329,500	66	42
Public	University of California - Los Angeles	920,183	9	7	934,135	9	7
Public	University of California - Riverside	128,506	129	89	126,916	130	90
Public	University of California - San Diego	1,060,207	5	4	1,066,979	4	3
Public	Univ. of California - San Francisco	1,084,031	4	3	1,042,841	5	4
Public	Univ. of California - Santa Barbara	225,614	89	59	225,976	86	57
Public	University of California - Santa Cruz	147,536	119	80	145,092	118	79
Public	University of Central Florida	143,063	120	81	108,560	139	97
Private	University of Chicago	378,322	56	20	389,900	54	20
Public	University of Cincinnati - Cincinnati	399,571	52	34	414,738	48	30
Public	University of Colorado - Boulder	362,882	58	38	369,663	58	37
Public	University of Colorado - Denver	401,230	51	33	400,815	52	34
Public	University of Connecticut - Health Ctr.	105,047	142	99	102,829	141	99
Public	University of Connecticut - Storrs	142,332	121	82	133,297	127	88
Private	University of Dayton	83,409	154	45	82,349	157	45
Public	University of Delaware	169,641	109	74	170,470	110	74
Public	University of Florida	652,341	26	17	642,502	27	18
Public	University of Georgia	313,445	70	45	308,486	69	45
Public	University of Hawaii - Manoa	319,818	67	43	326,402	67	43
Public	University of Houston - Univ. Park	122,163	133	92	112,469	136	95

2012 Total Research x $1000	2012 National Rank	2012 Control Rank	2011 Total Research x $1000	2011 National Rank	2011 Control Rank	2010 Total Research x $1000	2010 National Rank	2010 Control Rank
239,571	81	52	227,752	84	55	215,400	88	59
84,338	151	107	99,863	141	99	87,278	149	106
699,556	19	12	677,082	21	14	674,763	17	11
264,980	77	28	255,483	78	28	231,862	80	28
528,140	33	21	520,001	34	21	477,145	36	22
92,348	147	44	84,346	156	45	83,601	152	44
115,235	133	40	109,197	138	41	97,288	142	42
292,896	71	25	272,491	73	26	265,750	74	26
80,300	159	46	79,212	162	47	73,398	164	47
420,737	47	30	415,502	47	29	407,170	44	26
75,670	165	118	91,789	149	106	95,064	145	103
398,673	53	20	400,768	51	20	387,298	48	19
854,580	10	3	868,393	10	3	810,300	9	3
218,209	90	60	206,207	95	62	201,846	92	63
126,288	128	89	117,131	132	93	115,543	129	91
669,968	24	16	682,553	20	13	666,516	19	13
100,506	144	43	104,923	139	42	103,064	140	41
159,140	112	37	154,760	114	37	153,113	108	37
154,196	114	38	154,530	115	38	151,686	109	38
151,392	116	78	175,365	103	68	134,126	120	82
135,673	122	83	146,987	119	81	356,517	54	33
340,930	63	40	337,783	62	39	337,976	60	37
449,108	39	24	497,680	36	22	483,862	34	21
83,076	157	112	72,988	167	120	73,266	165	118
121,640	130	91	132,608	124	86	127,808	124	86
615,434	27	18	597,988	27	18	577,958	26	18
129,056	127	88	122,066	129	91	119,518	128	90
696,904	20	13	670,926	22	15	659,572	20	14
704,999	18	11	698,193	17	11	669,282	18	12
335,874	64	41	328,870	64	41	311,105	65	41
969,682	8	6	942,450	8	6	899,677	8	6
129,609	126	87	125,902	128	90	121,541	127	89
1,065,306	4	3	1,003,584	6	4	937,982	6	4
1,032,673	5	4	995,226	7	5	935,509	7	5
222,916	87	57	217,877	87	57	217,952	87	58
149,824	118	80	149,702	117	79	136,964	119	81
102,562	141	99	97,309	145	103	108,662	131	92
411,864	49	18	446,512	39	16	432,943	40	16
408,294	50	32	419,456	46	28	393,518	47	29
373,512	58	36	372,034	56	35	335,983	61	38
422,844	46	29	407,517	49	31	376,917	49	30
102,530	142	100	98,638	142	100	99,066	141	100
147,938	119	81	148,614	118	80	131,321	122	84
79,877	161	47	89,037	152	44	91,943	148	43
161,327	111	75	160,503	110	74	147,204	112	74
649,988	26	17	686,048	19	12	636,607	22	15
311,498	68	44	239,594	82	53	225,406	82	54
312,311	67	43	318,316	68	44	303,085	66	42
105,844	138	97	98,231	143	101	106,646	132	93

Total Research

	Institutions with Over $40 Million in Federal Research, Alphabetically	2014 Total Research x $1000	2014 National Rank	2014 Control Rank	2013 Total Research x $1000	2013 National Rank	2013 Control Rank
Public	University of Idaho	92,512	148	104	93,941	145	103
Public	University of Illinois - Chicago	339,644	63	39	358,797	62	40
Public	Univ. of Illinois - Urbana-Champaign	598,531	31	19	721,587	21	13
Public	University of Iowa	436,852	45	28	423,097	46	29
Public	University of Kansas - Lawrence	169,884	108	73	179,848	101	66
Public	University of Kansas Medical Center	81,302	156	111	87,202	153	109
Public	University of Kentucky	322,313	66	42	332,366	65	41
Public	University of Louisville	163,199	111	76	160,338	112	76
Public	University of Maine - Orono	100,493	145	101	77,169	162	115
Public	University of Maryland - Baltimore	390,682	53	35	412,387	50	32
Public	Univ. of Maryland - Baltimore County	64,329	171	123	62,887	180	132
Public	University of Maryland - College Park	472,235	42	26	487,345	37	22
Public	Univ. of Massachusetts - Amherst	183,210	99	65	172,217	108	73
Public	U. of Mass. Med. Sch. - Worcester	241,869	84	54	245,923	80	51
Private	University of Miami	342,852	62	24	338,568	63	23
Public	University of Michigan - Ann Arbor	1,279,603	2	1	1,304,074	2	1
Public	University of Minnesota - Twin Cities	850,880	12	8	834,181	14	9
Public	University of Missouri - Columbia	233,613	86	56	232,760	84	55
Public	University of Nebraska - Lincoln	254,879	81	52	245,170	82	53
Public	University of Nebraska Medical Ctr.	139,126	123	84	137,485	121	82
Public	University of Nevada - Reno	81,028	157	112	85,085	154	110
Public	Univ. of New Hampshire - Durham	130,951	126	86	134,535	124	85
Public	Univ. of New Mexico - Albuquerque	221,817	90	60	220,840	90	60
Public	Univ. of North Carolina - Chapel Hill	955,601	8	6	942,467	8	6
Public	University of North Dakota	67,199	166	119	68,636	170	122
Private	University of Notre Dame	160,461	113	37	156,234	115	37
Public	University of Oklahoma - Norman	120,322	134	93	129,078	128	89
Public	University of Oklahoma HSC	106,782	141	98	91,838	149	106
Public	University of Oregon	77,655	160	114	78,654	160	114
Private	University of Pennsylvania	792,314	17	7	790,265	16	7
Public	University of Pittsburgh - Pittsburgh	835,838	14	9	846,556	12	8
Public	University of Rhode Island	84,393	153	109	94,381	144	102
Private	University of Rochester	347,161	61	23	382,399	55	21
Public	Univ. of South Carolina - Columbia	181,363	100	66	178,800	102	67
Public	University of South Florida - Tampa	436,578	46	29	410,092	51	33
Private	University of Southern California	650,506	27	10	610,382	30	11
Public	University of Tennessee - Knoxville	170,471	107	72	175,264	106	71
Public	University of Tennessee HSC	67,841	165	118	71,897	166	119
Public	University of Texas - Austin	526,173	35	21	572,959	31	20
Public	University of Texas HSC - Houston	233,737	85	55	233,256	83	54
Public	Univ. of Texas HSC - San Antonio	172,716	105	70	175,983	104	69
Public	U. of Texas MD Anderson Cancer Ctr.	794,980	16	10	718,096	22	14
Public	U. of Texas Med. Branch - Galveston	178,014	102	68	180,198	100	65
Public	Univ. of Texas SW Med. Ctr. - Dallas	434,627	47	30	440,620	42	27
Public	University of Utah	476,017	41	25	486,245	39	24
Public	University of Vermont	109,343	139	96	115,054	134	93
Public	University of Virginia	337,732	64	40	366,103	60	39
Public	University of Washington - Seattle	1,091,135	3	2	1,111,508	3	2
Public	University of Wisconsin - Madison	984,830	7	5	997,523	6	5

2012 Total Research x $1000	2012 National Rank	2012 Control Rank	2011 Total Research x $1000	2011 National Rank	2011 Control Rank	2010 Total Research x $1000	2010 National Rank	2010 Control Rank
95,327	146	103	94,345	148	105	85,475	150	107
381,918	56	35	373,750	55	34	355,581	56	35
558,022	30	19	522,769	33	20	493,386	32	20
432,980	42	27	433,088	41	25	435,118	39	24
172,615	104	69	156,028	113	77	148,879	110	72
83,695	153	108	118,139	131	92	103,113	139	99
354,132	61	38	364,175	57	36	350,857	57	36
165,319	109	73	166,918	105	70	162,447	104	69
91,673	148	104	111,129	135	96	106,238	133	94
414,754	48	31	391,685	52	32	355,910	55	34
65,628	174	126	83,155	157	112	81,894	155	111
498,417	35	22	485,078	37	23	440,556	38	23
178,207	103	68	176,545	102	67	164,850	103	68
256,090	78	50	262,714	75	48	232,039	79	52
361,772	60	23	321,830	66	24	278,664	72	25
1,247,680	2	1	1,212,990	2	1	1,128,686	2	1
806,832	14	9	824,489	13	8	764,916	13	8
234,975	85	56	130,269	126	88	133,120	121	83
238,471	82	53	220,141	86	56	180,544	101	66
141,619	121	82	133,036	122	84	138,219	118	80
83,137	155	110	86,372	155	111	94,420	146	104
152,276	115	77	128,348	127	89	103,801	138	98
216,218	91	61	217,206	89	59	207,906	90	61
864,748	9	7	762,620	15	10	746,828	14	9
79,792	162	115	74,636	165	118	76,262	161	116
143,328	120	39	121,466	130	39	104,288	137	40
115,529	132	93	87,260	153	109	105,217	135	96
101,648	143	101	76,777	163	116	95,970	144	102
87,656	150	106	87,161	154	110	83,545	153	109
813,210	13	5	851,522	11	4	793,523	11	4
839,793	12	8	880,425	9	7	806,014	10	7
97,845	145	102	101,202	140	98	84,523	151	108
388,401	55	21	428,144	44	18	412,704	43	18
186,559	99	64	196,820	98	64	218,771	86	57
394,694	54	34	343,366	61	38	330,528	62	39
593,003	29	11	579,717	29	11	574,366	27	9
165,708	108	72	151,814	116	78	193,089	95	64
77,749	164	117	81,216	159	113	81,900	154	110
549,312	31	20	558,377	30	19	531,412	30	19
236,250	84	55	261,172	76	49	240,772	78	51
184,298	100	65	198,655	97	63	207,115	91	62
685,814	22	14	663,279	23	16	599,529	25	17
180,888	101	66	193,555	99	65	188,399	99	65
435,085	41	26	431,883	42	26	419,220	41	25
425,558	44	28	410,392	48	30	375,420	50	31
115,569	131	92	132,107	125	87	129,612	123	85
363,569	59	37	287,259	70	46	271,843	73	48
1,065,414	3	2	1,112,526	3	2	995,036	3	2
1,030,605	6	5	1,022,723	4	3	940,286	5	3

Total Research

	Institutions with Over $40 Million in Federal Research, Alphabetically	2014 Total Research x $1000	2014 National Rank	2014 Control Rank	2013 Total Research x $1000	2013 National Rank	2013 Control Rank
Public	Utah State University	167,256	110	75	156,774	114	78
Private	Vanderbilt University	659,418	25	9	548,086	33	13
Public	Virginia Commonwealth University	177,540	103	69	175,880	105	70
Public	Virginia Polytechnic Inst. and St. Univ.	502,486	36	22	487,121	38	23
Private	Wake Forest University	176,380	104	35	182,721	99	35
Public	Washington State Univ. - Pullman	287,942	77	49	273,037	75	49
Private	Washington University in St. Louis	646,756	28	11	665,484	26	9
Public	Wayne State University	213,253	93	61	217,984	91	61
Private	Weill Cornell Medical College	293,791	75	27	284,936	73	26
Public	West Virginia University	156,946	114	77	159,865	113	77
Private	Woods Hole Oceanographic Inst.	220,016	91	31	198,232	96	33
Private	Yale University	764,002	18	8	787,609	17	8
Private	Yeshiva University	306,826	72	26	271,166	76	27

2012 Total Research x $1000	2012 National Rank	2012 Control Rank	2011 Total Research x $1000	2011 National Rank	2011 Control Rank	2010 Total Research x $1000	2010 National Rank	2010 Control Rank
155,305	113	76	172,563	104	69	147,612	111	73
533,878	32	12	534,806	31	12	478,345	35	14
179,310	102	67	185,566	101	66	176,422	102	67
448,054	40	25	445,302	40	24	393,888	46	28
203,730	96	33	208,460	94	33	192,034	96	32
288,693	74	47	363,678	58	37	285,120	70	46
689,035	21	8	707,404	16	6	693,749	16	6
221,666	89	59	252,620	79	51	248,753	76	49
292,782	72	26	264,966	74	27	261,049	75	27
161,961	110	74	159,206	112	76	146,944	114	76
204,352	95	32	198,775	96	34	181,746	100	35
654,824	25	9	654,259	24	8	621,125	23	8
289,027	73	27	283,673	71	25	314,240	64	24

Federal Research

	Institutions with Over $40 Million in Federal Research, Alphabetically	2014 Federal Research x $1000	2014 National Rank	2014 Control Rank	2013 Federal Research x $1000	2013 National Rank	2013 Control Rank
Public	Arizona State University	186,126	65	39	190,066	67	41
Public	Auburn University	49,739	149	103	56,809	144	99
Public	Augusta University	47,771	151	105	47,913	154	108
Private	Baylor College of Medicine	264,641	47	22	285,230	43	19
Private	Boston University	254,285	48	23	265,476	48	23
Private	Brandeis University	45,800	153	47	43,963	160	47
Private	Brown University	125,005	84	33	120,977	86	32
Private	California Institute of Technology	276,447	42	19	272,223	46	22
Private	Carnegie Mellon University	198,247	61	25	215,560	57	24
Private	Case Western Reserve University	328,548	29	14	347,628	28	14
Public	Clemson University	44,673	155	108	47,825	155	109
Public	Cleveland State University	44,139	156	109	50,002	152	106
Private	Cold Spring Harbor Laboratory	41,845	158	48	41,002	163	48
Public	Colorado State Univ. - Fort Collins	206,958	56	33	213,355	58	34
Private	Columbia University	591,523	8	4	619,557	7	4
Private	Cornell University	299,320	36	17	299,951	35	16
Private	Dartmouth College	145,080	76	30	154,917	75	30
Private	Drexel University	75,557	122	41	74,047	125	42
Private	Duke University	556,847	10	5	580,416	10	5
Private	Emory University	329,254	27	13	364,136	26	13
Public	Florida International University	68,946	126	84	57,858	139	95
Public	Florida State University	140,995	79	49	132,583	81	50
Public	George Mason University	53,775	143	98	57,154	141	97
Private	George Washington University	139,148	82	32	119,441	91	33
Private	Georgetown University	99,567	103	36	113,703	98	35
Public	Georgia Institute of Technology	510,422	14	8	520,754	14	8
Private	Harvard University	554,944	11	6	575,868	11	6
Private	Icahn School of Med. at Mount Sinai	300,667	35	16	277,517	45	21
Public	Indiana University - Bloomington	80,109	117	79	82,005	120	82
Public	Indiana U. - Purdue U. - Indianapolis	142,589	78	48	151,962	76	46
Public	Iowa State University	115,285	90	57	120,934	87	55
Private	Johns Hopkins University	1,936,953	1	1	1,881,959	1	1
Public	Kansas State University	64,565	129	87	67,524	132	90
Public	Louisiana State Univ. - Baton Rouge	93,584	105	68	93,281	109	72
Private	Massachusetts Inst. of Technology	480,991	16	7	487,647	19	8
Private	Medical College of Wisconsin	111,241	97	35	116,765	95	34
Public	Medical University of South Carolina	118,649	89	56	127,472	84	53
Public	Michigan State University	247,970	49	26	246,131	52	29
Public	Mississippi State University	70,615	125	83	73,834	126	84
Public	Montana State University - Bozeman	66,770	128	86	66,451	133	91
Public	Naval Postgraduate School	89,284	109	72	86,538	115	78
Public	New Jersey Institute of Technology	51,853	146	100	55,017	147	101
Public	New Mexico State Univ. - Las Cruces	80,247	116	78	86,546	114	77
Private	New York University	314,712	31	15	283,382	44	20
Public	North Carolina State University	177,722	70	44	174,440	70	44
Private	Northeastern University	77,401	120	40	82,587	119	38
Private	Northwestern University	385,888	24	12	389,757	25	12
Public	Ohio State University - Columbus	416,177	21	12	425,547	22	13
Public	Oregon Health & Science University	246,050	50	27	244,867	53	30

2012 Federal Research x $1000	2012 National Rank	2012 Control Rank	2011 Federal Research x $1000	2011 National Rank	2011 Control Rank	2010 Federal Research x $1000	2010 National Rank	2010 Control Rank
182,188	68	42	178,153	68	42	164,890	67	42
55,118	149	103	59,061	146	102	53,648	147	102
55,106	150	104	54,254	155	108	51,727	153	108
268,753	47	23	295,529	43	21	284,072	41	22
273,204	44	21	300,923	40	20	298,467	37	20
44,061	162	47	47,793	162	48	43,282	164	47
127,665	85	32	123,649	92	33	120,749	91	33
322,295	34	16	340,131	30	16	325,751	30	16
209,307	60	25	200,878	65	25	179,136	64	25
358,722	26	14	352,938	28	15	333,438	27	15
48,182	157	111	49,365	161	114	59,374	137	94
46,205	159	113	42,292	168	120	24,894	206	150
43,874	163	48	55,450	152	47			
245,573	53	30	230,661	56	33	205,890	59	36
631,961	6	3	634,973	7	3	561,531	8	4
298,596	41	20	314,371	37	19	290,640	40	21
147,218	79	31	131,518	87	32	117,909	95	35
85,584	119	38	81,424	123	39	75,339	122	40
585,636	10	5	584,161	9	5	513,469	13	5
360,934	25	13	369,945	25	13	336,948	26	14
54,204	153	107	61,687	139	95	52,784	149	104
131,998	84	53	136,332	81	51	127,571	84	54
57,504	145	99	61,016	141	97	59,591	136	93
111,068	96	36	115,463	99	36	120,844	90	32
113,229	94	35	122,802	93	34	119,509	94	34
482,349	16	9	426,088	22	11	370,532	23	12
574,346	11	6	530,908	14	6	467,237	15	7
271,722	45	22	295,291	44	22	302,770	36	19
72,501	133	91	69,298	136	93	67,483	131	89
165,374	73	45	154,966	77	47	147,375	76	46
117,144	93	59	116,109	97	62	108,181	99	63
1,845,845	1	1	1,875,410	1	1	1,731,818	1	1
73,247	131	89	74,414	131	89	66,400	133	91
91,238	114	77	96,050	113	75	94,611	110	73
478,955	18	8	482,544	17	8	451,050	17	9
125,325	87	33	133,929	84	31	121,750	88	31
136,907	81	50	143,464	80	50	131,650	80	50
250,416	52	29	222,937	60	36	198,735	60	37
96,132	111	74	97,987	110	73	105,224	102	65
78,409	125	85	78,431	127	86	84,735	114	76
120,209	90	57	88,950	116	78	86,765	113	75
57,513	143	98	52,873	157	110	47,832	158	112
90,338	115	78	90,283	115	77	98,050	105	68
300,271	40	19	289,172	45	23	250,006	48	23
171,464	72	44	152,790	78	48	137,124	78	48
75,733	129	42	65,757	138	44	56,727	142	44
385,377	24	12	393,449	24	12	356,193	24	12
416,304	23	12	471,331	18	10	384,633	21	11
242,219	55	32	268,777	49	26	247,054	49	26

Federal Research

	Institutions with Over $40 Million in Federal Research, Alphabetically	2014 Federal Research x $1000	2014 National Rank	2014 Control Rank	2013 Federal Research x $1000	2013 National Rank	2013 Control Rank
Public	Oregon State University	143,815	77	47	148,174	78	48
Public	Penn. St. Univ. - Hershey Med. Ctr.	54,404	142	97	55,619	146	100
Public	Pennsylvania State Univ. - Univ. Park	461,896	18	10	500,567	16	9
Private	Princeton University	163,805	72	28	156,070	73	29
Public	Purdue University - West Lafayette	227,857	53	30	258,596	49	26
Private	Rensselaer Polytechnic Institute	58,940	136	44	60,765	137	44
Private	Rice University	73,782	124	42	79,742	123	40
Private	Rockefeller University	81,820	114	38	80,384	122	39
Private	Rush University	53,501	144	46	57,063	142	45
Public	Rutgers University - New Brunswick	355,116	25	13	288,374	40	22
Public	San Diego State University	44,807	154	107	45,175	157	111
Private	Scripps Research Institute	292,268	37	18	308,628	33	15
Private	Stanford University	608,342	4	2	625,144	5	2
Public	Stony Brook University	111,386	96	62	118,432	93	60
Public	Temple University	118,892	88	55	124,764	85	54
Public	Texas A&M Univ. - College Station	266,877	45	25	270,334	47	25
Private	Thomas Jefferson University	54,676	141	45	56,247	145	46
Private	Tufts University	115,046	91	34	112,495	99	36
Private	Tulane University	94,287	104	37	97,873	107	37
Public	Uniformed Services Univ. of the HS	213,389	55	32	119,647	90	58
Public	University at Albany	104,861	99	64	113,736	97	63
Public	University at Buffalo	185,144	66	40	200,212	62	37
Public	University of Alabama - Birmingham	276,112	44	24	286,873	41	23
Public	University of Alabama - Huntsville	73,913	123	82	83,396	118	81
Public	University of Alaska - Fairbanks	83,483	113	76	92,602	111	74
Public	University of Arizona	286,595	38	20	334,680	31	17
Public	Univ. of Arkansas for Med. Sciences	55,556	139	95	64,856	135	92
Public	University of California - Berkeley	309,305	33	18	305,932	34	19
Public	University of California - Davis	327,697	30	16	344,632	29	15
Public	University of California - Irvine	180,431	69	43	196,256	65	40
Public	University of California - Los Angeles	458,157	19	11	489,820	17	10
Public	University of California - Riverside	56,327	137	93	57,032	143	98
Public	University of California - San Diego	597,270	7	4	630,009	4	3
Public	Univ. of California - San Francisco	544,697	12	6	566,117	12	6
Public	Univ. of California - Santa Barbara	119,816	86	53	131,392	82	51
Public	University of California - Santa Cruz	89,206	110	73	88,600	112	75
Public	University of Central Florida	64,323	130	88	68,691	131	89
Private	University of Chicago	276,237	43	20	294,862	38	18
Public	University of Cincinnati - Cincinnati	243,705	51	28	256,816	50	27
Public	University of Colorado - Boulder	302,877	34	19	309,072	32	18
Public	University of Colorado - Denver	277,209	41	23	290,443	39	21
Public	Univ. of Connecticut - Health Center	59,277	135	92	59,929	138	94
Public	University of Connecticut - Storrs	80,317	115	77	86,471	116	79
Private	University of Dayton	63,881	131	43	66,396	134	43
Public	University of Delaware	111,933	95	61	114,048	96	62
Public	University of Florida	279,920	40	22	285,778	42	24
Public	University of Georgia	122,145	85	52	127,487	83	52
Public	University of Hawaii - Manoa	202,574	59	35	225,263	55	32
Public	University of Houston - Univ. Park	55,574	138	94	57,569	140	96

2012 Federal Research x $1000	2012 National Rank	2012 Control Rank	2011 Federal Research x $1000	2011 National Rank	2011 Control Rank	2010 Federal Research x $1000	2010 National Rank	2010 Control Rank
155,667	78	48	146,069	79	49	135,081	79	49
56,615	146	100	59,039	147	103	53,063	148	103
469,597	19	11	400,294	23	12	410,238	19	10
160,985	75	30	162,491	73	29	149,164	75	30
255,691	51	28	246,116	51	28	221,679	54	31
62,063	139	45	58,951	148	45	54,559	145	45
76,431	128	41	78,249	128	42	69,176	129	42
84,616	121	39	97,710	111	38	88,705	112	38
57,512	144	46	57,978	149	46	51,304	154	46
273,498	43	23	235,178	54	31	218,910	56	33
51,690	155	109	59,769	143	99	53,746	146	101
309,471	36	17	317,201	36	18	313,746	33	18
607,578	8	4	633,287	8	4	576,553	7	3
123,198	89	56	124,938	89	57	120,090	92	59
85,062	120	82	84,581	119	81	76,170	121	82
259,506	50	27	281,063	47	24	276,977	44	22
68,976	136	43	80,027	124	40	77,817	119	39
120,042	92	34	120,864	95	35	115,159	97	36
101,130	108	37	110,222	103	37	106,021	100	37
110,276	100	64	117,781	96	61	72,125	127	86
112,161	95	60	124,848	90	58	123,404	86	56
186,747	67	41	176,923	69	43	164,477	68	43
303,677	39	21	340,342	29	14	320,704	32	15
75,715	130	88	70,197	134	92	71,461	128	87
97,472	110	73	100,638	107	70	97,889	106	69
328,369	33	18	324,751	35	18	307,038	34	16
69,883	135	93	75,924	130	88	72,217	126	85
333,179	30	16	326,120	34	17	303,201	35	17
356,540	27	13	359,704	27	13	329,041	29	14
204,062	62	37	204,134	63	39	189,343	63	39
527,899	14	8	545,882	13	8	522,423	11	7
61,304	141	96	59,351	145	101	58,159	139	96
653,549	5	3	635,223	6	4	578,889	6	4
559,329	12	6	570,116	10	5	514,693	12	8
134,984	82	51	132,490	86	55	127,696	83	53
91,409	113	76	95,015	114	76	81,598	116	78
72,620	132	90	66,736	137	94	67,795	130	88
329,119	31	15	365,824	26	14	348,537	25	13
266,507	48	25	286,003	46	23	261,982	47	25
319,019	35	19	313,531	38	19	282,008	42	20
308,023	37	20	299,230	41	21	275,573	45	23
61,568	140	95	56,351	151	105	55,341	144	100
88,834	116	79	84,901	118	80	73,359	124	84
64,369	138	44	69,847	135	43	72,567	125	41
110,760	97	61	112,523	102	66	102,637	103	66
295,745	42	22	296,950	42	22	269,765	46	24
133,525	83	52	134,273	83	53	116,625	96	61
193,722	66	40	201,700	64	40	196,275	62	38
54,657	151	105	57,090	150	104	50,148	156	110

Federal Research

	Institutions with Over $40 Million in Federal Research, Alphabetically	2014 Federal Research x $1000	2014 National Rank	2014 Control Rank	2013 Federal Research x $1000	2013 National Rank	2013 Control Rank
Public	University of Idaho	49,423	150	104	52,430	149	103
Public	University of Illinois - Chicago	201,646	60	36	219,473	56	33
Public	Univ. of Illinois - Urbana-Champaign	336,172	26	14	459,791	20	12
Public	University of Iowa	234,122	52	29	252,161	51	28
Public	University of Kansas - Lawrence	88,725	111	74	99,374	105	69
Public	University of Kansas Medical Center	42,461	157	110	48,183	153	107
Public	University of Kentucky	140,450	80	50	148,758	77	47
Public	University of Louisville	63,258	132	89	72,047	128	86
Public	University of Maine - Orono	50,338	148	102	33,903	170	121
Public	University of Maryland - Baltimore	220,700	54	31	237,749	54	31
Public	Univ. of Maryland - Baltimore County	46,993	152	106	44,257	158	112
Public	University of Maryland - College Park	328,828	28	15	341,942	30	16
Public	Univ. of Massachusetts - Amherst	102,682	101	66	103,233	104	68
Public	U. of Mass. Med. Sch. - Worcester	183,582	68	42	189,159	68	42
Private	University of Miami	202,818	58	24	204,315	61	25
Public	University of Michigan - Ann Arbor	733,779	3	2	802,114	3	2
Public	University of Minnesota - Twin Cities	483,542	15	9	489,318	18	11
Public	University of Missouri - Columbia	102,784	100	65	108,305	100	64
Public	University of Nebraska - Lincoln	93,190	106	69	96,177	108	71
Public	University of Nebraska Medical Ctr.	76,195	121	81	80,750	121	83
Public	University of Nevada - Reno	50,904	147	101	53,898	148	102
Public	Univ. of New Hampshire - Durham	89,640	107	70	92,778	110	73
Public	Univ. of New Mexico - Albuquerque	151,082	75	46	155,684	74	45
Public	Univ. of North Carolina - Chapel Hill	601,933	6	3	614,627	8	4
Public	University of North Dakota	40,191	160	112	46,397	156	110
Private	University of Notre Dame	79,192	119	39	79,268	124	41
Public	University of Oklahoma - Norman	53,223	145	99	68,902	130	88
Public	University of Oklahoma HSC	55,133	140	96	50,860	151	105
Public	University of Oregon	62,824	133	90	61,856	136	93
Private	University of Pennsylvania	606,115	5	3	623,939	6	3
Public	University of Pittsburgh - Pittsburgh	565,409	9	5	601,358	9	5
Public	University of Rhode Island	61,836	134	91	70,900	129	87
Private	University of Rochester	265,686	46	21	298,781	36	17
Public	Univ. of South Carolina - Columbia	87,844	112	75	87,562	113	76
Public	University of South Florida - Tampa	205,155	57	34	207,441	60	36
Private	University of Southern California	421,887	20	9	423,708	23	10
Public	University of Tennessee - Knoxville	106,778	98	63	104,558	103	67
Public	University of Tennessee HSC	41,830	159	111	42,269	162	115
Public	University of Texas - Austin	313,955	32	17	352,788	27	14
Public	University of Texas HSC - Houston	136,145	83	51	144,235	80	49
Public	Univ. of Texas HSC - San Antonio	89,303	108	71	99,198	106	70
Public	U. of Texas MD Anderson Cancer Ctr.	158,986	73	45	182,971	69	43
Public	U. of Texas Med. Branch - Galveston	101,761	102	67	108,287	101	65
Public	Univ. of Texas SW Med. Ctr. - Dallas	185,137	67	41	198,114	63	38
Public	University of Utah	284,125	39	21	297,099	37	20
Public	University of Vermont	79,727	118	80	85,028	117	80
Public	University of Virginia	192,907	63	38	212,051	59	35
Public	University of Washington - Seattle	849,713	2	1	869,623	2	1
Public	University of Wisconsin - Madison	522,251	13	7	533,220	13	7

2012 Federal Research x $1000	2012 National Rank	2012 Control Rank	2011 Federal Research x $1000	2011 National Rank	2011 Control Rank	2010 Federal Research x $1000	2010 National Rank	2010 Control Rank
53,765	154	108	52,812	158	111	45,082	161	115
243,622	54	31	245,323	52	29	229,131	51	28
348,536	28	14	312,796	39	20	294,236	38	18
265,780	49	26	280,989	48	25	280,089	43	21
99,034	109	72	78,884	126	85	81,211	117	79
48,018	158	112	71,840	132	90	56,247	143	99
157,813	77	47	175,801	70	44	167,192	66	41
79,252	124	84	84,557	120	82	83,593	115	77
39,428	166	118	59,644	144	100	48,270	157	111
229,858	56	33	228,637	57	34	206,686	57	34
44,669	161	115	61,110	140	96	58,597	138	95
340,180	29	15	333,879	33	16	293,835	39	19
106,470	104	68	106,315	104	67	97,131	107	70
202,149	63	38	208,244	62	38	178,293	65	40
222,535	58	24	223,870	59	24	196,435	61	24
773,766	3	2	801,194	3	2	729,779	3	2
480,531	17	10	482,639	16	9	420,102	18	9
110,446	99	63	113,072	100	64	113,362	98	62
103,294	106	70	104,240	105	68	95,190	109	72
84,196	122	83	86,295	117	79	80,784	118	80
55,150	148	102	55,374	153	106	58,115	140	97
109,728	102	66	96,552	112	74	76,191	120	81
159,302	76	46	161,950	74	45	147,003	77	47
597,629	9	5	559,620	12	7	541,910	9	5
54,411	152	106	53,913	156	109	52,381	151	106
82,244	123	40	79,003	125	41	61,645	134	43
64,427	137	94	46,027	164	116	52,332	152	107
59,704	142	97	42,654	167	119	47,733	159	113
71,157	134	92	71,344	133	91	66,809	132	90
656,425	4	2	689,571	4	2	626,816	4	2
620,070	7	4	647,060	5	3	581,148	5	3
78,194	126	86	77,668	129	87	60,963	135	92
307,390	38	18	337,312	31	17	321,258	31	17
93,237	112	75	100,045	108	71	119,890	93	60
218,772	59	35	220,931	61	37	219,634	55	32
433,136	20	9	443,458	20	10	402,372	20	10
103,147	107	71	99,712	109	72	96,018	108	71
48,473	156	110	51,840	160	113	52,650	150	105
328,560	32	17	334,240	32	15	331,439	28	13
146,424	80	49	156,790	76	46	150,324	74	45
106,177	105	69	121,200	94	60	121,723	89	58
196,753	65	39	236,400	53	30	206,664	58	35
109,867	101	65	128,098	88	56	128,840	82	52
207,513	61	36	231,639	55	32	232,027	50	27
271,629	46	24	263,623	50	27	226,489	52	29
87,843	117	80	101,465	106	69	98,588	104	67
225,558	57	34	227,937	58	35	224,607	53	30
876,941	2	1	921,399	2	1	809,433	2	1
557,688	13	7	568,389	11	6	522,473	10	6

Federal Research

	Institutions with Over $40 Million in Federal Research, Alphabetically	2014 Federal Research x $1000	2014 National Rank	2014 Control Rank	2013 Federal Research x $1000	2013 National Rank	2013 Control Rank
Public	Utah State University	114,075	92	58	106,074	102	66
Private	Vanderbilt University	408,743	23	11	432,752	21	9
Public	Virginia Commonwealth University	119,507	87	54	119,293	92	59
Public	Virginia Polytechnic Inst. and St. Univ.	198,092	62	37	197,462	64	39
Private	Wake Forest University	153,069	74	29	156,506	72	28
Public	Washington State Univ. - Pullman	112,568	94	60	119,921	89	57
Private	Washington University in St. Louis	410,115	22	10	402,702	24	11
Public	Wayne State University	112,608	93	59	118,217	94	61
Private	Weill Cornell Medical College	139,514	81	31	144,352	79	31
Public	West Virginia University	67,450	127	85	72,677	127	85
Private	Woods Hole Oceanographic Inst.	177,616	71	27	158,672	71	27
Private	Yale University	475,585	17	8	502,439	15	7
Private	Yeshiva University	186,885	64	26	193,831	66	26

2012 Federal Research x $1000	2012 National Rank	2012 Control Rank	2011 Federal Research x $1000	2011 National Rank	2011 Control Rank	2010 Federal Research x $1000	2010 National Rank	2010 Control Rank
107,054	103	67	112,611	101	65	89,750	111	74
430,445	22	11	434,213	21	11	377,185	22	11
124,836	88	55	134,431	82	52	125,713	85	55
181,371	69	43	187,269	67	41	161,636	70	44
172,779	70	27	173,004	71	27	159,084	71	27
120,146	91	58	115,775	98	63	105,333	101	64
432,434	21	10	460,282	19	9	466,993	16	8
125,965	86	54	133,925	85	54	131,418	81	51
172,428	71	28	161,792	75	30	156,065	72	28
77,981	127	87	84,061	121	83	74,465	123	83
161,115	74	29	165,819	72	28	153,066	73	29
517,072	15	7	518,195	15	7	475,010	14	6
201,397	64	26	192,241	66	26	163,399	69	26

Research by Major Discipline		2014 Total Research by Major Discipline					
Institutions with Over $40 Million in Federal Research, Alphabetically		Percent Life Science	Percent Physical Science	Percent Enviro Science	Percent Eng Science	Percent Computer Science	Percent Math
Public	Arizona State University	20.6%	6.6%	9.8%	27.7%	3.3%	1.4%
Public	Auburn University	55.2%	4.1%	2.1%	33.0%	0.0%	0.5%
Public	Augusta University	99.9%	0.1%	0.0%	0.0%	0.0%	0.0%
Private	Baylor College of Medicine	100.0%	0.0%	0.0%	0.0%	0.0%	0.0%
Private	Boston University	68.5%	9.7%	2.0%	13.0%	1.3%	0.8%
Private	Brandeis University	44.2%	13.3%	0.0%	0.0%	3.7%	1.4%
Private	Brown University	48.2%	10.1%	3.0%	15.3%	4.1%	7.6%
Private	California Institute of Technology	18.2%	58.7%	6.5%	13.8%	0.0%	2.6%
Private	Carnegie Mellon University	4.3%	5.2%	0.2%	35.9%	44.2%	2.5%
Private	Case Western Reserve University	81.9%	2.5%	0.2%	13.0%	0.1%	0.2%
Public	Clemson University	31.0%	7.4%	0.0%	48.2%	7.6%	2.4%
Public	Cleveland State University	62.8%	1.6%	0.0%	32.2%	0.0%	0.4%
Private	Cold Spring Harbor Laboratory	100.0%	0.0%	0.0%	0.0%	0.0%	0.0%
Public	Colorado State University - Fort Collins	42.0%	4.3%	35.6%	12.0%	1.3%	1.2%
Private	Columbia University	69.3%	4.7%	13.7%	7.5%	2.9%	0.4%
Private	Cornell University	45.2%	19.1%	4.1%	19.1%	3.3%	0.6%
Private	Dartmouth College	78.1%	4.5%	1.4%	8.9%	2.3%	0.6%
Private	Drexel University	57.4%	1.4%	0.0%	32.3%	5.2%	0.5%
Private	Duke University	84.1%	1.7%	1.8%	7.5%	0.4%	1.2%
Private	Emory University	93.1%	4.1%	0.2%	1.0%	0.1%	0.5%
Public	Florida International University	40.9%	4.9%	4.2%	25.2%	10.2%	0.3%
Public	Florida State University	13.1%	31.9%	10.1%	18.7%	2.5%	2.0%
Public	George Mason University	18.0%	5.4%	11.4%	9.5%	14.0%	2.4%
Private	George Washington University	72.6%	2.4%	0.7%	6.5%	2.6%	0.6%
Private	Georgetown University	82.3%	3.1%	0.0%	0.0%	1.0%	0.1%
Public	Georgia Institute of Technology	2.7%	7.0%	2.2%	70.2%	13.7%	1.0%
Private	Harvard University	60.2%	7.7%	3.9%	6.5%	0.2%	1.2%
Private	Icahn School of Medicine at Mount Sinai	100.0%	0.0%	0.0%	0.0%	0.0%	0.0%
Public	Indiana University - Bloomington	26.1%	20.6%	3.4%	0.0%	16.8%	1.6%
Public	Indiana Univ. - Purdue Univ. - Indianapolis	89.4%	0.4%	0.2%	2.5%	0.9%	0.3%
Public	Iowa State University	50.1%	6.1%	1.6%	30.6%	1.5%	4.2%
Private	Johns Hopkins University	38.7%	8.6%	1.6%	42.0%	5.3%	2.1%
Public	Kansas State University	68.0%	5.5%	0.4%	14.3%	2.5%	0.5%
Public	Louisiana State University - Baton Rouge	56.1%	7.7%	11.2%	14.6%	1.0%	0.7%
Private	Massachusetts Institute of Technology	14.4%	13.1%	7.0%	49.5%	9.4%	1.1%
Private	Medical College of Wisconsin	100.0%	0.0%	0.0%	0.0%	0.0%	0.0%
Public	Medical University of South Carolina	100.0%	0.0%	0.0%	0.0%	0.0%	0.0%
Public	Michigan State University	51.1%	24.3%	0.6%	8.8%	2.5%	1.9%
Public	Mississippi State University	53.8%	4.3%	2.0%	20.3%	2.9%	0.7%
Public	Montana State University - Bozeman	37.3%	16.6%	11.1%	18.7%	0.8%	0.9%
Public	Naval Postgraduate School	0.3%	11.6%	11.7%	33.3%	12.7%	4.6%
Public	New Jersey Institute of Technology	1.1%	12.8%	0.8%	51.9%	5.4%	4.5%
Public	New Mexico State University - Las Cruces	28.0%	9.3%	2.2%	54.6%	2.1%	0.8%
Private	New York University	82.5%	2.6%	1.1%	2.3%	2.5%	2.1%
Public	North Carolina State University	43.0%	5.0%	5.9%	34.1%	2.9%	4.7%
Private	Northeastern University	23.6%	17.9%	2.6%	36.2%	7.8%	1.0%
Private	Northwestern University	70.2%	6.8%	0.3%	14.0%	0.0%	0.3%
Public	Ohio State University - Columbus	62.7%	4.7%	1.5%	20.3%	3.6%	1.0%
Public	Oregon Health & Science University	91.5%	0.0%	2.6%	2.9%	0.0%	0.0%

Percent Psychology	Percent Social Science	Percent Other Science	2014 Federal Research by Major Discipline								
			Percent Life Science	Percent Physical Science	Percent Enviro Science	Percent Eng Science	Percent Computer Science	Percent Math	Percent Psychology	Percent Social Science	Percent Other Science
3.6%	13.3%	13.6%	26.8%	7.7%	14.6%	25.6%	4.5%	1.9%	5.2%	9.5%	4.2%
0.3%	2.8%	1.9%	36.6%	7.9%	5.2%	43.8%	0.0%	0.4%	0.4%	5.1%	0.6%
0.0%	0.0%	0.0%	99.9%	0.1%	0.0%	0.0%	0.0%	0.0%	0.0%	0.0%	0.0%
0.0%	0.0%	0.0%	100.0%	0.0%	0.0%	0.0%	0.0%	0.0%	0.0%	0.0%	0.0%
3.7%	0.9%	0.1%	68.7%	9.7%	2.3%	12.3%	1.5%	0.9%	4.2%	0.3%	0.0%
5.0%	32.4%	0.0%	45.1%	14.5%	0.0%	0.0%	4.4%	1.7%	6.0%	28.2%	0.0%
3.1%	5.9%	2.7%	50.7%	9.9%	2.2%	14.3%	3.4%	9.4%	4.8%	2.2%	3.2%
0.0%	0.3%	0.0%	18.6%	62.2%	6.8%	9.4%	0.0%	2.9%	0.0%	0.0%	0.0%
3.4%	2.5%	1.8%	4.0%	5.5%	0.0%	34.9%	45.8%	2.5%	3.8%	2.2%	1.3%
0.4%	1.5%	0.2%	85.9%	2.3%	0.2%	10.0%	0.1%	0.1%	0.4%	1.0%	0.0%
0.3%	2.9%	0.1%	17.6%	10.8%	0.0%	53.6%	12.2%	1.7%	0.8%	3.3%	0.0%
0.1%	2.9%	0.0%	79.9%	1.2%	0.0%	17.5%	0.0%	0.4%	0.1%	0.8%	0.0%
0.0%	0.0%	0.0%	100.0%	0.0%	0.0%	0.0%	0.0%	0.0%	0.0%	0.0%	0.0%
0.7%	1.5%	1.4%	37.9%	4.3%	42.8%	9.8%	1.7%	1.4%	0.8%	1.4%	0.0%
0.5%	1.0%	0.0%	68.0%	5.8%	13.2%	7.9%	3.3%	0.4%	0.6%	0.7%	0.0%
2.0%	6.5%	0.2%	36.1%	30.9%	3.0%	20.0%	4.5%	0.8%	1.4%	3.2%	0.1%
2.2%	1.1%	0.9%	77.6%	5.2%	1.5%	8.9%	2.6%	0.7%	2.1%	0.5%	0.9%
3.0%	0.2%	0.0%	50.2%	1.2%	0.0%	38.1%	6.5%	0.7%	3.3%	0.1%	0.0%
1.0%	2.3%	0.0%	76.0%	2.7%	2.0%	12.1%	0.7%	2.1%	1.3%	3.1%	0.0%
0.5%	0.5%	0.0%	93.8%	3.1%	0.2%	1.4%	0.0%	0.6%	0.5%	0.5%	0.0%
7.3%	7.0%	0.0%	44.1%	5.9%	4.5%	23.3%	9.6%	0.5%	7.4%	4.7%	0.0%
13.6%	5.8%	2.2%	14.6%	25.7%	7.4%	24.1%	2.7%	2.3%	17.8%	3.5%	1.8%
8.0%	31.2%	0.0%	17.5%	7.6%	15.3%	13.5%	20.7%	2.9%	9.0%	13.4%	0.0%
1.8%	10.3%	2.5%	80.5%	2.1%	0.3%	5.1%	2.2%	0.4%	2.0%	5.3%	2.1%
1.0%	11.9%	0.5%	88.2%	4.2%	0.0%	0.0%	1.5%	0.1%	1.4%	4.6%	0.0%
0.9%	1.5%	0.8%	2.1%	7.1%	2.3%	71.1%	14.4%	0.5%	0.9%	1.1%	0.6%
0.8%	7.4%	12.0%	61.1%	8.6%	4.2%	7.9%	0.2%	1.5%	0.7%	3.6%	12.1%
0.0%	0.0%	0.0%	100.0%	0.0%	0.0%	0.0%	0.0%	0.0%	0.0%	0.0%	0.0%
7.6%	17.1%	6.9%	32.6%	21.7%	3.3%	0.0%	22.6%	1.9%	10.8%	6.8%	0.3%
0.9%	3.0%	2.3%	92.2%	0.6%	0.3%	3.3%	0.8%	0.5%	1.1%	0.7%	0.5%
0.7%	4.3%	0.7%	46.7%	7.2%	1.6%	31.8%	1.7%	4.8%	0.3%	5.2%	0.7%
0.2%	0.4%	1.3%	32.4%	9.2%	1.6%	46.6%	5.8%	2.3%	0.2%	0.4%	1.4%
1.8%	3.4%	3.6%	60.1%	11.5%	0.5%	14.8%	4.4%	0.7%	3.0%	4.1%	0.8%
0.4%	2.7%	5.4%	52.5%	13.9%	9.6%	13.6%	1.9%	1.5%	0.9%	2.8%	3.1%
0.1%	2.6%	2.8%	14.1%	19.2%	8.1%	44.5%	10.4%	1.4%	0.1%	1.1%	1.2%
0.0%	0.0%	0.0%	100.0%	0.0%	0.0%	0.0%	0.0%	0.0%	0.0%	0.0%	0.0%
0.0%	0.0%	0.0%	100.0%	0.0%	0.0%	0.0%	0.0%	0.0%	0.0%	0.0%	0.0%
1.6%	6.7%	2.6%	45.3%	31.1%	0.3%	10.0%	2.5%	2.2%	2.2%	5.5%	0.8%
0.6%	11.3%	4.3%	44.5%	3.7%	3.3%	28.6%	4.3%	0.3%	0.2%	9.4%	5.7%
0.6%	2.2%	11.9%	28.9%	20.2%	16.0%	16.8%	0.9%	1.4%	0.6%	1.5%	13.7%
0.2%	10.7%	14.9%	0.3%	11.7%	11.6%	33.5%	12.7%	4.0%	0.2%	10.9%	14.9%
0.0%	0.3%	23.2%	1.0%	14.1%	1.0%	58.5%	1.4%	3.3%	0.0%	0.1%	20.6%
0.1%	0.3%	2.6%	16.4%	6.5%	2.5%	69.6%	2.8%	1.2%	0.0%	0.3%	0.8%
4.4%	2.6%	0.0%	82.5%	3.5%	0.0%	1.3%	2.7%	2.8%	5.8%	1.3%	0.0%
0.6%	3.0%	0.8%	33.8%	7.4%	7.7%	34.4%	5.8%	6.5%	0.6%	2.7%	1.1%
4.5%	6.5%	0.0%	21.0%	17.5%	2.1%	37.0%	10.1%	1.3%	5.3%	5.7%	0.0%
0.7%	3.0%	4.6%	69.4%	7.2%	0.3%	14.8%	0.0%	0.4%	0.8%	2.5%	4.6%
1.1%	2.4%	2.7%	64.7%	6.2%	1.6%	16.8%	2.2%	1.6%	1.6%	3.1%	2.1%
0.7%	0.0%	2.4%	91.1%	0.0%	3.0%	2.5%	0.0%	0.0%	0.7%	0.0%	2.6%

Research by Major Discipline		2014 Total Research by Major Discipline					
	Institutions with Over $40 Million in Federal Research, Alphabetically	Percent Life Science	Percent Physical Science	Percent Enviro Science	Percent Eng Science	Percent Computer Science	Percent Math
Public	Oregon State University	50.7%	1.6%	20.3%	16.2%	2.8%	0.4%
Public	Pennsylvania St. Univ. - Hershey Med. Ctr.	100.0%	0.0%	0.0%	0.0%	0.0%	0.0%
Public	Pennsylvania State University - Univ. Park	23.8%	7.4%	8.4%	43.1%	7.5%	1.5%
Private	Princeton University	16.2%	24.4%	7.1%	29.5%	4.1%	3.7%
Public	Purdue University - West Lafayette	41.2%	5.8%	1.0%	40.9%	4.2%	1.4%
Private	Rensselaer Polytechnic Institute	5.3%	10.8%	1.9%	68.0%	8.7%	1.6%
Private	Rice University	8.4%	24.4%	2.9%	40.2%	6.4%	5.6%
Private	Rockefeller University	94.8%	2.5%	0.2%	0.0%	2.0%	0.5%
Private	Rush University	95.2%	0.0%	0.0%	0.0%	0.0%	0.0%
Public	Rutgers University - New Brunswick	59.3%	7.7%	6.1%	10.3%	2.7%	2.7%
Public	San Diego State University	46.4%	12.7%	2.7%	6.9%	2.4%	3.8%
Private	Scripps Research Institute	100.0%	0.0%	0.0%	0.0%	0.0%	0.0%
Private	Stanford University	64.8%	9.9%	3.7%	14.6%	2.7%	0.9%
Public	Stony Brook University	48.7%	15.0%	12.9%	9.4%	3.3%	3.0%
Public	Temple University	81.1%	5.6%	0.3%	2.7%	2.1%	0.4%
Public	Texas A&M University - College Station	31.1%	6.2%	16.8%	39.7%	1.2%	1.7%
Private	Thomas Jefferson University	100.0%	0.0%	0.0%	0.0%	0.0%	0.0%
Private	Tufts University	68.0%	4.1%	0.1%	13.0%	1.5%	1.9%
Private	Tulane University	87.3%	2.4%	0.9%	4.5%	0.0%	1.3%
Public	Uniformed Services University of the HS	99.9%	0.0%	0.0%	0.0%	0.0%	0.0%
Public	University at Albany	75.8%	3.2%	5.3%	0.0%	5.1%	0.1%
Public	University at Buffalo	65.9%	4.6%	0.9%	22.2%	3.6%	0.3%
Public	University of Alabama - Birmingham	94.1%	0.7%	0.1%	4.2%	0.2%	0.1%
Public	University of Alabama - Huntsville	1.7%	9.1%	13.2%	48.5%	26.2%	0.5%
Public	University of Alaska - Fairbanks	13.7%	7.6%	49.4%	17.6%	1.6%	0.0%
Public	University of Arizona	48.1%	28.6%	5.4%	9.5%	1.5%	0.7%
Public	University of Arkansas for Medical Sciences	100.0%	0.0%	0.0%	0.0%	0.0%	0.0%
Public	University of California - Berkeley	29.2%	16.9%	1.4%	26.2%	0.8%	1.0%
Public	University of California - Davis	72.9%	4.4%	3.9%	12.3%	1.2%	0.5%
Public	University of California - Irvine	62.6%	10.9%	3.4%	11.8%	4.3%	1.6%
Public	University of California - Los Angeles	73.3%	5.9%	2.6%	8.0%	1.7%	1.1%
Public	University of California - Riverside	55.1%	10.4%	7.1%	17.8%	3.9%	0.5%
Public	University of California - San Diego	56.7%	6.7%	17.1%	11.3%	3.3%	0.5%
Public	University of California - San Francisco	97.1%	2.9%	0.0%	0.0%	0.0%	0.0%
Public	University of California - Santa Barbara	12.5%	18.7%	11.4%	40.0%	5.5%	0.6%
Public	University of California - Santa Cruz	14.8%	20.7%	15.9%	40.6%	2.4%	0.5%
Public	University of Central Florida	17.5%	21.2%	6.4%	24.0%	9.1%	2.9%
Private	University of Chicago	67.8%	14.4%	2.2%	0.9%	5.3%	1.4%
Public	University of Cincinnati - Cincinnati	85.2%	2.0%	0.4%	9.7%	0.0%	0.4%
Public	University of Colorado - Boulder	7.8%	26.0%	26.6%	25.9%	2.3%	0.5%
Public	University of Colorado - Denver	95.7%	0.2%	0.1%	2.6%	0.0%	0.3%
Public	University of Connecticut - Health Center	100.0%	0.0%	0.0%	0.0%	0.0%	0.0%
Public	University of Connecticut - Storrs	29.0%	7.0%	6.7%	30.3%	2.7%	1.2%
Private	University of Dayton	1.2%	1.6%	0.2%	93.7%	2.9%	0.0%
Public	University of Delaware	29.6%	9.5%	11.1%	33.7%	3.3%	1.2%
Public	University of Florida	76.7%	3.9%	2.3%	13.1%	0.7%	0.3%
Public	University of Georgia	69.9%	3.8%	5.6%	2.9%	1.2%	1.7%
Public	University of Hawaii - Manoa	38.5%	10.7%	26.7%	5.4%	5.5%	0.0%
Public	University of Houston - University Park	18.6%	13.8%	6.6%	43.5%	4.1%	1.9%

Percent Psychology	Percent Social Science	Percent Other Science	2014 Federal Research by Major Discipline								
			Percent Life Science	Percent Physical Science	Percent Enviro Science	Percent Eng Science	Percent Computer Science	Percent Math	Percent Psychology	Percent Social Science	Percent Other Science
0.0%	2.2%	5.7%	39.3%	1.5%	27.8%	17.9%	3.8%	0.4%	0.0%	1.7%	7.6%
0.0%	0.0%	0.0%	100.0%	0.0%	0.0%	0.0%	0.0%	0.0%	0.0%	0.0%	0.0%
3.3%	4.9%	0.0%	17.2%	7.4%	8.3%	48.4%	10.1%	1.7%	3.5%	3.4%	0.0%
5.2%	9.6%	0.1%	17.8%	24.9%	7.1%	30.9%	4.9%	4.9%	4.2%	5.4%	0.0%
0.7%	4.5%	0.3%	31.6%	8.5%	1.7%	46.5%	6.6%	1.9%	0.9%	2.3%	0.0%
2.6%	1.0%	0.0%	4.0%	10.2%	2.5%	66.0%	10.2%	2.3%	4.0%	0.8%	0.0%
0.5%	6.9%	4.7%	9.5%	26.6%	3.4%	42.6%	9.1%	6.5%	0.6%	0.9%	1.0%
0.0%	0.0%	0.0%	95.2%	4.1%	0.4%	0.0%	0.0%	0.2%	0.0%	0.0%	0.0%
4.8%	0.0%	0.0%	94.4%	0.0%	0.0%	0.0%	0.0%	0.0%	5.6%	0.0%	0.0%
2.8%	7.8%	0.6%	59.1%	9.8%	5.4%	11.3%	2.7%	3.1%	2.4%	6.0%	0.2%
16.7%	6.1%	2.4%	58.9%	4.4%	3.3%	5.6%	2.0%	2.1%	18.5%	3.5%	1.6%
0.0%	0.0%	0.0%	100.0%	0.0%	0.0%	0.0%	0.0%	0.0%	0.0%	0.0%	0.0%
1.5%	1.8%	0.0%	63.5%	11.2%	1.9%	16.4%	3.2%	1.2%	1.5%	1.1%	0.0%
1.5%	0.7%	5.6%	49.3%	15.9%	12.6%	10.7%	4.5%	2.8%	2.6%	0.4%	1.2%
6.1%	1.2%	0.4%	78.4%	6.6%	0.3%	2.0%	2.8%	0.5%	7.8%	1.3%	0.2%
0.5%	2.3%	0.6%	29.0%	7.2%	30.7%	27.3%	1.9%	2.2%	0.5%	0.9%	0.3%
0.0%	0.0%	0.0%	100.0%	0.0%	0.0%	0.0%	0.0%	0.0%	0.0%	0.0%	0.0%
5.7%	5.7%	0.0%	67.7%	4.8%	0.2%	13.8%	1.8%	2.4%	2.3%	7.1%	0.0%
0.6%	3.1%	0.0%	90.8%	2.6%	0.8%	2.7%	0.0%	1.4%	0.9%	1.0%	0.0%
0.1%	0.0%	0.0%	99.9%	0.0%	0.0%	0.0%	0.0%	0.0%	0.1%	0.0%	0.0%
1.7%	8.9%	0.0%	82.0%	2.4%	3.4%	0.0%	4.9%	0.1%	1.2%	6.1%	0.0%
0.9%	1.3%	0.2%	57.7%	5.1%	1.1%	29.5%	3.7%	0.3%	1.6%	1.0%	0.0%
0.5%	0.1%	0.0%	92.9%	0.9%	0.1%	5.0%	0.3%	0.1%	0.6%	0.1%	0.0%
0.3%	0.6%	0.0%	0.9%	7.3%	12.8%	49.5%	29.0%	0.2%	0.2%	0.3%	0.0%
0.0%	1.2%	8.9%	12.7%	10.4%	59.3%	6.9%	1.7%	0.1%	0.0%	1.4%	7.5%
0.8%	3.9%	1.5%	42.5%	35.7%	5.2%	9.1%	2.5%	0.5%	0.7%	2.8%	1.0%
0.0%	0.0%	0.0%	100.0%	0.0%	0.0%	0.0%	0.0%	0.0%	0.0%	0.0%	0.0%
1.5%	7.3%	15.6%	31.5%	24.6%	2.1%	22.8%	0.0%	1.7%	1.5%	4.7%	11.1%
0.6%	3.4%	0.8%	74.7%	6.0%	2.7%	10.3%	1.8%	0.9%	0.7%	2.8%	0.0%
1.9%	3.4%	0.0%	60.6%	13.7%	4.1%	11.5%	3.9%	2.2%	2.2%	1.6%	0.0%
1.4%	3.8%	2.1%	70.4%	8.4%	3.2%	9.0%	2.1%	2.0%	1.7%	1.3%	1.9%
1.6%	2.6%	1.0%	46.6%	18.1%	8.8%	15.0%	7.0%	0.9%	2.7%	0.8%	0.0%
1.8%	1.7%	0.9%	58.7%	8.8%	14.7%	10.9%	2.4%	0.7%	2.2%	1.1%	0.4%
0.0%	0.0%	0.0%	97.3%	2.7%	0.0%	0.0%	0.0%	0.0%	0.0%	0.0%	0.0%
3.0%	6.2%	2.0%	11.2%	22.4%	8.1%	41.9%	5.9%	1.1%	4.2%	5.1%	0.0%
0.3%	2.5%	2.5%	17.5%	14.1%	14.8%	48.6%	2.6%	0.6%	0.2%	1.5%	0.0%
2.2%	10.4%	6.3%	17.5%	24.7%	6.4%	21.4%	15.3%	1.1%	2.7%	2.8%	8.2%
2.7%	5.3%	0.0%	68.1%	16.1%	2.6%	0.9%	6.4%	1.7%	2.6%	1.7%	0.0%
0.6%	1.5%	0.2%	91.8%	2.0%	0.2%	4.5%	0.0%	0.3%	0.6%	0.6%	0.0%
4.3%	4.2%	2.3%	7.1%	27.4%	30.0%	22.5%	2.6%	0.6%	4.9%	2.4%	2.6%
0.3%	0.8%	0.0%	95.3%	0.3%	0.1%	3.1%	0.0%	0.5%	0.4%	0.4%	0.0%
0.0%	0.0%	0.0%	100.0%	0.0%	0.0%	0.0%	0.0%	0.0%	0.0%	0.0%	0.0%
12.7%	4.8%	5.7%	35.2%	9.0%	7.2%	25.6%	3.2%	1.3%	14.4%	4.2%	0.0%
0.0%	0.0%	0.3%	1.4%	1.9%	0.2%	93.4%	2.9%	0.0%	0.0%	0.0%	0.1%
2.2%	8.5%	1.0%	22.3%	11.3%	12.8%	39.2%	4.0%	1.6%	2.9%	5.5%	0.5%
1.0%	2.0%	0.0%	68.7%	5.6%	3.3%	16.8%	1.3%	0.4%	1.8%	1.9%	0.0%
5.6%	5.5%	3.8%	73.8%	4.7%	6.3%	2.7%	1.2%	1.1%	8.0%	2.2%	0.0%
0.1%	2.1%	11.0%	30.8%	11.6%	30.7%	7.2%	8.2%	0.0%	0.2%	1.8%	9.5%
9.5%	1.7%	0.3%	20.6%	10.1%	2.3%	45.1%	3.9%	3.2%	13.5%	1.3%	0.0%

Research by Major Discipline		2014 Total Research by Major Discipline					
Institutions with Over $40 Million in Federal Research, Alphabetically		Percent Life Science	Percent Physical Science	Percent Enviro Science	Percent Eng Science	Percent Computer Science	Percent Math
Public	University of Idaho	64.6%	2.6%	6.1%	15.7%	2.6%	0.2%
Public	University of Illinois - Chicago	73.8%	3.7%	0.9%	6.2%	3.1%	0.9%
Public	University of Illinois - Urbana-Champaign	34.9%	10.9%	1.4%	28.9%	16.6%	0.7%
Public	University of Iowa	77.7%	4.7%	0.6%	11.0%	0.5%	0.3%
Public	University of Kansas - Lawrence	62.5%	10.0%	10.6%	11.6%	0.6%	0.5%
Public	University of Kansas Medical Center	100.0%	0.0%	0.0%	0.0%	0.0%	0.0%
Public	University of Kentucky	71.7%	2.8%	0.9%	14.0%	1.0%	0.6%
Public	University of Louisville	81.0%	1.5%	0.2%	15.1%	0.3%	0.1%
Public	University of Maine - Orono	39.1%	4.0%	20.2%	25.3%	0.6%	0.1%
Public	University of Maryland - Baltimore	97.8%	0.0%	0.5%	1.7%	0.0%	0.0%
Public	University of Maryland - Baltimore County	17.5%	12.4%	22.9%	15.5%	9.8%	1.9%
Public	University of Maryland - College Park	20.1%	18.1%	8.2%	23.5%	7.8%	1.2%
Public	University of Massachusetts - Amherst	38.1%	17.2%	2.2%	24.5%	10.1%	1.1%
Public	Univ. of Mass. Med. Sch. - Worcester	100.0%	0.0%	0.0%	0.0%	0.0%	0.0%
Private	University of Miami	74.0%	2.0%	18.7%	1.6%	0.5%	0.3%
Public	University of Michigan - Ann Arbor	59.4%	4.1%	1.4%	19.6%	0.7%	1.3%
Public	University of Minnesota - Twin Cities	69.9%	5.5%	1.8%	12.5%	1.8%	1.5%
Public	University of Missouri - Columbia	75.3%	3.2%	0.5%	14.2%	0.7%	1.0%
Public	University of Nebraska - Lincoln	51.1%	10.1%	1.5%	15.7%	4.1%	2.2%
Public	University of Nebraska Medical Center	100.0%	0.0%	0.0%	0.0%	0.0%	0.0%
Public	University of Nevada - Reno	57.4%	8.1%	16.3%	14.5%	1.3%	0.1%
Public	University of New Hampshire - Durham	26.1%	1.9%	44.9%	18.3%	0.3%	0.2%
Public	University of New Mexico - Albuquerque	59.4%	4.5%	2.5%	15.5%	2.0%	0.7%
Public	University of North Carolina - Chapel Hill	74.8%	3.1%	3.5%	0.5%	2.4%	0.8%
Public	University of North Dakota	23.1%	2.4%	12.9%	59.3%	0.1%	0.0%
Private	University of Notre Dame	15.4%	24.7%	1.4%	40.9%	4.3%	1.8%
Public	University of Oklahoma - Norman	25.1%	10.8%	32.8%	21.2%	3.0%	0.4%
Public	Univ. of Oklahoma Health Science Center	100.0%	0.0%	0.0%	0.0%	0.0%	0.0%
Public	University of Oregon	42.9%	23.8%	6.4%	1.1%	6.3%	0.8%
Private	University of Pennsylvania	82.7%	3.2%	0.2%	5.8%	2.0%	0.4%
Public	University of Pittsburgh - Pittsburgh	86.5%	3.3%	1.4%	4.3%	0.8%	0.4%
Public	University of Rhode Island	24.4%	4.7%	45.4%	6.8%	0.5%	0.0%
Private	University of Rochester	64.5%	3.6%	0.4%	26.0%	0.8%	0.2%
Public	University of South Carolina - Columbia	58.5%	7.8%	4.1%	18.8%	0.5%	2.5%
Public	University of South Florida - Tampa	66.5%	2.3%	4.3%	16.4%	1.5%	0.4%
Private	University of Southern California	62.4%	2.9%	2.5%	10.8%	15.2%	0.6%
Public	University of Tennessee - Knoxville	10.7%	11.0%	3.9%	37.9%	16.3%	0.5%
Public	Univ. of Tennessee Health Science Center	98.4%	0.0%	0.0%	0.8%	0.0%	0.0%
Public	University of Texas - Austin	14.0%	15.7%	13.0%	39.3%	11.3%	1.9%
Public	University of Texas HSC - Houston	100.0%	0.0%	0.0%	0.0%	0.0%	0.0%
Public	University of Texas HSC - San Antonio	100.0%	0.0%	0.0%	0.0%	0.0%	0.0%
Public	Univ. of Texas MD Anderson Cancer Ctr.	92.9%	1.8%	0.0%	0.0%	0.0%	2.1%
Public	Univ. of Texas Medical Branch - Galveston	97.3%	0.0%	0.0%	2.7%	0.0%	0.0%
Public	Univ. of Texas SW Medical Center - Dallas	100.0%	0.0%	0.0%	0.0%	0.0%	0.0%
Public	University of Utah	67.6%	3.9%	2.6%	15.7%	6.6%	1.2%
Public	University of Vermont	79.9%	1.4%	0.7%	6.9%	0.6%	1.0%
Public	University of Virginia	66.4%	7.3%	1.6%	17.5%	1.9%	0.4%
Public	University of Washington - Seattle	69.4%	4.1%	10.3%	11.8%	1.7%	0.6%
Public	University of Wisconsin - Madison	63.6%	7.3%	5.0%	15.0%	2.2%	0.6%

Percent Psychology	Percent Social Science	Percent Other Science	2014 Federal Research by Major Discipline								
			Percent Life Science	Percent Physical Science	Percent Enviro Science	Percent Eng Science	Percent Computer Science	Percent Math	Percent Psychology	Percent Social Science	Percent Other Science
0.2%	2.5%	5.3%	58.8%	3.1%	8.0%	16.2%	3.8%	0.3%	0.2%	2.1%	7.4%
3.9%	3.8%	3.7%	78.4%	3.7%	0.7%	4.9%	3.1%	1.1%	4.1%	2.5%	1.5%
3.0%	2.9%	0.7%	25.2%	13.4%	2.1%	31.4%	22.5%	0.9%	2.6%	1.8%	0.1%
2.0%	2.2%	0.9%	77.9%	7.2%	0.3%	9.8%	0.7%	0.3%	2.8%	1.0%	0.0%
0.8%	1.9%	1.5%	52.2%	14.7%	12.6%	12.4%	1.1%	0.8%	1.4%	2.6%	2.1%
0.0%	0.0%	0.0%	100.0%	0.0%	0.0%	0.0%	0.0%	0.0%	0.0%	0.0%	0.0%
3.3%	2.8%	2.9%	70.1%	3.7%	0.7%	13.8%	0.9%	1.0%	6.4%	1.5%	1.9%
1.2%	0.6%	0.0%	79.0%	2.4%	0.1%	15.0%	0.7%	0.1%	2.0%	0.6%	0.0%
0.0%	1.8%	8.8%	37.7%	2.4%	20.9%	22.9%	0.0%	0.2%	0.0%	2.8%	13.0%
0.0%	0.0%	0.0%	98.2%	0.0%	0.4%	1.5%	0.0%	0.0%	0.0%	0.0%	0.0%
3.6%	16.1%	0.3%	7.3%	13.1%	27.5%	18.6%	11.9%	2.2%	3.4%	16.0%	0.0%
1.2%	19.8%	0.0%	17.5%	20.4%	10.6%	20.7%	7.2%	1.3%	1.3%	21.1%	0.0%
2.8%	2.5%	1.5%	32.3%	20.5%	2.8%	24.8%	12.7%	1.3%	3.4%	1.2%	0.9%
0.0%	0.0%	0.0%	100.0%	0.0%	0.0%	0.0%	0.0%	0.0%	0.0%	0.0%	0.0%
2.8%	0.2%	0.0%	68.5%	2.3%	23.1%	1.8%	0.7%	0.3%	3.1%	0.2%	0.0%
1.7%	11.7%	0.1%	56.5%	4.4%	1.3%	23.8%	0.9%	0.9%	1.6%	10.5%	0.1%
3.0%	3.9%	0.1%	68.5%	7.0%	1.4%	11.6%	2.2%	1.9%	3.8%	3.6%	0.0%
0.9%	4.2%	0.0%	74.2%	5.8%	1.0%	9.5%	1.4%	2.2%	1.6%	4.3%	0.0%
5.9%	5.3%	4.1%	39.2%	15.2%	2.1%	17.9%	5.5%	2.2%	9.4%	3.5%	5.1%
0.0%	0.0%	0.0%	100.0%	0.0%	0.0%	0.0%	0.0%	0.0%	0.0%	0.0%	0.0%
0.9%	1.3%	0.1%	54.1%	9.8%	14.9%	16.5%	1.7%	0.2%	1.1%	1.6%	0.1%
0.6%	5.2%	2.6%	23.6%	1.9%	55.1%	13.2%	0.3%	0.2%	0.6%	4.5%	0.6%
3.7%	5.7%	6.0%	59.4%	5.6%	3.3%	16.7%	2.3%	0.9%	4.4%	2.5%	4.9%
4.9%	9.9%	0.1%	74.2%	3.6%	3.1%	0.5%	2.3%	1.1%	4.2%	11.0%	0.0%
0.0%	0.1%	2.1%	30.9%	2.2%	16.6%	50.0%	0.1%	0.0%	0.0%	0.1%	0.2%
3.1%	3.8%	4.5%	15.6%	32.7%	0.0%	40.4%	4.2%	2.2%	3.6%	0.1%	1.2%
0.9%	5.7%	0.0%	26.2%	15.3%	37.2%	14.5%	2.9%	0.9%	1.2%	1.9%	0.0%
0.0%	0.0%	0.0%	100.0%	0.0%	0.0%	0.0%	0.0%	0.0%	0.0%	0.0%	0.0%
13.4%	3.8%	1.6%	43.9%	23.2%	6.1%	0.1%	7.1%	0.9%	14.6%	2.2%	1.9%
1.9%	3.1%	0.6%	81.8%	3.7%	0.3%	6.5%	2.3%	0.4%	2.1%	2.6%	0.2%
1.7%	0.5%	1.0%	86.9%	2.6%	1.5%	4.1%	0.7%	0.4%	2.2%	0.5%	1.0%
1.8%	5.3%	11.0%	25.8%	5.2%	44.7%	6.3%	0.7%	0.0%	1.8%	4.9%	10.6%
4.4%	0.0%	0.2%	60.8%	3.9%	0.4%	28.8%	0.9%	0.2%	4.9%	0.0%	0.2%
4.1%	3.6%	0.1%	53.3%	8.0%	5.7%	17.7%	0.9%	4.6%	6.2%	3.6%	0.0%
2.6%	5.6%	0.4%	72.2%	2.2%	3.7%	11.0%	0.7%	0.4%	3.5%	6.0%	0.3%
1.5%	4.1%	0.0%	57.7%	2.1%	2.9%	10.7%	21.6%	0.7%	1.7%	2.4%	0.0%
0.8%	4.5%	14.3%	9.9%	12.6%	4.4%	35.6%	20.5%	0.7%	1.0%	4.0%	11.4%
0.0%	0.0%	0.8%	99.5%	0.0%	0.0%	0.0%	0.0%	0.0%	0.0%	0.0%	0.5%
1.6%	2.8%	0.4%	15.4%	17.2%	6.8%	38.6%	16.2%	1.5%	2.0%	2.0%	0.1%
0.0%	0.0%	0.0%	100.0%	0.0%	0.0%	0.0%	0.0%	0.0%	0.0%	0.0%	0.0%
0.0%	0.0%	0.0%	100.0%	0.0%	0.0%	0.0%	0.0%	0.0%	0.0%	0.0%	0.0%
2.1%	1.1%	0.0%	87.8%	3.7%	0.0%	0.0%	0.0%	3.2%	3.8%	1.5%	0.0%
0.0%	0.0%	0.0%	98.2%	0.0%	0.0%	1.8%	0.0%	0.0%	0.0%	0.0%	0.0%
0.0%	0.0%	0.0%	100.0%	0.0%	0.0%	0.0%	0.0%	0.0%	0.0%	0.0%	0.0%
0.8%	1.6%	0.0%	69.9%	4.8%	2.9%	10.3%	8.1%	1.3%	0.8%	1.8%	0.0%
2.7%	0.4%	6.2%	79.0%	1.7%	0.5%	6.5%	0.6%	1.0%	3.3%	0.2%	7.2%
1.9%	2.0%	0.9%	62.2%	9.8%	1.8%	19.2%	2.7%	0.6%	2.6%	0.4%	0.7%
0.9%	1.1%	0.0%	67.9%	4.8%	11.6%	11.5%	1.7%	0.7%	0.9%	1.0%	0.0%
0.5%	5.0%	0.9%	54.9%	9.8%	7.0%	18.6%	2.9%	0.8%	0.6%	4.9%	0.5%

Research by Major Discipline		2014 Total Research by Major Discipline					
Institutions with Over $40 Million in Federal Research, Alphabetically		Percent Life Science	Percent Physical Science	Percent Enviro Science	Percent Eng Science	Percent Computer Science	Percent Math
Public	Utah State University	33.0%	2.6%	1.6%	52.3%	1.2%	0.3%
Private	Vanderbilt University	83.4%	4.5%	0.5%	8.5%	0.0%	0.2%
Public	Virginia Commonwealth University	85.2%	4.2%	0.5%	4.0%	0.1%	1.2%
Public	Virginia Polytechnic Inst. and State Univ.	42.2%	3.0%	1.5%	45.5%	4.2%	0.7%
Private	Wake Forest University	97.6%	1.8%	0.0%	0.0%	0.3%	0.0%
Public	Washington State University - Pullman	63.5%	9.0%	2.6%	14.7%	2.2%	0.8%
Private	Washington University in St. Louis	90.6%	2.2%	1.4%	3.2%	0.8%	0.1%
Public	Wayne State University	74.5%	7.9%	0.2%	10.1%	1.8%	0.4%
Private	Weill Cornell Medical College	100.0%	0.0%	0.0%	0.0%	0.0%	0.0%
Public	West Virginia University	60.2%	5.9%	5.7%	24.6%	0.3%	0.4%
Private	Woods Hole Oceanographic Institution	0.0%	0.0%	64.4%	35.6%	0.0%	0.0%
Private	Yale University	83.8%	5.6%	0.8%	5.2%	1.2%	0.5%
Private	Yeshiva University	99.9%	0.1%	0.0%	0.0%	0.0%	0.0%

Percent Psychology	Percent Social Science	Percent Other Science	2014 Federal Research by Major Discipline								
			Percent Life Science	Percent Physical Science	Percent Enviro Science	Percent Eng Science	Percent Computer Science	Percent Math	Percent Psychology	Percent Social Science	Percent Other Science
7.9%	1.0%	0.1%	21.7%	2.2%	2.1%	63.8%	0.8%	0.2%	8.6%	0.5%	0.2%
1.7%	0.9%	0.2%	78.0%	6.0%	0.8%	11.6%	0.0%	0.3%	2.2%	1.0%	0.1%
3.6%	1.0%	0.0%	82.9%	5.7%	0.3%	4.5%	0.2%	1.7%	4.3%	0.3%	0.0%
0.9%	1.6%	0.5%	38.0%	4.0%	1.7%	47.4%	5.4%	0.9%	1.4%	0.4%	0.8%
0.3%	0.0%	0.0%	97.8%	1.6%	0.0%	0.0%	0.3%	0.0%	0.2%	0.0%	0.0%
1.1%	4.9%	1.2%	57.8%	16.0%	2.3%	17.1%	0.8%	1.2%	1.1%	3.3%	0.3%
1.1%	0.2%	0.5%	88.4%	2.6%	2.1%	4.0%	1.1%	0.1%	1.1%	0.1%	0.5%
2.1%	1.6%	1.4%	76.1%	7.2%	0.2%	9.8%	2.4%	0.6%	2.9%	0.8%	0.0%
0.0%	0.0%	0.0%	100.0%	0.0%	0.0%	0.0%	0.0%	0.0%	0.0%	0.0%	0.0%
0.4%	2.4%	0.2%	53.3%	7.6%	7.1%	29.5%	0.5%	0.5%	0.1%	1.1%	0.3%
0.0%	0.0%	0.0%	0.0%	0.0%	62.4%	37.6%	0.0%	0.0%	0.0%	0.0%	0.0%
1.4%	1.0%	0.5%	84.6%	5.4%	0.6%	5.5%	1.4%	0.6%	0.9%	0.7%	0.4%
0.0%	0.0%	0.0%	99.9%	0.1%	0.0%	0.0%	0.0%	0.0%	0.0%	0.0%	0.0%

Endowment Assets

	Institutions with Over $40 Million in Federal Research, Alphabetically	2015 Endowment Assets x $1000	2015 National Rank	2015 Control Rank	2014 Endowment Assets x $1000	2014 National Rank	2014 Control Rank
Public	Arizona State University	643,188	143	51	625,833	143	51
Public	Auburn University	641,993	144	52	621,106	147	55
Public	Augusta University	210,595	297	120	212,697	293	119
Private	Baylor College of Medicine	1,095,326	80	53	1,021,458	84	56
Private	Boston University	1,644,117	53	36	1,616,004	53	35
Private	Brandeis University	915,087	94	59	861,152	99	63
Private	Brown University	3,073,349	31	21	2,999,749	30	21
Private	California Institute of Technology	2,198,887	39	25	2,093,842	41	27
Private	Carnegie Mellon University	1,739,474	52	35	1,599,900	54	36
Private	Case Western Reserve University	1,775,999	51	34	1,758,570	49	33
Public	Clemson University	648,611	141	50	623,262	146	54
Public	Cleveland State University	74,900	568	200	72,300	576	203
Private	Cold Spring Harbor Laboratory						
Public	Colorado State Univ. - Fort Collins	281,355	252	99	284,495	242	97
Private	Columbia University	9,639,065	11	8	9,223,047	11	8
Private	Cornell University	4,760,560	19	15	4,646,134	19	15
Private	Dartmouth College	4,663,491	21	17	4,468,219	21	17
Private	Drexel University	668,386	137	89	660,150	136	87
Private	Duke University	7,296,545	14	11	7,036,776	14	11
Private	Emory University	6,684,305	16	13	6,681,479	15	12
Public	Florida International University	178,750	340	133	176,500	339	133
Public	Florida State University	605,275	150	56	624,557	145	53
Public	George Mason University	72,245	584	206	69,554	595	214
Private	George Washington University	1,616,357	56	37	1,576,508	56	38
Private	Georgetown University	1,528,869	60	39	1,461,276	62	41
Public	Georgia Institute of Technology	1,858,977	45	16	1,889,014	45	16
Private	Harvard University	36,448,817	1	1	35,883,891	1	1
Private	Icahn School of Med. at Mount Sinai	717,372	129	83	691,221	131	84
Public	Indiana University - Bloomington	960,625	91	33	961,054	89	31
Public	Indiana U. - Purdue U. - Indianapolis	825,184	106	40	834,834	104	39
Public	Iowa State University	786,205	114	43	777,018	112	43
Private	Johns Hopkins University	3,412,617	28	20	3,451,947	26	19
Public	Kansas State University	488,936	172	67	473,987	170	66
Public	Louisiana State Univ. - Baton Rouge	427,852	194	78	425,417	186	73
Private	Massachusetts Inst. of Technology	13,474,743	5	5	12,425,131	5	5
Private	Medical College of Wisconsin	778,315	116	73	748,637	122	75
Public	Medical University of South Carolina	322,644	227	91	312,580	227	91
Public	Michigan State University	2,673,652	34	13	2,548,913	34	13
Public	Mississippi State University	449,106	183	74	456,610	176	69
Public	Montana State University - Bozeman	142,661	392	148	141,066	388	148
Public	Naval Postgraduate School	5,086	1129	480	5,182	1021	419
Public	New Jersey Institute of Technology	99,257	474	171	98,117	471	171
Public	New Mexico State Univ. - Las Cruces	221,005	287	117	222,581	283	114
Private	New York University	3,576,180	26	19	3,422,227	27	20
Public	North Carolina State University	983,979	89	32	885,055	93	34
Private	Northeastern University	729,400	125	80	713,200	127	80
Private	Northwestern University	10,193,037	7	6	9,778,112	8	6
Public	Ohio State University - Columbus	3,633,887	24	6	3,547,566	24	6
Public	Oregon Health & Science University	571,341	153	58	522,384	160	60

2013 Endowment Assets x $1000	2013 National Rank	2013 Control Rank	2012 Endowment Assets x $1000	2012 National Rank	2012 Control Rank	2011 Endowment Assets x $1000	2011 National Rank	2011 Control Rank
552,789	141	51	500,667	138	50	514,724	138	49
522,145	147	56	461,727	148	57	450,361	152	59
142,208	354	139	117,426	382	145	121,259	378	142
873,721	85	57	789,997	86	58	838,207	84	57
1,403,061	54	36	1,157,075	59	40	1,159,583	60	41
766,205	99	62	674,522	97	64	703,666	97	63
2,699,948	29	21	2,460,131	28	21	2,496,926	29	21
1,849,880	38	24	1,746,526	37	24	1,772,369	37	24
1,371,365	56	38	987,054	68	46	1,017,338	69	46
1,595,300	47	31	1,600,013	44	29	1,703,164	41	27
528,697	146	55	482,866	142	53	473,748	145	53
61,707	589	209	54,300	606	216	53,900	604	210
245,887	243	97	225,362	244	95	221,231	251	96
8,197,880	8	6	7,654,152	8	6	7,789,578	7	6
4,133,842	19	15	3,850,426	19	15	3,960,058	19	15
3,733,596	21	17	3,486,383	21	17	3,413,406	22	18
586,938	137	89	555,381	131	84	525,211	137	89
6,040,973	14	11	5,555,196	14	11	5,747,377	14	11
5,816,046	15	12	5,461,158	15	12	5,400,367	15	12
149,384	344	132	132,554	351	137	136,237	352	134
548,095	143	52	497,709	139	51	525,260	136	48
59,261	606	218	55,165	600	213	51,608	618	215
1,375,202	55	37	1,305,892	53	36	1,331,101	53	36
1,286,323	61	40	1,140,486	60	41	1,160,291	59	40
1,714,876	45	16	1,608,248	43	15	1,619,718	45	15
32,334,293	1	1	30,435,375	1	1	31,728,080	1	1
630,518	128	81	594,968	120	77	607,498	117	76
835,123	89	30	772,185	88	29	835,119	85	28
709,877	109	41	634,979	109	40	653,518	108	37
673,515	115	44	604,897	115	43	612,283	115	41
2,987,298	25	19	2,678,721	25	20	2,598,467	26	20
364,675	191	78	329,240	193	78	337,460	193	76
383,443	183	73	357,602	178	70	364,076	179	69
10,857,976	5	5	10,308,274	5	5	9,712,628	5	5
597,865	134	86	470,510	146	91	487,921	143	92
272,319	227	89	239,472	229	89	230,286	243	90
1,997,985	36	14	1,721,100	38	14	1,718,101	40	14
394,925	178	70	343,857	184	73	346,676	187	74
121,755	395	149	119,821	376	143	115,687	396	149
4,461	1010	408	4,466	1131	472	4,143	1110	466
82,965	486	174	74,248	495	175	74,978	500	173
197,387	282	113	181,134	282	114	186,737	285	113
2,949,000	27	20	2,755,000	24	19	2,827,000	24	19
769,404	97	37	635,326	107	39	617,632	114	40
616,618	130	83	566,767	128	82	588,400	126	82
7,883,323	10	7	7,118,595	9	7	7,182,745	9	7
3,149,169	24	6	2,366,033	30	9	2,120,714	32	11
463,969	156	60	433,288	154	60	455,721	151	58

Endowment Assets

	Institutions with Over $40 Million in Federal Research, Alphabetically	2015 Endowment Assets x $1000	2015 National Rank	2015 Control Rank	2014 Endowment Assets x $1000	2014 National Rank	2014 Control Rank
Public	Oregon State University	505,369	168	65	511,427	162	62
Public	Penn. St. Univ. - Hershey Med. Ctr.	436,288	190	75	381,158	206	85
Public	Pennsylvania State Univ. - Univ. Park	1,854,222	46	17	1,739,032	51	17
Private	Princeton University	22,723,473	3	3	20,995,518	4	4
Public	Purdue University - West Lafayette	2,397,902	35	14	2,443,494	35	14
Private	Rensselaer Polytechnic Institute	676,546	136	88	659,035	137	88
Private	Rice University	5,557,479	18	14	5,527,693	18	14
Private	Rockefeller University	1,987,027	44	29	1,985,942	44	29
Private	Rush University	555,610	156	98	554,269	152	95
Public	Rutgers University - New Brunswick	710,802	130	47	763,561	116	45
Public	San Diego State University	209,372	299	122	190,608	324	129
Private	Scripps Research Institute						
Private	Stanford University	22,222,957	4	4	21,446,006	3	3
Public	Stony Brook University	247,397	274	108	214,446	288	116
Public	Temple University	386,230	206	84	374,758	210	86
Public	Texas A&M Univ. - College Station	9,856,983	10	3	10,540,226	7	2
Private	Thomas Jefferson University	437,750	188	114	375,697	208	123
Private	Tufts University	1,593,019	57	38	1,590,045	55	37
Private	Tulane University	1,220,464	68	45	1,183,924	70	46
Public	Uniformed Services Univ. of the HS						
Public	University at Albany	54,810	675	244	49,522	687	250
Public	University at Buffalo	619,296	148	54	624,791	144	52
Public	University of Alabama - Birmingham	388,405	205	83	406,098	195	80
Public	University of Alabama - Huntsville	65,978	620	224	70,419	591	212
Public	University of Alaska - Fairbanks	189,476	323	129	194,276	318	127
Public	University of Arizona	767,940	118	44	760,679	117	46
Public	Univ. of Arkansas for Med. Sciences	32,632	838	309	32,764	804	300
Public	University of California - Berkeley	4,045,451	23	5	3,913,416	23	5
Public	University of California - Davis	1,013,936	87	30	946,302	90	32
Public	University of California - Irvine	512,904	166	63	387,157	204	84
Public	University of California - Los Angeles	3,493,903	27	8	3,226,030	28	8
Public	University of California - Riverside	185,335	331	131	179,669	337	131
Public	University of California - San Diego	951,367	92	34	752,079	120	47
Public	Univ. of California - San Francisco	2,124,970	41	15	1,993,470	43	15
Public	Univ. of California - Santa Barbara	265,930	260	104	257,987	264	103
Public	University of California - Santa Cruz	164,331	359	141	152,855	365	144
Public	University of Central Florida	150,627	376	145	154,595	362	143
Private	University of Chicago	7,549,710	13	10	7,545,544	13	10
Public	University of Cincinnati - Cincinnati	1,195,899	71	25	1,183,922	71	25
Public	University of Colorado - Boulder	598,355	152	57	510,646	164	63
Public	University of Colorado - Denver	491,942	171	66	419,832	188	75
Public	Univ. of Connecticut - Health Center	103,450	460	168	103,885	453	165
Public	University of Connecticut - Storrs	279,699	255	102	280,876	247	99
Private	University of Dayton	500,407	169	104	510,107	165	102
Public	University of Delaware	1,341,373	65	22	1,310,133	64	22
Public	University of Florida	1,555,703	58	20	1,519,522	57	19
Public	University of Georgia	1,004,987	88	31	975,890	87	30
Public	University of Hawaii - Manoa	280,210	254	101	272,280	255	101
Public	University of Houston - Univ. Park	707,437	131	48	683,950	132	48

2013 Endowment Assets x $1000	2013 National Rank	2013 Control Rank	2012 Endowment Assets x $1000	2012 National Rank	2012 Control Rank	2011 Endowment Assets x $1000	2011 National Rank	2011 Control Rank
443,826	164	64	403,606	165	67	411,964	161	63
309,312	215	85	284,793	212	82	258,771	226	87
1,411,236	53	18	1,299,369	54	18	1,276,602	55	19
18,200,433	4	4	16,954,128	4	4	17,109,508	3	3
2,182,171	34	13	1,916,968	34	13	2,001,601	34	13
616,836	129	82	583,350	124	80	621,916	113	74
4,836,728	18	14	4,418,595	18	14	4,451,452	18	14
1,772,394	42	28	1,692,300	39	25	1,746,363	38	25
500,797	150	93	457,217	150	93	435,492	155	95
729,431	102	39	645,556	103	37	642,626	110	38
158,406	333	128	136,408	345	134	135,191	353	135
18,688,868	3	3	17,035,804	3	3	16,502,606	4	4
180,716	298	119	155,172	320	124	139,026	347	131
323,837	210	83	277,479	214	83	280,731	217	83
8,072,055	9	3	7,034,588	10	3	6,328,932	12	3
336,658	205	124	314,152	200	121	332,026	195	118
1,440,527	52	35	1,351,166	52	35	1,403,883	52	35
1,047,813	73	49	960,972	72	48	1,014,985	70	47
40,522	714	259	35,190	744	268	35,454	738	263
554,392	140	50	511,020	137	49	494,791	141	50
374,260	188	76	349,290	181	72	310,735	208	80
65,986	568	200	61,788	563	193	52,080	615	214
211,332	270	109	192,485	273	111	196,797	274	107
611,746	131	48	563,655	129	47	552,351	132	47
29,496	797	290	27,388	819	303	26,368	818	297
3,330,553	23	5	3,031,896	23	5	2,937,250	23	5
790,060	91	32	713,180	92	33	731,284	93	33
330,104	208	82	300,220	206	81	301,211	212	82
2,626,965	30	9	2,449,838	29	8	2,640,412	25	6
148,777	345	133	138,816	341	130	140,528	345	129
642,605	122	46	567,772	127	46	568,697	129	45
1,716,203	44	15	1,541,415	46	16	1,549,933	46	16
226,034	261	104	206,032	257	102	222,018	250	95
124,926	384	147	116,800	385	146	118,701	390	145
135,475	364	143	122,609	367	142	127,129	367	140
6,668,974	13	10	6,570,875	12	9	6,575,126	11	9
1,045,606	74	25	976,814	70	24	1,004,368	71	24
495,900	151	58	431,593	155	61	447,211	153	60
389,636	179	71	339,727	186	75	321,678	204	79
92,927	456	164	84,059	460	164	82,767	467	165
251,247	240	95	227,272	240	93	229,562	245	92
442,252	165	101	397,794	168	101	414,504	160	98
1,171,166	65	22	1,087,870	63	21	1,138,204	61	20
1,359,643	57	19	1,263,277	55	19	1,295,313	54	18
786,171	93	34	674,164	98	34	745,765	92	32
235,383	253	99	211,970	250	98	215,119	255	98
637,475	125	47	579,264	126	45	589,762	125	44

Endowment Assets

	Institutions with Over $40 Million in Federal Research, Alphabetically	2015 Endowment Assets x $1000	2015 National Rank	2015 Control Rank	2014 Endowment Assets x $1000	2014 National Rank	2014 Control Rank
Public	University of Idaho	239,603	276	109	240,980	272	108
Public	University of Illinois - Chicago	302,121	239	97	299,522	235	94
Public	Univ. of Illinois - Urbana-Champaign	1,530,658	59	21	1,488,828	59	21
Public	University of Iowa	1,263,043	67	23	1,251,356	65	23
Public	University of Kansas - Lawrence	1,170,313	73	26	1,147,213	76	26
Public	University of Kansas Medical Center	330,089	224	89	323,573	222	89
Public	University of Kentucky	1,142,722	77	27	1,136,833	78	27
Public	University of Louisville	844,288	104	39	876,825	94	35
Public	University of Maine - Orono	280,878	253	100	285,360	241	96
Public	University of Maryland - Baltimore	256,008	269	105	250,194	269	106
Public	Univ. of Maryland - Baltimore County	75,752	565	198	73,012	572	202
Public	University of Maryland - College Park	482,628	173	68	471,391	171	67
Public	Univ. of Massachusetts - Amherst	303,984	238	96	307,098	232	93
Public	Univ. of Mass. Med. Sch. - Worcester	194,251	319	127	211,880	295	120
Private	University of Miami	887,329	97	61	865,435	98	62
Public	University of Michigan - Ann Arbor	9,952,113	9	2	9,731,460	9	3
Public	University of Minnesota - Twin Cities	3,297,460	29	9	3,176,456	29	9
Public	University of Missouri - Columbia	857,471	101	38	804,003	106	40
Public	University of Nebraska - Lincoln	906,156	95	36	1,005,716	86	29
Public	University of Nebraska Medical Ctr.	226,077	283	114	232,088	277	110
Public	University of Nevada - Reno	306,587	234	93	295,334	237	95
Public	Univ. of New Hampshire - Durham	346,926	217	87	333,203	220	88
Public	Univ. of New Mexico - Albuquerque	403,670	202	81	412,772	192	79
Public	Univ. of North Carolina - Chapel Hill	2,988,806	32	11	2,695,663	33	12
Public	University of North Dakota	230,600	280	112	226,800	281	113
Private	University of Notre Dame	8,566,952	12	9	8,039,756	12	9
Public	University of Oklahoma - Norman	1,066,117	82	28	1,045,426	82	28
Public	University of Oklahoma HSC	456,907	179	72	448,040	179	71
Public	University of Oregon	719,111	128	46	627,004	142	50
Private	University of Pennsylvania	10,133,569	8	7	9,582,335	10	7
Public	University of Pittsburgh - Pittsburgh	3,588,775	25	7	3,492,839	25	7
Public	University of Rhode Island	131,655	407	153	132,234	405	152
Private	University of Rochester	2,050,199	43	28	2,015,283	42	28
Public	Univ. of South Carolina - Columbia	625,186	147	53	596,379	148	56
Public	University of South Florida - Tampa	417,415	196	80	417,335	189	76
Private	University of Southern California	4,709,511	20	16	4,593,014	20	16
Public	University of Tennessee - Knoxville	608,873	149	55	854,073	101	37
Public	University of Tennessee HSC						
Public	University of Texas - Austin	10,507,795	6	1	11,340,760	6	1
Public	University of Texas HSC - Houston	306,094	236	95	256,097	267	104
Public	Univ. of Texas HSC - San Antonio	476,632	175	70	485,459	169	65
Public	U. of Texas MD Anderson Cancer Ctr.	1,200,742	70	24	1,236,742	67	24
Public	U. of Texas Med. Branch - Galveston	531,562	163	61	549,315	154	58
Public	Univ. of Texas SW Med. Ctr. - Dallas	1,620,501	55	19	1,661,474	52	18
Public	University of Utah	1,023,004	86	29	844,761	103	38
Public	University of Vermont	453,653	181	73	394,454	202	82
Public	University of Virginia	6,180,515	17	4	5,945,952	17	4
Public	University of Washington - Seattle	3,076,226	30	10	2,832,753	31	10
Public	University of Wisconsin - Madison	2,792,622	33	12	2,699,253	32	11

The Center for Measuring University Performance

2013 Endowment Assets x $1000	2013 National Rank	2013 Control Rank	2012 Endowment Assets x $1000	2012 National Rank	2012 Control Rank	2011 Endowment Assets x $1000	2011 National Rank	2011 Control Rank
209,398	272	110	188,511	277	112	192,003	280	111
245,900	242	96	217,195	246	96	219,987	252	97
1,310,300	60	21	1,137,035	61	20	1,132,626	62	21
1,094,803	69	24	981,104	69	23	1,044,097	68	23
1,005,416	78	26	922,220	75	25	982,848	73	25
283,579	220	87	260,113	220	87	267,595	221	84
995,295	79	27	900,158	78	26	915,924	76	26
788,529	92	33	726,244	91	32	772,157	90	31
252,345	237	94	226,401	242	94	230,206	244	91
230,006	258	102	206,582	256	101	198,619	270	104
66,825	562	195	59,996	573	199	57,886	582	201
433,821	167	65	408,984	162	66	417,452	157	61
272,087	228	90	233,317	235	92	210,101	261	99
171,437	314	124	144,846	333	125	137,750	348	132
777,947	94	60	678,694	95	62	719,852	95	61
8,382,311	7	2	7,691,052	7	2	7,834,752	6	1
2,757,476	28	8	2,494,050	27	7	2,503,305	28	8
692,853	112	43	622,209	113	42	559,516	130	46
870,173	86	29	790,011	85	28	807,025	87	29
200,809	278	111	182,310	281	113	186,237	286	114
259,775	232	92	238,286	231	90	235,404	240	89
231,504	255	100	214,879	249	97	227,225	246	93
371,362	189	77	343,321	185	74	349,145	183	72
2,381,151	31	10	2,179,177	31	10	2,260,970	30	9
162,785	332	127	140,260	338	128	122,283	376	141
6,856,301	12	9	6,329,866	13	10	6,259,598	13	10
927,019	83	28	820,724	82	27	845,469	83	27
397,294	174	69	351,739	179	71	366,554	178	68
558,437	139	49	477,599	144	54	467,211	148	56
7,741,396	11	8	6,754,658	11	8	6,582,029	10	8
2,975,896	26	7	2,618,436	26	6	2,527,398	27	7
102,885	430	158	93,659	433	156	97,659	429	155
1,730,829	43	29	1,581,773	45	30	1,622,812	44	30
544,399	145	54	513,936	135	48	494,358	142	51
363,924	192	79	334,132	190	77	349,320	182	71
3,868,355	20	16	3,488,933	20	16	3,517,173	20	16
726,483	104	40	647,826	100	36	590,551	123	43
9,145,142	6	1	8,209,163	6	1	7,441,482	8	2
227,043	260	103	201,989	264	106	191,856	281	112
432,031	168	66	412,085	160	64	411,599	162	64
1,111,653	67	23	1,056,878	64	22	1,059,791	66	22
495,887	152	59	473,427	145	55	472,297	146	54
1,450,655	51	17	1,465,375	48	17	1,452,473	50	17
745,553	101	38	670,411	99	35	668,683	103	36
374,316	187	75	325,555	195	79	343,050	189	75
5,166,660	17	4	4,788,852	17	4	4,760,515	17	4
2,346,693	32	11	2,111,332	32	11	2,154,494	31	10
2,334,560	33	12	2,082,181	33	12	2,066,958	33	12

Endowment Assets

	Institutions with Over $40 Million in Federal Research, Alphabetically	2015 Endowment Assets x $1000	2015 National Rank	2015 Control Rank	2014 Endowment Assets x $1000	2014 National Rank	2014 Control Rank
Public	Utah State University	314,688	231	92	282,465	245	98
Private	Vanderbilt University	4,133,542	22	18	4,086,040	22	18
Public	Virginia Commonwealth University	1,638,147	54	18	1,509,431	58	20
Public	Virginia Polytechnic Inst. and St. Univ.	817,759	107	41	796,437	109	42
Private	Wake Forest University	1,167,400	75	49	1,148,026	75	50
Public	Washington State Univ. - Pullman	885,777	98	37	868,091	96	36
Private	Washington University in St. Louis	6,818,748	15	12	6,643,379	16	13
Public	Wayne State University	306,319	235	94	311,337	228	92
Private	Weill Cornell Medical College	1,276,986	66	44	1,243,814	66	43
Public	West Virginia University	533,599	162	60	533,627	158	59
Private	Woods Hole Oceanographic Inst.						
Private	Yale University	25,572,100	2	2	23,894,800	2	2
Private	Yeshiva University	1,061,440	84	56	1,094,558	79	52

2013 Endowment Assets x $1000	2013 National Rank	2013 Control Rank	2012 Endowment Assets x $1000	2012 National Rank	2012 Control Rank	2011 Endowment Assets x $1000	2011 National Rank	2011 Control Rank
242,025	246	98	209,188	252	99	208,986	263	100
3,673,434	22	18	3,399,293	22	18	3,414,514	21	17
1,326,915	59	20	438,140	153	59	349,699	181	70
660,340	119	45	594,776	121	44	600,648	122	42
1,061,639	70	46	1,000,133	67	45	1,058,250	67	45
777,628	95	35	737,409	89	30	722,717	94	34
5,651,860	16	13	5,225,992	16	13	5,280,143	16	13
276,234	225	88	247,111	226	88	251,309	229	88
1,138,386	66	44	1,096,528	62	42	1,099,348	64	43
460,640	158	61	417,504	159	63	392,001	169	66
20,780,000	2	2	19,345,000	2	2	19,374,000	2	2
1,183,499	64	43	1,054,052	65	43	1,125,032	63	42

Annual Giving

	Institutions with Over $40 Million in Federal Research, Alphabetically	2015 Annual Giving x $1000	2015 National Rank	2015 Control Rank	2014 Annual Giving x $1000	2014 National Rank	2014 Control Rank
Public	Arizona State University	130,775	61	32	99,212	78	44
Public	Auburn University	106,353	82	48	86,579	88	50
Public	Augusta University	12,151	348	164	61,007	123	76
Private	Baylor College of Medicine	61,656	119	44	84,211	93	39
Private	Boston University	140,393	56	26	132,583	55	27
Private	Brandeis University	60,196	120	45	56,905	126	49
Private	Brown University	187,754	37	21	201,731	33	20
Private	California Institute of Technology	161,929	47	23	113,370	71	33
Private	Carnegie Mellon University	139,563	57	27	137,573	50	24
Private	Case Western Reserve University	132,826	58	28	124,509	62	30
Public	Clemson University	81,861	103	63	61,721	121	75
Public	Cleveland State University	17,732	266	130	14,179	309	156
Private	Cold Spring Harbor Laboratory						
Public	Colorado State Univ. - Fort Collins	41,342	154	92	143,239	47	24
Private	Columbia University	552,682	6	5	469,969	9	7
Private	Cornell University	434,465	17	14	341,851	19	13
Private	Dartmouth College	218,832	32	19	254,944	27	17
Private	Drexel University	88,916	95	38	89,966	86	38
Private	Duke University	472,008	11	9	437,382	12	9
Private	Emory University	228,034	31	18	268,926	26	16
Public	Florida International University	23,312	212	110	21,459	226	121
Public	Florida State University	68,634	112	70	55,725	128	78
Public	George Mason University	53,164	128	80	48,467	139	83
Private	George Washington University	248,030	28	16	98,515	79	35
Private	Georgetown University	172,452	43	22	134,685	52	25
Public	Georgia Institute of Technology	119,118	73	42	141,888	48	25
Private	Harvard University	1,045,872	2	2	1,155,610	1	1
Private	Icahn School of Med. at Mount Sinai	109,733	78	33	150,420	45	23
Public	Indiana University - Bloomington	211,471	34	15	190,593	35	15
Public	Indiana U. - Purdue U. - Indianapolis	121,989	68	38	135,910	51	27
Public	Iowa State University	105,512	83	49	64,854	116	71
Private	Johns Hopkins University	582,675	5	4	614,606	5	5
Public	Kansas State University	98,094	88	53	156,335	42	20
Public	Louisiana State Univ. - Baton Rouge	130,763	62	33	110,644	73	40
Private	Massachusetts Inst. of Technology	439,404	16	13	375,031	18	12
Private	Medical College of Wisconsin	20,907	230	112	16,704	270	131
Public	Medical University of South Carolina	31,498	178	103	38,853	156	90
Public	Michigan State University	131,499	60	31	117,566	65	34
Public	Mississippi State University	56,857	125	78	66,002	114	70
Public	Montana State University - Bozeman	13,299	331	161	12,185	337	165
Public	Naval Postgraduate School						
Public	New Jersey Institute of Technology	8,821	443	199	8,918	420	195
Public	New Mexico State Univ. - Las Cruces	16,568	282	142	13,928	313	157
Private	New York University	439,662	15	12	455,718	10	8
Public	North Carolina State University	119,150	72	41	117,535	66	35
Private	Northeastern University	59,857	122	46	39,543	154	65
Private	Northwestern University	536,831	8	7	616,351	4	4
Public	Ohio State University - Columbus	359,798	21	6	332,627	20	7
Public	Oregon Health & Science University	141,018	55	30	153,281	43	21

2013 Annual Giving x $1000	2013 National Rank	2013 Control Rank	2012 Annual Giving x $1000	2012 National Rank	2012 Control Rank	2011 Annual Giving x $1000	2011 National Rank	2011 Control Rank
108,011	65	38	98,844	66	41	103,404	59	34
67,911	105	64	63,712	106	68	61,263	105	66
33,894	165	95	4,664	593	242	6,710	480	199
100,540	74	29	80,736	83	30	68,407	96	36
116,562	58	26	86,181	76	27	89,499	72	27
54,556	123	48	60,768	108	39	61,745	104	39
176,416	35	19	178,065	32	18	160,512	33	19
103,446	72	28	99,983	65	25	156,525	34	20
112,164	60	27	79,141	85	32	79,074	87	32
94,238	79	31	90,584	73	26	85,029	76	29
75,666	98	60	71,304	96	62	63,062	102	65
6,163	515	220	5,265	556	230	10,294	368	171
112,473	59	33	29,925	166	98	35,054	155	88
646,663	4	4	490,311	5	5	495,562	5	5
326,497	16	11	263,358	19	11	245,242	22	12
160,165	41	20	170,847	34	19	146,757	40	22
64,953	108	42	67,459	103	37	51,468	115	46
423,658	9	9	350,944	11	10	349,658	12	9
204,171	32	17	211,589	26	15	147,370	38	21
24,706	197	111	15,267	269	138	40,548	137	83
61,270	115	72	54,942	116	74	49,913	118	71
44,617	134	80	44,111	133	82	44,408	128	78
84,436	85	34	73,070	94	34	81,452	82	30
131,044	47	23	113,721	52	22	206,525	28	16
102,717	73	45	118,429	50	29	118,184	48	25
792,256	2	2	650,243	2	2	639,153	2	2
127,027	51	24	103,111	60	23	94,316	67	26
160,548	40	21	122,489	46	25	152,282	37	17
127,341	50	27	164,444	36	17	131,301	43	21
62,288	114	71	60,716	109	70	63,290	101	64
518,571	5	5	479,654	6	6	485,410	6	6
108,060	64	37	75,373	88	56	66,897	98	61
96,895	78	48	105,784	55	33	91,248	70	44
403,539	11	10	379,058	10	9	534,343	4	4
13,263	322	161	19,197	218	101	20,611	222	106
43,841	138	82	40,197	139	85	40,178	139	85
130,964	48	25	122,883	45	24	107,694	56	32
65,925	106	65	51,332	122	78	43,197	132	80
16,659	263	138	10,602	358	171	10,293	369	172
10,023	384	179	8,442	418	190	6,379	498	206
12,499	335	165	12,060	321	158	10,873	352	164
449,344	7	7	395,510	9	8	337,852	13	10
131,378	46	24	100,324	64	40	94,757	65	40
46,828	130	53	34,512	151	61	36,276	150	64
295,601	18	12	233,746	25	14	228,623	24	14
290,595	20	8	334,509	13	3	255,698	20	10
121,027	56	31	91,560	72	47	101,446	60	35

Annual Giving

	Institutions with Over $40 Million in Federal Research, Alphabetically	2015 Annual Giving x $1000	2015 National Rank	2015 Control Rank	2014 Annual Giving x $1000	2014 National Rank	2014 Control Rank
Public	Oregon State University	99,318	87	52	97,217	81	46
Public	Penn. St. Univ. - Hershey Med. Ctr.	35,023	171	100	38,772	157	91
Public	Pennsylvania State Univ. - Univ. Park	155,658	50	26	172,319	39	18
Private	Princeton University	549,840	7	6	240,931	29	18
Public	Purdue University - West Lafayette	172,219	44	22	129,490	59	30
Private	Rensselaer Polytechnic Institute	38,364	164	68	53,230	133	53
Private	Rice University	122,186	67	30	104,113	76	34
Private	Rockefeller University	18,562	262	133	13,457	321	163
Private	Rush University	3,689	681	402	3,960	659	390
Public	Rutgers University - New Brunswick	127,846	63	34	105,811	74	41
Public	San Diego State University	76,036	107	66	79,854	98	58
Private	Scripps Research Institute						
Private	Stanford University	1,625,036	1	1	928,458	2	2
Public	Stony Brook University	86,687	98	59	78,655	102	60
Public	Temple University	58,792	124	77	60,787	124	77
Public	Texas A&M Univ. - College Station	255,179	26	11	317,549	22	8
Private	Thomas Jefferson University	38,809	162	67	29,305	188	82
Private	Tufts University	62,131	118	43	69,847	107	43
Private	Tulane University	88,422	96	39	78,768	100	42
Public	Uniformed Services Univ. of the HS						
Public	University at Albany	9,439	419	191	9,948	391	182
Public	University at Buffalo	30,565	184	105	33,300	172	100
Public	University of Alabama - Birmingham	76,612	106	65	80,004	97	57
Public	University of Alabama - Huntsville	2,032	803	348	3,329	701	291
Public	University of Alaska - Fairbanks	27,865	190	106	20,328	233	123
Public	University of Arizona	190,184	36	16	186,192	37	16
Public	Univ. of Arkansas for Med. Sciences	16,815	273	134	25,062	201	111
Public	University of California - Berkeley	366,116	20	5	389,935	17	6
Public	University of California - Davis	185,840	38	17	133,393	54	28
Public	University of California - Irvine	66,617	114	72	97,241	80	45
Public	University of California - Los Angeles	473,205	10	2	430,276	15	5
Public	University of California - Riverside	16,985	272	133	22,692	214	116
Public	University of California - San Diego	171,059	46	24	150,446	44	22
Public	Univ. of California - San Francisco	608,580	4	1	444,938	11	3
Public	Univ. of California - Santa Barbara	63,413	116	74	67,505	110	67
Public	University of California - Santa Cruz	24,831	202	109	40,855	151	89
Public	University of Central Florida	32,779	176	102	23,116	213	115
Private	University of Chicago	443,792	13	10	405,350	16	11
Public	University of Cincinnati - Cincinnati	119,700	71	40	140,645	49	26
Public	University of Colorado - Boulder	151,553	52	27	67,726	109	66
Public	University of Colorado - Denver	171,102	45	23	66,852	111	68
Public	Univ. of Connecticut - Health Center	8,475	451	202	5,395	567	238
Public	University of Connecticut - Storrs	40,751	156	94	30,570	183	104
Private	University of Dayton	28,219	189	84	20,199	237	113
Public	University of Delaware	44,896	147	89	48,905	136	82
Public	University of Florida	215,580	33	14	215,184	30	12
Public	University of Georgia	104,108	84	50	96,088	82	47
Public	University of Hawaii - Manoa	90,650	93	56	92,519	84	48
Public	University of Houston - Univ. Park	95,602	91	55	85,269	91	53

2013 Annual Giving x $1000	2013 National Rank	2013 Control Rank	2012 Annual Giving x $1000	2012 National Rank	2012 Control Rank	2011 Annual Giving x $1000	2011 National Rank	2011 Control Rank
81,027	88	54	101,634	62	39	82,837	80	51
39,174	150	84	32,677	158	94	48,701	121	72
174,105	36	17	145,186	38	18	216,450	25	11
242,551	25	15	246,035	23	13	236,173	23	13
121,592	55	30	170,449	35	16	155,438	35	15
41,814	143	61	32,058	159	65	49,752	119	48
122,673	53	25	80,676	84	31	85,807	75	28
37,562	156	68	28,192	173	73	34,544	158	69
	1058	507	7,474	455	254	15,019	274	135
90,313	80	49	69,238	99	64	79,145	86	55
72,452	102	61	60,561	110	71	54,833	109	68
931,569	1	1	1,034,849	1	1	709,423	1	1
97,892	77	47	82,276	81	52	44,784	127	77
63,014	112	69	36,757	147	88	44,248	129	79
254,628	23	10	180,886	30	13	184,051	31	14
31,469	176	75	30,299	164	68	27,733	182	80
52,260	124	49	48,937	126	47	62,313	103	38
77,824	95	37	53,572	119	43	47,830	123	50
8,389	430	195	18,928	220	118	20,924	220	116
28,700	185	106	68,104	101	66	32,727	162	92
63,762	110	67	70,130	97	63	91,447	69	43
2,435	788	329	7,227	463	203	13,526	302	151
14,461	295	148	17,829	232	124	13,993	295	147
151,363	42	22	180,317	31	14	147,314	39	18
27,370	190	109	20,608	206	116	19,516	234	122
340,919	15	5	405,435	8	1	283,347	16	6
104,743	69	42	93,977	69	44	111,235	51	28
77,210	97	59	77,236	87	55	94,487	66	41
419,647	10	1	344,201	12	2	415,030	8	1
25,450	193	110	33,837	153	91	34,940	156	89
167,404	38	19	135,543	40	20	116,151	49	26
385,745	12	2	329,477	14	4	409,448	9	2
60,999	116	73	105,362	57	35	47,467	124	74
23,684	202	114	22,766	194	109	20,117	226	118
38,839	152	86	14,858	277	141	19,660	232	121
289,447	21	13	255,764	21	12	246,748	21	11
105,037	67	40	105,168	58	36	109,759	54	30
63,377	111	68	86,295	75	49	110,646	52	29
51,596	125	76	133,993	42	22	81,136	83	53
6,879	484	210	6,242	497	211	5,801	518	216
38,982	151	85	35,371	149	90	32,875	161	91
18,071	243	113	17,308	239	114	15,969	262	127
46,844	129	77	45,796	131	81	29,981	173	99
210,951	31	15	173,385	33	15	201,029	30	13
85,814	84	51	81,568	82	53	77,852	88	56
62,465	113	70	50,267	124	79	48,300	122	73
84,201	86	52	72,850	95	61	75,076	91	59

Annual Giving

	Institutions with Over $40 Million in Federal Research, Alphabetically	2015 Annual Giving x $1000	2015 National Rank	2015 Control Rank	2014 Annual Giving x $1000	2014 National Rank	2014 Control Rank
Public	University of Idaho	19,358	254	126	26,912	193	108
Public	University of Illinois - Chicago	62,590	117	75	66,508	112	69
Public	Univ. of Illinois - Urbana-Champaign	177,235	40	19	177,193	38	17
Public	University of Iowa	159,532	48	25	146,748	46	23
Public	University of Kansas - Lawrence	176,704	42	21	129,794	57	29
Public	University of Kansas Medical Center	44,176	148	90	32,448	177	102
Public	University of Kentucky	118,190	74	43	105,565	75	42
Public	University of Louisville	86,309	100	61	85,065	92	54
Public	University of Maine - Orono	21,682	221	115	22,644	215	117
Public	University of Maryland - Baltimore	69,153	109	67	62,004	120	74
Public	Univ. of Maryland - Baltimore County	7,663	476	212	9,143	411	192
Public	University of Maryland - College Park	122,694	66	37	81,788	95	56
Public	Univ. of Massachusetts - Amherst	35,327	170	99	33,918	169	99
Public	Univ. of Mass. Med. Sch. - Worcester	8,328	458	204	4,855	600	247
Private	University of Miami	193,809	35	20	186,528	36	21
Public	University of Michigan - Ann Arbor	394,310	18	4	432,596	13	4
Public	University of Minnesota - Twin Cities	344,303	22	7	287,361	24	10
Public	University of Missouri - Columbia	108,689	79	46	118,745	64	33
Public	University of Nebraska - Lincoln	177,321	39	18	116,724	68	37
Public	University of Nebraska Medical Ctr.	89,054	94	57	83,219	94	55
Public	University of Nevada - Reno	100,048	85	51	38,414	158	92
Public	Univ. of New Hampshire - Durham	9,605	413	188	18,350	257	134
Public	Univ. of New Mexico - Albuquerque	68,992	110	68	73,517	106	64
Public	Univ. of North Carolina - Chapel Hill	301,177	25	10	298,804	23	9
Public	University of North Dakota	9,284	427	194	9,079	416	193
Private	University of Notre Dame	379,869	19	15	320,316	21	14
Public	University of Oklahoma - Norman	252,475	27	12	126,639	61	32
Public	University of Oklahoma HSC	64,872	115	73	34,274	167	97
Public	University of Oregon	145,109	54	29	68,221	108	65
Private	University of Pennsylvania	517,198	9	8	483,569	7	6
Public	University of Pittsburgh - Pittsburgh	124,602	65	36	117,068	67	36
Public	University of Rhode Island	17,563	267	131	14,627	299	151
Private	University of Rochester	108,217	80	34	120,038	63	31
Public	Univ. of South Carolina - Columbia	113,506	76	44	115,683	69	38
Public	University of South Florida - Tampa	59,903	121	76	37,419	160	93
Private	University of Southern California	653,025	3	3	731,933	3	3
Public	University of Tennessee - Knoxville	119,749	70	39	111,303	72	39
Public	University of Tennessee HSC	16,692	278	139			
Public	University of Texas - Austin	310,212	24	9	529,391	6	1
Public	University of Texas HSC - Houston	46,346	144	87	37,179	161	94
Public	Univ. of Texas HSC - San Antonio	42,764	151	91	44,606	143	85
Public	U. of Texas MD Anderson Cancer Ctr.	176,908	41	20	163,188	40	19
Public	U. of Texas Med. Branch - Galveston	41,039	155	93	40,965	150	88
Public	Univ. of Texas SW Med. Ctr. - Dallas	149,243	53	28	127,930	60	31
Public	University of Utah	126,244	64	35	194,893	34	14
Public	University of Vermont	40,458	157	95	37,119	162	95
Public	University of Virginia	233,218	30	13	214,412	31	13
Public	University of Washington - Seattle	447,021	12	3	478,072	8	2
Public	University of Wisconsin - Madison	330,454	23	8	249,661	28	11

2013 Annual Giving x $1000	2013 National Rank	2013 Control Rank	2012 Annual Giving x $1000	2012 National Rank	2012 Control Rank	2011 Annual Giving x $1000	2011 National Rank	2011 Control Rank
17,759	248	133	16,534	250	130	16,493	253	132
55,700	121	75	59,017	114	72	80,095	84	54
169,548	37	18	137,059	39	19	126,987	44	22
122,102	54	29	104,392	59	37	123,346	46	24
135,754	45	23	121,186	47	26	104,911	57	33
33,938	163	94	30,296	165	97	26,228	189	104
78,903	93	57	73,788	91	58	77,666	89	57
123,415	52	28	73,547	92	59	86,211	74	47
18,944	234	126	25,367	186	106	18,850	238	125
109,647	63	36	77,984	86	54	84,143	78	49
21,057	220	120	11,776	325	159	11,606	331	158
79,118	92	56	93,736	71	46	96,727	63	38
31,914	174	100	32,017	160	95	31,724	166	94
10,158	379	175	3,584	672	270	8,669	403	181
180,538	34	18	163,978	37	20	171,938	32	18
351,552	14	4	291,335	17	7	270,351	18	8
219,905	28	12	254,855	22	10	257,082	19	9
103,979	71	44	88,689	74	48	83,098	79	50
120,093	57	32	109,388	54	32	89,261	73	46
70,505	103	62	62,028	107	69	66,762	99	62
28,426	186	107	23,554	192	108	23,069	208	112
20,880	221	121	16,501	251	131	4,974	560	232
65,919	107	66	64,063	105	67	65,882	100	63
272,767	22	9	286,710	18	8	274,947	17	7
9,080	400	186	7,869	440	196	8,067	424	187
247,928	24	14	203,250	28	17	205,160	29	17
162,048	39	20	115,172	51	30	125,031	45	23
32,210	172	99	23,801	191	107	31,347	168	96
185,648	33	16	109,529	53	31	93,096	68	42
506,607	6	6	440,603	7	7	437,718	7	7
127,859	49	26	118,700	49	28	114,482	50	27
12,649	334	164	12,719	311	153	18,911	237	124
90,023	81	32	85,415	79	29	72,118	93	33
107,008	66	39	85,566	78	50	75,785	90	58
36,520	158	90	43,613	135	83	81,492	81	52
674,512	3	3	491,854	4	4	402,411	10	8
104,164	70	43	124,196	44	23	100,706	62	37
290,987	19	7	258,308	20	9	354,339	11	3
39,323	149	83	48,552	127	80	41,844	134	81
37,617	155	88	36,599	148	89	32,025	163	93
212,506	30	14	186,667	29	12	153,732	36	16
29,682	180	104	55,947	115	73	26,704	187	103
104,866	68	41	120,844	48	27	139,808	42	20
213,984	29	13	134,011	41	21	140,718	41	19
37,003	157	89	21,728	200	114	29,069	176	101
224,541	27	11	237,221	24	11	216,162	26	12
322,231	17	6	295,564	16	6	334,494	14	4
360,689	13	3	315,278	15	5	315,768	15	5

Annual Giving

Institutions with Over $40 Million in Federal Research, Alphabetically		2015 Annual Giving x $1000	2015 National Rank	2015 Control Rank	2014 Annual Giving x $1000	2014 National Rank	2014 Control Rank
Public	Utah State University	52,076	130	81	33,941	168	98
Private	Vanderbilt University	121,909	69	31	157,510	41	22
Public	Virginia Commonwealth University	67,256	113	71	64,190	117	72
Public	Virginia Polytechnic Inst. and St. Univ.	86,391	99	60	78,141	103	61
Private	Wake Forest University	99,763	86	35	91,772	85	37
Public	Washington State Univ. - Pullman	106,370	81	47	85,672	89	51
Private	Washington University in St. Louis	246,714	29	17	274,498	25	15
Public	Wayne State University	47,983	141	84			
Private	Weill Cornell Medical College	156,176	49	24	204,237	32	19
Public	West Virginia University	110,384	77	45	85,323	90	52
Private	Woods Hole Oceanographic Inst.						
Private	Yale University	440,807	14	11	430,309	14	10
Private	Yeshiva University	59,420	123	47	63,153	118	46

2013 Annual Giving x $1000	2013 National Rank	2013 Control Rank	2012 Annual Giving x $1000	2012 National Rank	2012 Control Rank	2011 Annual Giving x $1000	2011 National Rank	2011 Control Rank
32,488	170	97	27,664	177	102	30,705	170	98
145,433	44	22	126,367	43	21	119,441	47	23
59,238	117	74	101,716	61	38	47,432	125	75
86,970	83	50	75,120	89	57	91,001	71	45
79,631	90	35	73,797	90	33	110,603	53	24
45,336	132	78	105,469	56	34	101,026	61	36
233,019	26	16	205,687	27	16	215,071	27	15
			53,761	118	76	51,344	116	70
148,460	43	21	67,578	102	36	70,289	95	35
99,034	76	46	83,933	80	51	84,984	77	48
444,171	8	8	543,905	3	3	580,325	3	3
75,591	99	39	86,032	77	28	79,567	85	31

National Academy Membership

	Institutions with Over $40 Million in Federal Research, Alphabetically	2015 National Academy Membership	2015 National Rank	2015 Control Rank	2014 National Academy Membership	2014 National Rank	2014 Control Rank
Public	Arizona State University	22	55	29	22	53	28
Public	Auburn University	1	163	100	1	165	102
Public	Augusta University	0	221	136	0	222	137
Private	Baylor College of Medicine	24	50	24	24	50	25
Private	Boston University	20	58	28	21	55	26
Private	Brandeis University	11	70	34	11	68	33
Private	Brown University	22	55	27	19	60	29
Private	California Institute of Technology	112	12	8	113	11	7
Private	Carnegie Mellon University	39	31	18	37	32	18
Private	Case Western Reserve University	20	58	28	20	57	28
Public	Clemson University	2	142	87	2	140	85
Public	Cleveland State University	0	221	136	0	222	137
Private	Cold Spring Harbor Laboratory	5	104	43	4	108	44
Public	Colorado State Univ. - Fort Collins	9	77	41	8	81	44
Private	Columbia University	134	6	4	131	6	4
Private	Cornell University	62	20	12	61	20	12
Private	Dartmouth College	15	62	31	13	66	32
Private	Drexel University	7	92	39	7	89	39
Private	Duke University	66	19	11	65	19	11
Private	Emory University	32	35	20	28	41	20
Public	Florida International University	1	163	100	1	165	102
Public	Florida State University	7	92	54	6	96	55
Public	George Mason University	2	142	87	2	140	85
Private	George Washington University	12	68	33	10	72	35
Private	Georgetown University	9	77	37	10	72	35
Public	Georgia Institute of Technology	31	38	18	26	46	24
Private	Harvard University	371	1	1	370	1	1
Private	Icahn School of Med. at Mount Sinai	17	61	30	16	61	30
Public	Indiana University - Bloomington	8	84	47	8	81	44
Public	Indiana U.. - Purdue U. - Indianapolis	6	99	58	6	96	55
Public	Iowa State University	8	84	47	5	103	61
Private	Johns Hopkins University	97	15	9	95	15	9
Public	Kansas State University	1	163	100	1	165	102
Public	Louisiana State Univ. - Baton Rouge	3	119	73	3	117	72
Private	Massachusetts Inst. of Technology	268	3	3	265	3	3
Private	Medical College of Wisconsin	3	119	47	3	117	46
Public	Medical University of South Carolina	3	119	73	3	117	72
Public	Michigan State University	13	65	34	12	67	35
Public	Mississippi State University	1	163	100	2	140	85
Public	Montana State University - Bozeman	0	221	136	0	222	137
Public	Naval Postgraduate School	3	119	73	3	117	72
Public	New Jersey Institute of Technology	1	163	100	2	140	85
Public	New Mexico State Univ. - Las Cruces	0	221	136	0	222	137
Private	New York University	59	21	13	53	23	13
Public	North Carolina State University	20	58	31	20	57	30
Private	Northeastern University	3	119	47	3	117	46
Private	Northwestern University	43	28	17	43	28	17
Public	Ohio State University - Columbus	32	35	16	32	36	17
Public	Oregon Health & Science University	10	73	37	10	72	38

2013 National Academy Membership	2013 National Rank	2013 Control Rank	2012 National Academy Membership	2012 National Rank	2012 Control Rank	2011 National Academy Membership	2011 National Rank	2011 Control Rank
21	54	29	20	54	29	20	53	29
1	165	101	1	163	99	2	133	78
0	220	137	0	220	136	0	218	137
22	51	25	21	52	25	21	51	23
20	56	27	19	56	27	18	55	25
12	67	33	12	66	32	11	67	34
18	58	29	17	60	29	15	60	29
111	10	7	110	9	6	109	8	6
37	31	18	32	33	18	34	32	18
19	57	28	18	58	28	18	55	25
2	137	82	2	136	81	1	163	100
0	220	137	0	220	136	0	218	137
4	105	44	4	105	44	3	109	47
5	101	59	5	100	58	5	98	57
125	6	4	120	6	4	115	6	4
61	20	12	61	19	11	62	18	10
14	64	31	15	62	30	15	60	29
6	95	41	7	88	40	6	93	41
63	18	10	62	18	10	60	19	11
27	41	20	27	43	21	25	44	21
1	165	101	1	163	99	2	133	78
6	95	55	7	88	49	7	88	49
2	137	82	2	136	81	2	133	78
10	69	35	11	68	34	9	72	35
10	69	35	11	68	34	8	80	37
26	43	22	30	36	18	30	35	17
356	1	1	355	1	1	352	1	1
16	61	30	14	63	31	13	64	31
8	83	46	10	70	35	10	69	35
6	95	55	6	96	55	7	88	49
7	90	51	7	88	49	8	80	44
91	15	9	90	15	9	84	15	9
1	165	101	0	220	136	0	218	137
3	115	69	2	136	81	2	133	78
270	3	3	269	3	3	268	3	3
3	115	47	3	113	49	3	109	47
3	115	69	3	113	65	3	109	63
10	69	35	9	73	37	8	80	44
2	137	82	1	163	99	1	163	100
0	220	137	0	220	136	0	218	137
3	115	69	3	113	65	3	109	63
2	137	82	2	136	81	2	133	78
0	220	137	0	220	136	0	218	137
52	23	13	45	25	15	41	26	16
18	58	30	19	56	30	18	55	31
3	115	47	3	113	49	3	109	47
43	28	17	42	27	17	40	27	17
32	34	16	30	36	18	28	39	20
9	74	37	9	73	37	9	72	38

National Academy Membership

	Institutions with Over $40 Million in Federal Research, Alphabetically	2015 National Academy Membership	2015 National Rank	2015 Control Rank	2014 National Academy Membership	2014 National Rank	2014 Control Rank
Public	Oregon State University	5	104	62	4	108	65
Public	Penn. St. Univ. - Hershey Med. Ctr.	2	142	87	2	140	85
Public	Pennsylvania State Univ. - Univ. Park	27	43	22	27	43	22
Private	Princeton University	120	7	5	124	7	5
Public	Purdue University - West Lafayette	27	43	22	27	43	22
Private	Rensselaer Polytechnic Institute	7	92	39	7	89	39
Private	Rice University	25	48	23	25	48	24
Private	Rockefeller University	51	24	14	47	25	15
Private	Rush University	2	142	56	2	140	56
Public	Rutgers University - New Brunswick	39	31	14	36	33	15
Public	San Diego State University	0	221	136	0	222	137
Private	Scripps Research Institute	26	46	22	28	41	20
Private	Stanford University	320	2	2	316	2	2
Public	Stony Brook University	14	63	32	15	63	33
Public	Temple University	4	111	68	3	117	72
Public	Texas A&M Univ. - College Station	27	43	22	24	50	26
Private	Thomas Jefferson University	4	111	44	3	117	46
Private	Tufts University	11	70	34	11	68	33
Private	Tulane University	1	163	64	1	165	64
Public	Uniformed Services Univ. of the HS	4	111	68	4	108	65
Public	University at Albany	2	142	87	2	140	85
Public	University at Buffalo	8	84	47	7	89	51
Public	University of Alabama - Birmingham	8	84	47	8	81	44
Public	University of Alabama - Huntsville	0	221	136	0	222	137
Public	University of Alaska - Fairbanks	2	142	87	1	165	102
Public	University of Arizona	31	38	18	30	37	18
Public	Univ. of Arkansas for Med. Sciences	1	163	100	1	165	102
Public	University of California - Berkeley	230	4	1	230	4	1
Public	University of California - Davis	45	27	11	46	27	11
Public	University of California - Irvine	31	38	18	30	37	18
Public	University of California - Los Angeles	101	14	6	100	14	6
Public	University of California - Riverside	8	84	47	8	81	44
Public	University of California - San Diego	117	8	3	118	8	3
Public	Univ. of California - San Francisco	135	5	2	132	5	2
Public	Univ. of California - Santa Barbara	56	22	9	58	21	9
Public	University of California - Santa Cruz	10	73	37	11	68	36
Public	University of Central Florida	1	163	100	1	165	102
Private	University of Chicago	69	17	10	67	18	10
Public	University of Cincinnati - Cincinnati	8	84	47	8	81	44
Public	University of Colorado - Boulder	30	41	21	30	37	18
Public	University of Colorado - Denver	14	63	32	15	63	33
Public	Univ. of Connecticut - Health Center	4	111	68	4	108	65
Public	University of Connecticut - Storrs	1	163	100	1	165	102
Private	University of Dayton	0	221	86	0	222	86
Public	University of Delaware	7	92	54	7	89	51
Public	University of Florida	25	48	26	25	48	25
Public	University of Georgia	6	99	58	6	96	55
Public	University of Hawaii - Manoa	10	73	37	8	81	44
Public	University of Houston - Univ. Park	9	77	41	9	78	41

2013 National Academy Membership	2013 National Rank	2013 Control Rank	2012 National Academy Membership	2012 National Rank	2012 Control Rank	2011 National Academy Membership	2011 National Rank	2011 Control Rank
4	105	62	3	113	65	3	109	63
2	137	82	1	163	99	1	163	100
26	43	22	24	47	25	23	47	25
120	7	5	117	7	5	114	7	5
25	47	25	26	45	24	25	44	24
8	83	38	8	83	38	8	80	37
25	47	23	23	49	23	18	55	25
46	26	16	46	24	14	48	24	14
2	137	56	2	136	56	2	133	56
37	31	14	34	32	15	35	30	13
0	220	137	0	220	136	0	218	137
26	43	22	26	45	22	26	41	20
310	2	2	297	2	2	294	2	2
14	64	34	14	63	33	11	67	34
3	115	69	2	136	81	2	133	78
22	51	27	23	49	27	22	49	27
3	115	47	4	105	44	5	98	42
11	68	34	10	70	36	9	72	35
1	165	65	2	136	56	2	133	56
4	105	62	4	105	62	3	109	63
2	137	82	2	136	81	2	133	78
7	90	51	7	88	49	7	88	49
7	90	51	7	88	49	5	98	57
0	220	137	1	163	99	1	163	100
1	165	101	1	163	99	1	163	100
28	40	21	28	40	22	26	41	22
1	165	101	1	163	99	1	163	100
227	4	1	230	4	1	228	4	1
44	27	11	41	28	11	39	28	11
30	38	19	31	35	17	34	32	15
95	14	6	94	14	6	95	13	5
8	83	46	7	88	49	6	93	53
117	8	3	115	8	3	109	8	3
129	5	2	125	5	2	118	5	2
57	21	9	60	20	9	57	21	9
9	74	37	9	73	37	9	72	38
1	165	101	1	163	99	1	163	100
63	18	10	60	20	12	58	20	12
9	74	37	9	73	37	10	69	35
30	38	19	29	39	21	26	41	22
15	62	32	16	61	32	15	60	32
4	105	62	4	105	62	4	102	60
1	165	101	1	163	99	1	163	100
0	220	84	0	220	85	0	218	82
7	90	51	8	83	46	8	80	44
24	49	26	24	47	25	23	47	25
6	95	55	6	96	55	6	93	53
9	74	37	9	73	37	9	72	38
9	74	37	9	73	37	8	80	44

National Academy Membership

	Institutions with Over $40 Million in Federal Research, Alphabetically	2015 National Academy Membership	2015 National Rank	2015 Control Rank	2014 National Academy Membership	2014 National Rank	2014 Control Rank
Public	University of Idaho	0	221	136	0	222	137
Public	University of Illinois - Chicago	6	99	58	7	89	51
Public	Univ. of Illinois - Urbana-Champaign	56	22	9	55	22	10
Public	University of Iowa	22	55	29	22	53	28
Public	University of Kansas - Lawrence	5	104	62	5	103	61
Public	University of Kansas Medical Center	3	119	73	3	117	72
Public	University of Kentucky	3	119	73	3	117	72
Public	University of Louisville	2	142	87	2	140	85
Public	University of Maine - Orono	1	163	100	1	165	102
Public	University of Maryland - Baltimore	9	77	41	9	78	41
Public	Univ. of Maryland - Baltimore County	0	221	136	0	222	137
Public	University of Maryland - College Park	26	46	25	30	37	18
Public	Univ. of Massachusetts - Amherst	7	92	54	7	89	51
Public	Univ. of Mass. Med. Sch. - Worcester	7	92	54	6	96	55
Private	University of Miami	11	70	34	10	72	35
Public	University of Michigan - Ann Arbor	108	13	5	106	13	5
Public	University of Minnesota - Twin Cities	41	29	12	40	29	12
Public	University of Missouri - Columbia	9	77	41	8	81	44
Public	University of Nebraska - Lincoln	3	119	73	2	140	85
Public	University of Nebraska Medical Ctr.	1	163	100	1	165	102
Public	University of Nevada - Reno	2	142	87	2	140	85
Public	Univ. of New Hampshire - Durham	0	221	136	0	222	137
Public	Univ. of New Mexico - Albuquerque	5	104	62	4	108	65
Public	Univ. of North Carolina - Chapel Hill	38	33	15	38	30	13
Public	University of North Dakota	0	221	136	0	222	137
Private	University of Notre Dame	4	111	44	3	117	46
Public	University of Oklahoma - Norman	1	163	100	1	165	102
Public	University of Oklahoma HSC	1	163	100	1	165	102
Public	University of Oregon	9	77	41	10	72	38
Private	University of Pennsylvania	117	8	6	114	10	6
Public	University of Pittsburgh - Pittsburgh	32	35	16	33	35	16
Public	University of Rhode Island	2	142	87	2	140	85
Private	University of Rochester	24	50	24	26	46	23
Public	Univ. of South Carolina - Columbia	1	163	100	2	140	85
Public	University of South Florida - Tampa	8	84	47	6	96	55
Private	University of Southern California	50	25	15	51	24	14
Public	University of Tennessee - Knoxville	5	104	62	5	103	61
Public	University of Tennessee HSC	0	221	136	0	222	137
Public	University of Texas - Austin	69	17	8	72	17	8
Public	University of Texas HSC - Houston	3	119	73	3	117	72
Public	Univ. of Texas HSC - San Antonio	5	104	62	4	108	65
Public	U. of Texas MD Anderson Cancer Ctr.	12	68	36	11	68	36
Public	U. of Texas Med. Branch - Galveston	3	119	73	3	117	72
Public	Univ. of Texas SW Med. Ctr. - Dallas	40	30	13	38	30	13
Public	University of Utah	23	54	28	20	57	30
Public	University of Vermont	2	142	87	2	140	85
Public	University of Virginia	24	50	27	24	50	26
Public	University of Washington - Seattle	115	10	4	116	9	4
Public	University of Wisconsin - Madison	77	16	7	75	16	7

2013 National Academy Membership	2013 National Rank	2013 Control Rank	2012 National Academy Membership	2012 National Rank	2012 Control Rank	2011 National Academy Membership	2011 National Rank	2011 Control Rank
0	220	137	0	220	136	0	218	137
8	83	46	8	83	46	6	93	53
57	21	9	55	22	10	57	21	9
22	51	27	21	52	28	22	49	27
5	101	59	6	96	55	6	93	53
2	137	82	2	136	81	2	133	78
3	115	69	3	113	65	3	109	63
2	137	82	2	136	81	2	133	78
1	165	101	1	163	99	2	133	78
9	74	37	9	73	37	9	72	38
0	220	137	0	220	136	0	218	137
31	36	18	30	36	18	30	35	17
8	83	46	8	83	46	9	72	38
5	101	59	5	100	58	5	98	57
10	69	35	9	73	37	8	80	37
100	13	5	95	13	5	89	14	6
39	29	12	38	29	12	39	28	11
8	83	46	7	88	49	7	88	49
2	137	82	3	113	65	2	133	78
1	165	101	1	163	99	1	163	100
2	137	82	3	113	65	3	109	63
0	220	137	0	220	136	0	218	137
3	115	69	3	113	65	3	109	63
34	33	15	35	31	14	31	34	16
0	220	137	0	220	136	0	218	137
4	105	44	4	105	44	3	109	47
1	165	101	1	163	99	1	163	100
1	165	101	1	163	99	1	163	100
9	74	37	9	73	37	8	80	44
114	9	6	110	9	6	103	12	8
32	34	16	32	33	16	28	39	20
2	137	82	2	136	81	2	133	78
27	41	20	28	40	19	29	37	19
2	137	82	2	136	81	2	133	78
3	115	69	3	113	65	3	109	63
50	24	14	50	23	13	50	23	13
4	105	62	3	113	65	1	163	100
0	220	137	0	220	136	0	218	137
69	17	8	67	17	8	68	16	7
3	115	69	3	113	65	3	109	63
4	105	62	3	113	65	3	109	63
9	74	37	5	100	58	3	109	63
3	115	69	2	136	81	2	133	78
38	30	13	37	30	13	35	30	13
17	60	31	18	58	31	19	54	30
2	137	82	2	136	81	3	109	63
26	43	22	27	43	23	29	37	19
110	12	4	109	12	4	104	11	4
70	16	7	68	16	7	67	17	8

National Academy Membership

Institutions with Over $40 Million in Federal Research, Alphabetically		2015 National Academy Membership	2015 National Rank	2015 Control Rank	2014 National Academy Membership	2014 National Rank	2014 Control Rank
Public	Utah State University	0	221	136	0	222	137
Private	Vanderbilt University	36	34	19	34	34	19
Public	Virginia Commonwealth University	6	99	58	6	96	55
Public	Virginia Polytechnic Inst. and St. Univ.	13	65	34	16	61	32
Private	Wake Forest University	7	92	39	6	96	42
Public	Washington State Univ. - Pullman	9	77	41	9	78	41
Private	Washington University in St. Louis	46	26	16	47	25	15
Public	Wayne State University	3	119	73	3	117	72
Private	Weill Cornell Medical College	28	42	21	27	43	22
Public	West Virginia University	2	142	87	1	165	102
Private	Woods Hole Oceanographic Inst.	3	119	47	3	117	46
Private	Yale University	114	11	7	111	12	8
Private	Yeshiva University	13	65	32	14	65	31

2013 National Academy Membership	2013 National Rank	2013 Control Rank	2012 National Academy Membership	2012 National Rank	2012 Control Rank	2011 National Academy Membership	2011 National Rank	2011 Control Rank
0	220	137	0	220	136	1	163	100
31	36	19	28	40	19	25	44	21
6	95	55	5	100	58	4	102	60
15	62	32	14	63	33	14	63	33
5	101	43	5	100	43	4	102	43
9	74	37	9	73	37	9	72	38
48	25	15	44	26	16	43	25	15
2	137	82	2	136	81	2	133	78
24	49	24	20	54	26	18	55	25
1	165	101	1	163	99	1	163	100
3	115	47	3	113	49	3	109	47
111	10	7	110	9	6	109	8	6
13	66	32	12	66	32	13	64	31

Faculty Awards

Institutions with Over $40 Million in Federal Research, Alphabetically		2015 Faculty Awards	2015 National Rank	2015 Control Rank	2014 Faculty Awards	2014 National Rank	2014 Control Rank
Public	Arizona State University	23	24	10	9	62	38
Public	Auburn University	3	144	92	2	195	126
Public	Augusta University	0	473	285	0	474	282
Private	Baylor College of Medicine	6	98	33	3	153	53
Private	Boston University	16	40	18	16	34	18
Private	Brandeis University	9	76	29	4	126	42
Private	Brown University	20	29	16	17	30	16
Private	California Institute of Technology	16	40	18	12	48	22
Private	Carnegie Mellon University	13	49	24	10	58	24
Private	Case Western Reserve University	11	58	26	4	126	42
Public	Clemson University	3	144	92	5	109	71
Public	Cleveland State University	2	178	115	1	259	163
Private	Cold Spring Harbor Laboratory	2	178	115	4	126	85
Public	Colorado State Univ. - Fort Collins	11	58	33	7	78	50
Private	Columbia University	34	8	4	25	19	11
Private	Cornell University	30	12	7	24	20	12
Private	Dartmouth College	6	98	33	6	90	34
Private	Drexel University	5	110	39	4	126	42
Private	Duke University	30	12	7	33	7	4
Private	Emory University	19	33	17	26	17	10
Public	Florida International University	13	49	26	5	109	71
Public	Florida State University	9	76	48	7	78	50
Public	George Mason University	5	110	72	5	109	71
Private	George Washington University	14	45	21	11	54	23
Private	Georgetown University	4	127	45	7	78	29
Public	Georgia Institute of Technology	21	27	12	16	34	17
Private	Harvard University	84	1	1	90	1	1
Private	Icahn School of Med. at Mount Sinai	6	98	33	8	68	27
Public	Indiana University - Bloomington	15	42	23	18	29	14
Public	Indiana U. - Purdue U. - Indianapolis	3	144	92	5	109	71
Public	Iowa State University	6	98	66	6	90	57
Private	Johns Hopkins University	33	9	5	32	11	7
Public	Kansas State University	2	178	115	4	126	85
Public	Louisiana State Univ. - Baton Rouge	5	110	72	4	126	85
Private	Massachusetts Inst. of Technology	41	5	3	42	3	3
Private	Medical College of Wisconsin	0	473	189	0	474	193
Public	Medical University of South Carolina	1	263	167	1	259	163
Public	Michigan State University	11	58	33	13	42	23
Public	Mississippi State University	4	127	83	1	259	163
Public	Montana State University - Bozeman	2	178	115	1	259	163
Public	Naval Postgraduate School	0	473	285	1	259	163
Public	New Jersey Institute of Technology	0	473	285	0	474	282
Public	New Mexico State Univ. - Las Cruces	6	98	66	2	195	126
Private	New York University	27	22	13	29	13	8
Public	North Carolina State University	11	58	33	12	48	27
Private	Northeastern University	14	45	21	9	62	25
Private	Northwestern University	33	9	5	28	15	9
Public	Ohio State University - Columbus	17	38	21	13	42	23
Public	Oregon Health & Science University	8	85	56	5	109	71

2013 Faculty Awards	2013 National Rank	2013 Control Rank	2012 Faculty Awards	2012 National Rank	2012 Control Rank	2011 Faculty Awards	2011 National Rank	2011 Control Rank
5	119	76	14	45	26	13	52	32
1	264	168	3	156	101	4	132	87
1	264	168	0	551	314	0	530	307
5	119	44	4	129	46	5	108	42
21	22	11	23	24	13	18	35	17
11	58	23	7	97	36	11	61	24
16	36	18	11	56	22	16	42	19
10	67	25	16	37	19	12	57	23
10	67	25	12	50	21	14	47	20
11	58	23	8	84	31	11	61	24
4	135	86	6	101	64	6	93	59
0	523	306	4	129	84	1	273	176
2	194	128	2	189	122	0	530	307
8	75	46	5	117	73	4	132	87
32	9	4	37	7	4	37	9	5
19	28	14	21	30	15	27	17	10
12	51	21	6	101	38	6	93	35
7	88	32	8	84	31	2	191	70
20	25	12	30	13	6	22	25	11
18	31	16	22	25	14	22	25	11
4	135	86	8	84	54	5	108	67
2	194	128	7	97	62	11	61	38
3	156	100	2	189	122	2	191	122
12	51	21	13	47	20	6	93	35
4	135	50	10	67	26	5	108	42
15	39	20	22	25	12	23	24	14
87	1	1	93	1	1	101	1	1
7	88	32	6	101	38	3	157	53
17	33	17	12	50	30	18	35	19
4	135	86	8	84	54	7	83	52
10	67	43	11	56	35	5	108	67
24	19	8	27	17	8	30	14	8
3	156	100	2	189	122	5	108	67
5	119	76	5	117	73	3	157	105
29	12	5	29	14	7	38	8	4
1	264	97	1	271	98	1	273	98
1	264	168	3	156	101	4	132	87
16	36	19	13	47	28	18	35	19
1	264	168	3	156	101	5	108	67
4	135	86	2	189	122	2	191	122
0	523	306	1	271	174	0	530	307
4	135	86	0	551	314	2	191	122
1	264	168	5	117	73	2	191	122
25	18	7	25	19	10	30	14	8
14	44	24	12	50	30	14	47	28
8	75	30	8	84	31	6	93	35
22	21	10	25	19	10	34	10	6
29	12	8	11	56	35	24	21	11
7	88	57	10	67	42	8	78	49

Faculty Awards

	Institutions with Over $40 Million in Federal Research, Alphabetically	2015 Faculty Awards	2015 National Rank	2015 Control Rank	2014 Faculty Awards	2014 National Rank	2014 Control Rank
Public	Oregon State University	5	110	72	6	90	57
Public	Penn. St. Univ. - Hershey Med. Ctr.	2	178	115	2	195	126
Public	Pennsylvania State Univ. - Univ. Park	19	33	17	14	38	20
Private	Princeton University	22	26	15	24	20	12
Public	Purdue University - West Lafayette	19	33	17	15	36	18
Private	Rensselaer Polytechnic Institute	5	110	39	5	109	39
Private	Rice University	6	98	33	7	78	29
Private	Rockefeller University	7	90	31	7	78	29
Private	Rush University	0	473	189	0	474	193
Public	Rutgers University - New Brunswick	20	29	14	21	26	11
Public	San Diego State University	3	144	92	3	153	101
Private	Scripps Research Institute	8	85	30	13	42	20
Private	Stanford University	56	2	2	46	2	2
Public	Stony Brook University	10	67	40	11	54	32
Public	Temple University	10	67	40	8	68	42
Public	Texas A&M Univ. - College Station	14	45	25	6	90	57
Private	Thomas Jefferson University	1	263	97	1	259	97
Private	Tufts University	6	98	33	6	90	34
Private	Tulane University	4	127	45	3	153	53
Public	Uniformed Services Univ. of the HS	2	178	115	2	195	126
Public	University at Albany	4	127	83	5	109	71
Public	University at Buffalo	6	98	66	6	90	57
Public	University of Alabama - Birmingham	0	473	285	4	126	85
Public	University of Alabama - Huntsville	2	178	115	1	259	163
Public	University of Alaska - Fairbanks	2	178	115	3	153	101
Public	University of Arizona	9	76	48	10	58	35
Public	Univ. of Arkansas for Med. Sciences	0	473	285	1	259	163
Public	University of California - Berkeley	45	3	1	42	3	1
Public	University of California - Davis	12	54	30	8	68	42
Public	University of California - Irvine	20	29	14	15	36	18
Public	University of California - Los Angeles	29	19	8	28	15	7
Public	University of California - Riverside	7	90	60	9	62	38
Public	University of California - San Diego	29	19	8	19	28	13
Public	Univ. of California - San Francisco	31	11	5	33	7	4
Public	Univ. of California - Santa Barbara	12	54	30	10	58	35
Public	University of California - Santa Cruz	8	85	56	5	109	71
Public	University of Central Florida	7	90	60	7	78	50
Private	University of Chicago	25	23	14	24	20	12
Public	University of Cincinnati - Cincinnati	10	67	40	9	62	38
Public	University of Colorado - Boulder	21	27	12	12	48	27
Public	University of Colorado - Denver	5	110	72	8	68	42
Public	Univ. of Connecticut - Health Center	3	144	92	3	153	101
Public	University of Connecticut - Storrs	9	76	48	5	109	71
Private	University of Dayton	0	473	189	0	474	193
Public	University of Delaware	9	76	48	12	48	27
Public	University of Florida	23	24	10	21	26	11
Public	University of Georgia	6	98	66	17	30	15
Public	University of Hawaii - Manoa	4	127	83	5	109	71
Public	University of Houston - Univ. Park	4	127	83	7	78	50

2013 Faculty Awards	2013 National Rank	2013 Control Rank	2012 Faculty Awards	2012 National Rank	2012 Control Rank	2011 Faculty Awards	2011 National Rank	2011 Control Rank
8	75	46	15	40	21	7	83	52
2	194	128	3	156	101	0	530	307
21	22	12	20	32	16	26	19	9
17	33	17	21	30	15	20	29	14
14	44	24	22	25	12	24	21	11
7	88	32	8	84	31	4	132	46
6	102	39	9	70	27	11	61	24
7	88	32	11	56	22	8	78	30
0	523	218	0	551	236	0	530	224
20	25	14	16	37	19	14	47	28
5	119	76	6	101	64	4	132	87
10	67	25	11	56	22	13	52	21
48	3	2	44	2	2	44	3	2
11	58	36	4	129	84	11	61	38
8	75	46	8	84	54	7	83	52
18	31	16	22	25	12	19	32	17
1	264	97	1	271	98	2	191	70
8	75	30	4	129	46	7	83	32
3	156	57	5	117	45	6	93	35
2	194	128	2	189	122	1	273	176
2	194	128	4	129	84	2	191	122
13	47	27	8	84	54	7	83	52
1	264	168	0	551	314	7	83	52
1	264	168	1	271	174	0	530	307
3	156	100	5	117	73	1	273	176
12	51	31	15	40	21	19	32	17
1	264	168	1	271	174	0	530	307
32	9	6	40	5	2	31	12	5
14	44	24	14	45	26	17	39	22
15	39	20	13	47	28	14	47	28
33	8	5	28	16	9	27	17	8
9	72	44	11	56	35	15	46	27
35	7	4	35	8	4	43	4	2
40	4	2	32	11	6	39	6	4
11	58	36	11	56	35	12	57	35
4	135	86	2	189	122	5	108	67
6	102	64	7	97	62	4	132	87
24	19	8	26	18	9	20	29	14
11	58	36	10	67	42	10	69	43
19	28	15	12	50	30	12	57	35
6	102	64	9	70	44	10	69	43
3	156	100	1	271	174	1	273	176
8	75	46	6	101	64	5	108	67
0	523	218	0	551	236	1	273	98
6	102	64	11	56	35	5	108	67
15	39	20	20	32	16	18	35	19
8	75	46	12	50	30	6	93	59
11	58	36	5	117	73	5	108	67
5	119	76	15	40	21	5	108	67

Faculty Awards

	Institutions with Over $40 Million in Federal Research, Alphabetically	2015 Faculty Awards	2015 National Rank	2015 Control Rank	2014 Faculty Awards	2014 National Rank	2014 Control Rank
Public	University of Idaho	2	178	115	0	474	282
Public	University of Illinois - Chicago	11	58	33	12	48	27
Public	Univ. of Illinois - Urbana-Champaign	30	12	6	35	5	2
Public	University of Iowa	10	67	40	11	54	32
Public	University of Kansas - Lawrence	11	58	33	14	38	20
Public	University of Kansas Medical Center	0	473	285	1	259	163
Public	University of Kentucky	10	67	40	9	62	38
Public	University of Louisville	5	110	72	3	153	101
Public	University of Maine - Orono	1	263	167	1	259	163
Public	University of Maryland - Baltimore	3	144	92	4	126	85
Public	Univ. of Maryland - Baltimore County	2	178	115	4	126	85
Public	University of Maryland - College Park	20	29	14	14	38	20
Public	Univ. of Massachusetts - Amherst	17	38	21	10	58	35
Public	Univ. of Mass. Med. Sch. - Worcester	12	54	30	12	48	27
Private	University of Miami	7	90	31	8	68	27
Public	University of Michigan - Ann Arbor	42	4	2	34	6	3
Public	University of Minnesota - Twin Cities	35	7	4	26	17	8
Public	University of Missouri - Columbia	9	76	48	7	78	50
Public	University of Nebraska - Lincoln	3	144	92	4	126	85
Public	University of Nebraska Medical Ctr.	0	473	285	0	474	282
Public	University of Nevada - Reno	0	473	285	3	153	101
Public	Univ. of New Hampshire - Durham	3	144	92	6	90	57
Public	Univ. of New Mexico - Albuquerque	10	67	40	8	68	42
Public	Univ. of North Carolina - Chapel Hill	19	33	17	24	20	9
Public	University of North Dakota	2	178	115	2	195	126
Private	University of Notre Dame	14	45	21	14	38	19
Public	University of Oklahoma - Norman	9	76	48	6	90	57
Public	University of Oklahoma HSC	0	473	285	0	474	282
Public	University of Oregon	11	58	33	6	90	57
Private	University of Pennsylvania	30	12	7	33	7	4
Public	University of Pittsburgh - Pittsburgh	13	49	26	24	20	9
Public	University of Rhode Island	2	178	115	2	195	126
Private	University of Rochester	12	54	25	3	153	53
Public	Univ. of South Carolina - Columbia	9	76	48	6	90	57
Public	University of South Florida - Tampa	13	49	26	8	68	42
Private	University of Southern California	30	12	7	23	25	15
Public	University of Tennessee - Knoxville	8	85	56	7	78	50
Public	University of Tennessee HSC	2	178	115	2	195	126
Public	University of Texas - Austin	19	33	17	17	30	15
Public	University of Texas HSC - Houston	2	178	115	5	109	71
Public	Univ. of Texas HSC - San Antonio	0	473	285	1	259	163
Public	U. of Texas MD Anderson Cancer Ctr.	3	144	92	2	195	126
Public	U. of Texas Med. Branch - Galveston	0	473	285	0	474	282
Public	Univ. of Texas SW Med. Ctr. - Dallas	13	49	26	13	42	23
Public	University of Utah	10	67	40	13	42	23
Public	University of Vermont	5	110	72	6	90	57
Public	University of Virginia	15	42	23	11	54	32
Public	University of Washington - Seattle	39	6	3	30	12	5
Public	University of Wisconsin - Madison	30	12	6	29	13	6

2013 Faculty Awards	2013 National Rank	2013 Control Rank	2012 Faculty Awards	2012 National Rank	2012 Control Rank	2011 Faculty Awards	2011 National Rank	2011 Control Rank
4	135	86	1	271	174	1	273	176
8	75	46	11	56	35	10	69	43
29	12	8	24	23	11	24	21	11
12	51	31	15	40	21	14	47	28
8	75	46	11	56	35	12	57	35
2	194	128	1	271	174	1	273	176
12	51	31	8	84	54	13	52	32
5	119	76	9	70	44	5	108	67
2	194	128	3	156	101	5	108	67
6	102	64	6	101	64	4	132	87
3	156	100	3	156	101	3	157	105
11	58	36	16	37	19	17	39	22
12	51	31	8	84	54	6	93	59
13	47	27	15	40	21	16	42	24
7	88	32	7	97	36	8	78	30
50	2	1	40	5	2	47	2	1
32	9	6	33	10	5	25	20	10
6	102	64	9	70	44	4	132	87
9	72	44	6	101	64	7	83	52
0	523	306	0	551	314	0	530	307
6	102	64	4	129	84	2	191	122
2	194	128	5	117	73	5	108	67
7	88	57	6	101	64	6	93	59
21	22	12	25	19	10	28	16	7
1	264	168	1	271	174	4	132	87
15	39	20	9	70	27	7	83	32
3	156	100	5	117	73	6	93	59
0	523	306	0	551	314	0	530	307
7	88	57	9	70	44	11	61	38
29	12	5	35	8	5	34	10	6
28	16	10	22	25	12	20	29	16
4	135	86	4	129	84	4	132	87
6	102	39	6	101	38	13	52	21
8	75	46	9	70	44	9	74	47
7	88	57	5	117	73	8	78	49
19	28	14	25	19	10	22	25	11
11	58	36	9	70	44	9	74	47
3	156	100	2	189	122	3	157	105
17	33	17	31	12	7	22	25	15
1	264	168	2	189	122	2	191	122
1	264	168	2	189	122	2	191	122
1	264	168	1	271	174	2	191	122
1	264	168	2	189	122	2	191	122
15	39	20	17	36	18	16	42	24
13	47	27	12	50	30	11	61	38
6	102	64	9	70	44	6	93	59
11	58	36	8	84	54	16	42	24
39	5	3	42	4	1	43	4	2
26	17	11	29	14	8	31	12	5

Faculty Awards

	Institutions with Over $40 Million in Federal Research, Alphabetically	2015 Faculty Awards	2015 National Rank	2015 Control Rank	2014 Faculty Awards	2014 National Rank	2014 Control Rank
Public	Utah State University	3	144	92	4	126	85
Private	Vanderbilt University	15	42	20	13	42	20
Public	Virginia Commonwealth University	6	98	66	6	90	57
Public	Virginia Polytechnic Inst. and St. Univ.	10	67	40	8	68	42
Private	Wake Forest University	3	144	53	6	90	34
Public	Washington State Univ. - Pullman	7	90	60	6	90	57
Private	Washington University in St. Louis	29	19	12	17	30	16
Public	Wayne State University	5	110	72	8	68	42
Private	Weill Cornell Medical College	10	67	28	9	62	25
Public	West Virginia University	8	85	56	5	109	71
Private	Woods Hole Oceanographic Inst.	1	263	97	1	259	97
Private	Yale University	30	12	7	33	7	4
Private	Yeshiva University	5	110	39	7	78	29

2013 Faculty Awards	2013 National Rank	2013 Control Rank	2012 Faculty Awards	2012 National Rank	2012 Control Rank	2011 Faculty Awards	2011 National Rank	2011 Control Rank
7	88	57	2	189	122	10	69	43
16	36	18	19	34	17	17	39	18
13	47	27	9	70	44	11	61	38
7	88	57	8	84	54	13	52	32
7	88	32	9	70	27	7	83	32
8	75	46	9	70	44	6	93	59
20	25	12	18	35	18	19	32	16
6	102	64	4	129	84	5	108	67
9	72	29	8	84	31	9	74	28
8	75	46	6	101	64	2	191	122
2	194	67	1	271	98	0	530	224
37	6	3	44	2	2	39	6	3
7	88	32	9	70	27	10	69	27

Doctorates Awarded

	Institutions with Over $40 Million in Federal Research, Alphabetically	2015 Doctorates	2015 National Rank	2015 Control Rank	2014 Doctorates	2014 National Rank	2014 Control Rank
Public	Arizona State University	687	14	12	596	20	16
Public	Auburn University	257	80	58	249	83	59
Public	Augusta University	29	314	191	28	315	194
Private	Baylor College of Medicine	111	157	50	105	166	52
Private	Boston University	484	36	11	513	27	9
Private	Brandeis University	100	170	55	97	172	54
Private	Brown University	215	94	26	227	91	26
Private	California Institute of Technology	182	110	32	181	107	33
Private	Carnegie Mellon University	333	62	19	341	57	18
Private	Case Western Reserve University	197	101	30	199	98	28
Public	Clemson University	237	88	64	216	92	66
Public	Cleveland State University	59	232	154	38	282	177
Private	Cold Spring Harbor Laboratory	0	622	335	0	613	329
Public	Colorado State Univ. - Fort Collins	251	81	59	230	90	65
Private	Columbia University	564	24	7	636	16	3
Private	Cornell University	487	34	9	505	28	10
Private	Dartmouth College	85	192	65	95	176	55
Private	Drexel University	213	96	27	183	106	32
Private	Duke University	485	35	10	557	23	7
Private	Emory University	264	78	22	271	74	22
Public	Florida International University	189	108	77	159	120	83
Public	Florida State University	424	46	31	410	47	32
Public	George Mason University	249	82	60	256	81	58
Private	George Washington University	222	91	25	238	87	25
Private	Georgetown University	114	154	48	133	133	41
Public	Georgia Institute of Technology	526	29	21	553	25	18
Private	Harvard University	745	9	1	746	10	1
Private	Icahn School of Med. at Mount Sinai	28	320	127	45	260	91
Public	Indiana University - Bloomington	538	26	19	458	40	28
Public	Indiana U. - Purdue U. - Indianapolis	69	216	143	61	219	143
Public	Iowa State University	336	60	42	347	55	38
Private	Johns Hopkins University	535	27	8	477	35	11
Public	Kansas State University	190	107	76	166	118	81
Public	Louisiana State Univ. - Baton Rouge	331	63	44	345	56	39
Private	Massachusetts Inst. of Technology	606	20	5	594	21	5
Private	Medical College of Wisconsin	26	330	134	47	254	87
Public	Medical University of South Carolina	191	106	75	174	110	76
Public	Michigan State University	577	22	17	602	19	15
Public	Mississippi State University	146	127	91	138	129	90
Public	Montana State University - Bozeman	79	204	136	56	231	152
Public	Naval Postgraduate School	15	395	225	30	303	186
Public	New Jersey Institute of Technology	65	224	149	52	241	160
Public	New Mexico State Univ. - Las Cruces	131	138	97	114	152	106
Private	New York University	438	39	12	476	36	12
Public	North Carolina State University	512	31	23	494	31	21
Private	Northeastern University	157	121	35	186	103	31
Private	Northwestern University	438	39	12	446	42	13
Public	Ohio State University - Columbus	832	4	4	747	9	9
Public	Oregon Health & Science University	43	268	171	46	256	169

2013 Doctorates	2013 National Rank	2013 Control Rank	2012 Doctorates	2012 National Rank	2012 Control Rank	2011 Doctorates	2011 National Rank	2011 Control Rank
611	19	15	545	21	16	490	27	18
237	80	59	247	74	53	204	90	63
22	340	199	23	320	191	73	179	119
85	179	61	83	174	59	75	175	59
488	31	11	507	24	7	491	26	9
93	168	56	82	177	60	88	160	52
205	96	29	232	81	24	216	86	25
236	81	22	172	107	31	168	101	30
295	67	19	284	62	18	270	66	20
168	109	33	186	101	29	213	87	26
187	103	73	220	87	62	192	94	67
44	251	163	35	272	172	46	236	153
8	459	212	5	482	233	0	539	273
232	83	61	235	80	57	203	91	64
627	18	4	558	20	5	568	19	5
490	29	10	501	25	8	495	24	7
91	172	57	73	187	66	82	167	54
207	94	28	163	112	32	170	100	29
495	28	9	450	36	11	329	54	17
227	87	24	243	78	23	224	81	23
156	115	80	151	118	86	148	116	82
370	52	36	428	42	30	429	35	26
249	77	56	212	90	65	194	93	66
228	86	23	224	86	25	222	82	24
131	136	41	116	143	46	102	149	48
488	31	21	483	29	20	449	30	21
686	14	2	691	12	2	653	13	2
35	277	103	41	250	91	39	252	90
479	36	24	468	33	23	409	40	29
48	241	159	35	272	172	57	209	138
363	53	37	376	49	34	358	49	35
530	24	7	479	30	10	426	37	11
158	113	78	162	113	81	162	106	75
305	65	47	322	58	41	255	71	51
587	20	5	573	18	4	609	17	4
40	263	96	38	262	96	19	340	137
137	128	90	130	135	95	96	155	106
499	27	19	491	27	19	484	28	19
131	136	96	135	131	93	139	122	87
49	236	155	53	227	147	56	213	141
19	358	208	12	392	221	17	346	206
67	201	135	65	201	130	64	194	129
132	135	95	102	154	106	105	148	101
440	40	13	448	37	12	428	36	10
488	31	21	446	38	26	395	43	31
177	105	32	125	139	43	132	125	37
481	35	12	378	48	15	382	44	13
807	5	5	756	7	6	782	5	5
41	259	167	57	220	144	56	213	141

Doctorates Awarded

	Institutions with Over $40 Million in Federal Research, Alphabetically	2015 Doctorates	2015 National Rank	2015 Control Rank	2014 Doctorates	2014 National Rank	2014 Control Rank
Public	Oregon State University	215	94	69	186	103	73
Public	Penn. St. Univ. - Hershey Med. Ctr.	26	330	197	22	348	207
Public	Pennsylvania State Univ. - Univ. Park	673	17	14	638	15	13
Private	Princeton University	371	51	17	389	50	17
Public	Purdue University - West Lafayette	717	12	11	732	11	10
Private	Rensselaer Polytechnic Institute	164	119	34	135	131	40
Private	Rice University	176	113	33	191	101	30
Private	Rockefeller University	28	320	127	23	340	138
Private	Rush University	17	382	162	9	444	203
Public	Rutgers University - New Brunswick	597	21	16	369	52	35
Public	San Diego State University	140	129	92	80	189	129
Private	Scripps Research Institute						
Private	Stanford University	688	13	2	729	12	2
Public	Stony Brook University	347	57	40	301	67	48
Public	Temple University	197	101	72	238	87	63
Public	Texas A&M Univ. - College Station	740	10	9	709	13	11
Private	Thomas Jefferson University	21	352	143	27	321	124
Private	Tufts University	116	153	47	128	136	42
Private	Tulane University	123	147	45	110	159	50
Public	Uniformed Services Univ. of the HS						
Public	University at Albany	164	119	86	186	103	73
Public	University at Buffalo	342	58	41	360	53	36
Public	University of Alabama - Birmingham	170	115	82	166	118	81
Public	University of Alabama - Huntsville	33	294	181	30	303	186
Public	University of Alaska - Fairbanks	40	273	173	49	249	166
Public	University of Arizona	528	28	20	460	39	27
Public	Univ. of Arkansas for Med. Sciences	38	281	176	40	278	174
Public	University of California - Berkeley	826	6	6	937	1	1
Public	University of California - Davis	553	25	18	504	29	19
Public	University of California - Irvine	390	49	33	414	44	31
Public	University of California - Los Angeles	774	7	7	795	7	7
Public	University of California - Riverside	272	75	55	264	78	56
Public	University of California - San Diego	505	32	24	487	34	24
Public	Univ. of California - San Francisco	130	139	98	138	129	90
Public	Univ. of California - Santa Barbara	349	56	39	360	53	36
Public	University of California - Santa Cruz	151	124	88	179	108	75
Public	University of Central Florida	286	72	52	266	76	54
Private	University of Chicago	392	48	16	401	48	16
Public	University of Cincinnati - Cincinnati	213	96	70	265	77	55
Public	University of Colorado - Boulder	434	43	30	380	51	34
Public	University of Colorado - Denver	103	168	114	120	146	101
Public	University of Connecticut - Health Ctr.	16	389	222	28	315	194
Public	University of Connecticut - Storrs	323	66	47	274	73	52
Private	University of Dayton	34	290	110	27	321	124
Public	University of Delaware	237	88	64	207	96	70
Public	University of Florida	754	8	8	796	6	6
Public	University of Georgia	467	37	26	463	38	26
Public	University of Hawaii - Manoa	239	87	63	194	100	71
Public	University of Houston - Univ. Park	326	64	45	275	72	51

2013 Doctorates	2013 National Rank	2013 Control Rank	2012 Doctorates	2012 National Rank	2012 Control Rank	2011 Doctorates	2011 National Rank	2011 Control Rank
215	91	65	197	98	71	172	99	71
20	353	204	32	280	177	36	263	167
662	17	14	629	17	14	634	14	12
319	61	17	351	51	16	350	52	15
684	15	13	649	14	12	668	12	11
150	119	36	136	129	38	131	126	38
178	104	31	190	100	28	178	98	28
17	374	164	40	253	93	23	312	122
12	411	182	7	451	208	34	270	102
417	45	31	414	43	31	407	41	30
82	184	122	48	234	153	59	204	135
764	9	1	764	6	1	762	7	1
309	64	46	263	70	50	298	61	43
208	93	66	216	89	64	233	77	56
693	13	12	663	13	11	619	15	13
24	320	128	17	352	149	20	334	135
121	146	47	143	125	36	138	123	36
130	140	44	120	140	44	99	152	49
154	118	83	158	116	84	154	110	78
335	55	39	305	60	43	313	58	40
147	123	86	174	106	76	153	111	79
28	303	183	37	266	169	30	278	173
52	226	149	50	230	150	46	236	153
441	39	27	446	38	26	445	31	22
29	300	181	32	280	177	28	288	178
937	1	1	892	1	1	920	1	1
580	21	16	566	19	15	507	22	16
435	42	29	413	44	32	374	45	32
784	6	6	725	9	8	728	9	8
255	75	55	263	70	50	235	76	55
489	30	20	523	22	17	484	28	19
136	129	91	134	132	94	119	137	94
387	50	34	346	52	36	354	50	36
160	111	77	172	107	77	148	116	82
238	78	57	229	82	58	245	75	54
413	46	15	401	45	13	396	42	12
230	84	62	242	79	56	220	83	59
386	51	35	344	53	37	353	51	37
122	145	99	107	151	103	93	157	107
23	328	195	29	291	180	75	175	117
272	72	52	265	68	49	219	84	60
30	295	115	23	320	130	18	342	139
202	97	68	228	84	60	211	88	62
742	11	10	696	11	10	774	6	6
440	40	28	453	35	25	443	32	23
229	85	63	196	99	72	251	72	52
317	62	45	301	61	44	284	64	46

Doctorates Awarded

Institutions with Over $40 Million in Federal Research, Alphabetically		2015 Doctorates	2015 National Rank	2015 Control Rank	2014 Doctorates	2014 National Rank	2014 Control Rank
Public	University of Idaho	80	201	134	87	184	125
Public	University of Illinois - Chicago	314	68	49	328	61	43
Public	Univ. of Illinois - Urbana-Champaign	829	5	5	804	5	5
Public	University of Iowa	453	38	27	490	33	23
Public	University of Kansas - Lawrence	365	53	36	290	68	49
Public	University of Kansas Medical Center	25	336	199	38	282	177
Public	University of Kentucky	295	69	50	328	61	43
Public	University of Louisville	170	115	82	148	126	87
Public	University of Maine - Orono	69	216	143	77	194	130
Public	University of Maryland - Baltimore	81	199	132	63	215	141
Public	Univ. of Maryland - Baltimore County	100	170	116	102	170	117
Public	University of Maryland - College Park	654	18	15	620	17	14
Public	Univ. of Massachusetts - Amherst	268	76	56	287	70	50
Public	Univ. of Mass. Med. Sch. - Worcester	61	230	152	58	228	150
Private	University of Miami	208	98	28	173	111	35
Public	University of Michigan - Ann Arbor	882	2	2	881	3	3
Public	University of Minnesota - Twin Cities	725	11	10	778	8	8
Public	University of Missouri - Columbia	435	42	29	390	49	33
Public	University of Nebraska - Lincoln	325	65	46	313	65	46
Public	University of Nebraska Medical Ctr.	81	199	132	52	241	160
Public	University of Nevada - Reno	109	158	108	118	147	102
Public	Univ. of New Hampshire - Durham	75	211	140	75	197	131
Public	Univ. of New Mexico - Albuquerque	222	91	67	231	89	64
Public	Univ. of North Carolina - Chapel Hill	519	30	22	557	23	17
Public	University of North Dakota	87	187	125	59	224	147
Private	University of Notre Dame	244	83	23	206	97	27
Public	University of Oklahoma - Norman	218	93	68	210	95	69
Public	University of Oklahoma HSC	29	314	191	33	296	183
Public	University of Oregon	199	100	71	155	123	84
Private	University of Pennsylvania	566	23	6	535	26	8
Public	University of Pittsburgh - Pittsburgh	438	39	28	496	30	20
Public	University of Rhode Island	93	181	122	101	171	118
Private	University of Rochester	267	77	21	281	71	21
Public	Univ. of South Carolina - Columbia	358	54	37	325	63	45
Public	University of South Florida - Tampa	321	67	48	330	58	40
Private	University of Southern California	685	16	3	594	21	5
Public	University of Tennessee - Knoxville	353	55	38	458	40	28
Public	University of Tennessee HSC						
Public	University of Texas - Austin	899	1	1	892	2	2
Public	University of Texas HSC - Houston	153	123	87	141	128	89
Public	Univ. of Texas HSC - San Antonio	66	223	148	54	237	157
Public	U. of Texas MD Anderson Cancer Ctr.						
Public	U. of Texas Med. Branch - Galveston	39	278	174	45	260	170
Public	Univ. of Texas SW Med. Ctr. - Dallas	88	186	124	92	179	122
Public	University of Utah	384	50	34	330	58	40
Public	University of Vermont	79	204	136	71	203	136
Public	University of Virginia	366	52	35	424	43	30
Public	University of Washington - Seattle	687	14	12	663	14	12
Public	University of Wisconsin - Madison	857	3	3	813	4	4

2013 Doctorates	2013 National Rank	2013 Control Rank	2012 Doctorates	2012 National Rank	2012 Control Rank	2011 Doctorates	2011 National Rank	2011 Control Rank
95	164	110	58	216	141	63	196	131
352	54	38	342	55	38	326	56	39
809	4	4	869	2	2	794	4	4
538	23	17	437	40	28	432	34	25
325	57	41	273	64	46	299	60	42
37	270	172	29	291	180	36	263	167
305	65	47	322	58	41	261	69	49
138	127	89	185	102	73	156	109	77
45	248	161	59	212	137	52	222	146
81	186	124	75	183	120	63	196	131
95	164	110	72	188	122	97	154	105
696	12	11	632	16	13	582	18	14
295	67	49	268	67	48	258	70	50
52	226	149	66	199	128	66	190	126
163	110	34	181	104	30	166	102	31
885	2	2	857	4	4	797	3	3
772	7	7	734	8	7	723	10	9
411	47	32	367	50	35	365	48	34
325	57	41	246	75	54	287	63	45
42	255	165	40	253	161	39	252	163
125	143	98	111	147	100	106	146	100
64	204	137	58	216	141	60	201	134
202	97	68	202	97	70	165	105	74
530	24	18	495	26	18	506	23	17
72	200	134	68	195	127	52	222	146
214	92	27	210	92	26	159	107	32
206	95	67	218	88	63	186	97	70
24	320	193	24	316	189	27	292	179
169	107	75	170	109	78	149	114	81
527	26	8	514	23	6	543	20	6
435	42	29	479	30	21	519	21	15
97	162	109	89	167	113	81	168	114
290	70	20	265	68	20	276	65	19
334	56	40	279	63	45	289	62	44
295	67	49	270	66	47	269	67	47
663	16	3	634	15	3	616	16	3
484	34	23	461	34	24	371	47	33
849	3	3	867	3	3	801	2	2
117	148	100	127	137	96	108	144	99
51	230	153	56	223	145	38	256	164
52	226	149	40	253	161	45	239	156
89	175	117	98	158	108	85	165	112
324	59	43	339	56	39	304	59	41
84	180	119	62	207	135	58	206	136
399	48	33	393	46	33	421	38	27
763	10	9	708	10	9	723	10	9
772	7	7	813	5	5	761	8	7

Doctorates Awarded

	Institutions with Over $40 Million in Federal Research, Alphabetically	2015 Doctorates	2015 National Rank	2015 Control Rank	2014 Doctorates	2014 National Rank	2014 Control Rank
Public	Utah State University	102	169	115	109	161	110
Private	Vanderbilt University	340	59	18	318	64	19
Public	Virginia Commonwealth University	282	73	53	329	60	42
Public	Virginia Polytechnic Inst. and St. Univ.	488	33	25	494	31	21
Private	Wake Forest University	53	248	89	53	239	81
Public	Washington State Univ. - Pullman	281	74	54	260	80	57
Private	Washington University in St. Louis	292	70	20	261	79	23
Public	Wayne State University	242	84	61	244	84	60
Private	Weill Cornell Medical College	68	220	74	70	205	68
Public	West Virginia University	183	109	78	155	123	84
Private	Woods Hole Oceanographic Inst.						
Private	Yale University	426	45	15	413	45	14
Private	Yeshiva University	96	177	59	124	138	44

2013 Doctorates	2013 National Rank	2013 Control Rank	2012 Doctorates	2012 National Rank	2012 Control Rank	2011 Doctorates	2011 National Rank	2011 Control Rank
105	155	106	94	161	111	111	142	98
310	63	18	273	64	19	322	57	18
324	59	43	333	57	40	329	54	38
479	36	24	469	32	22	414	39	28
50	233	79	57	220	77	58	206	71
268	74	54	203	95	68	197	92	65
255	75	21	251	73	21	248	73	21
223	88	64	229	82	58	231	78	57
73	196	64	57	220	77	60	201	68
158	113	78	162	113	81	166	102	72
398	49	16	390	47	14	342	53	16
131	136	41	129	136	41	122	134	41

Postdoctoral Appointees

	Institutions with Over $40 Million in Federal Research, Alphabetically	2014 Postdocs	2014 National Rank	2014 Control Rank	2013 Postdocs	2013 National Rank	2013 Control Rank
Public	Arizona State University	253	68	42	257	69	42
Public	Auburn University	40	175	121	36	176	125
Public	Augusta University	188	91	57	139	107	71
Private	Baylor College of Medicine	594	31	16	596	29	14
Private	Boston University	444	45	23	464	39	20
Private	Brandeis University	102	128	45	116	118	40
Private	Brown University	244	71	27	259	68	27
Private	California Institute of Technology	552	34	18	579	31	16
Private	Carnegie Mellon University	215	81	30	194	87	31
Private	Case Western Reserve University	190	90	34	224	81	29
Public	Clemson University	65	144	95	42	166	116
Public	Cleveland State University	3	314	210	8	264	185
Private	Cold Spring Harbor Laboratory	153	104	38	0	335	112
Public	Colorado State Univ. - Fort Collins	297	63	37	290	60	34
Private	Columbia University	1,274	6	5	1,232	7	5
Private	Cornell University	466	39	21	437	41	21
Private	Dartmouth College	222	78	28	228	76	28
Private	Drexel University	74	140	49	69	140	45
Private	Duke University	656	23	11	732	19	8
Private	Emory University	674	20	9	712	21	10
Public	Florida International University	64	146	97	49	156	108
Public	Florida State University	211	83	53	212	85	56
Public	George Mason University	33	186	130	32	188	134
Private	George Washington University	94	133	47	80	135	44
Private	Georgetown University	127	116	40	115	119	41
Public	Georgia Institute of Technology	217	80	51	267	65	39
Private	Harvard University	5,761	1	1	5,809	1	1
Private	Icahn School of Med. at Mount Sinai	670	21	10	621	26	12
Public	Indiana University - Bloomington	144	108	69	117	117	78
Public	Indiana U. - Purdue U. - Indianapolis	249	69	43	219	82	53
Public	Iowa State University	331	55	32	299	59	33
Private	Johns Hopkins University	1,715	3	3	1,693	3	3
Public	Kansas State University	142	111	72	136	109	73
Public	Louisiana State Univ. - Baton Rouge	141	112	73	149	102	66
Private	Massachusetts Inst. of Technology	1,516	4	4	1,406	4	4
Private	Medical College of Wisconsin	175	94	35	122	112	38
Public	Medical University of South Carolina	173	95	60	179	91	57
Public	Michigan State University	450	43	21	446	40	20
Public	Mississippi State University	46	166	114	41	169	119
Public	Montana State University - Bozeman	38	178	124	42	166	116
Public	Naval Postgraduate School	16	227	159	24	202	145
Public	New Jersey Institute of Technology	24	202	142	39	170	120
Public	New Mexico State Univ. - Las Cruces	28	195	137	24	202	145
Private	New York University	596	30	15	593	30	15
Public	North Carolina State University	473	38	18	490	36	18
Private	Northeastern University	117	122	43	105	126	42
Private	Northwestern University	708	18	8	716	20	9
Public	Ohio State University - Columbus	629	28	15	625	25	14
Public	Oregon Health & Science University	270	65	39	280	64	38

2012 Postdocs	2012 National Rank	2012 Control Rank	2011 Postdocs	2011 National Rank	2011 Control Rank	2010 Postdocs	2010 National Rank	2010 Control Rank
221	77	50	204	83	53	210	84	56
45	162	113	42	169	117	39	174	122
143	107	71	156	104	68	123	115	76
588	29	14	572	31	14	494	34	16
530	35	17	600	28	12	870	16	8
128	118	40	102	122	40	111	118	40
274	67	26	279	65	27	271	67	27
623	25	12	573	30	13	588	27	13
241	72	27	234	73	28	200	87	30
219	78	28	194	87	32	160	99	34
45	162	113	44	166	114	47	161	109
9	262	184	12	247	173	11	257	184
0	342	113	0	340	111	0	345	110
313	57	34	233	74	46	242	69	42
1,283	6	5	1,276	7	6	1,358	6	4
386	44	21	487	38	19	426	40	21
208	83	31	199	86	31	191	91	31
63	141	46	54	151	48	73	137	43
747	19	8	784	19	9	807	19	9
678	22	11	691	23	11	672	23	12
55	150	104	51	154	106	40	172	120
235	73	46	218	78	49	241	71	44
31	183	128	31	187	132	28	195	139
98	126	42	68	138	44	62	146	45
131	117	39	112	119	39	126	113	39
307	60	36	295	62	36	273	66	40
6,019	1	1	6,120	1	1	5,827	1	1
579	31	15	536	35	17	502	33	15
316	56	33	125	113	76	126	113	75
20	215	157	239	71	44	217	80	52
158	99	65	152	105	69	278	65	39
1,775	3	3	1,649	3	3	1,721	3	3
112	121	81	103	121	82	74	136	94
138	110	73	158	102	66	167	98	65
1,398	5	4	1,345	4	4	1,286	7	5
133	114	38	136	111	37	141	108	37
186	90	57	194	87	56	188	92	61
429	40	20	455	40	20	445	38	19
35	177	124	41	171	119	40	172	120
41	169	119	56	147	101	62	146	102
0	342	230	0	340	230	0	345	236
17	232	167	36	177	123	18	225	161
29	188	132	24	201	144	14	242	174
623	25	12	493	37	18	489	35	17
371	48	26	318	54	29	231	74	47
96	130	43	100	124	41	96	127	41
742	20	9	813	17	8	741	20	10
616	28	15	617	27	16	597	26	14
303	62	38	298	60	34	306	57	31

Postdoctoral Appointees

	Institutions with Over $40 Million in Federal Research, Alphabetically	2014 Postdocs	2014 National Rank	2014 Control Rank	2013 Postdocs	2013 National Rank	2013 Control Rank
Public	Oregon State University	201	85	54	237	70	43
Public	Penn. St. Univ. - Hershey Med. Ctr.	91	134	87	95	127	85
Public	Pennsylvania State Univ. - Univ. Park	365	50	27	380	44	23
Private	Princeton University	464	41	22	527	34	17
Public	Purdue University - West Lafayette	358	51	28	289	61	35
Private	Rensselaer Polytechnic Institute	82	137	48	85	131	43
Private	Rice University	206	84	31	182	90	34
Private	Rockefeller University	298	62	26	303	57	26
Private	Rush University	33	186	57	33	186	54
Public	Rutgers University - New Brunswick	345	54	31	237	70	43
Public	San Diego State University	32	188	131	30	192	138
Private	Scripps Research Institute	648	24	12	0	335	112
Private	Stanford University	2,048	2	2	1,976	2	2
Public	Stony Brook University	224	77	50	236	72	45
Public	Temple University	192	89	56	156	100	64
Public	Texas A&M Univ. - College Station	386	48	25	341	51	28
Private	Thomas Jefferson University	119	121	42	134	110	37
Private	Tufts University	194	88	33	194	87	31
Private	Tulane University	124	117	41	162	96	36
Public	Uniformed Services Univ. of the HS	36	181	127	42	166	116
Public	University at Albany	69	141	92	80	135	92
Public	University at Buffalo	301	60	35	266	66	40
Public	University of Alabama - Birmingham	228	75	48	226	78	50
Public	University of Alabama - Huntsville	19	217	151	14	236	168
Public	University of Alaska - Fairbanks	47	163	111	50	155	107
Public	University of Arizona	451	42	20	303	57	32
Public	Univ. of Arkansas for Med. Sciences	57	150	100	54	148	100
Public	University of California - Berkeley	1,148	10	4	1,255	6	2
Public	University of California - Davis	765	17	10	779	15	8
Public	University of California - Irvine	315	57	33	325	53	29
Public	University of California - Los Angeles	1,088	11	5	1,084	11	5
Public	University of California - Riverside	141	112	73	143	104	68
Public	University of California - San Diego	1,338	5	1	1,275	5	1
Public	Univ. of California - San Francisco	1,051	12	6	1,047	12	6
Public	Univ. of California - Santa Barbara	285	64	38	281	63	37
Public	University of California - Santa Cruz	120	120	79	122	112	75
Public	University of Central Florida	47	163	111	52	150	102
Private	University of Chicago	583	32	17	598	28	13
Public	University of Cincinnati - Cincinnati	466	39	19	468	38	19
Public	University of Colorado - Boulder	879	14	7	836	14	7
Public	University of Colorado - Denver	267	66	40	285	62	36
Public	University of Connecticut - Health Ctr.	104	127	83	122	112	75
Public	University of Connecticut - Storrs	121	119	78	115	119	79
Private	University of Dayton	10	265	82	7	269	81
Public	University of Delaware	166	100	63	131	111	74
Public	University of Florida	644	25	13	677	23	12
Public	University of Georgia	231	74	47	228	76	49
Public	University of Hawaii - Manoa	243	72	45	265	67	41
Public	University of Houston - Univ. Park	258	67	41	219	82	53

2012 Postdocs	2012 National Rank	2012 Control Rank	2011 Postdocs	2011 National Rank	2011 Control Rank	2010 Postdocs	2010 National Rank	2010 Control Rank
214	81	52	189	91	58	179	94	62
100	125	84	88	128	86	109	119	79
401	41	21	380	47	24	372	49	26
457	39	20	471	39	20	484	36	18
306	61	37	297	61	35	349	51	27
80	136	44	77	134	43	92	129	42
158	99	35	165	99	35	179	94	33
309	58	24	318	54	26	320	54	26
36	176	53	51	154	49	61	150	47
243	71	45	240	70	43	220	78	50
31	183	128	46	161	111	43	164	112
0	342	113	0	340	111	0	345	110
1,887	2	2	1,798	2	2	1,777	2	2
222	76	49	202	84	54	172	97	64
159	98	64	110	120	81	101	125	85
320	55	32	316	56	30	304	58	32
145	104	36	163	100	36	152	103	35
201	85	32	205	82	30	186	93	32
143	107	37	124	116	38	138	110	38
71	137	93	71	136	93	64	144	100
92	131	88	86	129	87	106	122	82
264	68	42	299	59	33	285	62	36
226	74	47	245	69	42	237	73	46
8	267	186	15	237	168	18	225	161
58	148	102	52	153	105	44	163	111
308	59	35	270	67	40	310	56	30
41	169	119	33	183	129	31	190	135
1,533	4	1	1,286	6	1	1,253	9	3
757	18	11	819	15	8	860	17	9
379	45	24	369	48	25	387	46	23
1,009	12	6	1,062	12	6	1,121	12	6
133	114	77	167	98	64	241	71	44
1,219	8	2	1,260	8	2	1,514	4	1
1,066	11	5	1,091	11	5	1,094	13	7
300	63	39	291	63	37	334	53	28
141	109	72	150	106	70	155	102	68
55	150	104	65	142	98	58	153	105
565	33	16	562	32	15	570	30	14
465	38	19	410	45	22	280	64	38
776	17	10	770	20	11	741	20	11
300	63	39	284	64	38	282	63	37
125	119	79	116	118	80	96	127	87
134	111	74	125	113	76	121	116	77
11	254	74	14	240	72	8	274	80
133	114	77	124	116	79	120	117	78
674	23	12	625	26	15	648	25	13
245	70	44	279	65	39	219	79	51
339	53	30	238	72	45	216	81	53
198	87	55	213	79	50	209	85	57

Postdoctoral Appointees

Institutions with Over $40 Million in Federal Research, Alphabetically		2014 Postdocs	2014 National Rank	2014 Control Rank	2013 Postdocs	2013 National Rank	2013 Control Rank
Public	University of Idaho	56	154	103	51	153	105
Public	University of Illinois - Chicago	238	73	46	232	74	47
Public	Univ. of Illinois - Urbana-Champaign	525	35	17	562	32	16
Public	University of Iowa	355	53	30	352	48	26
Public	University of Kansas - Lawrence	154	103	66	155	101	65
Public	University of Kansas Medical Center	111	125	81	113	121	80
Public	University of Kentucky	155	102	65	217	84	55
Public	University of Louisville	97	130	85	92	128	86
Public	University of Maine - Orono	14	238	163	15	233	167
Public	University of Maryland - Baltimore	358	51	28	352	48	26
Public	Univ. of Maryland - Baltimore County	63	147	98	58	146	98
Public	University of Maryland - College Park	437	46	23	379	45	24
Public	Univ. of Massachusetts - Amherst	153	104	67	165	94	60
Public	U. of Mass. Med. Sch. - Worcester	315	57	33	315	56	31
Private	University of Miami	198	87	32	202	86	30
Public	University of Michigan - Ann Arbor	1,238	7	2	1,227	8	3
Public	University of Minnesota - Twin Cities	679	19	11	660	24	13
Public	University of Missouri - Columbia	184	93	59	225	79	51
Public	University of Nebraska - Lincoln	201	85	54	157	99	63
Public	University of Nebraska Medical Ctr.	110	126	82	112	122	81
Public	University of Nevada - Reno	65	144	95	80	135	92
Public	Univ. of New Hampshire - Durham	45	168	115	34	181	129
Public	Univ. of New Mexico - Albuquerque	139	114	75	83	134	91
Public	Univ. of North Carolina - Chapel Hill	802	15	8	778	16	9
Public	University of North Dakota	21	209	146	22	211	153
Private	University of Notre Dame	171	96	36	186	89	33
Public	University of Oklahoma - Norman	145	107	68	142	105	69
Public	University of Oklahoma HSC	89	135	88	84	133	90
Public	University of Oregon	85	136	89	89	130	88
Private	University of Pennsylvania	919	13	7	947	13	7
Public	University of Pittsburgh - Pittsburgh	659	22	12	741	17	10
Public	University of Rhode Island	27	197	139	36	176	125
Private	University of Rochester	222	78	28	325	53	25
Public	Univ. of South Carolina - Columbia	144	108	69	119	116	77
Public	University of South Florida - Tampa	300	61	36	321	55	30
Private	University of Southern California	480	37	20	486	37	19
Public	University of Tennessee - Knoxville	143	110	71	149	102	66
Public	University of Tennessee HSC	113	124	80	106	125	84
Public	University of Texas - Austin	370	49	26	361	47	25
Public	University of Texas HSC - Houston	212	82	52	229	75	48
Public	Univ. of Texas HSC - San Antonio	165	101	64	169	92	58
Public	U. of Texas MD Anderson Cancer Ctr.	640	26	14	604	27	15
Public	U. of Texas Med. Branch - Galveston	131	115	76	137	108	72
Public	Univ. of Texas SW Med. Ctr. - Dallas	571	33	16	552	33	17
Public	University of Utah	429	47	24	384	42	21
Public	University of Vermont	95	132	86	85	131	89
Public	University of Virginia	447	44	22	384	42	21
Public	University of Washington - Seattle	1,184	9	3	1,187	10	4
Public	University of Wisconsin - Madison	767	16	9	738	18	11

The Top American Research Universities

2012 Postdocs	2012 National Rank	2012 Control Rank	2011 Postdocs	2011 National Rank	2011 Control Rank	2010 Postdocs	2010 National Rank	2010 Control Rank
43	165	116	50	156	107	42	167	115
251	69	43	257	68	41	254	68	41
558	34	18	548	34	18	513	31	17
363	49	27	368	50	27	383	47	24
184	91	58	172	95	61	142	107	71
134	111	74	125	113	76	103	123	83
344	52	29	303	58	32	320	54	29
114	120	80	135	112	75	134	111	73
22	208	151	14	240	169	25	203	147
350	50	28	343	52	28	378	48	25
45	162	113	36	177	123	80	134	92
399	42	22	431	42	21	396	43	21
165	94	60	209	80	51	215	83	55
324	54	31	386	46	23	403	41	20
219	78	28	227	76	29	227	76	28
1,080	10	4	1,121	10	4	1,174	11	5
580	30	16	640	25	14	671	24	12
199	86	54	219	77	48	286	61	35
163	96	62	159	101	65	159	100	66
145	104	69	148	108	72	148	104	69
53	153	106	66	141	97	65	143	99
48	158	110	46	161	111	37	177	125
70	139	95	193	89	57	224	77	49
850	14	7	878	14	7	844	18	10
20	215	157	8	268	190	12	251	180
182	92	34	182	93	34	147	105	36
134	111	74	80	133	91	108	120	80
90	132	89	81	132	90	68	141	97
90	132	89	67	140	96	80	134	92
956	13	7	978	13	7	1,042	14	7
841	15	8	818	16	9	891	15	8
50	156	108	50	156	107	47	161	109
214	81	30	413	43	22	356	50	24
97	127	85	144	109	73	147	105	70
289	66	41	304	57	31	293	59	33
506	36	18	447	41	21	427	39	20
145	104	69	171	96	62	179	94	62
156	101	66	149	107	71	108	120	80
372	47	25	369	48	25	287	60	34
224	75	48	209	80	51	216	81	53
173	93	59	171	96	62	139	109	72
621	27	14	509	36	19	581	29	16
150	102	67	157	103	67	200	87	58
572	32	17	582	29	17	585	28	15
389	43	23	732	21	12	508	32	18
85	135	92	68	138	95	87	130	88
658	24	13	643	24	13	396	43	21
1,190	9	3	1,186	9	3	1,175	10	4
798	16	9	797	18	10	1,369	5	2

Postdoctoral Appointees

	Institutions with Over $40 Million in Federal Research, Alphabetically	2014 Postdocs	2014 National Rank	2014 Control Rank	2013 Postdocs	2013 National Rank	2013 Control Rank
Public	Utah State University	47	163	111	45	160	111
Private	Vanderbilt University	634	27	13	678	22	11
Public	Virginia Commonwealth University	249	69	43	225	79	51
Public	Virginia Polytechnic Inst. and St. Univ.	226	76	49	235	73	46
Private	Wake Forest University	152	106	39	164	95	35
Public	Washington State Univ. - Pullman	169	97	61	166	93	59
Private	Washington University in St. Louis	625	29	14	350	50	23
Public	Wayne State University	185	92	58	158	98	62
Private	Weill Cornell Medical College	322	56	24	334	52	24
Public	West Virginia University	67	143	94	38	172	121
Private	Woods Hole Oceanographic Inst.	97	130	46	120	115	39
Private	Yale University	1,201	8	6	1,214	9	6
Private	Yeshiva University	303	59	25	365	46	22

2012 Postdocs	2012 National Rank	2012 Control Rank	2011 Postdocs	2011 National Rank	2011 Control Rank	2010 Postdocs	2010 National Rank	2010 Control Rank
22	208	151	22	212	153	31	190	135
711	21	10	720	22	10	681	22	11
217	80	51	232	75	47	242	69	42
202	84	53	202	84	54	200	87	58
188	89	33	192	90	33	206	86	29
190	88	56	184	92	59	194	90	60
374	46	22	559	33	16	484	36	18
164	95	61	138	110	74	131	112	74
347	51	23	344	51	24	339	52	25
46	161	112	93	127	85	81	133	91
107	122	41	99	125	42	71	138	44
1,256	7	6	1,307	5	5	1,283	8	6
293	65	25	321	53	25	393	45	23

SAT Scores

Institutions with Over $40 Million in Federal Research, Alphabetically		2014 Median SAT	2014 National Rank	2014 Control Rank	2013 Median SAT	2013 National Rank	2013 Control Rank
Public	Arizona State University	1145	273	92	1145	309	93
Public	Auburn University	1220	143	38	1220	155	38
Public	Augusta University	1030	673	237	1015	841	286
Private	Baylor College of Medicine						
Private	Boston University	1300	82	71	1285	94	82
Private	Brandeis University	1365	51	47	1350	58	53
Private	Brown University	1440	23	23	1435	24	24
Private	California Institute of Technology	1550	1	1	1545	1	1
Private	Carnegie Mellon University	1440	23	23	1435	24	24
Private	Case Western Reserve University	1370	46	44	1375	42	42
Public	Clemson University	1245	114	27	1245	125	28
Public	Cleveland State University	1010	790	288	1030	727	233
Private	Cold Spring Harbor Laboratory						
Public	Colorado State Univ. - Fort Collins	1130	286	98	1130	324	97
Private	Columbia University	1480	8	8	1480	8	8
Private	Cornell University	1420	28	28	1420	29	29
Private	Dartmouth College	1455	18	18	1455	17	17
Private	Drexel University	1200	174	122	1190	201	146
Private	Duke University	1460	13	13	1455	17	17
Private	Emory University	1370	46	44	1365	46	46
Public	Florida International University	1080	475	166	1150	276	80
Public	Florida State University	1240	118	29	1220	155	38
Public	George Mason University	1150	252	80	1150	276	80
Private	George Washington University	1295	93	80	1295	91	79
Private	Georgetown University	1420	28	28	1405	33	33
Public	Georgia Institute of Technology	1400	35	1	1360	50	2
Private	Harvard University	1505	3	3	1505	3	3
Private	Icahn School of Med. at Mount Sinai						
Public	Indiana University - Bloomington	1175	213	65	1175	225	64
Public	Indiana U. - Purdue U. - Indianapolis	1000	868	320	1005	929	319
Public	Iowa State University	1150	252	80	1150	276	80
Private	Johns Hopkins University	1435	26	26	1415	30	30
Public	Kansas State University						
Public	Louisiana State Univ. - Baton Rouge	1170	215	66	1170	231	66
Private	Massachusetts Inst. of Technology	1495	6	6	1500	5	5
Private	Medical College of Wisconsin						
Public	Medical University of South Carolina						
Public	Michigan State University	1170	215	66	1170	231	66
Public	Mississippi State University	1130	286	98	1110	367	109
Public	Montana State University - Bozeman	1130	286	98	1110	367	109
Public	Naval Postgraduate School						
Public	New Jersey Institute of Technology	1165	234	72	1140	316	94
Public	New Mexico State Univ. - Las Cruces	990	899	333	990	972	339
Private	New York University	1345	59	54	1355	54	51
Public	North Carolina State University	1245	114	27	1225	151	36
Private	Northeastern University	1420	28	28	1390	35	35
Private	Northwestern University	1475	10	10	1470	11	11
Public	Ohio State University - Columbus	1300	82	12	1300	82	10
Public	Oregon Health & Science University						

2012 Median SAT	2012 National Rank	2012 Control Rank	2011 Median SAT	2011 National Rank	2011 Control Rank	2010 Median SAT	2010 National Rank	2010 Control Rank
1105	421	127	1095	439	130	1080	507	160
1220	152	35	1220	154	35	1220	147	32
0	1421	546	0	1416	544	0	1433	542
1275	104	89	1275	101	87	1260	107	91
1340	63	58	1340	60	56	1360	46	46
1425	24	24	1390	35	35	1430	21	21
1525	1	1	1525	1	1	1525	1	1
1420	27	27	1410	26	26	1400	26	26
1370	45	45	1340	60	56	1350	49	49
1235	136	26	1235	138	27	1220	147	32
1010	859	285	990	972	342	970	1071	377
1130	322	97	1130	316	93	1130	322	92
1485	9	9	1480	8	8	1460	10	10
1415	29	29	1400	29	29	1400	26	26
1455	13	13	1465	10	10	1450	13	13
1220	152	118	1205	176	133	1210	166	129
1440	18	18	1440	16	16	1435	19	19
1375	43	43	1405	28	28	1390	33	33
1140	310	91	1070	531	168	1075	518	162
1220	152	35	1205	176	44	1190	201	50
1150	284	81	1150	277	79	1145	304	86
1295	87	75	1300	81	73	1290	84	75
1390	35	35	1395	32	32	1400	26	26
1355	55	4	1335	65	6	1330	61	4
1500	2	2	1490	5	5	1490	2	2
1165	262	75	1165	256	74	1170	232	61
1005	928	320	995	964	340	1005	931	316
1150	284	81	1150	277	79	1150	278	80
1405	32	32	1400	29	29	1395	30	30
1170	229	64	1170	234	64	1170	232	61
1490	7	7	1490	5	5	1485	5	5
1170	229	64	1170	234	64	1170	232	61
1090	451	140	1090	449	134	1070	535	167
1110	381	112	1130	316	93	1110	375	107
1140	310	91	1120	355	102	1125	353	102
990	969	344	990	972	342	990	971	334
1350	59	54	1360	49	48	1345	52	51
1185	216	57	1185	220	57	1180	224	57
1370	45	45	1340	60	56	1310	69	64
1440	18	18	1455	14	14	1445	14	14
1260	111	20	1260	110	18	1260	107	17

SAT Scores

Institutions with Over $40 Million in Federal Research, Alphabetically		2014 Median SAT	2014 National Rank	2014 Control Rank	2013 Median SAT	2013 National Rank	2013 Control Rank
Public	Oregon State University	1105	393	132	1100	435	131
Public	Penn. St. Univ. - Hershey Med. Ctr.						
Public	Pennsylvania State Univ. - Univ. Park	1190	184	56	1195	193	51
Private	Princeton University	1500	5	5	1505	3	3
Public	Purdue University - West Lafayette	1205	164	49	1200	192	50
Private	Rensselaer Polytechnic Institute	1395	37	36	1389	38	38
Private	Rice University	1470	12	12	1460	12	12
Private	Rockefeller University						
Private	Rush University						
Public	Rutgers University - New Brunswick	1215	157	43	1210	172	43
Public	San Diego State University	1110	347	115	1090	455	140
Private	Scripps Research Institute						
Private	Stanford University	1475	10	10	1475	10	10
Public	Stony Brook University	1250	112	26	1250	122	27
Public	Temple University	1120	335	111	1120	351	106
Public	Texas A&M Univ. - College Station	1195	179	53	1180	221	62
Private	Thomas Jefferson University						
Private	Tufts University	1440	23	23	1445	20	20
Private	Tulane University	1360	54	50	1360	50	49
Public	Uniformed Services Univ. of the HS						
Public	University at Albany	1095	416	142	1100	435	131
Public	University at Buffalo	1150	252	80	1155	270	77
Public	University of Alabama - Birmingham	1110	347	115	1150	276	80
Public	University of Alabama - Huntsville	1220	143	38	1190	201	56
Public	University of Alaska - Fairbanks						
Public	University of Arizona				1107	421	124
Public	Univ. of Arkansas for Med. Sciences						
Public	University of California - Berkeley	1370	46	3	1355	54	4
Public	University of California - Davis	1205	164	49	1195	193	51
Public	University of California - Irvine	1160	240	73	1130	324	97
Public	University of California - Los Angeles	1325	66	8	1300	82	10
Public	University of California - Riverside	1130	286	98	1090	455	140
Public	University of California - San Diego	1310	79	11	1280	99	16
Public	Univ. of California - San Francisco						
Public	Univ. of California - Santa Barbara	1235	133	33	1215	167	41
Public	University of California - Santa Cruz	1130	286	98	1095	448	138
Public	University of Central Florida	1185	209	62	1180	221	62
Private	University of Chicago	1518	2	2	1515	2	2
Public	University of Cincinnati - Cincinnati	1170	215	66	1130	324	97
Public	University of Colorado - Boulder	1220	143	38	1205	179	46
Public	University of Colorado - Denver	1050	560	192	1070	532	174
Public	Univ. of Connecticut - Health Center						
Public	University of Connecticut - Storrs	1240	118	29	1230	147	34
Private	University of Dayton	1205	164	116	1205	179	134
Public	University of Delaware	1190	184	56	1170	231	66
Public	University of Florida	1265	104	22	1265	110	20
Public	University of Georgia	1235	133	33	1235	142	32
Public	University of Hawaii - Manoa	1085	466	161	1085	503	159
Public	University of Houston - Univ. Park	1145	273	92	1140	316	94

2012 Median SAT	2012 National Rank	2012 Control Rank	2011 Median SAT	2011 National Rank	2011 Control Rank	2010 Median SAT	2010 National Rank	2010 Control Rank
1090	451	140	1090	449	134	1085	497	154
1195	194	49	1195	197	51	1195	195	48
1500	2	2	1500	2	2	1490	2	2
1180	221	61	1170	234	64	1165	254	73
1365	49	48	1375	45	44	1365	42	42
1445	15	15	1430	20	20	1440	15	15
1195	194	49	1195	197	51	1190	201	50
1085	504	155	1085	498	156	1040	712	223
1475	11	11	1455	14	14	1455	11	11
1235	136	26	1230	143	28	1210	166	38
1110	381	112	1110	372	107	1110	375	107
1195	194	49	1210	169	39	1215	159	36
1435	21	21	1430	20	20	1425	22	22
1360	50	49	1325	67	61	1315	66	62
1105	421	127	1115	368	105	1120	357	104
1155	276	78	1155	269	77	1155	275	78
1110	381	112	1110	372	107	1110	375	107
1170	229	64	1170	234	64	1170	232	61
1095	440	135	1100	427	122	1085	497	154
1370	45	1	1360	49	2	1345	52	2
1210	173	42	1210	169	39	1195	195	48
1160	267	77	1185	220	57	1180	224	57
1300	77	8	1300	81	9	1275	100	14
1080	513	157	1050	625	201	1060	600	185
1235	136	26	1270	104	15	1265	105	15
1215	167	37	1205	176	44	1200	191	46
1140	310	91	1135	312	90	1150	278	80
1180	221	61	1185	220	57	1180	224	57
1485	9	9	1485	7	7	1480	7	7
1130	322	97	1140	303	87	1130	322	92
1170	229	64	1190	200	53	1170	232	61
1070	531	163	1050	625	201	1050	634	198
1230	141	31	1220	154	35	1220	147	32
1205	179	136	1205	176	133	1170	232	172
1185	216	57	1205	176	44	1185	217	55
1265	109	18	1260	110	18	1265	105	15
1215	167	37	1225	145	30	1230	140	29
1080	513	157	1090	449	134	1095	433	127
1130	322	97	1110	372	107	1090	447	137

SAT Scores

	Institutions with Over $40 Million in Federal Research, Alphabetically	2014 Median SAT	2014 National Rank	2014 Control Rank	2013 Median SAT	2013 National Rank	2013 Control Rank
Public	University of Idaho	1040	650	229	1070	532	174
Public	University of Illinois - Chicago	1130	286	98	1090	455	140
Public	Univ. of Illinois - Urbana-Champaign	1300	82	12	1280	99	16
Public	University of Iowa	1170	215	66	1205	179	46
Public	University of Kansas - Lawrence	1150	252	80	1150	276	80
Public	University of Kansas Medical Center						
Public	University of Kentucky	1150	252	80	1150	276	80
Public	University of Louisville	1150	252	80	1150	276	80
Public	University of Maine - Orono	1075	481	168	1085	503	159
Public	University of Maryland - Baltimore						
Public	Univ. of Maryland - Baltimore County	1210	162	47	1210	172	43
Public	University of Maryland - College Park	1315	77	10	1310	75	7
Public	Univ. of Massachusetts - Amherst	1215	157	43	1210	172	43
Public	Univ. of Mass. Med. Sch. - Worcester						
Private	University of Miami	1320	70	62	1325	67	61
Public	University of Michigan - Ann Arbor	1390	38	2	1340	61	6
Public	University of Minnesota - Twin Cities	1260	107	23	1260	111	21
Public	University of Missouri - Columbia	1170	215	66	1170	231	66
Public	University of Nebraska - Lincoln	1150	252	80	1150	276	80
Public	University of Nebraska Medical Ctr.						
Public	University of Nevada - Reno	1075	481	168	1075	521	168
Public	Univ. of New Hampshire - Durham	1100	403	138	1100	435	131
Public	Univ. of New Mexico - Albuquerque	1050	560	192	1030	727	233
Public	Univ. of North Carolina - Chapel Hill	1320	70	9	1305	78	8
Public	University of North Dakota	1090	420	144	1090	455	140
Private	University of Notre Dame	1460	13	13	1460	12	12
Public	University of Oklahoma - Norman	1190	184	56	1190	201	56
Public	University of Oklahoma HSC						
Public	University of Oregon	1110	347	115	1105	423	125
Private	University of Pennsylvania	1455	18	18	1450	19	19
Public	University of Pittsburgh - Pittsburgh	1270	103	21	1255	118	26
Public	University of Rhode Island	1070	491	172	1070	532	174
Private	University of Rochester				1350	58	53
Public	Univ. of South Carolina - Columbia	1210	162	47	1195	193	51
Public	University of South Florida - Tampa	1160	240	73	1170	231	66
Private	University of Southern California	1380	43	41	1380	41	41
Public	University of Tennessee - Knoxville	1205	164	49	1205	179	46
Public	University of Tennessee HSC						
Public	University of Texas - Austin	1290	94	14	1260	111	21
Public	University of Texas HSC - Houston						
Public	Univ. of Texas HSC - San Antonio						
Public	U. of Texas MD Anderson Cancer Ctr.						
Public	U. of Texas Med. Branch - Galveston						
Public	U. of Texas SW Medical Ctr. - Dallas						
Public	University of Utah	1130	286	98	1110	367	109
Public	University of Vermont	1185	209	62	1185	218	61
Public	University of Virginia	1355	56	5	1355	54	4
Public	University of Washington - Seattle	1230	137	36	1230	147	34
Public	University of Wisconsin - Madison	1280	97	17	1260	111	21

2012 Median SAT	2012 National Rank	2012 Control Rank	2011 Median SAT	2011 National Rank	2011 Control Rank	2010 Median SAT	2010 National Rank	2010 Control Rank
1070	531	163	1070	531	168	1070	535	167
1090	451	140	1090	449	134	1090	447	137
1280	95	14	1280	96	14	1280	91	12
1150	284	81	1170	234	64	1170	232	61
1150	284	81	1150	277	79	1130	322	92
1170	229	64	1150	277	79	1150	278	80
1130	322	97	1110	372	107	1130	322	92
1065	582	183	1075	520	164	1060	600	185
1225	149	34	1210	169	39	1205	172	40
1300	77	8	1290	88	11	1290	84	10
1190	202	53	1185	220	57	1160	265	76
1325	68	62	1315	73	67	1295	82	73
1340	63	6	1390	35	1	1300	75	9
1240	125	24	1240	125	25	1240	130	26
1170	229	64	1170	234	64	1170	232	61
1170	229	64	1150	277	79	1150	278	80
1065	582	183	1055	611	198	1045	702	220
1095	440	135	1100	427	122	1105	419	123
1030	729	242	1030	707	228	1030	737	230
1300	77	8	1305	79	8	1310	69	6
1090	451	140	1090	449	134	1050	634	198
1440	18	18	1460	11	11	1440	15	15
1190	202	53	1190	200	53	1190	201	50
1108	420	126	1105	417	118	1110	375	107
1445	15	15	1440	16	16	1440	15	15
1275	104	16	1270	104	15	1260	107	17
1055	611	194	1060	596	195	1045	702	220
1340	63	58	1345	56	53	1325	62	58
1195	194	49	1185	220	57	1190	201	50
1170	229	64	1155	269	77	1130	322	92
1375	43	43	1385	41	40	1370	41	41
1205	179	44	1205	176	44	1205	172	40
1255	119	23	1250	117	23	1230	140	29
1110	381	112	1110	372	107	1110	375	107
1185	216	57	1185	220	57	1183	223	56
1360	50	2	1350	53	3	1335	59	3
1215	167	37	1225	145	30	1215	159	36
1260	111	20	1260	110	18	1260	107	17

SAT Scores

Institutions with Over $40 Million in Federal Research, Alphabetically		2014 Median SAT	2014 National Rank	2014 Control Rank	2013 Median SAT	2013 National Rank	2013 Control Rank
Public	Utah State University	1070	491	172	1090	455	140
Private	Vanderbilt University	1460	13	13	1460	12	12
Public	Virginia Commonwealth University	1105	393	132	1105	423	125
Public	Virginia Polytechnic Inst. and St. Univ.	1215	157	43	1220	155	38
Private	Wake Forest University						
Public	Washington State Univ. - Pullman	1030	673	237	1030	727	233
Private	Washington University in St. Louis	1460	13	13	1460	12	12
Public	Wayne State University	1070	491	172	1050	616	203
Private	Weill Cornell Medical College						
Public	West Virginia University	1090	420	144	1035	714	227
Private	Woods Hole Oceanographic Inst.						
Private	Yale University	1505	3	3	1500	5	5
Private	Yeshiva University	1240	118	90	1235	142	111

2012 Median SAT	2012 National Rank	2012 Control Rank	2011 Median SAT	2011 National Rank	2011 Control Rank	2010 Median SAT	2010 National Rank	2010 Control Rank
1070	531	163	1090	449	134	1110	375	107
1460	12	12	1440	16	16	1420	23	23
1105	421	127	1080	505	158	1095	433	127
1215	167	37	1210	169	39	1220	147	32
1050	627	201	1065	582	188	1085	497	154
1490	7	7	1460	11	11	1465	9	9
1030	729	242	1010	831	277	970	1071	377
1055	611	194	1090	449	134	1070	535	167
1495	4	4	1500	2	2	1490	2	2
1220	152	118	1225	145	116	1218	158	123

National Merit and Achievement Scholars

	Institutions with Over $40 Million in Federal Research, Alphabetically	2015 National Merits	2015 National Rank	2015 Control Rank	2014 National Merits	2014 National Rank	2014 Control Rank
Public	Arizona State University	112	17	7	118	17	5
Public	Auburn University	64	30	14	74	27	10
Public	Augusta University	3	193	87	0	343	146
Private	Baylor College of Medicine						
Private	Boston University	35	60	31	36	61	34
Private	Brandeis University	12	114	59	15	107	55
Private	Brown University	76	24	14	104	22	14
Private	California Institute of Technology	45	48	27	43	51	30
Private	Carnegie Mellon University	51	44	25	38	58	32
Private	Case Western Reserve University	60	34	19	51	42	26
Public	Clemson University	55	41	19	43	51	22
Public	Cleveland State University	1	247	107	0	343	146
Private	Cold Spring Harbor Laboratory						
Public	Colorado State Univ. - Fort Collins	4	173	80	5	170	76
Private	Columbia University	78	23	13	103	23	15
Private	Cornell University	72	26	16	92	24	16
Private	Dartmouth College	64	30	17	63	33	20
Private	Drexel University	7	143	77	5	170	95
Private	Duke University	108	19	11	127	16	12
Private	Emory University	58	38	21	54	39	23
Public	Florida International University	0	326	139	1	257	111
Public	Florida State University	22	84	41	14	110	54
Public	George Mason University	1	247	107	1	257	111
Private	George Washington University	17	96	48	20	94	48
Private	Georgetown University	32	68	36	35	62	35
Public	Georgia Institute of Technology	59	36	17	57	36	15
Private	Harvard University	209	4	3	309	3	2
Private	Icahn School of Med. at Mount Sinai						
Public	Indiana University - Bloomington	68	28	12	48	47	19
Public	Indiana U. - Purdue U. - Indianapolis	0	326	139	0	343	146
Public	Iowa State University	33	64	31	43	51	22
Private	Johns Hopkins University	47	45	26	43	51	30
Public	Kansas State University	9	128	60	6	159	68
Public	Louisiana State Univ. - Baton Rouge	27	74	34	25	84	42
Private	Massachusetts Inst. of Technology	139	14	9	185	10	9
Private	Medical College of Wisconsin						
Public	Medical University of South Carolina	0	326	139	0	343	146
Public	Michigan State University	43	51	23	45	48	20
Public	Mississippi State University	37	56	27	41	55	24
Public	Montana State University - Bozeman	7	143	67	8	144	66
Public	Naval Postgraduate School						
Public	New Jersey Institute of Technology	0	326	139	1	257	111
Public	New Mexico State Univ. - Las Cruces	0	326	139	0	343	146
Private	New York University	12	114	59	20	94	48
Public	North Carolina State University	5	158	73	11	124	59
Private	Northeastern University	85	22	12	114	18	13
Private	Northwestern University	206	5	4	228	8	7
Public	Ohio State University - Columbus	18	93	46	16	103	51
Public	Oregon Health & Science University	0	326	139	0	343	146

2013 National Merits	2013 National Rank	2013 Control Rank	2012 National Merits	2012 National Rank	2012 Control Rank	2011 National Merits	2011 National Rank	2011 Control Rank
120	19	6	99	24	8	125	21	9
70	33	13	62	39	18	198	10	2
0	355	147	0	369	144	0	386	160
34	59	31	44	52	29	30	74	41
17	100	52	7	156	86	14	118	64
101	22	15	101	23	16	106	25	16
43	51	30	51	47	26	36	62	34
32	64	34	38	61	35	36	62	34
66	37	23	59	41	22	25	84	46
39	55	25	43	54	24	39	58	26
0	355	147	0	369	144	1	271	112
9	137	60	6	166	74	9	147	65
103	21	14	128	20	14	111	24	15
87	26	16	66	33	20	86	30	18
70	33	21	79	28	18	75	36	23
4	187	103	5	178	101	5	177	102
167	13	11	135	19	13	112	23	14
53	47	28	53	45	25	55	40	24
2	229	96	1	257	107	1	271	112
16	105	51	14	112	52	28	80	37
1	258	108	1	257	107	1	271	112
17	100	52	19	94	51	12	132	72
28	74	40	39	59	33	35	66	36
176	11	1	127	21	7	136	20	8
321	2	2	322	1	1	307	1	1
67	36	14	65	35	15	87	29	12
0	355	147	0	369	144	0	386	160
38	58	28	36	66	30	34	69	32
33	62	33	32	71	39	34	69	38
8	146	64	12	120	55	6	164	73
43	51	22	38	61	27	36	62	29
212	9	9	191	12	10	160	19	12
0	355	147	0	369	144	0	386	160
39	55	25	40	58	26	37	60	28
32	64	31	17	101	46	13	125	59
10	130	57	11	131	63	10	143	64
1	258	108	0	369	144	0	386	160
1	258	108	0	369	144	1	271	112
26	80	43	28	76	42	113	22	13
10	130	57	12	120	55	6	164	73
151	16	13	105	22	15	102	26	17
259	4	4	240	7	6	247	4	4
22	87	42	62	39	18	92	27	10
0	355	147	0	369	144	0	386	160

National Merit and Achievement Scholars

	Institutions with Over $40 Million in Federal Research, Alphabetically	2015 National Merits	2015 National Rank	2015 Control Rank	2014 National Merits	2014 National Rank	2014 Control Rank
Public	Oregon State University	4	173	80	13	115	57
Public	Penn. St. Univ. - Hershey Med. Ctr.						
Public	Pennsylvania State Univ. - Univ. Park	21	85	42	24	87	44
Private	Princeton University	146	11	8	179	11	10
Public	Purdue University - West Lafayette	94	21	10	28	75	36
Private	Rensselaer Polytechnic Institute	19	90	46	32	67	37
Private	Rice University	59	36	20	64	31	18
Private	Rockefeller University						
Private	Rush University	0	326	188	0	343	198
Public	Rutgers University - New Brunswick	35	60	30	35	62	28
Public	San Diego State University	0	326	139	0	343	146
Private	Scripps Research Institute						
Private	Stanford University	176	7	6	249	5	4
Public	Stony Brook University	25	77	37	11	124	59
Public	Temple University	1	247	107	1	257	111
Public	Texas A&M Univ. - College Station	142	13	5	165	12	2
Private	Thomas Jefferson University						
Private	Tufts University	55	41	23	64	31	18
Private	Tulane University	33	64	34	44	50	29
Public	Uniformed Services Univ. of the HS						
Public	University at Albany	0	326	139	0	343	146
Public	University at Buffalo	1	247	107	2	223	98
Public	University of Alabama - Birmingham	24	79	38	21	92	46
Public	University of Alabama - Huntsville	2	217	91	1	257	111
Public	University of Alaska - Fairbanks	0	326	139	1	257	111
Public	University of Arizona	65	29	13	71	28	11
Public	Univ. of Arkansas for Med. Sciences	0	326	139	0	343	146
Public	University of California - Berkeley	129	16	6	114	18	6
Public	University of California - Davis	3	193	87	1	257	111
Public	University of California - Irvine	2	217	91	4	183	82
Public	University of California - Los Angeles	43	51	23	32	67	31
Public	University of California - Riverside	1	247	107	0	343	146
Public	University of California - San Diego	18	93	46	14	110	54
Public	Univ. of California - San Francisco						
Public	Univ. of California - Santa Barbara	4	173	80	3	203	92
Public	University of California - Santa Cruz	0	326	139	0	343	146
Public	University of Central Florida	69	27	11	84	26	9
Private	University of Chicago	294	1	1	315	1	1
Public	University of Cincinnati - Cincinnati	44	49	22	49	45	17
Public	University of Colorado - Boulder	5	158	73	6	159	68
Public	University of Colorado - Denver	0	326	139	0	343	146
Public	Univ. of Connecticut - Health Center						
Public	University of Connecticut - Storrs	2	217	91	1	257	111
Private	University of Dayton	4	173	94	3	203	112
Public	University of Delaware	3	193	87	4	183	82
Public	University of Florida	146	11	4	32	67	31
Public	University of Georgia	42	54	25	45	48	20
Public	University of Hawaii - Manoa	0	326	139	0	343	146
Public	University of Houston - Univ. Park	29	72	33	33	64	29

2013 National Merits	2013 National Rank	2013 Control Rank	2012 National Merits	2012 National Rank	2012 Control Rank	2011 National Merits	2011 National Rank	2011 Control Rank
5	173	79	11	131	63	9	147	65
16	105	51	23	84	39	26	83	38
192	10	10	216	9	8	190	12	9
20	93	45	16	103	48	22	88	42
29	71	38	21	87	47	18	104	55
74	29	19	162	13	11	178	13	10
0	355	209	0	369	226	0	386	227
24	85	40	24	83	38	35	66	31
0	355	147	0	369	144	0	386	160
219	8	8	242	6	5	201	9	8
14	114	55	12	120	55	4	189	81
0	355	147	0	369	144	1	271	112
158	14	3	137	18	6	163	18	7
69	35	22	51	47	26	81	34	22
30	69	37	39	59	33	43	50	29
0	355	147	0	369	144	0	386	160
1	258	108	1	257	107	2	231	96
27	77	36	12	120	55	15	113	52
2	229	96	1	257	107	1	271	112
0	355	147	0	369	144	0	386	160
72	31	12	85	26	10	90	28	11
0	355	147	0	369	144	0	386	160
111	20	7	92	25	9	74	37	14
3	204	90	2	231	97	1	271	112
0	355	147	2	231	97	1	271	112
18	98	48	27	78	35	36	62	29
0	355	147	0	369	144	1	271	112
15	110	54	12	120	55	14	118	55
1	258	108	4	188	83	0	386	160
1	258	108	0	369	144	0	386	160
64	38	15	68	32	13	76	35	13
333	1	1	316	2	2	265	2	2
30	69	33	38	61	27	42	52	22
6	160	72	6	166	74	8	152	68
0	355	147	0	369	144	0	386	160
5	173	79	1	257	107	3	211	88
2	229	134	4	188	106	5	177	102
2	229	96	2	231	97	5	177	76
23	86	41	147	15	3	166	16	6
61	43	19	56	43	20	40	57	25
0	355	147	0	369	144	1	271	112
26	80	38	30	74	33	21	89	43

National Merit and Achievement Scholars

Institutions with Over $40 Million in Federal Research, Alphabetically		2015 National Merits	2015 National Rank	2015 Control Rank	2014 National Merits	2014 National Rank	2014 Control Rank
Public	University of Idaho	23	80	39	23	88	45
Public	University of Illinois - Chicago	1	247	107	3	203	92
Public	Univ. of Illinois - Urbana-Champaign	26	75	35	39	57	26
Public	University of Iowa	20	87	43	26	81	40
Public	University of Kansas - Lawrence	26	75	35	30	73	34
Public	University of Kansas Medical Center						
Public	University of Kentucky	111	18	8	109	20	7
Public	University of Louisville	19	90	45	18	98	48
Public	University of Maine - Orono	2	217	91	2	223	98
Public	University of Maryland - Baltimore	0	326	139	0	343	146
Public	Univ. of Maryland - Baltimore County	2	217	91	9	136	63
Public	University of Maryland - College Park	61	33	15	63	33	14
Public	Univ. of Massachusetts - Amherst	1	247	107	3	203	92
Public	Univ. of Mass. Med. Sch. - Worcester						
Private	University of Miami	35	60	31	50	44	28
Public	University of Michigan - Ann Arbor	56	40	18	66	30	13
Public	University of Minnesota - Twin Cities	147	10	3	141	15	4
Public	University of Missouri - Columbia	18	93	46	30	73	34
Public	University of Nebraska - Lincoln	47	45	20	33	64	29
Public	University of Nebraska Medical Ctr.	0	326	139	0	343	146
Public	University of Nevada - Reno	16	98	50	14	110	54
Public	Univ. of New Hampshire - Durham	0	326	139	0	343	146
Public	Univ. of New Mexico - Albuquerque	14	106	55	19	97	47
Public	Univ. of North Carolina - Chapel Hill	20	87	43	49	45	17
Public	University of North Dakota	2	217	91	2	223	98
Private	University of Notre Dame	57	39	22	51	42	26
Public	University of Oklahoma - Norman	288	2	1	313	2	1
Public	University of Oklahoma HSC	0	326	139	0	343	146
Public	University of Oregon	6	152	69	10	132	61
Private	University of Pennsylvania	139	14	9	143	13	11
Public	University of Pittsburgh - Pittsburgh	16	98	50	28	75	36
Public	University of Rhode Island	0	326	139	0	343	146
Private	University of Rochester	37	56	30	28	75	40
Public	Univ. of South Carolina - Columbia	46	47	21	56	38	16
Public	University of South Florida - Tampa	9	128	60	9	136	63
Private	University of Southern California	226	3	2	240	6	5
Public	University of Tennessee - Knoxville	23	80	39	31	71	33
Public	University of Tennessee HSC						
Public	University of Texas - Austin	60	34	16	71	28	11
Public	University of Texas HSC - Houston	0	326	139	0	343	146
Public	Univ. of Texas HSC - San Antonio	0	326	139	0	343	146
Public	U. of Texas MD Anderson Cancer Ctr.	0	326	139	0	343	146
Public	U. of Texas Med. Branch - Galveston	0	326	139	0	343	146
Public	U. of Texas SW Medical Ctr. - Dallas	0	326	139	0	343	146
Public	University of Utah	33	64	31	26	81	40
Public	University of Vermont	10	120	57	10	132	61
Public	University of Virginia	36	59	29	38	58	27
Public	University of Washington - Seattle	12	114	56	18	98	48
Public	University of Wisconsin - Madison	15	102	53	16	103	51

2013 National Merits	2013 National Rank	2013 Control Rank	2012 National Merits	2012 National Rank	2012 Control Rank	2011 National Merits	2011 National Rank	2011 Control Rank
25	84	39	12	120	55	17	105	50
3	204	90	3	213	91	4	189	81
88	25	10	70	31	12	69	38	15
16	105	51	23	84	39	25	84	39
28	74	35	37	65	29	38	59	27
97	23	8	71	30	11	30	74	34
17	100	49	19	94	44	23	87	41
2	229	96	8	147	68	2	231	96
0	355	147	0	369	144	0	386	160
9	137	60	5	178	78	8	152	68
62	40	17	66	33	14	64	39	16
1	258	108	1	257	107	2	231	96
62	40	24	41	56	32	49	44	26
63	39	16	53	45	21	48	45	19
135	17	4	143	17	5	168	14	4
12	122	56	29	75	34	25	84	39
51	48	20	46	50	22	44	49	21
0	355	147	0	369	144	0	386	160
8	146	64	16	103	48	11	137	62
0	355	147	0	369	144	1	271	112
21	89	43	16	103	48	11	137	62
47	50	21	147	15	3	168	14	4
6	160	72	4	188	83	2	231	96
56	45	26	57	42	23	54	41	25
176	11	1	196	11	2	207	8	1
0	355	147	0	369	144	0	386	160
10	130	57	8	147	68	14	118	55
152	15	12	153	14	12	165	17	11
29	71	34	27	78	35	30	74	34
0	355	147	0	369	144	1	271	112
26	80	43	31	72	40	37	60	33
62	40	17	46	50	22	48	45	19
8	146	64	25	82	37	20	94	46
250	5	5	270	3	3	260	3	3
41	54	24	21	87	41	20	94	46
74	29	11	63	38	17	53	43	18
0	355	147	0	369	144	0	386	160
0	355	147	0	369	144	0	386	160
0	355	147	0	369	144	0	386	160
0	355	147	0	369	144	0	386	160
33	62	30	21	87	41	19	99	48
9	137	60	7	156	71	4	189	81
39	55	25	35	69	32	41	55	24
19	96	47	13	116	54	14	118	55
20	93	45	21	87	41	21	89	43

National Merit and Achievement Scholars

	Institutions with Over $40 Million in Federal Research, Alphabetically	2015 National Merits	2015 National Rank	2015 Control Rank	2014 National Merits	2014 National Rank	2014 Control Rank
Public	Utah State University	1	247	107	1	257	111
Private	Vanderbilt University	206	5	4	260	4	3
Public	Virginia Commonwealth University	0	326	139	5	170	76
Public	Virginia Polytechnic Inst. and St. Univ.	4	173	80	4	183	82
Private	Wake Forest University	0	326	188	9	136	74
Public	Washington State Univ. - Pullman	5	158	73	6	159	68
Private	Washington University in St. Louis	32	68	36	223	9	8
Public	Wayne State University	7	143	67	9	136	63
Private	Weill Cornell Medical College						
Public	West Virginia University	10	120	57	27	80	39
Private	Woods Hole Oceanographic Inst.						
Private	Yale University	166	8	7	237	7	6
Private	Yeshiva University	0	326	188	2	223	126

2013 National Merits	2013 National Rank	2013 Control Rank	2012 National Merits	2012 National Rank	2012 Control Rank	2011 National Merits	2011 National Rank	2011 Control Rank
0	355	147	0	369	144	2	231	96
285	3	3	207	10	9	238	7	7
1	258	108	1	257	107	0	386	160
17	100	49	17	101	46	19	99	48
9	137	78	4	188	106	8	152	85
3	204	90	4	188	83	3	211	88
223	7	7	234	8	7	239	6	6
8	146	64	8	147	68	17	105	50
21	89	43	16	103	48	15	113	52
224	6	6	249	5	4	244	5	5
3	204	115	1	257	151	4	189	109

Change: Research		Total Research in Constant 1983 Dollars					
Institutions with Over $40 Million in Federal Research, Alphabetically		2014 Total Research x $1000	2005 Total Research x $1000	Net Change in Constant Dollars	Percent Change in Constant Dollars	Net Change in National Rank	Net Change in Control Rank
Public	Arizona State University	124,107	69,323	54,784	79.0%	40	28
Public	Auburn University	45,690	54,904	-9,214	-16.8%	-18	-13
Public	Augusta University	20,908	27,941	-7,032	-25.2%	-19	-14
Private	Baylor College of Medicine	161,848	190,496	-28,648	-15.0%	-14	-7
Private	Boston University	115,390	102,380	13,011	12.7%	3	0
Private	Brandeis University	21,864	22,483	-618	-2.8%	0	0
Private	Brown University	95,194	57,420	37,774	65.8%	27	6
Private	California Institute of Technology	116,788	110,206	6,583	6.0%	-1	0
Private	Carnegie Mellon University	81,687	83,183	-1,496	-1.8%	-5	-4
Private	Case Western Reserve University	136,126	134,399	1,727	1.3%	-7	0
Public	Clemson University	38,112	72,730	-34,619	-47.6%	-45	-34
Public	Cleveland State University	19,987	6,597	13,390	203.0%	81	63
Private	Cold Spring Harbor Laboratory	25,023					
Public	Colorado State Univ. - Fort Collins	98,017	98,098	-82	-0.1%	-6	-2
Private	Columbia University	275,478	222,362	53,117	23.9%	4	1
Private	Cornell University	189,443	177,916	11,527	6.5%	-3	-1
Private	Dartmouth College	66,642	74,378	-7,736	-10.4%	-10	-3
Private	Drexel University	40,588	36,567	4,021	11.0%	6	-1
Private	Duke University	336,341	261,951	74,390	28.4%	4	2
Private	Emory University	179,862	138,571	41,291	29.8%	6	2
Public	Florida International University	35,052	31,844	3,207	10.1%	5	7
Public	Florida State University	75,456	71,788	3,668	5.1%	6	5
Public	George Mason University	27,879	17,704	10,175	57.5%	33	26
Private	George Washington University	69,568	44,734	24,834	55.5%	32	6
Private	Georgetown University	53,149	51,471	1,677	3.3%	-2	0
Public	Georgia Institute of Technology	234,873	176,663	58,210	32.9%	9	5
Private	Harvard University	285,652	185,720	99,931	53.8%	14	5
Private	Icahn School of Med. at Mount Sinai	151,124	93,564	57,560	61.5%	28	6
Public	Indiana University - Bloomington	56,213	51,022	5,191	10.2%	7	6
Public	Indiana U. - Purdue U. - Indianapolis	103,260	76,532	26,727	34.9%	14	9
Public	Iowa State University	96,947	87,024	9,923	11.4%	1	3
Private	Johns Hopkins University	726,399	599,607	126,793	21.1%	0	0
Public	Kansas State University	58,145	51,247	6,898	13.5%	10	8
Public	Louisiana State Univ. - Baton Rouge	92,111	98,314	-6,203	-6.3%	-13	-6
Private	Massachusetts Inst. of Technology	265,774	241,182	24,592	10.2%	-3	-1
Private	Medical College of Wisconsin	65,126	59,612	5,514	9.3%	1	-2
Public	Medical University of South Carolina	79,110	73,959	5,151	7.0%	6	5
Public	Michigan State University	160,605	138,600	22,004	15.9%	0	0
Public	Mississippi State University	65,302	74,681	-9,379	-12.6%	-12	-8
Public	Montana State University - Bozeman	34,125	45,461	-11,336	-24.9%	-22	-15
Public	Naval Postgraduate School	29,806	21,323	8,483	39.8%	21	17
Public	New Jersey Institute of Technology	30,774	31,945	-1,170	-3.7%	-3	0
Public	New Mexico State Univ. - Las Cruces	42,107	52,090	-9,982	-19.2%	-19	-14
Private	New York University	159,989	114,705	45,284	39.5%	14	4
Public	North Carolina State University	143,612	125,668	17,944	14.3%	5	4
Private	Northeastern University	36,451	26,377	10,074	38.2%	19	2
Private	Northwestern University	202,672	160,822	41,851	26.0%	2	1
Public	Ohio State University - Columbus	245,500	252,886	-7,386	-2.9%	-8	-4
Public	Oregon Health & Science University	102,106	110,755	-8,649	-7.8%	-14	-9

Federal Research in Constant 1983 Dollars						Non-Federal Research in Constant 1983 Dollars					
2014 Federal Research x $1000	2005 Federal Research x $1000	Net Change in Constant Dollars	Percent Change in Constant Dollars	Net Change in National Rank	Net Change in Control Rank	2014 Non-Federal Research x $1000	2005 Non-Federal Research x $1000	Net Change in Constant Dollars	Percent Change in Constant Dollars	Net Change in National Rank	Net Change in Control Rank
60,696	39,265	21,431	54.6%	32	23	63,412	30,059	33,353	111.0%	27	25
16,220	21,313	-5,093	-23.9%	-15	-11	29,470	33,591	-4,121	-12.3%	-21	-12
15,578	17,405	-1,827	-10.5%	3	1	5,330	10,535	-5,205	-49.4%	-52	-37
86,299	124,855	-38,556	-30.9%	-26	-11	75,549	65,641	9,908	15.1%	-9	-8
82,922	95,038	-12,116	-12.7%	-8	-3	32,468	7,342	25,126	342.2%	92	17
14,935	16,524	-1,589	-9.6%	5	4	6,929	5,959	970	16.3%	-2	-2
40,764	37,733	3,031	8.0%	16	3	54,430	19,687	34,743	176.5%	48	8
90,149	103,564	-13,414	-13.0%	-10	-3	26,639	6,642	19,997	301.1%	80	15
64,648	72,222	-7,573	-10.5%	-7	-1	17,039	10,962	6,077	55.4%	18	-2
107,140	88,245	18,894	21.4%	16	7	28,986	46,154	-17,167	-37.2%	-42	-15
14,568	23,601	-9,033	-38.3%	-27	-21	23,544	49,129	-25,585	-52.1%	-65	-42
14,394	2,993	11,401	381.0%	122	92	5,593	3,604	1,989	55.2%	21	20
13,646						11,377					
67,489	64,058	3,431	5.4%	5	2	30,528	34,040	-3,513	-10.3%	-19	-10
192,896	188,209	4,687	2.5%	2	1	82,583	34,153	48,430	141.8%	37	9
97,608	100,692	-3,083	-3.1%	0	2	91,835	77,225	14,610	18.9%	-2	-4
47,311	50,803	-3,493	-6.9%	-2	-1	19,331	23,575	-4,243	-18.0%	-32	-15
24,639	26,000	-1,361	-5.2%	-2	-1	15,949	10,566	5,382	50.9%	9	-2
181,588	156,389	25,199	16.1%	5	3	154,753	105,563	49,190	46.6%	7	0
107,370	110,830	-3,461	-3.1%	2	1	72,493	27,741	44,752	161.3%	37	4
22,483	21,317	1,167	5.5%	7	7	12,568	10,528	2,040	19.4%	-2	3
45,978	43,917	2,062	4.7%	4	4	29,478	27,871	1,607	5.8%	-12	-4
17,536	15,148	2,388	15.8%	20	13	10,343	2,556	7,787	304.6%	81	64
45,376	32,717	12,659	38.7%	25	7	24,192	12,017	12,175	101.3%	34	2
32,469	41,666	-9,197	-22.1%	-13	-3	20,680	9,805	10,875	110.9%	40	4
166,449	101,802	64,646	63.5%	20	9	68,424	74,860	-6,436	-8.6%	-21	-9
180,967	164,420	16,547	10.1%	3	1	104,685	21,301	83,384	391.5%	81	21
98,048	79,458	18,590	23.4%	17	7	53,077	14,106	38,970	276.3%	76	12
26,124	28,494	-2,371	-8.3%	-3	-4	30,090	22,528	7,562	33.6%	5	9
46,498	42,741	3,757	8.8%	9	9	56,761	33,791	22,970	68.0%	13	13
37,594	40,701	-3,107	-7.6%	2	1	59,353	46,323	13,030	28.1%	-1	4
631,640	530,459	101,181	19.1%	0	0	94,759	69,147	25,612	37.0%	7	-1
21,055	24,428	-3,374	-13.8%	-3	-1	37,090	26,819	10,271	38.3%	5	9
30,518	25,038	5,480	21.9%	19	16	61,593	73,276	-11,683	-15.9%	-23	-11
156,851	189,890	-33,039	-17.4%	-7	-3	108,923	51,292	57,630	112.4%	23	7
36,276	42,717	-6,442	-15.1%	-9	-4	28,851	16,895	11,956	70.8%	21	1
38,691	44,934	-6,242	-13.9%	-7	-4	40,418	29,025	11,393	39.3%	3	7
80,863	64,978	15,885	24.4%	10	8	79,742	73,622	6,120	8.3%	-8	-2
23,028	35,078	-12,051	-34.4%	-21	-17	42,274	39,603	2,671	6.7%	-9	-1
21,774	29,737	-7,963	-26.8%	-17	-14	12,351	15,724	-3,372	-21.4%	-32	-19
29,116	17,891	11,225	62.7%	39	30	690	3,432	-2,742	-79.9%	-131	-84
16,909	14,833	2,076	14.0%	21	15	13,865	17,112	-3,247	-19.0%	-35	-23
26,169	37,895	-11,726	-30.9%	-17	-14	15,939	14,195	1,744	12.3%	-10	-1
102,628	79,647	22,981	28.9%	20	7	57,362	35,058	22,304	63.6%	10	-2
57,955	45,321	12,634	27.9%	10	6	85,657	80,347	5,309	6.6%	-8	-2
25,240	15,168	10,072	66.4%	42	12	11,211	11,209	2	0.0%	-14	-9
125,838	101,380	24,458	24.1%	11	6	76,834	59,441	17,393	29.3%	-3	-5
135,715	122,120	13,595	11.1%	1	-1	109,784	130,766	-20,981	-16.0%	-11	-10
80,237	90,180	-9,943	-11.0%	-9	-6	21,869	20,575	1,294	6.3%	-13	-5

Change: Research		Total Research in Constant 1983 Dollars					
Institutions with Over $40 Million in Federal Research, Alphabetically		2014 Total Research x $1000	2005 Total Research x $1000	Net Change in Constant Dollars	Percent Change in Constant Dollars	Net Change in National Rank	Net Change in Control Rank
Public	Oregon State University	74,826	74,882	-57	-0.1%	-4	-3
Public	Penn. St. Univ. - Hershey Med. Ctr.	26,999	25,988	1,011	3.9%	3	2
Public	Pennsylvania State Univ. - Univ. Park	229,220	233,892	-4,672	-2.0%	-10	-7
Private	Princeton University	93,829	84,048	9,780	11.6%	-2	-4
Public	Purdue University - West Lafayette	163,851	151,579	12,273	8.1%	-3	-2
Private	Rensselaer Polytechnic Institute	34,190	27,232	6,958	25.6%	12	0
Private	Rice University	44,486	26,206	18,280	69.8%	33	6
Private	Rockefeller University	103,168	82,528	20,640	25.0%	10	2
Private	Rush University	26,268	34,758	-8,490	-24.4%	-20	-5
Public	Rutgers University - New Brunswick	204,489	114,408	90,081	78.7%	26	17
Public	San Diego State University	25,264	30,685	-5,421	-17.7%	-14	-9
Private	Scripps Research Institute	125,950	137,120	-11,170	-8.1%	-13	-2
Private	Stanford University	297,483	296,897	586	0.2%	-3	-1
Public	Stony Brook University	68,579	88,164	-19,584	-22.2%	-21	-12
Public	Temple University	67,358	34,496	32,862	95.3%	46	37
Public	Texas A&M Univ. - College Station	239,773	199,234	40,539	20.3%	3	4
Private	Thomas Jefferson University	38,603	44,598	-5,995	-13.4%	-10	-3
Private	Tufts University	51,006	54,416	-3,410	-6.3%	-9	-3
Private	Tulane University	48,518	57,710	-9,191	-15.9%	-15	-6
Public	Uniformed Services Univ. of the HS	85,598	32,682	52,916	161.9%	63	51
Public	University at Albany	42,208	107,857	-65,648	-60.9%	-67	-48
Public	University at Buffalo	120,684	110,998	9,686	8.7%	-1	-1
Public	University of Alabama - Birmingham	137,443	132,288	5,155	3.9%	-4	-5
Public	University of Alabama - Huntsville	28,043	22,676	5,367	23.7%	16	13
Public	University of Alaska - Fairbanks	49,682	57,929	-8,247	-14.2%	-15	-9
Public	University of Arizona	187,789	220,206	-32,417	-14.7%	-13	-7
Public	Univ. of Arkansas for Med. Sciences	42,862	38,007	4,855	12.8%	11	12
Public	University of California - Berkeley	231,037	230,305	732	0.3%	-8	-5
Public	University of California - Davis	228,169	227,160	1,009	0.4%	-8	-5
Public	University of California - Irvine	105,107	114,940	-9,833	-8.6%	-12	-7
Public	University of California - Los Angeles	300,072	326,270	-26,198	-8.0%	-5	-4
Public	University of California - Riverside	41,906	50,758	-8,853	-17.4%	-15	-11
Public	University of California - San Diego	345,734	299,446	46,288	15.5%	1	1
Public	Univ. of California - San Francisco	353,503	313,321	40,182	12.8%	1	1
Public	Univ. of California - Santa Barbara	73,573	68,530	5,042	7.4%	7	6
Public	University of California - Santa Cruz	48,111	43,863	4,249	9.7%	8	8
Public	University of Central Florida	46,653	42,652	4,001	9.4%	9	9
Private	University of Chicago	123,371	122,086	1,285	1.1%	-6	-1
Public	University of Cincinnati - Cincinnati	130,300	118,791	11,509	9.7%	0	-1
Public	University of Colorado - Boulder	118,336	108,571	9,764	9.0%	1	0
Public	University of Colorado - Denver	130,841	104,360	26,481	25.4%	11	8
Public	Univ. of Connecticut - Health Center	34,256	49,333	-15,078	-30.6%	-26	-19
Public	University of Connecticut - Storrs	46,414	42,025	4,389	10.4%	9	9
Private	University of Dayton	27,200	28,010	-810	-2.9%	-1	-2
Public	University of Delaware	55,320	45,824	9,496	20.7%	12	10
Public	University of Florida	212,728	220,414	-7,685	-3.5%	-7	-5
Public	University of Georgia	102,214	131,570	-29,355	-22.3%	-24	-17
Public	University of Hawaii - Manoa	104,293	95,789	8,503	8.9%	2	4
Public	University of Houston - Univ. Park	39,837	33,528	6,310	18.8%	9	9

Federal Research in Constant 1983 Dollars						Non-Federal Research in Constant 1983 Dollars					
2014 Federal Research x $1000	2005 Federal Research x $1000	Net Change in Constant Dollars	Percent Change in Constant Dollars	Net Change in National Rank	Net Change in Control Rank	2014 Non-Federal Research x $1000	2005 Non-Federal Research x $1000	Net Change in Constant Dollars	Percent Change in Constant Dollars	Net Change in National Rank	Net Change in Control Rank
46,898	45,280	1,618	3.6%	4	4	27,928	29,602	-1,675	-5.7%	-24	-13
17,741	14,891	2,850	19.1%	24	17	9,258	11,096	-1,839	-16.6%	-20	-10
150,624	134,022	16,602	12.4%	0	-2	78,595	99,870	-21,274	-21.3%	-22	-14
53,417	49,853	3,563	7.1%	4	2	40,412	34,195	6,217	18.2%	-7	-6
74,304	62,441	11,863	19.0%	10	7	89,547	89,138	409	0.5%	-8	-2
19,220	17,583	1,637	9.3%	15	4	14,969	9,649	5,321	55.1%	15	-1
24,060	22,731	1,329	5.8%	5	0	20,426	3,475	16,951	487.8%	104	20
26,682	35,530	-8,848	-24.9%	-11	0	76,486	46,998	29,488	62.7%	12	-1
17,447	20,412	-2,965	-14.5%	-6	-2	8,821	14,346	-5,525	-38.5%	-39	-16
115,803	50,863	64,941	127.7%	48	32	88,686	63,545	25,141	39.6%	7	9
14,612	14,672	-60	-0.4%	14	9	10,653	16,014	-5,361	-33.5%	-39	-24
95,309	113,364	-18,055	-15.9%	-9	-5	30,641	23,756	6,886	29.0%	2	-6
198,380	238,663	-40,282	-16.9%	-1	0	99,102	58,234	40,868	70.2%	16	3
36,323	52,237	-15,914	-30.5%	-25	-18	32,256	35,927	-3,671	-10.2%	-21	-10
38,771	22,421	16,350	72.9%	43	34	28,587	12,075	16,512	136.8%	45	40
87,029	88,427	-1,398	-1.6%	-2	-2	152,744	110,807	41,937	37.8%	2	3
17,830	35,787	-17,957	-50.2%	-39	-8	20,773	8,811	11,962	135.8%	50	7
37,517	40,782	-3,266	-8.0%	0	0	13,489	13,633	-144	-1.1%	-17	-10
30,747	39,299	-8,552	-21.8%	-8	-2	17,771	18,411	-639	-3.5%	-20	-10
69,586	20,772	48,815	235.0%	81	61	16,012	11,910	4,102	34.4%	2	6
34,195	43,167	-8,972	-20.8%	-14	-9	8,013	64,690	-56,677	-87.6%	-150	-109
60,375	63,080	-2,704	-4.3%	-4	-4	60,309	47,918	12,391	25.9%	-4	3
90,040	119,787	-29,747	-24.8%	-18	-9	47,403	12,501	34,902	279.2%	76	63
24,103	17,591	6,512	37.0%	27	21	3,940	5,085	-1,145	-22.5%	-32	-24
27,224	37,226	-10,002	-26.9%	-12	-11	22,458	20,703	1,755	8.5%	-12	-4
93,459	121,604	-28,146	-23.1%	-15	-8	94,331	98,601	-4,271	-4.3%	-8	-4
18,117	24,525	-6,408	-26.1%	-14	-10	24,745	13,482	11,263	83.5%	30	29
100,864	120,836	-19,971	-16.5%	-9	-5	130,173	109,469	20,703	18.9%	-1	0
106,862	99,673	7,189	7.2%	7	2	121,307	127,487	-6,180	-4.8%	-7	-6
58,839	67,081	-8,242	-12.3%	-13	-11	46,268	47,859	-1,590	-3.3%	-18	-7
149,405	195,145	-45,740	-23.4%	-13	-7	150,667	131,125	19,542	14.9%	-6	-5
18,368	21,977	-3,609	-16.4%	-5	-3	23,538	28,781	-5,244	-18.2%	-34	-19
194,770	192,677	2,093	1.1%	1	1	150,964	106,769	44,195	41.4%	3	4
177,626	182,312	-4,686	-2.6%	-1	0	175,877	131,009	44,868	34.2%	0	0
39,072	43,173	-4,101	-9.5%	-2	1	34,501	25,358	9,143	36.1%	8	12
29,090	25,874	3,216	12.4%	12	9	19,021	17,989	1,032	5.7%	-12	-4
20,976	16,617	4,358	26.2%	27	19	25,677	26,035	-358	-1.4%	-21	-9
90,081	102,030	-11,950	-11.7%	-10	-3	33,290	20,055	13,235	66.0%	26	1
79,472	84,162	-4,690	-5.6%	-5	-3	50,828	34,629	16,199	46.8%	4	8
98,768	96,896	1,872	1.9%	4	0	19,568	11,675	7,892	67.6%	22	23
90,398	88,297	2,101	2.4%	3	1	40,443	16,063	24,380	151.8%	52	44
19,330	29,013	-9,683	-33.4%	-22	-18	14,926	20,321	-5,395	-26.5%	-43	-27
26,191	26,781	-590	-2.2%	4	3	20,223	15,244	4,980	32.7%	4	10
20,832	24,412	-3,581	-14.7%	-4	-2	6,368	3,598	2,770	77.0%	27	3
36,501	31,032	5,470	17.6%	14	9	18,819	14,792	4,026	27.2%	0	7
91,282	96,225	-4,943	-5.1%	-1	-2	121,446	124,189	-2,743	-2.2%	-5	-4
39,831	42,762	-2,930	-6.9%	1	4	62,383	88,808	-26,425	-29.8%	-30	-16
66,059	78,964	-12,905	-16.3%	-6	-5	38,233	16,825	21,408	127.2%	42	36
18,123	15,475	2,648	17.1%	21	14	21,715	18,053	3,662	20.3%	-3	2

Change: Research		Total Research in Constant 1983 Dollars					
Institutions with Over $40 Million in Federal Research, Alphabetically		2014 Total Research x $1000	2005 Total Research x $1000	Net Change in Constant Dollars	Percent Change in Constant Dollars	Net Change in National Rank	Net Change in Control Rank
Public	University of Idaho	30,168	37,796	-7,628	-20.2%	-11	-6
Public	University of Illinois - Chicago	110,758	132,181	-21,423	-16.2%	-18	-12
Public	Univ. of Illinois - Urbana-Champaign	195,181	207,530	-12,349	-6.0%	-9	-4
Public	University of Iowa	142,457	138,770	3,687	2.7%	-7	-5
Public	University of Kansas - Lawrence	55,399	48,318	7,082	14.7%	10	8
Public	University of Kansas Medical Center	26,513	30,633	-4,120	-13.5%	-8	-4
Public	University of Kentucky	105,106	127,353	-22,247	-17.5%	-19	-13
Public	University of Louisville	53,219	53,303	-83	-0.2%	-4	-4
Public	University of Maine - Orono	32,771	31,175	1,596	5.1%	1	4
Public	University of Maryland - Baltimore	127,401	126,416	986	0.8%	-5	-5
Public	Univ. of Maryland - Baltimore County	20,978	24,281	-3,304	-13.6%	-10	-9
Public	University of Maryland - College Park	153,996	140,641	13,355	9.5%	-5	-4
Public	Univ. of Massachusetts - Amherst	59,745	52,945	6,799	12.8%	9	8
Public	Univ. of Mass. Med. Sch. - Worcester	78,873	73,238	5,636	7.7%	6	5
Private	University of Miami	111,804	87,035	24,769	28.5%	12	0
Public	University of Michigan - Ann Arbor	417,279	335,931	81,348	24.2%	0	0
Public	University of Minnesota - Twin Cities	277,472	227,947	49,525	21.7%	3	2
Public	University of Missouri - Columbia	76,181	91,664	-15,483	-16.9%	-14	-7
Public	University of Nebraska - Lincoln	83,116	83,179	-63	-0.1%	-3	0
Public	University of Nebraska Medical Ctr.	45,369	51,191	-5,822	-11.4%	-11	-8
Public	University of Nevada - Reno	26,423	39,694	-13,271	-33.4%	-23	-17
Public	Univ. of New Hampshire - Durham	42,703	45,009	-2,306	-5.1%	-3	0
Public	Univ. of New Mexico - Albuquerque	72,335	74,215	-1,881	-2.5%	-3	-3
Public	Univ. of North Carolina - Chapel Hill	311,621	183,161	128,460	70.1%	19	11
Public	University of North Dakota	21,914	19,435	2,478	12.8%	11	9
Private	University of Notre Dame	52,326	29,597	22,730	76.8%	38	5
Public	University of Oklahoma - Norman	39,237	43,994	-4,757	-10.8%	-8	-6
Public	University of Oklahoma HSC	34,822	28,128	6,694	23.8%	11	12
Public	University of Oregon	25,323	21,868	3,455	15.8%	9	7
Private	University of Pennsylvania	258,374	272,014	-13,640	-5.0%	-8	-4
Public	University of Pittsburgh - Pittsburgh	272,567	216,973	55,594	25.6%	7	5
Public	University of Rhode Island	27,521	25,023	2,498	10.0%	7	4
Private	University of Rochester	113,209	143,418	-30,209	-21.1%	-25	-8
Public	Univ. of South Carolina - Columbia	59,142	50,755	8,388	16.5%	15	13
Public	University of South Florida - Tampa	142,368	107,653	34,715	32.2%	15	11
Private	University of Southern California	212,130	184,823	27,307	14.8%	-1	0
Public	University of Tennessee - Knoxville	55,591	70,837	-15,246	-21.5%	-13	-9
Public	University of Tennessee HSC	22,123	30,358	-8,235	-27.1%	-15	-9
Public	University of Texas - Austin	171,585	170,680	905	0.5%	-4	-2
Public	University of Texas HSC - Houston	76,222	63,388	12,834	20.2%	12	11
Public	Univ. of Texas HSC - San Antonio	56,323	59,128	-2,806	-4.7%	-5	-2
Public	U. of Texas MD Anderson Cancer Ctr.	259,243	159,384	99,859	62.7%	17	10
Public	U. of Texas Med. Branch - Galveston	58,050	72,368	-14,317	-19.8%	-10	-7
Public	Univ. of Texas SW Med. Ctr. - Dallas	141,732	133,228	8,504	6.4%	-4	-5
Public	University of Utah	155,229	101,620	53,609	52.8%	23	17
Public	University of Vermont	35,657	48,047	-12,391	-25.8%	-20	-14
Public	University of Virginia	110,134	97,620	12,515	12.8%	4	6
Public	University of Washington - Seattle	355,819	293,833	61,986	21.1%	5	4
Public	University of Wisconsin - Madison	321,153	331,451	-10,297	-3.1%	-4	-3

Federal Research in Constant 1983 Dollars						Non-Federal Research in Constant 1983 Dollars					
2014 Federal Research x $1000	2005 Federal Research x $1000	Net Change in Constant Dollars	Percent Change in Constant Dollars	Net Change in National Rank	Net Change in Control Rank	2014 Non-Federal Research x $1000	2005 Non-Federal Research x $1000	Net Change in Constant Dollars	Percent Change in Constant Dollars	Net Change in National Rank	Net Change in Control Rank
16,117	19,607	-3,490	-17.8%	-10	-8	14,051	18,189	-4,138	-22.7%	-38	-25
65,757	82,297	-16,540	-20.1%	-11	-8	45,001	49,884	-4,883	-9.8%	-26	-14
109,626	120,431	-10,805	-9.0%	-1	0	85,555	87,099	-1,544	-1.8%	-10	-4
76,347	89,852	-13,505	-15.0%	-10	-7	66,110	48,918	17,192	35.1%	0	6
28,933	26,865	2,068	7.7%	7	5	26,466	21,452	5,014	23.4%	-5	3
13,847	19,137	-5,290	-27.6%	-15	-13	12,666	11,496	1,170	10.2%	-9	-1
45,801	59,302	-13,502	-22.8%	-15	-11	59,306	68,051	-8,745	-12.9%	-24	-12
20,628	27,868	-7,240	-26.0%	-17	-13	32,591	25,434	7,157	28.1%	4	9
16,415	12,023	4,392	36.5%	32	25	16,356	19,152	-2,796	-14.6%	-29	-17
71,970	53,686	18,284	34.1%	16	12	55,431	72,730	-17,299	-23.8%	-30	-16
15,324	18,014	-2,690	-14.9%	-5	-5	5,653	6,267	-614	-9.8%	-15	-8
107,231	81,402	25,829	31.7%	22	14	46,765	59,238	-12,473	-21.1%	-30	-16
33,485	27,792	5,692	20.5%	15	11	26,260	25,153	1,107	4.4%	-17	-5
59,866	54,271	5,595	10.3%	0	-1	19,007	18,966	41	0.2%	-18	-8
66,139	64,811	1,328	2.0%	2	2	45,665	22,224	23,441	105.5%	29	2
239,285	230,290	8,995	3.9%	1	0	177,993	105,640	72,353	68.5%	8	8
157,683	132,801	24,882	18.7%	5	1	119,789	95,146	24,643	25.9%	1	1
33,518	39,885	-6,367	-16.0%	-6	-5	42,663	51,780	-9,116	-17.6%	-30	-17
30,389	31,006	-617	-2.0%	4	2	52,727	52,173	554	1.1%	-22	-11
24,847	20,467	4,380	21.4%	16	13	20,522	30,724	-10,203	-33.2%	-47	-30
16,600	25,055	-8,455	-33.7%	-24	-18	9,823	14,639	-4,816	-32.9%	-36	-20
29,232	32,665	-3,433	-10.5%	1	-1	13,472	12,345	1,127	9.1%	-14	-5
49,268	53,805	-4,537	-8.4%	-6	-4	23,067	20,410	2,656	13.0%	-9	-1
196,290	133,018	63,272	47.6%	13	6	115,331	50,143	65,188	130.0%	26	18
13,106	13,328	-222	-1.7%	12	8	8,807	6,107	2,700	44.2%	14	14
25,825	21,210	4,614	21.8%	16	4	26,502	8,387	18,115	216.0%	66	10
17,356	17,497	-141	-0.8%	7	5	21,881	26,497	-4,616	-17.4%	-31	-18
17,979	18,956	-977	-5.2%	4	3	16,843	9,172	7,671	83.6%	31	30
20,487	18,092	2,395	13.2%	13	10	4,836	3,776	1,060	28.1%	5	6
197,654	193,232	4,422	2.3%	2	0	60,719	78,782	-18,062	-22.9%	-29	-14
184,380	174,553	9,827	5.6%	3	2	88,187	42,420	45,767	107.9%	28	23
20,165	17,497	2,667	15.2%	18	13	7,356	7,525	-169	-2.3%	-14	-7
86,640	106,939	-20,298	-19.0%	-16	-6	26,569	36,480	-9,911	-27.2%	-39	-16
28,646	27,034	1,612	6.0%	5	3	30,497	23,721	6,776	28.6%	1	7
66,901	59,213	7,688	13.0%	9	6	75,467	48,440	27,027	55.8%	6	10
137,577	137,101	476	0.3%	-3	1	74,553	47,722	26,831	56.2%	8	-4
34,820	29,550	5,270	17.8%	14	10	20,770	41,287	-20,516	-49.7%	-60	-39
13,641	19,700	-6,059	-30.8%	-20	-16	8,482	10,658	-2,176	-20.4%	-25	-15
102,381	105,706	-3,325	-3.1%	-1	-1	69,204	64,975	4,230	6.5%	-12	-2
44,397	46,725	-2,328	-5.0%	-5	-3	31,825	16,663	15,162	91.0%	35	31
29,122	39,505	-10,384	-26.3%	-13	-10	27,201	19,623	7,578	38.6%	8	10
51,845	66,844	-14,998	-22.4%	-16	-12	207,398	92,540	114,858	124.1%	14	13
33,184	48,688	-15,503	-31.8%	-25	-20	24,866	23,680	1,186	5.0%	-16	-5
60,373	83,914	-23,541	-28.1%	-20	-15	81,359	49,314	32,045	65.0%	11	11
92,653	70,041	22,612	32.3%	16	10	62,576	31,579	30,997	98.2%	24	22
25,999	33,174	-7,175	-21.6%	-12	-12	9,658	14,874	-5,216	-35.1%	-39	-23
62,907	82,481	-19,574	-23.7%	-15	-11	47,227	15,139	32,089	212.0%	63	54
277,091	251,803	25,288	10.0%	0	0	78,728	42,029	36,699	87.3%	22	19
170,306	198,340	-28,034	-14.1%	-8	-4	150,847	133,111	17,736	13.3%	-6	-5

Change: Research	Total Research in Constant 1983 Dollars					
Institutions with Over $40 Million in Federal Research, Alphabetically	2014 Total Research x $1000	2005 Total Research x $1000	Net Change in Constant Dollars	Percent Change in Constant Dollars	Net Change in National Rank	Net Change in Control Rank
Public	Utah State University	54,542	54,663	-121	-0.2%	-5	-4
Private	Vanderbilt University	215,036	145,535	69,501	47.8%	10	5
Public	Virginia Commonwealth University	57,896	60,677	-2,782	-4.6%	-5	-2
Public	Virginia Polytechnic Inst. and St. Univ.	163,861	120,435	43,426	36.1%	15	10
Private	Wake Forest University	57,518	76,894	-19,376	-25.2%	-23	-6
Public	Washington State Univ. - Pullman	93,898	75,866	18,032	23.8%	6	5
Private	Washington University in St. Louis	210,907	220,876	-9,969	-4.5%	-10	-4
Public	Wayne State University	69,542	93,995	-24,453	-26.0%	-23	-13
Private	Weill Cornell Medical College	95,805	74,090	21,716	29.3%	13	4
Public	West Virginia University	51,180	47,925	3,255	6.8%	6	6
Private	Woods Hole Oceanographic Inst.	71,747	48,805	22,942	47.0%	26	6
Private	Yale University	249,141	179,251	69,890	39.0%	10	3
Private	Yeshiva University	100,056	80,196	19,860	24.8%	8	2

Federal Research in Constant 1983 Dollars						Non-Federal Research in Constant 1983 Dollars					
2014 Federal Research x $1000	2005 Federal Research x $1000	Net Change in Constant Dollars	Percent Change in Constant Dollars	Net Change in National Rank	Net Change in Control Rank	2014 Non-Federal Research x $1000	2005 Non-Federal Research x $1000	Net Change in Constant Dollars	Percent Change in Constant Dollars	Net Change in National Rank	Net Change in Control Rank
37,200	38,482	-1,282	-3.3%	6	5	17,342	16,182	1,161	7.2%	-9	-1
133,291	116,988	16,304	13.9%	4	1	81,745	28,547	53,198	186.3%	46	9
38,971	40,418	-1,447	-3.6%	6	5	18,925	20,260	-1,335	-6.6%	-24	-12
64,598	45,617	18,980	41.6%	17	12	99,263	74,817	24,446	32.7%	5	5
49,916	58,842	-8,926	-15.2%	-7	-2	7,602	18,052	-10,450	-57.9%	-73	-20
36,708	33,316	3,392	10.2%	11	7	57,189	42,550	14,640	34.4%	-1	4
133,739	166,410	-32,672	-19.6%	-9	-4	77,169	54,465	22,703	41.7%	1	-2
36,721	50,077	-13,356	-26.7%	-18	-13	32,820	43,918	-11,098	-25.3%	-27	-15
45,496	51,181	-5,686	-11.1%	-9	-3	50,310	22,908	27,401	119.6%	31	2
21,995	25,952	-3,956	-15.2%	-6	-4	29,185	21,973	7,212	32.8%	4	7
57,921	41,840	16,080	38.4%	18	5	13,827	6,965	6,862	98.5%	26	2
155,088	138,171	16,917	12.2%	-1	1	94,053	41,080	52,973	129.0%	35	7
60,943	66,819	-5,876	-8.8%	-6	-1	39,113	13,377	25,736	192.4%	64	10

Change: Private Support & Doctorates	Endowment Assets in Constant 1998 Dollars					
Institutions with Over $40 Million in Federal Research, Alphabetically	2015 Endowment Assets x $1000	2006 Endowment Assets x $1000	Net Change in Constant Dollars	Percent Change in Constant Dollars	Net Change in National Rank	Net Change in Control Rank
Public Arizona State University	379,159	288,122	91,037	31.6%	-2	-1
Public Auburn University	378,455	244,647	133,808	54.7%	21	12
Public Augusta University	124,146	83,027	41,119	49.5%	48	1
Private Baylor College of Medicine	645,695	773,145	-127,450	-16.5%	-24	-15
Private Boston University	969,207	668,509	300,698	45.0%	14	10
Private Brandeis University	539,444	423,031	116,412	27.5%	9	10
Private Brown University	1,811,739	1,581,209	230,530	14.6%	-5	-1
Private California Institute of Technology	1,296,244	1,153,757	142,487	12.3%	-4	-1
Private Carnegie Mellon University	1,025,420	685,706	339,714	49.5%	13	9
Private Case Western Reserve University	1,046,951	1,166,633	-119,682	-10.3%	-17	-11
Public Clemson University	382,356	250,851	131,505	52.4%	21	12
Public Cleveland State University	44,154	23,792	20,361	85.6%	94	19
Private Cold Spring Harbor Laboratory						
Public Colorado State Univ. - Fort Collins	165,859	111,094	54,765	49.3%	42	9
Private Columbia University	5,682,229	4,333,417	1,348,812	31.1%	-4	-2
Private Cornell University	2,806,350	2,584,856	221,494	8.6%	0	0
Private Dartmouth College	2,749,128	2,256,615	492,513	21.8%	-1	-1
Private Drexel University	394,014	384,453	9,561	2.5%	-23	-10
Private Duke University	4,301,313	3,282,435	1,018,879	31.0%	1	1
Private Emory University	3,940,398	3,554,140	386,258	10.9%	-4	-4
Public Florida International University	105,373	58,591	46,783	79.8%	74	7
Public Florida State University	356,810	365,365	-8,555	-2.3%	-30	-17
Public George Mason University	42,588	34,141	8,447	24.7%	-27	-18
Private George Washington University	952,842	703,306	249,536	35.5%	6	4
Private Georgetown University	901,268	609,016	292,252	48.0%	12	11
Public Georgia Institute of Technology	1,095,867	966,562	129,305	13.4%	0	-3
Private Harvard University	21,486,578	21,102,682	383,895	1.8%	0	0
Private Icahn School of Med. at Mount Sinai	422,891					
Public Indiana University - Bloomington	566,288	484,297	81,991	16.9%	-2	-4
Public Indiana U. - Purdue U. - Indianapolis	486,446	447,044	39,402	8.8%	-10	-7
Public Iowa State University	463,468	361,994	101,474	28.0%	8	-2
Private Johns Hopkins University	2,011,738	1,715,577	296,161	17.3%	-4	-1
Public Kansas State University	288,228	214,957	73,271	34.1%	16	3
Public Louisiana State Univ. - Baton Rouge	252,219	242,435	9,784	4.0%	-28	-13
Private Massachusetts Inst. of Technology	7,943,361	6,107,015	1,836,346	30.1%	0	0
Private Medical College of Wisconsin	458,817	322,698	136,119	42.2%	18	15
Public Medical University of South Carolina	190,199	83,721	106,477	127.2%	113	29
Public Michigan State University	1,576,118	764,679	811,439	106.1%	23	6
Public Mississippi State University	264,748	173,352	91,396	52.7%	24	2
Public Montana State University - Bozeman	84,099	67,763	16,335	24.1%	-5	-12
Public Naval Postgraduate School	2,998					
Public New Jersey Institute of Technology	58,512	42,715	15,797	37.0%	19	-7
Public New Mexico State Univ. - Las Cruces	130,282	105,587	24,695	23.4%	16	-5
Private New York University	2,108,158	1,295,176	812,982	62.8%	4	2
Public North Carolina State University	580,056	300,895	279,161	92.8%	51	17
Private Northeastern University	429,981	434,858	-4,877	-1.1%	-27	-15
Private Northwestern University	6,008,795	3,751,660	2,257,136	60.2%	4	2
Public Ohio State University - Columbus	2,142,176	1,457,293	684,883	47.0%	3	1
Public Oregon Health & Science University	336,806	267,526	69,279	25.9%	-2	-2

Annual Giving in Constant 1998 Dollars						Doctorates Awarded					
2015 Annual Giving x $1000	2006 Annual Giving x $1000	Net Change in Constant Dollars	Percent Change in Constant Dollars	Net Change in National Rank	Net Change in Control Rank	2015 Doctorates Awarded	2006 Doctorates Awarded	Net Change in Doctorates	Percent Change in Doctorates	Net Change in National Rank	Net Change in Control Rank
77,092	108,561	-31,470	-29.0%	-28	-17	687	314	373	118.8%	37	24
62,695	42,812	19,884	46.4%	11	6	257	164	93	56.7%	18	9
7,163	6,681	482	7.2%	55	13	29	13	16	123.1%	94	13
36,346	40,083	-3,737	-9.3%	-19	-2	111	45	66	146.7%	89	54
82,762	69,407	13,355	19.2%	-1	1	484	491	-7	-1.4%	-14	-3
35,486	58,316	-22,831	-39.1%	-57	-16	100	93	7	7.5%	-11	6
110,681	92,258	18,423	20.0%	1	-2	215	209	6	2.9%	-16	0
95,457	85,760	9,698	11.3%	-4	0	182	177	5	2.8%	-21	-2
82,272	52,912	29,360	55.5%	17	7	333	245	88	35.9%	8	2
78,301	48,257	30,044	62.3%	24	8	197	243	-46	-18.9%	-29	-8
48,257	36,952	11,305	30.6%	4	0	237	136	101	74.3%	33	17
10,453	4,801	5,652	117.7%	235	75	59	30	29	96.7%	68	13
24,371	23,135	1,236	5.3%	-5	-6	251	186	65	34.9%	4	-3
325,806	275,336	50,470	18.3%	1	2	564	579	-15	-2.6%	-6	-1
256,117	207,526	48,591	23.4%	-5	-5	487	476	11	2.3%	-10	0
129,001	115,618	13,384	11.6%	-1	-1	85	60	25	41.7%	20	18
52,416	31,581	20,835	66.0%	26	10	213	141	72	51.1%	22	12
278,249	242,318	35,930	14.8%	-3	-1	485	271	214	79.0%	26	9
134,426	83,852	50,574	60.3%	15	7	264	204	60	29.4%	1	5
13,742	10,138	3,604	35.5%	76	29	189	88	101	114.8%	59	28
40,460	36,669	3,791	10.3%	-4	-6	424	325	99	30.5%	2	3
31,340	16,992	14,348	84.4%	70	28	249	163	86	52.8%	18	8
146,214	38,947	107,266	275.4%	73	27	222	278	-56	-20.1%	-33	-7
101,660	71,663	29,997	41.9%	8	4	114	84	30	35.7%	19	17
70,220	69,901	319	0.5%	-19	-14	526	400	126	31.5%	2	-2
616,542	434,188	182,354	42.0%	0	0	745	627	118	18.8%	5	3
64,688						28	11	17	154.5%	117	98
124,662	49,161	75,501	153.6%	46	30	538	389	149	38.3%	10	3
71,913	28,811	43,101	149.6%	61	39	69	63	6	9.5%	-15	-20
62,199	40,327	21,873	54.2%	16	9	336	281	55	19.6%	-3	-2
343,487	275,380	68,107	24.7%	1	2	535	408	127	31.1%	3	4
57,826	38,803	19,023	49.0%	14	6	190	160	30	18.8%	-5	-6
77,085	47,808	29,277	61.2%	24	16	331	252	79	31.3%	5	4
259,029	171,904	87,124	50.7%	4	0	606	602	4	0.7%	-4	0
12,325						26	30	-4	-13.3%	-30	0
18,568	21,792	-3,224	-14.8%	-17	-8	191	29	162	558.6%	205	95
77,519	66,145	11,373	17.2%	-3	-1	577	463	114	24.6%	3	-1
33,517	53,000	-19,483	-36.8%	-52	-38	146	111	35	31.5%	13	-1
7,840						79	40	39	97.5%	59	16
						15	9	6	66.7%	60	-5
5,200	5,036	164	3.3%	38	1	65	75	-10	-13.3%	-38	-33
9,767	76,632	-66,865	-87.3%	-234	-119	131	79	52	65.8%	44	17
259,181	204,285	54,896	26.9%	-2	-2	438	440	-2	-0.5%	-13	-2
70,239	100,931	-30,692	-30.4%	-37	-24	512	369	143	38.8%	8	2
35,286	14,235	21,050	147.9%	105	66	157	102	55	53.9%	29	21
316,462	184,933	131,529	71.1%	7	4	438	423	15	3.5%	-12	-1
212,101	153,195	58,906	38.5%	1	3	832	664	168	25.3%	6	4
83,130						43	61	-18	-29.5%	-61	-45

Change: Private Support & Doctorates		Endowment Assets in Constant 1998 Dollars					
Institutions with Over $40 Million in Federal Research, Alphabetically		2015 Endowment Assets x $1000	2006 Endowment Assets x $1000	Net Change in Constant Dollars	Percent Change in Constant Dollars	Net Change in National Rank	Net Change in Control Rank
Public	Oregon State University	297,915	279,772	18,143	6.5%	-23	-13
Public	Penn. St. Univ. - Hershey Med. Ctr.	257,192	145,200	111,991	77.1%	47	10
Public	Pennsylvania State Univ. - Univ. Park	1,093,064	714,190	378,874	53.0%	15	4
Private	Princeton University	13,395,487	9,520,168	3,875,319	40.7%	1	1
Public	Purdue University - West Lafayette	1,413,563	1,089,996	323,568	29.7%	1	-2
Private	Rensselaer Polytechnic Institute	398,824	498,376	-99,552	-20.0%	-51	-30
Private	Rice University	3,276,134	2,909,467	366,666	12.6%	-1	0
Private	Rockefeller University	1,171,352	1,293,172	-121,820	-9.4%	-13	-7
Private	Rush University	327,532	282,856	44,676	15.8%	-14	-6
Public	Rutgers University - New Brunswick	419,018	369,183	49,835	13.5%	-11	-9
Public	San Diego State University	123,425	71,512	51,913	72.6%	74	8
Private	Scripps Research Institute						
Private	Stanford University	13,100,433	10,278,997	2,821,437	27.4%	-1	-1
Public	Stony Brook University	145,841	55,861	89,979	161.1%	156	39
Public	Temple University	227,683	149,009	78,673	52.8%	24	-3
Public	Texas A&M Univ. - College Station	5,810,691	3,789,197	2,021,494	53.3%	0	0
Private	Thomas Jefferson University	258,054					
Private	Tufts University	939,085	887,008	52,076	5.9%	-8	-3
Private	Tulane University	719,464	626,404	93,059	14.9%	3	4
Public	Uniformed Services Univ. of the HS						
Public	University at Albany	32,310	14,664	17,647	120.3%	106	26
Public	University at Buffalo	365,075	364,631	444	0.1%	-27	-14
Public	University of Alabama - Birmingham	228,965	252,752	-23,787	-9.4%	-45	-23
Public	University of Alabama - Huntsville	38,894	19,824	19,070	96.2%	88	19
Public	University of Alaska - Fairbanks	111,696	128,311	-16,615	-12.9%	-63	-37
Public	University of Arizona	452,701	340,563	112,138	32.9%	11	0
Public	Univ. of Arkansas for Med. Sciences	19,237					
Public	University of California - Berkeley	2,384,793	1,798,307	586,487	32.6%	0	0
Public	University of California - Davis	597,715	402,852	194,863	48.4%	22	5
Public	University of California - Irvine	302,357	138,225	164,132	118.7%	82	25
Public	University of California - Los Angeles	2,059,656	1,395,429	664,226	47.6%	1	0
Public	University of California - Riverside	109,255	69,807	39,448	56.5%	51	3
Public	University of California - San Diego	560,831	308,307	252,524	81.9%	46	14
Public	Univ. of California - San Francisco	1,252,670	844,984	407,686	48.2%	9	0
Public	Univ. of California - Santa Barbara	156,766	110,810	45,956	41.5%	36	5
Public	University of California - Santa Cruz	96,873	71,119	25,754	36.2%	17	-10
Public	University of Central Florida	88,795	70,365	18,429	26.2%	3	-12
Private	University of Chicago	4,450,554	3,551,939	898,615	25.3%	0	0
Public	University of Cincinnati - Cincinnati	704,982	803,583	-98,600	-12.3%	-16	-7
Public	University of Colorado - Boulder	352,730	215,403	137,328	63.8%	35	12
Public	University of Colorado - Denver	290,000	146,474	143,526	98.0%	62	17
Public	Univ. of Connecticut - Health Center	60,984	71,053	-10,070	-14.2%	-83	-36
Public	University of Connecticut - Storrs	164,883	144,260	20,622	14.3%	-16	-16
Private	University of Dayton	294,990	257,929	37,061	14.4%	-12	-5
Public	University of Delaware	790,739	892,694	-101,954	-11.4%	-17	-8
Public	University of Florida	917,087	727,060	190,027	26.1%	2	0
Public	University of Georgia	592,440	378,637	213,803	56.5%	28	5
Public	University of Hawaii - Manoa	165,184	142,228	22,956	16.1%	-11	-14
Public	University of Houston - Univ. Park	417,034	255,129	161,906	63.5%	28	11

Annual Giving in Constant 1998 Dollars						Doctorates Awarded					
2015 Annual Giving x $1000	2006 Annual Giving x $1000	Net Change in Constant Dollars	Percent Change in Constant Dollars	Net Change in National Rank	Net Change in Control Rank	2015 Doctorates Awarded	2006 Doctorates Awarded	Net Change in Doctorates	Percent Change in Doctorates	Net Change in National Rank	Net Change in Control Rank
58,548	48,047	10,501	21.9%	-3	-5	215	166	49	29.5%	2	-4
20,646	21,199	-553	-2.6%	-6	-4	26	20	6	30.0%	28	-13
91,760	83,620	8,140	9.7%	-3	-4	673	646	27	4.2%	-4	-4
324,131	151,078	173,053	114.5%	16	8	371	288	83	28.8%	5	0
101,523	118,036	-16,513	-14.0%	-15	-9	717	566	151	26.7%	7	2
22,616	30,082	-7,467	-24.8%	-38	-17	164	146	18	12.3%	-7	3
72,029	50,864	21,165	41.6%	10	5	176	147	29	19.7%	-2	3
10,942	64,497	-53,555	-83.0%	-203	-105	28	28	0	0.0%	-4	18
2,175						17	30	-13	-43.3%	-82	-28
75,365	48,875	26,490	54.2%	18	12	597	393	204	51.9%	14	5
44,823	32,756	12,067	36.8%	10	5	140	49	91	185.7%	108	50
957,959	664,967	292,992	44.1%	0	0	688	677	11	1.6%	-4	0
51,102	26,319	24,783	94.2%	36	22	347	367	-20	-5.4%	-17	-14
34,658	30,566	4,092	13.4%	1	-2	197	383	-186	-48.6%	-64	-49
150,428	106,435	43,993	41.3%	8	5	740	535	205	38.3%	10	5
22,878	2,124	20,754	977.3%	591	395	21	17	4	23.5%	24	39
36,626	149,495	-112,869	-75.5%	-94	-28	116	105	11	10.5%	-8	7
52,125	53,370	-1,245	-2.3%	-25	-7	123	96	27	28.1%	10	14
5,564	62,564	-57,000	-91.1%	-359	-159	164	144	20	13.9%	-5	-9
18,018	20,772	-2,754	-13.3%	-13	-6	342	353	-11	-3.1%	-14	-11
45,163	54,937	-9,774	-17.8%	-39	-28	170	143	27	18.9%	2	-3
1,198	3,807	-2,610	-68.5%	-229	-118	33	31	2	6.5%	1	-17
16,426	14,771	1,655	11.2%	27	6	40	21	19	90.5%	80	8
112,113	88,320	23,793	26.9%	6	4	528	395	133	33.7%	6	0
9,912						38	20	18	90.0%	77	8
215,825	179,506	36,319	20.2%	-3	1	826	763	63	8.3%	-4	-4
109,553	56,684	52,869	93.3%	27	19	553	413	140	33.9%	3	-1
39,271	61,358	-22,087	-36.0%	-53	-39	390	266	124	46.6%	14	11
278,954	233,230	45,724	19.6%	0	0	774	708	66	9.3%	0	-1
10,013	22,095	-12,083	-54.7%	-114	-41	272	165	107	64.8%	22	11
100,839	134,958	-34,119	-25.3%	-20	-13	505	358	147	41.1%	11	5
358,758	146,840	211,918	144.3%	21	9	130	128	2	1.6%	-14	-13
37,382	40,552	-3,170	-7.8%	-18	-17	349	339	10	2.9%	-11	-8
14,638	19,012	-4,374	-23.0%	-21	-7	151	136	15	11.0%	-3	-7
19,323	22,696	-3,373	-14.9%	-22	-11	286	177	109	61.6%	17	8
261,615	173,048	88,567	51.2%	5	2	392	398	-6	-1.5%	-16	-3
70,563	51,601	18,962	36.7%	4	1	213	264	-51	-19.3%	-32	-25
89,340	25,742	63,599	247.1%	85	56	434	310	124	40.0%	10	8
100,865	30,890	69,974	226.5%	77	51	103	90	13	14.4%	-5	-13
4,996	6,939	-1,943	-28.0%	-58	-29	16	0	16		219	30
24,023	27,756	-3,733	-13.4%	-26	-16	323	307	16	5.2%	-12	-8
16,635	15,486	1,149	7.4%	19	14	34	29	5	17.2%	21	32
26,466	34,650	-8,184	-23.6%	-33	-20	237	222	15	6.8%	-12	-12
127,084	114,235	12,850	11.2%	-1	0	754	718	36	5.0%	-2	-3
61,372	50,709	10,663	21.0%	-6	-7	467	374	93	24.9%	1	-2
53,438	16,415	37,024	225.6%	109	54	239	156	83	53.2%	20	9
56,357	15,183	41,174	271.2%	119	56	326	236	90	38.1%	10	6

Change: Private Support & Doctorates		Endowment Assets in Constant 1998 Dollars					
Institutions with Over $40 Million in Federal Research, Alphabetically		2015 Endowment Assets x $1000	2006 Endowment Assets x $1000	Net Change in Constant Dollars	Percent Change in Constant Dollars	Net Change in National Rank	Net Change in Control Rank
Public	University of Idaho	141,246	123,776	17,470	14.1%	-6	-12
Public	University of Illinois - Chicago	178,100	118,810	59,290	49.9%	41	5
Public	Univ. of Illinois - Urbana-Champaign	902,323	630,606	271,717	43.1%	11	1
Public	University of Iowa	744,564	607,828	136,736	22.5%	6	0
Public	University of Kansas - Lawrence	689,900	597,346	92,554	15.5%	2	-2
Public	University of Kansas Medical Center	194,587	160,824	33,764	21.0%	-3	-11
Public	University of Kentucky	673,635	573,036	100,599	17.6%	1	-2
Public	University of Louisville	497,708	496,447	1,261	0.3%	-18	-11
Public	University of Maine - Orono	165,578	136,963	28,615	20.9%	-2	-11
Public	University of Maryland - Baltimore	150,917	126,088	24,829	19.7%	-2	-10
Public	Univ. of Maryland - Baltimore County	44,656	31,721	12,935	40.8%	18	-4
Public	University of Maryland - College Park	284,509	274,399	10,110	3.7%	-24	-13
Public	Univ. of Massachusetts - Amherst	179,199	77,865	101,334	130.1%	121	29
Public	Univ. of Mass. Med. Sch. - Worcester	114,511	36,084	78,427	217.3%	227	57
Private	University of Miami	523,080	452,793	70,287	15.5%	-3	1
Public	University of Michigan - Ann Arbor	5,866,771	4,125,021	1,741,750	42.2%	-1	0
Public	University of Minnesota - Twin Cities	1,943,853	1,623,300	320,553	19.7%	-4	-3
Public	University of Missouri - Columbia	505,479	465,744	39,735	8.5%	-9	-7
Public	University of Nebraska - Lincoln	534,179	547,214	-13,035	-2.4%	-13	-9
Public	University of Nebraska Medical Ctr.	133,272	126,280	6,992	5.5%	-18	-21
Public	University of Nevada - Reno	180,733	58,235	122,498	210.4%	181	48
Public	Univ. of New Hampshire - Durham	204,513	154,144	50,369	32.7%	7	-8
Public	Univ. of New Mexico - Albuquerque	237,963	201,528	36,436	18.1%	-6	-8
Public	Univ. of North Carolina - Chapel Hill	1,761,901	838,702	923,199	110.1%	20	5
Public	University of North Dakota	135,939					
Private	University of Notre Dame	5,050,218	3,237,848	1,812,370	56.0%	4	4
Public	University of Oklahoma - Norman	628,476	483,578	144,898	30.0%	8	2
Public	University of Oklahoma HSC	269,347	217,260	52,087	24.0%	7	-4
Public	University of Oregon	423,916	267,004	156,912	58.8%	24	11
Private	University of Pennsylvania	5,973,739	3,877,623	2,096,116	54.1%	1	0
Public	University of Pittsburgh - Pittsburgh	2,115,583	1,315,726	799,856	60.8%	4	2
Public	University of Rhode Island	77,611	58,234	19,376	33.3%	9	-11
Private	University of Rochester	1,208,592	1,088,332	120,260	11.0%	-6	-3
Public	Univ. of South Carolina - Columbia	368,547	281,192	87,355	31.1%	-4	-2
Public	University of South Florida - Tampa	246,066	240,711	5,355	2.2%	-29	-14
Private	University of Southern California	2,776,257	2,237,519	538,737	24.1%	1	1
Public	University of Tennessee - Knoxville	358,931	457,960	-99,030	-21.6%	-56	-23
Public	University of Tennessee HSC						
Public	University of Texas - Austin	6,194,345	4,574,683	1,619,662	35.4%	0	0
Public	University of Texas HSC - Houston	180,442	114,687	65,756	57.3%	49	9
Public	Univ. of Texas HSC - San Antonio	280,975	252,682	28,292	11.2%	-14	-9
Public	U. of Texas MD Anderson Cancer Ctr.	707,837	334,049	373,788	111.9%	61	21
Public	U. of Texas Med. Branch - Galveston	313,356	315,399	-2,043	-0.6%	-28	-14
Public	U. of Texas SW Medical Ctr. - Dallas	955,285	834,472	120,813	14.5%	-2	-2
Public	University of Utah	603,061	371,538	231,523	62.3%	32	8
Public	University of Vermont	267,428	206,237	61,191	29.7%	12	-1
Public	University of Virginia	3,643,414	2,640,542	1,002,872	38.0%	1	0
Public	University of Washington - Seattle	1,813,435	1,233,018	580,418	47.1%	2	0
Public	University of Wisconsin - Madison	1,646,251	1,196,153	450,098	37.6%	0	-1

Annual Giving in Constant 1998 Dollars						Doctorates Awarded					
2015 Annual Giving x $1000	2006 Annual Giving x $1000	Net Change in Constant Dollars	Percent Change in Constant Dollars	Net Change in National Rank	Net Change in Control Rank	2015 Doctorates Awarded	2006 Doctorates Awarded	Net Change in Doctorates	Percent Change in Doctorates	Net Change in National Rank	Net Change in Control Rank
11,412	17,518	-6,107	-34.9%	-62	-20	80	105	-25	-23.8%	-56	-42
36,897	31,951	4,946	15.5%	3	-2	314	311	3	1.0%	-16	-12
104,480	93,646	10,834	11.6%	-3	0	829	689	140	20.3%	3	2
94,044	74,604	19,440	26.1%	1	-1	453	364	89	24.5%	4	1
104,167	57,472	46,695	81.2%	22	14	365	271	94	34.7%	8	7
26,042	14,550	11,492	79.0%	74	23	25	30	-5	-16.7%	-36	-32
69,673	47,910	21,763	45.4%	11	5	295	256	39	15.2%	-4	-4
50,879	44,621	6,258	14.0%	-10	-9	170	144	26	18.1%	-1	-5
12,782	13,398	-617	-4.6%	12	3	69	38	31	81.6%	54	12
40,766	42,201	-1,436	-3.4%	-15	-12	81	150	-69	-46.0%	-90	-58
4,517	10,975	-6,458	-58.8%	-209	-81	100	89	11	12.4%	-5	-13
72,328	54,018	18,311	33.9%	4	2	654	602	52	8.6%	-2	-3
20,825	20,980	-154	-0.7%	-3	-1	268	253	15	5.9%	-10	-9
4,909						61	24	37	154.2%	104	25
114,250	115,640	-1,390	-1.2%	-5	-3	208	195	13	6.7%	-15	1
232,446	183,528	48,918	26.7%	-2	1	882	763	119	15.6%	0	0
202,967	194,851	8,116	4.2%	-8	-3	725	751	-26	-3.5%	-6	-6
64,072	65,336	-1,264	-1.9%	-21	-15	435	277	158	57.0%	17	12
104,531	50,346	54,185	107.6%	40	26	325	245	80	32.7%	5	4
52,497	27,462	25,036	91.2%	37	22	81	60	21	35.0%	13	-2
58,978	23,781	35,198	148.0%	60	33	109	97	12	12.4%	-3	-11
5,662	10,022	-4,360	-43.5%	-119	-45	75	55	20	36.4%	13	-4
40,671	35,381	5,289	14.9%	3	0	222	181	41	22.7%	-4	-9
177,544	172,655	4,888	2.8%	-6	-3	519	490	29	5.9%	-7	-7
5,473						87	110	-23	-20.9%	-46	-34
223,933	131,262	92,671	70.6%	8	1	244	160	84	52.5%	19	10
148,834	70,938	77,896	109.8%	25	14	218	157	61	38.9%	12	3
38,242	17,735	20,507	115.6%	73	32	29	25	4	16.0%	14	-16
85,542	51,457	34,084	66.2%	22	13	199	175	24	13.7%	-8	-9
304,888	298,849	6,039	2.0%	-5	-4	566	496	70	14.1%	-2	1
73,453	85,059	-11,606	-13.6%	-21	-15	438	412	26	6.3%	-10	-10
10,353	7,572	2,782	36.7%	100	36	93	67	26	38.8%	16	-1
63,794	48,160	15,634	32.5%	3	3	267	200	67	33.5%	3	7
66,912	38,149	28,763	75.4%	28	17	358	246	112	45.5%	15	12
35,313	33,824	1,489	4.4%	-5	-6	321	184	137	74.5%	19	9
384,958	296,113	88,846	30.0%	2	2	685	650	35	5.4%	-5	0
70,592	72,080	-1,488	-2.1%	-20	-14	353	317	36	11.4%	-5	-3
9,840											
182,870	128,808	54,062	42.0%	4	3	899	796	103	12.9%	0	0
27,321	26,025	1,296	5.0%	-8	-5	153	100	53	53.0%	28	8
25,209	17,876	7,334	41.0%	35	13	66	30	36	120.0%	77	19
104,287	70,225	34,062	48.5%	12	7						
24,192	26,455	-2,263	-8.6%	-22	-13	39	33	6	18.2%	2	-18
87,979	99,121	-11,142	-11.2%	-17	-10	88	63	25	39.7%	15	-1
74,421						384	276	108	39.1%	10	8
23,850	14,294	9,556	66.9%	69	20	79	61	18	29.5%	3	-10
137,482	157,894	-20,412	-12.9%	-9	-5	366	327	39	11.9%	-5	-2
263,519	230,801	32,718	14.2%	-1	0	687	612	75	12.3%	1	-1
194,803	237,870	-43,067	-18.1%	-14	-7	857	648	209	32.3%	9	6

Change: Private Support & Doctorates		Endowment Assets in Constant 1998 Dollars					
Institutions with Over $40 Million in Federal Research, Alphabetically		2015 Endowment Assets x $1000	2006 Endowment Assets x $1000	Net Change in Constant Dollars	Percent Change in Constant Dollars	Net Change in National Rank	Net Change in Control Rank
Public	Utah State University	185,509	80,511	104,998	130.4%	120	32
Private	Vanderbilt University	2,436,723	2,150,277	286,446	13.3%	0	0
Public	Virginia Commonwealth University	965,688	193,874	771,814	398.1%	146	56
Public	Virginia Polytechnic Inst. and St. Univ.	482,069	326,516	155,553	47.6%	26	5
Private	Wake Forest University	688,182	760,859	-72,677	-9.6%	-17	-10
Public	Washington State Univ. - Pullman	522,166	423,183	98,983	23.4%	3	-3
Private	Washington University in St. Louis	4,019,652	3,418,921	600,731	17.6%	-1	-1
Public	Wayne State University	180,575	147,420	33,155	22.5%	-3	-12
Private	Weill Cornell Medical College	752,783	568,755	184,028	32.4%	14	11
Public	West Virginia University	314,557	277,897	36,660	13.2%	-14	-6
Private	Woods Hole Oceanographic Inst.						
Private	Yale University	15,074,753	13,158,732	1,916,021	14.6%	0	0
Private	Yeshiva University	625,719	929,274	-303,555	-32.7%	-38	-23

Annual Giving in Constant 1998 Dollars						Doctorates Awarded					
2015 Annual Giving x $1000	2006 Annual Giving x $1000	Net Change in Constant Dollars	Percent Change in Constant Dollars	Net Change in National Rank	Net Change in Control Rank	2015 Doctorates Awarded	2006 Doctorates Awarded	Net Change in Doctorates	Percent Change in Doctorates	Net Change in National Rank	Net Change in Control Rank
30,699	22,849	7,850	34.4%	23	9	102	81	21	25.9%	8	-4
71,865	83,861	-11,995	-14.3%	-24	-7	340	253	87	34.4%	7	2
39,647	47,515	-7,868	-16.6%	-26	-21	282	197	85	43.1%	9	1
50,927	54,569	-3,642	-6.7%	-31	-22	488	366	122	33.3%	8	2
58,810	55,025	3,786	6.9%	-20	-5	53	39	14	35.9%	19	25
62,705	37,480	25,226	67.3%	24	15	281	170	111	65.3%	20	9
145,438	92,239	53,198	57.7%	10	3	292	303	-11	-3.6%	-15	-4
28,286	36,367	-8,081	-22.2%	-31	-19	242	187	55	29.4%	0	-6
92,066	88,940	3,126	3.5%	-8	-2	68	36	32	88.9%	56	47
65,071	44,470	20,602	46.3%	14	8	183	168	15	8.9%	-14	-14
259,856	316,341	-56,485	-17.9%	-11	-8	426	318	108	34.0%	4	0
35,028						96	121	-25	-20.7%	-44	-13

Change: Students		SAT Scores					
Institutions with Over $40 Million in Federal Research, Alphabetically		2014 Median SAT	2005 Median SAT	Net Change in SAT	Percent Change in SAT	Net Change in National Rank	Net Change in Control Rank
Public	Arizona State University	1145	1110	35	3.2%	147	14
Public	Auburn University	1220	1110	110	9.9%	277	68
Public	Augusta University	1030					
Private	Baylor College of Medicine						
Private	Boston University	1300	1300	0	0.0%	-1	5
Private	Brandeis University	1365	1350	15	1.1%	1	5
Private	Brown University	1440	1435	5	0.3%	-7	-7
Private	California Institute of Technology	1550	1510	40	2.6%	0	0
Private	Carnegie Mellon University	1440	1380	60	4.3%	12	12
Private	Case Western Reserve University	1370	1340	30	2.2%	11	12
Public	Clemson University	1245	1205	40	3.3%	68	10
Public	Cleveland State University	1010	960	50	5.2%	419	130
Private	Cold Spring Harbor Laboratory						
Public	Colorado State Univ. - Fort Collins	1130	1110	20	1.8%	134	8
Private	Columbia University	1480	1440	40	2.8%	4	4
Private	Cornell University	1420	1385	35	2.5%	2	2
Private	Dartmouth College	1455	1450	5	0.3%	-7	-7
Private	Drexel University	1200	1190	10	0.8%	40	45
Private	Duke University	1460	1430	30	2.1%	6	6
Private	Emory University	1370	1380	-10	-0.7%	-11	-9
Public	Florida International University	1080	1105	-25	-2.3%	-17	-44
Public	Florida State University	1240	1160	80	6.9%	146	29
Public	George Mason University	1150	1105	45	4.1%	206	42
Private	George Washington University	1295	1280	15	1.2%	0	3
Private	Georgetown University	1420	1390	30	2.2%	-1	-1
Public	Georgia Institute of Technology	1400	1335	65	4.9%	24	1
Private	Harvard University	1505	1490	15	1.0%	1	1
Private	Icahn School of Med. at Mount Sinai						
Public	Indiana University - Bloomington	1175	1110	65	5.9%	207	41
Public	Indiana U. - Purdue U. - Indianapolis	1000	995	5	0.5%	134	-1
Public	Iowa State University	1150	1110	40	3.6%	168	26
Private	Johns Hopkins University	1435	1385	50	3.6%	4	4
Public	Kansas State University		1070				
Public	Louisiana State Univ. - Baton Rouge	1170	1125	45	4.0%	145	19
Private	Massachusetts Inst. of Technology	1495	1500	-5	-0.3%	-3	-3
Private	Medical College of Wisconsin						
Public	Medical University of South Carolina						
Public	Michigan State University	1170	1125	45	4.0%	145	19
Public	Mississippi State University	1130	1070	60	5.6%	288	57
Public	Montana State University - Bozeman	1130	1070	60	5.6%	288	57
Public	Naval Postgraduate School						
Public	New Jersey Institute of Technology	1165	1125	40	3.6%	126	13
Public	New Mexico State Univ. - Las Cruces	990	970	20	2.1%	234	43
Private	New York University	1345	1330	15	1.1%	3	6
Public	North Carolina State University	1245	1195	50	4.2%	91	17
Private	Northeastern University	1420	1230	190	15.4%	118	91
Private	Northwestern University	1475	1410	65	4.6%	12	12
Public	Ohio State University - Columbus	1300	1180	120	10.2%	142	39
Public	Oregon Health & Science University						

National Merit and Achievement Scholars						Headcount Enrollment			
2015 National Merit Scholars	2006 National Merit Scholars	Net Change in Merit Scholars	Percent Change in Merit Scholars	Net Change in National Rank	Net Change in Control Rank	Fall 2014 Total Student Headcount	Fall 2005 Total Student Headcount	Net Change in Enrollment	Percent Change in Enrollment
112	190	-78	-41.1%	-7	-4	83,260	51,612	23,703	39.8%
64	31	33	106.5%	39	18	25,912	23,333	2,760	11.9%
3						7,988			
						1,584	1,340	297	23.1%
35	58	-23	-39.7%	-16	-5	32,112	30,957	3,063	10.5%
12	33	-21	-63.6%	-47	-22	5,945	5,189	960	19.3%
76	105	-29	-27.6%	-1	1	9,181	8,261	1,299	16.5%
45	30	15	50.0%	22	11	2,209	2,169	37	1.7%
51	27	24	88.9%	33	18	12,587	10,017	2,831	29.0%
60	51	9	17.6%	15	10	10,771	9,615	1,585	17.3%
55	46	9	19.6%	10	3	21,857	17,165	4,841	28.4%
1	0	1		177	63	16,936	15,482	922	5.8%
4	13	-9	-69.2%	-46	-22	31,354	27,780	3,168	11.2%
78	78	0	0.0%	9	7	27,589	21,983	6,267	29.4%
72	72	0	0.0%	8	5	21,679	19,642	2,059	10.5%
64	79	-15	-19.0%	1	2	6,298	5,780	616	10.8%
7	5	2	40.0%	58	43	26,359	18,466	9,359	55.1%
108	147	-39	-26.5%	-4	0	15,856	14,075	3,633	29.7%
58	61	-3	-4.9%	2	2	14,769	12,134	3,115	26.7%
0	0	0	0.0%	98	31	49,610	36,904	16,382	49.3%
22	17	5	29.4%	23	9	41,226	39,146	4,342	11.8%
1	1	0	0.0%	45	11	33,729	29,728	5,483	19.4%
17	13	4	30.8%	31	22	25,613	24,099	2,196	9.4%
32	60	-28	-46.7%	-26	-11	17,858	13,652	4,694	35.7%
59	117	-58	-49.6%	-14	-9	23,109	17,135	6,466	38.9%
209	362	-153	-42.3%	-3	-2	28,791	25,017	3,940	15.9%
						1,074	663	425	65.5%
68	59	9	15.3%	15	6	46,416	37,958	7,827	20.3%
0	1	-1	-100.0%	-34	-21	30,690	29,933	830	2.8%
33	50	-17	-34.0%	-14	-10	34,435	25,741	7,055	25.8%
47	40	7	17.5%	12	5	21,372	19,225	2,552	13.6%
9	9	0	0.0%	29	9	24,766	23,182	1,716	7.4%
27	45	-18	-40.0%	-21	-10	31,044	34,128	-890	-2.8%
139	159	-20	-12.6%	-1	0	11,319	10,206	979	9.5%
						1,209	1,325	-50	-4.0%
						2,898	2,499	595	25.8%
43	54	-11	-20.4%	-6	-4	50,081	45,166	5,539	12.4%
37	26	11	42.3%	25	10	20,138	16,101	3,965	24.5%
7	4	3	75.0%	68	19	14,982	12,143	2,977	24.8%
						2,869	2,285	836	41.1%
0	0	0	0.0%	98	31	10,646	8,058	1,876	21.4%
0	3	-3	-100.0%	-95	-44	15,829	16,072	-345	-2.1%
12	151	-139	-92.1%	-100	-49	49,274	40,004	11,086	29.0%
5	36	-31	-86.1%	-95	-44	33,989	30,148	4,135	13.9%
85	1	84	8400.0%	270	163	19,798	22,604	-3,146	-13.7%
206	203	3	1.5%	2	1	21,554	18,065	3,929	22.3%
18	120	-102	-85.0%	-72	-39	58,322	50,504	7,591	15.0%
						2,861	2,511	407	16.6%

Change: Students		SAT Scores					
Institutions with Over $40 Million in Federal Research, Alphabetically		2014 Median SAT	2005 Median SAT	Net Change in SAT	Percent Change in SAT	Net Change in National Rank	Net Change in Control Rank
Public	Oregon State University	1105	1080	25	2.3%	150	14
Public	Penn. St. Univ. - Hershey Med. Ctr.						
Public	Pennsylvania State Univ. - Univ. Park	1190	1190	0	0.0%	30	-8
Private	Princeton University	1500	1480	20	1.4%	0	0
Public	Purdue University - West Lafayette	1205	1145	60	5.2%	141	19
Private	Rensselaer Polytechnic Institute	1395	1320	75	5.7%	34	31
Private	Rice University	1470	1435	35	2.4%	4	4
Private	Rockefeller University						
Private	Rush University						
Public	Rutgers University - New Brunswick	1215	1195	20	1.7%	48	1
Public	San Diego State University	1110	1080	30	2.8%	196	31
Private	Scripps Research Institute						
Private	Stanford University	1475	1455	20	1.4%	-2	-2
Public	Stony Brook University	1250	1180	70	5.9%	112	25
Public	Temple University	1120	1090	30	2.8%	155	22
Public	Texas A&M Univ. - College Station	1195	1200	-5	-0.4%	12	-14
Private	Thomas Jefferson University						
Private	Tufts University	1440	1405	35	2.5%	1	1
Private	Tulane University	1360	1350	10	0.7%	-2	2
Public	Uniformed Services Univ. of the HS						
Public	University at Albany	1095	1130	-35	-3.1%	-67	-63
Public	University at Buffalo	1150	1160	-10	-0.9%	12	-22
Public	University of Alabama - Birmingham	1110	1070	40	3.7%	227	40
Public	University of Alabama - Huntsville	1220	1140	80	7.0%	173	33
Public	University of Alaska - Fairbanks		1045				
Public	University of Arizona		1125				
Public	Univ. of Arkansas for Med. Sciences						
Public	University of California - Berkeley	1370	1330	40	3.0%	16	0
Public	University of California - Davis	1205	1180	25	2.1%	60	2
Public	University of California - Irvine	1160	1200	-40	-3.3%	-49	-34
Public	University of California - Los Angeles	1325	1295	30	2.3%	18	-1
Public	University of California - Riverside	1130	1075	55	5.1%	269	51
Public	University of California - San Diego	1310	1260	50	4.0%	36	6
Public	Univ. of California - San Francisco						
Public	Univ. of California - Santa Barbara	1235	1180	55	4.7%	91	18
Public	University of California - Santa Cruz	1130	1165	-35	-3.0%	-30	-43
Public	University of Central Florida	1185	1140	45	3.9%	107	9
Private	University of Chicago	1518	1440	78	5.4%	10	10
Public	University of Cincinnati - Cincinnati	1170	1070	100	9.3%	359	89
Public	University of Colorado - Boulder	1220	1160	60	5.2%	121	20
Public	University of Colorado - Denver	1050	1030	20	1.9%	224	48
Public	Univ. of Connecticut - Health Ctr.						
Public	University of Connecticut - Storrs	1240	1185	55	4.6%	104	21
Private	University of Dayton	1205	1160	45	3.9%	100	91
Public	University of Delaware	1190	1205	-15	-1.2%	-2	-19
Public	University of Florida	1265	1260	5	0.4%	11	-5
Public	University of Georgia	1235	1225	10	0.8%	20	-5
Public	University of Hawaii - Manoa	1085	1105	-20	-1.8%	-8	-39
Public	University of Houston - Univ. Park	1145	1070	75	7.0%	301	63

National Merit and Achievement Scholars						Headcount Enrollment			
2015 National Merit Scholars	2006 National Merit Scholars	Net Change in Merit Scholars	Percent Change in Merit Scholars	Net Change in National Rank	Net Change in Control Rank	Fall 2014 Total Student Headcount	Fall 2005 Total Student Headcount	Net Change in Enrollment	Percent Change in Enrollment
4	11	-7	-63.6%	-31	-16	28,886	19,224	9,928	52.4%
						842	769	104	14.1%
21	24	-3	-12.5%	1	-1	47,040	40,709	5,245	12.5%
146	195	-49	-25.1%	-2	-1	8,088	6,773	1,400	20.9%
94	87	7	8.0%	7	1	39,752	40,151	-624	-1.5%
19	15	4	26.7%	27	18	6,835	6,514	-401	-5.5%
59	145	-86	-59.3%	-20	-8	6,621	5,095	1,816	37.8%
						209	200	33	18.8%
						2,457	1,452	1,204	96.1%
35	16	19	118.8%	51	22	48,378	34,449	13,060	37.0%
0	1	-1	-100.0%	-34	-21	33,483	31,802	680	2.1%
176	188	-12	-6.4%	4	2	16,963	19,042	-861	-4.8%
25	19	6	31.6%	25	9	24,607	22,011	2,263	10.1%
1	0	1		177	63	37,485	33,695	4,608	14.0%
142	139	3	2.2%	6	1	59,175	44,910	14,362	32.0%
						3,606	2,681	1,274	54.6%
55	52	3	5.8%	7	5	10,907	9,776	1,398	14.7%
33	24	9	37.5%	22	12	12,603		192	1.5%
0	0	0	0.0%	98	31	17,273	17,040	275	1.6%
1	2	-1	-50.0%	5	-5	29,995	27,220	2,740	10.1%
24	3	21	700.0%	152	57	18,698	16,572	2,341	14.3%
2	4	-2	-50.0%	-6	-5	7,348	7,084	297	4.2%
0	2	-2	-100.0%	-74	-37	8,620	8,228	-116	-1.3%
65	96	-31	-32.3%	-4	-4	42,236	37,036	5,153	13.9%
						2,890	2,328	720	33.2%
129	72	57	79.2%	18	8	37,565	33,547	4,500	13.6%
3	2	1	50.0%	59	15	34,508	28,815	5,106	17.4%
2	4	-2	-50.0%	-6	-5	30,051	24,400	5,778	23.8%
43	26	17	65.4%	30	14	41,845	35,625	4,790	12.9%
1	2	-1	-50.0%	5	-5	21,498	16,622	4,202	24.3%
18	13	5	38.5%	34	12	30,709	25,320	6,604	27.4%
						3,170	2,863	407	14.7%
4	2	2	100.0%	79	22	23,051	21,016	2,204	10.6%
0	1	-1	-100.0%	-34	-21	17,866	15,012	2,869	19.1%
69	28	41	146.4%	48	23	60,767	44,856	19,232	46.3%
294	202	92	45.5%	7	5	15,097	14,150	1,210	8.7%
44	34	10	29.4%	17	8	35,313	27,932	8,496	31.7%
5	10	-5	-50.0%	-8	-6	32,432	31,589	9	0.0%
0	0	0	0.0%	98	31	22,791	19,766	7,045	44.7%
						570	485	97	20.5%
2	2	0	0.0%	35	11	25,971	23,185	3,918	17.8%
4	11	-7	-63.6%	-31	-15	11,343	10,569	1,059	10.3%
3	14	-11	-78.6%	-73	-33	22,680	20,982	1,559	7.4%
146	280	-134	-47.9%	-9	-3	49,459	49,693	1,601	3.3%
42	64	-22	-34.4%	-17	-9	35,197	33,660	1,319	3.9%
0	1	-1	-100.0%	-34	-21	19,507	20,644	-355	-1.8%
29	11	18	163.6%	70	31	40,914	35,344	5,848	16.7%

Change: Students		SAT Scores					
Institutions with Over $40 Million in Federal Research, Alphabetically		2014 Median SAT	2005 Median SAT	Net Change in SAT	Percent Change in SAT	Net Change in National Rank	Net Change in Control Rank
Public	University of Idaho	1040	1070	-30	-2.8%	-76	-74
Public	University of Illinois - Chicago	1130	1070	60	5.6%	288	57
Public	Univ. of Illinois - Urbana-Champaign	1300	1260	40	3.2%	33	5
Public	University of Iowa	1170	1125	45	4.0%	145	19
Public	University of Kansas - Lawrence	1150	1110	40	3.6%	168	26
Public	University of Kansas Medical Center						
Public	University of Kentucky	1150	1110	40	3.6%	168	26
Public	University of Louisville	1150	1090	60	5.5%	238	53
Public	University of Maine - Orono	1075	1075	0	0.0%	74	-19
Public	University of Maryland - Baltimore						
Public	Univ. of Maryland - Baltimore County	1210	1215	-5	-0.4%	13	-12
Public	University of Maryland - College Park	1315	1275	40	3.1%	23	2
Public	Univ. of Massachusetts - Amherst	1215	1140	75	6.6%	159	28
Public	Univ. of Mass. Med. Sch. - Worcester						
Private	University of Miami	1320	1260	60	4.8%	45	37
Public	University of Michigan - Ann Arbor	1390	1280	110	8.6%	55	9
Public	University of Minnesota - Twin Cities	1260	1160	100	8.6%	157	35
Public	University of Missouri - Columbia	1170	1160	10	0.9%	49	-8
Public	University of Nebraska - Lincoln	1150	1140	10	0.9%	64	-9
Public	University of Nebraska Medical Ctr.						
Public	University of Nevada - Reno	1075	1060	15	1.4%	154	11
Public	Univ. of New Hampshire - Durham	1100	1130	-30	-2.7%	-54	-59
Public	Univ. of New Mexico - Albuquerque	1050	1010	40	4.0%	338	83
Public	Univ. of North Carolina - Chapel Hill	1320	1290	30	2.3%	18	-1
Public	University of North Dakota	1090	1030	60	5.8%	364	96
Private	University of Notre Dame	1460	1385	75	5.4%	17	17
Public	University of Oklahoma - Norman	1190	1160	30	2.6%		
Public	University of Oklahoma HSC						
Public	University of Oregon	1110	1115	-5	-0.4%	60	-12
Private	University of Pennsylvania	1455	1430	25	1.7%	1	1
Public	University of Pittsburgh - Pittsburgh	1270	1235	35	2.8%	36	4
Public	University of Rhode Island	1070	1085	-15	-1.4%	45	-28
Private	University of Rochester		1320				
Public	Univ. of South Carolina - Columbia	1210	1150	60	5.2%	133	19
Public	University of South Florida - Tampa	1160	1120	40	3.6%	157	27
Private	University of Southern California	1380	1355	25	1.8%	3	5
Public	University of Tennessee - Knoxville	1205	1125	80	7.1%	196	36
Public	University of Tennessee HSC						
Public	University of Texas - Austin	1290	1235	55	4.5%	45	11
Public	University of Texas HSC - Houston						
Public	Univ. of Texas HSC - San Antonio						
Public	U. of Texas MD Anderson Cancer Ctr.						
Public	U. of Texas Med. Branch - Galveston						
Public	Univ. of Texas SW Med. Ctr. - Dallas						
Public	University of Utah	1130	1090	40	3.7%	204	35
Public	University of Vermont	1185	1165	20	1.7%	47	-7
Public	University of Virginia	1355	1325	30	2.3%	12	-1
Public	University of Washington - Seattle	1230	1200	30	2.5%	54	3
Public	University of Wisconsin - Madison	1280	1260	20	1.6%	18	0

National Merit and Achievement Scholars						Headcount Enrollment			
2015 National Merit Scholars	2006 National Merit Scholars	Net Change in Merit Scholars	Percent Change in Merit Scholars	Net Change in National Rank	Net Change in Control Rank	Fall 2014 Total Student Headcount	Fall 2005 Total Student Headcount	Net Change in Enrollment	Percent Change in Enrollment
23	14	9	64.3%	40	15	11,702	12,476	-1,193	-9.3%
1	6	-5	-83.3%	-66	-32	27,969	24,812	2,205	8.6%
26	80	-54	-67.5%	-45	-23	45,140	41,938	4,682	11.6%
20	27	-7	-25.9%	-10	-8	29,970	28,426	225	0.8%
26	53	-27	-50.9%	-28	-15	23,288	26,934	-3,526	-13.1%
						3,892	2,015	2,126	120.4%
111	32	79	246.9%	50	23	29,203	25,672	3,806	15.0%
19	19	0	0.0%	12	1	21,561	20,726	956	4.6%
2	6	-4	-66.7%	-36	-16	11,286	11,435	64	0.6%
					6,276	5,526	799	14.6%	
2	2	0	0.0%	35	11	13,979	11,650	2,107	17.7%
61	62	-1	-1.6%	6	2	37,610	35,369	2,281	6.5%
1	1	0	0.0%	45	11	28,635	25,093	4,325	17.8%
						1,103	1,008	328	42.3%
35	28	7	25.0%	15	11	16,674	15,674	1,439	9.4%
56	71	-15	-21.1%	-4	-3	43,625	39,993	4,594	11.8%
147	75	72	96.0%	23	10	51,147	51,175	1,673	3.4%
18	26	-8	-30.8%	-12	-9	35,425	27,930	8,620	32.2%
47	46	1	2.2%	6	2	25,006	21,675	2,447	10.8%
						3,696	2,995	831	29.0%
16	1	15	1500.0%	194	68	19,934	16,336	4,400	28.3%
0	1	-1	-100.0%	-34	-21	15,117	14,511	-469	-3.0%
14	0	14		318	115	27,844	26,172	2,158	8.4%
20	170	-150	-88.2%	-75	-39	29,135	27,276	2,776	10.5%
2	6	-4	-66.7%	-36	-16	14,906	12,954	1,872	14.4%
57	61	-4	-6.6%	1	1	12,179	11,417	764	6.7%
288	143	145	101.4%	15	4	27,261	26,506	115	0.4%
						3,499	3,638	373	11.9%
6	10	-4	-40.0%	-2	-2	24,096	20,347	4,104	20.5%
139	125	14	11.2%	6	5	24,806	23,704	1,563	6.7%
16	20	-4	-20.0%	0	-5	28,617	26,559	1,822	6.8%
0	0	0	0.0%	98	31	16,571	15,095	1,780	12.0%
37	25	12	48.0%	29	15	11,060	8,588	2,594	30.6%
46	27	19	70.4%	30	14	32,971	27,065	7,683	30.4%
9	8	1	12.5%	34	12	41,938	42,660	993	2.4%
226	210	16	7.6%	3	2	42,453	32,836	10,847	34.3%
23	26	-3	-11.5%	1	-2	30,386	28,512	3,105	11.4%
60	259	-199	-76.8%	-30	-14	51,313	49,696	-113	-0.2%
						4,556	3,662	1,139	33.3%
						3,147	2,781	393	14.3%
						303	86	228	304.0%
						3,211	2,172	1,230	62.1%
						2,341	2,393	657	39.0%
33	18	15	83.3%	41	17	31,515	30,558	3,079	10.8%
10	6	4	66.7%	61	18	12,856	11,597	1,889	17.2%
36	38	-2	-5.3%	2	-1	23,732	23,765	655	2.8%
12	44	-32	-72.7%	-60	-31	44,784	39,251	5,649	14.4%
15	21	-6	-28.6%	-7	-10	42,598	40,793	1,719	4.2%

Change: Students		SAT Scores					
Institutions with Over $40 Million in Federal Research, Alphabetically		2014 Median SAT	2005 Median SAT	Net Change in SAT	Percent Change in SAT	Net Change in National Rank	Net Change in Control Rank
Public	Utah State University	1070	1110	-40	-3.6%	-71	-66
Private	Vanderbilt University	1460	1370	90	6.6%	28	28
Public	Virginia Commonwealth University	1105	1060	45	4.2%	242	47
Public	Virginia Polytechnic Inst. and St. Univ.	1215	1200	15	1.3%	34	-4
Private	Wake Forest University		1325				
Public	Washington State Univ. - Pullman	1030	1105	-75	-6.8%	-215	-115
Private	Washington University in St. Louis	1460	1440	20	1.4%	-1	-1
Public	Wayne State University	1070	950	120	12.6%	736	256
Private	Weill Cornell Medical College						
Public	West Virginia University	1090	1050	40	3.8%	250	53
Private	Woods Hole Oceanographic Inst.						
Private	Yale University	1505	1480	25	1.7%	2	2
Private	Yeshiva University	1240	1220	20	1.6%	44	43

National Merit and Achievement Scholars						Headcount Enrollment			
2015 National Merit Scholars	2006 National Merit Scholars	Net Change in Merit Scholars	Percent Change in Merit Scholars	Net Change in National Rank	Net Change in Control Rank	Fall 2014 Total Student Headcount	Fall 2005 Total Student Headcount	Net Change in Enrollment	Percent Change in Enrollment
1	2	-1	-50.0%	5	-5	27,662	14,458	11,202	68.1%
206	140	66	47.1%	13	9	12,686	11,479	1,594	14.4%
0	0	0	0.0%	98	31	30,848	29,168	4,217	15.8%
4	18	-14	-77.8%	-68	-32	31,224	27,979	3,469	12.5%
0	13	-13	-100.0%	-199	-118	7,788	6,716	1,344	20.9%
5	4	1	25.0%	53	13	28,686	23,544	5,974	26.3%
32	269	-237	-88.1%	-65	-34	14,348	13,383	1,328	10.2%
7	1	6	600.0%	149	51	27,578	32,160	-4,630	-14.4%
						1,023	818	292	39.9%
10	12	-2	-16.7%	16	5	29,175	26,051	4,915	20.3%
166	244	-78	-32.0%	-3	-4	12,336	11,483	865	7.5%
0	3	-3	-100.0%	-95	-51	6,348	6,240	329	5.5%

Institutional Characteristics

	Institutions with Over $40 Million in Federal Research, Alphabetically	State	Highest Degree Offered	Has a Medical School
Public	Arizona State University	AZ	Doctor's - Res/Sch & Prof Prac	
Public	Auburn University	AL	Doctor's - Res/Sch & Prof Prac	
Public	Augusta University	GA	Doctor's - Res/Sch & Prof Prac	Yes
Private	Baylor College of Medicine	TX	Doctor's - Res/Sch & Prof Prac	Yes
Private	Boston University	MA	Doctor's - Res/Sch & Prof Prac	Yes
Private	Brandeis University	MA	Doctor's - Research/Scholar	
Private	Brown University	RI	Doctor's - Res/Sch & Prof Prac	Yes
Private	California Institute of Technology	CA	Doctor's - Research/Scholar	
Private	Carnegie Mellon University	PA	Doctor's - Research/Scholar	
Private	Case Western Reserve University	OH	Doctor's - Res/Sch & Prof Prac	Yes
Public	Clemson University	SC	Doctor's - Research/Scholar	
Public	Cleveland State University	OH	Doctor's - Res/Sch & Prof Prac	
Private	Cold Spring Harbor Laboratory	NY	Doctor's - Research/Scholar	
Public	Colorado State University - Fort Collins	CO	Doctor's - Res/Sch & Prof Prac	
Private	Columbia University	NY	Doctor's - Res/Sch & Prof Prac	Yes
Private	Cornell University	NY	Doctor's - Res/Sch & Prof Prac	
Private	Dartmouth College	NH	Doctor's - Res/Sch & Prof Prac	Yes
Private	Drexel University	PA	Doctor's - Res/Sch & Prof Prac	Yes
Private	Duke University	NC	Doctor's - Res/Sch & Prof Prac	Yes
Private	Emory University	GA	Doctor's - Res/Sch & Prof Prac	Yes
Public	Florida International University	FL	Doctor's - Res/Sch & Prof Prac	Yes
Public	Florida State University	FL	Doctor's - Res/Sch & Prof Prac	Yes
Public	George Mason University	VA	Doctor's - Res/Sch & Prof Prac	
Private	George Washington University	DC	Doctor's - Res/Sch & Prof Prac	Yes
Private	Georgetown University	DC	Doctor's - Res/Sch & Prof Prac	Yes
Public	Georgia Institute of Technology	GA	Doctor's - Research/Scholar	
Private	Harvard University	MA	Doctor's - Res/Sch & Prof Prac	Yes
Private	Icahn School of Medicine at Mount Sinai	NY	Doctor's - Res/Sch & Prof Prac	Yes
Public	Indiana University - Bloomington	IN	Doctor's - Res/Sch & Prof Prac	
Public	Indiana University-Purdue University - Indianapolis	IN	Doctor's - Res/Sch & Prof Prac	Yes
Public	Iowa State University	IA	Doctor's - Res/Sch & Prof Prac	
Private	Johns Hopkins University	MD	Doctor's - Res/Sch & Prof Prac	Yes
Public	Kansas State University	KS	Doctor's - Res/Sch & Prof Prac	
Public	Louisiana State University - Baton Rouge	LA	Doctor's - Res/Sch & Prof Prac	
Private	Massachusetts Institute of Technology	MA	Doctor's - Research/Scholar	
Private	Medical College of Wisconsin	WI	Doctor's - Res/Sch & Prof Prac	Yes
Public	Medical University of South Carolina	SC	Doctor's - Res/Sch & Prof Prac	Yes
Public	Michigan State University	MI	Doctor's - Res/Sch & Prof Prac	Yes
Public	Mississippi State University	MS	Doctor's - Res/Sch & Prof Prac	
Public	Montana State University - Bozeman	MT	Doctor's - Res/Sch & Prof Prac	
Public	Naval Postgraduate School	CA	Doctor's - Research/Scholar	
Public	New Jersey Institute of Technology	NJ	Doctor's - Research/Scholar	
Public	New Mexico State University - Las Cruces	NM	Doctor's - Res/Sch & Prof Prac	
Private	New York University	NY	Doctor's - Res/Sch & Prof Prac	Yes
Public	North Carolina State University	NC	Doctor's - Res/Sch & Prof Prac	
Private	Northeastern University	MA	Doctor's - Res/Sch & Prof Prac	
Private	Northwestern University	IL	Doctor's - Res/Sch & Prof Prac	Yes
Public	Ohio State University - Columbus	OH	Doctor's - Res/Sch & Prof Prac	Yes
Public	Oregon Health & Science University	OR	Doctor's - Res/Sch & Prof Prac	Yes

Federal Land Grant Institution	Federal Research Focus	Total Student Enrollment Fall 2013
	Moderate Life Sciences and Moderate Engineering	83,260
Yes	Moderate Life Sciences and Moderate Engineering	25,912
	All Life Sciences	7,988
	All Life Sciences	1,584
	Strong Life Sciences	32,112
	Moderate Life Sciences and ModerateSocial Sciences	5,945
	Strong Life Sciences	9,181
	Strong Physical Sciences	2,209
	Moderate Computer Sciences and Moderate Engineering	12,587
	Heavy Life Sciences	10,771
Yes	Strong Engineering	21,857
	Heavy Life Sciences	16,936
	All Life Sciences	
Yes	Moderate Life Sciences and Moderate Environmental Sciences	31,354
	Strong Life Sciences	27,589
Yes	Moderate Life Sciences and Moderate Physical Sciences	21,679
	Heavy Life Sciences	6,298
	Strong Life Sciences and Moderate Engineering	26,359
	Heavy Life Sciences	15,856
	Heavy Life Sciences	14,769
	Moderate Life Sciences	49,610
	Moderate Physical Sciences	41,226
	Mixed	33,729
	Heavy Life Sciences	25,613
	Heavy Life Sciences	17,858
	Strong Engineering	23,109
	Strong Life Sciences	28,791
	All Life Sciences	1,074
	Moderate Life Sciences	46,416
	Heavy Life Sciences	30,690
Yes	Moderate Life Sciences and Moderate Engineering	34,435
	Moderate Life Sciences and Moderate Engineering	21,372
Yes	Strong Life Sciences	24,766
Yes-System	Strong Life Sciences	31,044
	Moderate Engineering	11,319
	All Life Sciences	1,209
	All Life Sciences	2,898
Yes	Moderate Life Sciences and Moderate Physical Sciences	50,081
Yes	Moderate Life Sciences and Moderate Engineering	20,138
Yes	Moderate Life Sciences	14,982
	Moderate Engineering	2,869
	Strong Engineering	10,646
Yes	Strong Engineering	15,829
	Heavy Life Sciences	49,274
Yes	Moderate Life Sciences and Moderate Engineering	33,989
	Moderate Engineering	19,798
	Strong Life Sciences	21,554
Yes	Strong Life Sciences	58,322
	Heavy Life Sciences	2,861

Institutional Characteristics

	Institutions with Over $40 Million in Federal Research, Alphabetically	State	Highest Degree Offered	Has a Medical School
Public	Oregon State University	OR	Doctor's - Res/Sch & Prof Prac	
Public	Pennsylvania State University - Hershey Medical Ctr.	PA	Doctor's - Res/Sch & Prof Prac	Yes
Public	Pennsylvania State University - University Park	PA	Doctor's - Res/Sch & Prof Prac	
Private	Princeton University	NJ	Doctor's - Research/Scholar	
Public	Purdue University - West Lafayette	IN	Doctor's - Res/Sch & Prof Prac	
Private	Rensselaer Polytechnic Institute	NY	Doctor's - Research/Scholar	
Private	Rice University	TX	Doctor's - Research/Scholar	
Private	Rockefeller University	NY	Doctor's - Research/Scholar	
Private	Rush University	IL	Doctor's - Res/Sch & Prof Prac	Yes
Public	Rutgers University - New Brunswick	NJ	Doctor's - Res/Sch & Prof Prac	Yes
Public	San Diego State University	CA	Doctor's - Other	
Private	Scripps Research Institute	CA	Doctor's - Research/Scholar	
Private	Stanford University	CA	Doctor's - Res/Sch & Prof Prac	Yes
Public	Stony Brook University	NY	Doctor's - Res/Sch & Prof Prac	Yes
Public	Temple University	PA	Doctor's - Res/Sch & Prof Prac	Yes
Public	Texas A&M University - College Station	TX	Doctor's - Res/Sch & Prof Prac	
Private	Thomas Jefferson University	PA	Doctor's - Res/Sch & Prof Prac	Yes
Private	Tufts University	MA	Doctor's - Res/Sch & Prof Prac	Yes
Private	Tulane University	LA	Doctor's - Res/Sch & Prof Prac	Yes
Public	Uniformed Services University of the Health Sciences	MD	Doctor's - Res/Sch & Prof Prac	
Public	University at Albany	NY	Doctor's - Research/Scholar	
Public	University at Buffalo	NY	Doctor's - Res/Sch & Prof Prac	Yes
Public	University of Alabama - Birmingham	AL	Doctor's - Res/Sch & Prof Prac	Yes
Public	University of Alabama - Huntsville	AL	Doctor's - Res/Sch & Prof Prac	
Public	University of Alaska - Fairbanks	AK	Doctor's - Research/Scholar	
Public	University of Arizona	AZ	Doctor's - Res/Sch & Prof Prac	Yes
Public	University of Arkansas for Medical Sciences	AR	Doctor's - Res/Sch & Prof Prac	Yes
Public	University of California - Berkeley	CA	Doctor's - Res/Sch & Prof Prac	
Public	University of California - Davis	CA	Doctor's - Res/Sch & Prof Prac	Yes
Public	University of California - Irvine	CA	Doctor's - Res/Sch & Prof Prac	Yes
Public	University of California - Los Angeles	CA	Doctor's - Res/Sch & Prof Prac	Yes
Public	University of California - Riverside	CA	Doctor's - Res/Sch & Prof Prac	
Public	University of California - San Diego	CA	Doctor's - Res/Sch & Prof Prac	Yes
Public	University of California - San Francisco	CA	Doctor's - Res/Sch & Prof Prac	Yes
Public	University of California - Santa Barbara	CA	Doctor's - Research/Scholar	
Public	University of California - Santa Cruz	CA	Doctor's - Research/Scholar	
Public	University of Central Florida	FL	Doctor's - Res/Sch & Prof Prac	Yes
Private	University of Chicago	IL	Doctor's - Res/Sch & Prof Prac	Yes
Public	University of Cincinnati - Cincinnati	OH	Doctor's - Res/Sch & Prof Prac	Yes
Public	University of Colorado - Boulder	CO	Doctor's - Res/Sch & Prof Prac	
Public	University of Colorado - Denver	CO	Doctor's - Res/Sch & Prof Prac	Yes
Public	University of Connecticut - Health Center	CT	Doctor's - Res/Sch & Prof Prac	Yes
Public	University of Connecticut - Storrs	CT	Doctor's - Res/Sch & Prof Prac	
Private	University of Dayton	OH	Doctor's - Res/Sch & Prof Prac	
Public	University of Delaware	DE	Doctor's - Res/Sch & Prof Prac	
Public	University of Florida	FL	Doctor's - Res/Sch & Prof Prac	Yes
Public	University of Georgia	GA	Doctor's - Res/Sch & Prof Prac	
Public	University of Hawaii - Manoa	HI	Doctor's - Res/Sch & Prof Prac	Yes
Public	University of Houston - University Park	TX	Doctor's - Res/Sch & Prof Prac	

Federal Land Grant Institution	Federal Research Focus	Total Student Enrollment Fall 2013
Yes	Moderate Life Sciences and Moderate Environmental Sciences	28,886
	All Life Sciences	842
Yes	Moderate Engineering	47,040
	Moderate Engineering	8,088
Yes	Moderate Life Sciences and Moderate Engineering	39,752
	Strong Engineering	6,835
	Moderate Physical Sciences and Moderate Engineering	6,621
	All Life Sciences	209
	Heavy Life Sciences	2,457
Yes	Strong Life Sciences	48,378
	Strong Life Sciences	33,483
	All Life Sciences	
	Strong Life Sciences	16,963
	Moderate Life Sciences	24,607
	Heavy Life Sciences	37,485
Yes	Moderate Life Sciences, Mod. Engineering and Mod. Environmental Sci	59,175
	All Life Sciences	3,606
	Strong Life Sciences	10,907
	Heavy Life Sciences	12,603
	All Life Sciences	
	Heavy Life Sciences	17,273
	Strong Life Sciences and Moderate Engineering	29,995
	Heavy Life Sciences	18,698
	Moderate Computer Sciences and Moderate Engineering	7,348
Yes-System	Strong Environmental Sciences	8,620
Yes	Moderate Life Sciences and Moderate Physical Sciences	42,236
	All Life Sciences	2,890
Yes-System	Moderate Life Sciences	37,565
Yes-System	Strong Life Sciences	34,508
No-System	Strong Life Sciences	30,051
No-System	Strong Life Sciences	41,845
Yes-System	Moderate Life Sciences	21,498
No-System	Strong Life Sciences	30,709
No-System	All Life Sciences	3,170
No-System	Moderate Engineering	23,051
No-System	Moderate Engineering	17,866
	Mixed	60,767
	Strong Life Sciences	15,097
	Heavy Life Sciences	35,313
	Moderate Environmental Sciences and Moderate Physical Sciences	32,432
	All Life Sciences	22,791
	All Life Sciences	570
Yes	Moderate Life Sciences and Moderate Engineering	25,971
	Heavy Engineering	11,343
Yes	Moderate Engineering	22,680
Yes	Strong Life Sciences	49,459
Yes	Strong Life Sciences	35,197
Yes	Moderate Life Sciences and Moderate Environmental Sciences	19,507
	Moderate Engineering	40,914

Institutional Characteristics

	Institutions with Over $40 Million in Federal Research, Alphabetically	State	Highest Degree Offered	Has a Medical School
Public	University of Idaho	ID	Doctor's - Res/Sch & Prof Prac	Yes
Public	University of Illinois - Chicago	IL	Doctor's - Res/Sch & Prof Prac	Yes
Public	University of Illinois - Urbana-Champaign	IL	Doctor's - Res/Sch & Prof Prac	
Public	University of Iowa	IA	Doctor's - Res/Sch & Prof Prac	Yes
Public	University of Kansas - Lawrence	KS	Doctor's - Res/Sch & Prof Prac	
Public	University of Kansas Medical Center	KS	Doctor's - Res/Sch & Prof Prac	Yes
Public	University of Kentucky	KY	Doctor's - Res/Sch & Prof Prac	Yes
Public	University of Louisville	KY	Doctor's - Res/Sch & Prof Prac	Yes
Public	University of Maine - Orono	ME	Doctor's - Research/Scholar	
Public	University of Maryland - Baltimore	MD	Doctor's - Res/Sch & Prof Prac	Yes
Public	University of Maryland - Baltimore County	MD	Doctor's - Research/Scholar	
Public	University of Maryland - College Park	MD	Doctor's - Res/Sch & Prof Prac	
Public	University of Massachusetts - Amherst	MA	Doctor's - Res/Sch & Prof Prac	
Public	University of Massachusetts Medical Sch. - Worcester	MA	Doctor's - Res/Sch & Prof Prac	Yes
Private	University of Miami	FL	Doctor's - Res/Sch & Prof Prac	Yes
Public	University of Michigan - Ann Arbor	MI	Doctor's - Res/Sch & Prof Prac	Yes
Public	University of Minnesota - Twin Cities	MN	Doctor's - Res/Sch & Prof Prac	Yes
Public	University of Missouri - Columbia	MO	Doctor's - Res/Sch & Prof Prac	Yes
Public	University of Nebraska - Lincoln	NE	Doctor's - Res/Sch & Prof Prac	
Public	University of Nebraska Medical Center	NE	Doctor's - Res/Sch & Prof Prac	Yes
Public	University of Nevada - Reno	NV	Doctor's - Res/Sch & Prof Prac	Yes
Public	University of New Hampshire - Durham	NH	Doctor's - Res/Sch & Prof Prac	
Public	University of New Mexico - Albuquerque	NM	Doctor's - Res/Sch & Prof Prac	Yes
Public	University of North Carolina - Chapel Hill	NC	Doctor's - Res/Sch & Prof Prac	Yes
Public	University of North Dakota	ND	Doctor's - Res/Sch & Prof Prac	Yes
Private	University of Notre Dame	IN	Doctor's - Res/Sch & Prof Prac	
Public	University of Oklahoma - Norman	OK	Doctor's - Res/Sch & Prof Prac	
Public	University of Oklahoma Health Sciences Center	OK	Doctor's - Res/Sch & Prof Prac	Yes
Public	University of Oregon	OR	Doctor's - Res/Sch & Prof Prac	
Private	University of Pennsylvania	PA	Doctor's - Res/Sch & Prof Prac	Yes
Public	University of Pittsburgh - Pittsburgh	PA	Doctor's - Res/Sch & Prof Prac	Yes
Public	University of Rhode Island	RI	Doctor's - Res/Sch & Prof Prac	
Private	University of Rochester	NY	Doctor's - Res/Sch & Prof Prac	Yes
Public	University of South Carolina - Columbia	SC	Doctor's - Res/Sch & Prof Prac	Yes
Public	University of South Florida - Tampa	FL	Doctor's - Res/Sch & Prof Prac	Yes
Private	University of Southern California	CA	Doctor's - Res/Sch & Prof Prac	Yes
Public	University of Tennessee - Knoxville	TN	Doctor's - Res/Sch & Prof Prac	Yes
Public	University of Tennessee Health Science Center	TN	Doctor's - Res/Sch & Prof Prac	
Public	University of Texas - Austin	TX	Doctor's - Res/Sch & Prof Prac	
Public	University of Texas Health Science Center - Houston	TX	Doctor's - Res/Sch & Prof Prac	Yes
Public	University of Texas Health Science Ctr. - San Antonio	TX	Doctor's - Res/Sch & Prof Prac	Yes
Public	University of Texas MD Anderson Cancer Center	TX	Master's	
Public	University of Texas Medical Branch - Galveston	TX	Doctor's - Res/Sch & Prof Prac	Yes
Public	University of Texas SW Medical Center - Dallas	TX	Doctor's - Res/Sch & Prof Prac	Yes
Public	University of Utah	UT	Doctor's - Res/Sch & Prof Prac	Yes
Public	University of Vermont	VT	Doctor's - Res/Sch & Prof Prac	Yes
Public	University of Virginia	VA	Doctor's - Res/Sch & Prof Prac	Yes
Public	University of Washington - Seattle	WA	Doctor's - Res/Sch & Prof Prac	Yes
Public	University of Wisconsin - Madison	WI	Doctor's - Res/Sch & Prof Prac	Yes

Federal Land Grant Institution	Federal Research Focus	Total Student Enrollment Fall 2013
Yes	Strong Life Sciences	11,702
	Heavy Life Sciences	27,969
Yes	Moderate Life Sciences and Moderate Engineering	45,140
	Heavy Life Sciences	29,970
	Strong Life Sciences	23,288
	All Life Sciences	3,892
Yes	Strong Life Sciences	29,203
	Heavy Life Sciences	21,561
Yes	Moderate Life Sciences	11,286
	All Life Sciences	6,276
	Moderate Environmental Sciences	13,979
Yes	Mixed	37,610
Yes	Moderate Life Sciences	28,635
	All Life Sciences	1,103
	Strong Life Sciences	16,674
	Strong Life Sciences	43,625
Yes	Strong Life Sciences	51,147
Yes-System	Strong Life Sciences	35,425
Yes-System	Moderate Life Sciences	25,006
No-System	All Life Sciences	3,696
Yes	Strong Life Sciences	19,934
Yes	Strong Environmental Sciences	15,117
	Strong Life Sciences	27,844
	Strong Life Sciences	29,135
	Moderate Life Sciences and Moderate Engineering	14,906
	Moderate Physical Sciences and Moderate Engineering	12,179
	Moderate Life Sciences and Moderate Environmental Sciences	27,261
	All Life Sciences	3,499
	Moderate Life Sciences	24,096
	Heavy Life Sciences	24,806
	Heavy Life Sciences	28,617
Yes	Moderate Life Sciences and Moderate Environmental Sciences	16,571
	Strong Life Sciences and Moderate Engineering	11,060
	Strong Life Sciences	32,971
	Strong Life Sciences	41,938
	Strong Life Sciences	42,453
Yes	Moderate Engineering	30,386
	All Life Sciences	
	Moderate Engineering	51,313
	All Life Sciences	4,556
	All Life Sciences	3,147
	Heavy Life Sciences	303
	All Life Sciences	3,211
	All Life Sciences	2,341
	Strong Life Sciences	31,515
Yes	Heavy Life Sciences	12,856
	Strong Life Sciences	23,732
	Strong Life Sciences	44,784
Yes	Strong Life Sciences	42,598

Institutional Characteristics

	Institutions with Over $40 Million in Federal Research, Alphabetically	State	Highest Degree Offered	Has a Medical School
Public	Utah State University	UT	Doctor's - Res/Sch & Prof Prac	
Private	Vanderbilt University	TN	Doctor's - Res/Sch & Prof Prac	Yes
Public	Virginia Commonwealth University	VA	Doctor's - Res/Sch & Prof Prac	Yes
Public	Virginia Polytechnic Institute and State University	VA	Doctor's - Res/Sch & Prof Prac	
Private	Wake Forest University	NC	Doctor's - Res/Sch & Prof Prac	Yes
Public	Washington State University - Pullman	WA	Doctor's - Res/Sch & Prof Prac	Yes
Private	Washington University in St. Louis	MO	Doctor's - Res/Sch & Prof Prac	Yes
Public	Wayne State University	MI	Doctor's - Res/Sch & Prof Prac	Yes
Private	Weill Cornell Medical College	NY	Doctor's - Res/Sch & Prof Prac	Yes
Public	West Virginia University	WV	Doctor's - Res/Sch & Prof Prac	Yes
Private	Woods Hole Oceanographic Institution	MA	Non-Degree Granting	
Private	Yale University	CT	Doctor's - Res/Sch & Prof Prac	Yes
Private	Yeshiva University	NY	Doctor's - Res/Sch & Prof Prac	Yes

	Federal Land Grant Institution	Federal Research Focus	Total Student Enrollment Fall 2013
	Yes	Strong Engineering	27,662
		Heavy Life Sciences	12,686
		Heavy Life Sciences	30,848
	Yes	Moderate Life Sciences and Moderate Engineering	31,224
		All Life Sciences	7,788
	Yes	Strong Life Sciences	28,686
		Heavy Life Sciences	14,348
		Heavy Life Sciences	27,578
		All Life Sciences	1,023
	Yes	Strong Life Sciences and Moderate Engineering	29,175
		Strong Environmental Sciences and Moderate Engineering	
		Heavy Life Sciences	12,336
		All Life Sciences	6,348

Student Characteristics	Fall 2014 Headcount Enrollment						
Institutions with Over $40 Million in Federal Research, Alphabetically	Total Student Enrollment	Total Undergraduate Students	%	Total Graduate Students	%	First-time, Full-time Students	Full-time Transfer Students
Public	Arizona State University	83,260	67,498	81.1%	15,762	18.9%	10,757	5,889
Public	Auburn University	25,912	20,629	79.6%	5,283	20.4%	4,552	1,140
Public	Augusta University	7,988	5,225	65.4%	2,763	34.6%	740	458
Private	Baylor College of Medicine	1,584			1,584	100.0%		
Private	Boston University	32,112	18,017	56.1%	14,095	43.9%	3,915	475
Private	Brandeis University	5,945	3,729	62.7%	2,216	37.3%	859	60
Private	Brown University	9,181	6,548	71.3%	2,633	28.7%	1,559	55
Private	California Institute of Technology	2,209	983	44.5%	1,226	55.5%	226	7
Private	Carnegie Mellon University	12,587	5,888	46.8%	6,699	53.2%	1,474	61
Private	Case Western Reserve University	10,771	4,911	45.6%	5,860	54.4%	1,282	32
Public	Clemson University	21,857	17,260	79.0%	4,597	21.0%	3,470	1,241
Public	Cleveland State University	16,936	11,826	69.8%	5,110	30.2%	1,562	1,083
Private	Cold Spring Harbor Laboratory							
Public	Colorado State Univ. - Fort Collins	31,354	23,598	75.3%	7,756	24.7%	4,253	1,210
Private	Columbia University	27,589	8,100	29.4%	19,489	70.6%	1,490	512
Private	Cornell University	21,679	14,282	65.9%	7,397	34.1%	3,225	553
Private	Dartmouth College	6,298	4,289	68.1%	2,009	31.9%	1,152	13
Private	Drexel University	26,359	16,896	64.1%	9,463	35.9%	2,925	959
Private	Duke University	15,856	6,626	41.8%	9,230	58.2%	1,721	13
Private	Emory University	14,769	7,829	53.0%	6,940	47.0%	1,823	206
Public	Florida International University	49,610	41,009	82.7%	8,601	17.3%	3,761	3,254
Public	Florida State University	41,226	32,948	79.9%	8,278	20.1%	5,944	1,884
Public	George Mason University	33,729	22,349	66.3%	11,380	33.7%	3,046	1,902
Private	George Washington University	25,613	10,740	41.9%	14,873	58.1%	2,410	384
Private	Georgetown University	17,858	7,595	42.5%	10,263	57.5%	1,575	148
Public	Georgia Institute of Technology	23,109	14,682	63.5%	8,427	36.5%	2,805	484
Private	Harvard University	28,791	10,338	35.9%	18,453	64.1%	1,650	11
Private	Icahn School of Medi. at Mount Sinai	1,074			1,074	100.0%		
Public	Indiana University - Bloomington	46,416	36,419	78.5%	9,997	21.5%	7,697	877
Public	Indiana U. - Purdue U. - Indianapolis	30,690	22,525	73.4%	8,165	26.6%	3,772	1,324
Public	Iowa State University	34,435	28,893	83.9%	5,542	16.1%	6,016	1,891
Private	Johns Hopkins University	21,372	6,357	29.7%	15,015	70.3%	1,470	248
Public	Kansas State University	24,766	20,327	82.1%	4,439	17.9%	3,691	1,287
Public	Louisiana State Univ. - Baton Rouge	31,044	25,572	82.4%	5,472	17.6%	5,652	886
Private	Massachusetts Inst. of Technology	11,319	4,512	39.9%	6,807	60.1%	1,043	16
Private	Medical College of Wisconsin	1,209			1,209	100.0%		
Public	Medical University of South Carolina	2,898	293	10.1%	2,605	89.9%		139
Public	Michigan State University	50,081	38,786	77.4%	11,295	22.6%	7,890	1,517
Public	Mississippi State University	20,138	16,536	82.1%	3,602	17.9%	2,964	1,582
Public	Montana State University - Bozeman	14,982	13,298	88.8%	1,684	11.2%	2,428	647
Public	Naval Postgraduate School	2,869			2,869	100.0%		
Public	New Jersey Institute of Technology	10,646	7,550	70.9%	3,096	29.1%	953	534
Public	New Mexico State Univ. - Las Cruces	15,829	12,784	80.8%	3,045	19.2%	1,848	564
Private	New York University	49,274	24,985	50.7%	24,289	49.3%	5,860	783
Public	North Carolina State University	33,989	24,473	72.0%	9,516	28.0%	4,493	1,136
Private	Northeastern University	19,798	13,510	68.2%	6,288	31.8%	2,944	460
Private	Northwestern University	21,554	9,048	42.0%	12,506	58.0%	2,043	55
Public	Ohio State University - Columbus	58,322	44,741	76.7%	13,581	23.3%	7,070	2,559
Public	Oregon Health & Science University	2,861	847	29.6%	2,014	70.4%		153

Fall 2014 Part-Time Enrollment			2014-2015 Degrees Awarded				
Percentage of Total Students Enrolled Part Time	Percentage of Under-graduates Enrolled Part Time	Percentage of Graduates Enrolled Part Time	Associate's Degrees	Bachelor's Degrees	Master's Degrees	Doctorate Degrees	Professional Degrees
21.5%	18.0%	36.2%	0	14,866	5,091	687	223
15.0%	8.6%	39.8%	0	4,638	1,107	257	262
20.1%	22.0%	16.7%	7	1,019	435	29	358
			0	0	56	111	183
19.5%	7.8%	34.5%	0	4,406	4,359	484	632
8.2%	0.5%	21.2%	0	1,479	776	100	0
4.6%	4.5%	5.0%	0	1,948	520	215	106
			0	228	123	182	0
8.5%	3.2%	13.1%	0	1,651	2,811	333	0
8.9%	3.0%	13.9%	0	1,055	1,215	197	458
11.0%	4.0%	37.1%	0	3,844	1,270	237	0
38.1%	26.7%	64.4%	0	2,420	1,461	59	147
24.7%	13.3%	59.3%	0	5,229	1,755	251	126
15.7%	7.5%	19.1%	0	2,652	7,522	564	723
0.4%	0.1%	0.9%	0	3,949	2,428	487	278
2.3%	1.4%	4.1%	0	1,289	602	85	88
27.2%	15.0%	48.9%	23	3,799	2,477	213	462
4.6%	0.4%	7.6%	0	2,183	2,458	485	316
9.6%	1.2%	19.0%	0	2,308	1,426	264	506
36.0%	37.5%	28.8%	72	9,061	3,187	189	283
14.7%	11.3%	27.9%	177	9,604	2,153	424	393
34.9%	20.3%	63.6%	0	5,109	2,943	249	154
32.6%	8.5%	50.0%	205	2,679	4,223	222	737
19.3%	4.9%	29.9%	0	2,222	3,466	114	864
17.4%	9.7%	30.8%	0	3,274	1,882	526	0
29.0%	30.4%	28.3%	12	1,823	4,229	745	789
			0	0	76	28	129
18.8%	13.9%	37.0%	14	7,798	2,487	538	279
29.1%	23.4%	44.9%	126	3,948	1,558	69	741
10.3%	5.0%	37.8%	0	6,144	903	336	147
37.3%	4.8%	51.0%	0	1,973	4,818	535	132
16.3%	10.2%	44.1%	43	3,883	1,109	190	113
11.5%	9.3%	22.0%	0	4,707	1,130	331	273
1.9%	0.8%	2.6%	0	1,280	1,734	606	0
15.7%		15.7%	0	0	49	26	191
7.2%	4.1%	7.6%	0	136	293	191	308
12.7%	8.9%	25.9%	0	8,299	2,138	577	627
15.6%	8.4%	48.4%	0	3,211	760	146	80
21.3%	15.5%	67.4%	57	2,239	528	79	0
43.0%		43.0%	0	0	1,324	15	0
27.4%	21.5%	41.8%	0	1,352	1,099	65	0
22.5%	16.6%	47.5%	21	2,616	794	131	0
19.0%	5.1%	33.4%	54	6,034	8,489	438	1,017
20.7%	12.5%	41.5%	173	5,555	2,338	512	79
5.9%	0.1%	18.4%	0	3,655	1,919	157	409
21.0%	7.2%	31.0%	0	2,875	5,210	438	545
13.2%	9.2%	26.3%	3	10,898	2,707	832	863
43.8%	76.2%	30.2%	0	354	252	43	228

Student Characteristics		Fall 2014 Headcount Enrollment						
Institutions with Over $40 Million in Federal Research, Alphabetically		Total Student Enrollment	Total Undergraduate Students	%	Total Graduate Students	%	First-time, Full-time Students	Full-time Transfer Students
Public	Oregon State University	28,886	23,903	82.7%	4,983	17.3%	3,453	1,361
Public	Penn. St. Univ. - Hershey Med. Ctr.	842			842	100.0%		
Public	Pennsylvania State Univ. - Univ. Park	47,040	40,541	86.2%	6,499	13.8%	8,166	445
Private	Princeton University	8,088	5,391	66.7%	2,697	33.3%	1,310	
Public	Purdue University - West Lafayette	39,752	30,237	76.1%	9,515	23.9%	6,533	822
Private	Rensselaer Polytechnic Institute	6,835	5,618	82.2%	1,217	17.8%	1,331	121
Private	Rice University	6,621	3,926	59.3%	2,695	40.7%	946	30
Private	Rockefeller University	209			209	100.0%		
Private	Rush University	2,457	143	5.8%	2,314	94.2%		48
Public	Rutgers University - New Brunswick	48,378	34,544	71.4%	13,834	28.6%	6,409	2,547
Public	San Diego State University	33,483	28,394	84.8%	5,089	15.2%	4,779	2,848
Private	Scripps Research Institute							
Private	Stanford University	16,963	7,019	41.4%	9,944	58.6%	1,677	29
Public	Stony Brook University	24,607	16,480	67.0%	8,127	33.0%	2,852	1,534
Public	Temple University	37,485	28,287	75.5%	9,198	24.5%	4,472	2,219
Public	Texas A&M Univ. - College Station	59,175	46,847	79.2%	12,328	20.8%	9,486	2,431
Private	Thomas Jefferson University	3,606	891	24.7%	2,715	75.3%		420
Private	Tufts University	10,907	5,177	47.5%	5,730	52.5%	1,350	30
Private	Tulane University	12,603	7,892	62.6%	4,711	37.4%	1,647	116
Public	Uniformed Services Univ. of the HS							
Public	University at Albany	17,273	12,929	74.9%	4,344	25.1%	2,546	1,267
Public	University at Buffalo	29,995	19,882	66.3%	10,113	33.7%	3,498	1,654
Public	University of Alabama - Birmingham	18,698	11,679	62.5%	7,019	37.5%	1,719	924
Public	University of Alabama - Huntsville	7,348	5,618	76.5%	1,730	23.5%	714	554
Public	University of Alaska - Fairbanks	8,620	7,484	86.8%	1,136	13.2%	739	263
Public	University of Arizona	42,236	32,987	78.1%	9,249	21.9%	7,050	1,642
Public	Univ. of Arkansas for Med. Sciences	2,890	732	25.3%	2,158	74.7%		35
Public	University of California - Berkeley	37,565	27,126	72.2%	10,439	27.8%	5,431	2,137
Public	University of California - Davis	34,508	27,565	79.9%	6,943	20.1%	5,331	3,055
Public	University of California - Irvine	30,051	24,489	81.5%	5,562	18.5%	5,426	1,983
Public	University of California - Los Angeles	41,845	29,633	70.8%	12,212	29.2%	5,753	3,115
Public	University of California - Riverside	21,498	18,790	87.4%	2,708	12.6%	4,273	1,263
Public	University of California - San Diego	30,709	24,810	80.8%	5,899	19.2%	4,913	2,402
Public	Univ. of California - San Francisco	3,170			3,170	100.0%		
Public	Univ. of California - Santa Barbara	23,051	20,238	87.8%	2,813	12.2%	4,725	1,546
Public	University of California - Santa Cruz	17,866	16,277	91.1%	1,589	8.9%	4,019	1,029
Public	University of Central Florida	60,767	52,671	86.7%	8,096	13.3%	6,216	4,345
Private	University of Chicago	15,097	5,738	38.0%	9,359	62.0%	1,445	21
Public	University of Cincinnati - Cincinnati	35,313	24,300	68.8%	11,013	31.2%	4,566	802
Public	University of Colorado - Boulder	32,432	26,557	81.9%	5,875	18.1%	5,814	1,215
Public	University of Colorado - Denver	22,791	13,509	59.3%	9,282	40.7%	1,248	1,561
Public	Univ. of Connecticut - Health Center	570	0	0.0%	570	100.0%	0	0
Public	University of Connecticut - Storrs	25,971	18,395	70.8%	7,576	29.2%	3,577	785
Private	University of Dayton	11,343	8,529	75.2%	2,814	24.8%	2,172	178
Public	University of Delaware	22,680	18,951	83.6%	3,729	16.4%	4,510	390
Public	University of Florida	49,459	32,829	66.4%	16,630	33.6%	6,475	1,498
Public	University of Georgia	35,197	26,882	76.4%	8,315	23.6%	5,240	1,281
Public	University of Hawaii - Manoa	19,507	14,126	72.4%	5,381	27.6%	1,808	1,286
Public	University of Houston - Univ. Park	40,914	33,037	80.7%	7,877	19.3%	3,908	3,112

Fall 2014 Part-Time Enrollment			2014-2015 Degrees Awarded				
Percentage of Total Students Enrolled Part Time	Percentage of Under-graduates Enrolled Part Time	Percentage of Graduates Enrolled Part Time	Associate's Degrees	Bachelor's Degrees	Master's Degrees	Doctorate Degrees	Professional Degrees
23.7%	22.7%	28.3%	0	4,854	874	215	140
5.0%		5.0%	0	0	30	26	129
3.9%	2.9%	10.2%	20	10,876	1,342	673	102
1.4%	2.2%		0	1,282	514	371	0
12.8%	6.0%	34.5%	67	7,346	1,859	717	256
2.4%	0.4%	11.8%	0	1,143	408	164	0
4.1%	1.4%	8.0%	0	1,265	711	176	0
			0	0	9	28	0
38.1%	33.6%	38.4%	0	58	493	17	183
15.3%	6.2%	38.1%	105	7,569	2,780	597	656
16.0%	11.6%	40.2%	0	6,965	1,610	140	0
			0	0	0	0	0
7.1%		12.2%	0	1,737	2,317	688	273
16.1%	6.6%	35.3%	0	4,363	1,865	347	253
15.1%	11.7%	25.9%	1	6,024	1,523	197	918
12.9%	10.5%	21.9%	0	10,305	2,545	740	349
27.1%	27.2%	27.1%	6	427	424	21	435
8.1%	1.0%	14.6%	0	1,769	1,184	116	473
18.3%	21.3%	13.4%	82	2,219	1,585	123	415
			0	0	0	0	0
16.6%	5.7%	48.9%	0	3,210	1,271	164	0
18.0%	8.6%	36.5%	0	4,983	2,509	342	686
34.0%	27.5%	45.0%	0	2,286	1,680	170	392
32.8%	23.4%	63.5%	0	1,143	424	33	13
52.8%	53.4%	49.0%	307	572	209	40	0
13.4%	10.5%	23.8%	0	7,076	1,702	528	411
28.4%	26.5%	29.1%	68	292	204	38	271
5.5%	3.0%	12.2%	0	8,516	2,386	826	339
3.9%	2.7%	8.6%	0	7,762	1,123	553	425
2.6%	1.4%	7.7%	0	6,763	1,412	390	202
3.1%	2.0%	5.8%	0	8,373	2,992	774	610
2.2%	1.8%	4.9%	0	4,729	521	272	0
3.1%	2.6%	4.9%	0	5,884	1,156	505	179
			0	0	312	130	453
2.2%	1.6%	6.9%	0	5,357	519	349	0
2.9%	2.8%	3.8%	0	4,225	288	151	0
33.7%	30.7%	52.7%	471	12,808	2,233	286	137
16.2%	1.1%	25.4%	0	1,659	2,644	392	287
25.6%	14.9%	49.2%	34	5,417	2,924	213	477
17.8%	8.3%	60.3%	0	5,851	1,225	434	172
46.7%	40.8%	55.3%	0	2,435	1,910	103	549
0.0%		0.0%	0	0	50	16	127
12.9%	3.9%	34.6%	20	5,692	1,694	323	294
12.7%	7.4%	28.9%	0	1,924	783	34	134
10.1%	7.8%	21.6%	325	4,500	891	237	37
15.3%	8.9%	27.8%	393	8,696	3,630	754	1,137
9.5%	5.6%	21.9%	0	7,447	1,598	467	425
25.5%	16.9%	48.2%	0	3,404	975	239	244
27.3%	27.4%	26.8%	0	6,425	2,075	326	453

Student Characteristics		Fall 2014 Headcount Enrollment						
Institutions with Over $40 Million in Federal Research, Alphabetically		Total Student Enrollment	Total Undergraduate Students	%	Total Graduate Students	%	First-time, Full-time Students	Full-time Transfer Students
Public	University of Idaho	11,702	9,283	79.3%	2,419	20.7%	1,554	521
Public	University of Illinois - Chicago	27,969	16,718	59.8%	11,251	40.2%	3,011	1,550
Public	Univ. of Illinois - Urbana-Champaign	45,140	32,959	73.0%	12,181	27.0%	6,926	1,320
Public	University of Iowa	29,970	22,354	74.6%	7,616	25.4%	4,347	983
Public	University of Kansas - Lawrence	23,288	18,811	80.8%	4,477	19.2%	3,977	1,096
Public	University of Kansas Medical Center	3,892	532	13.7%	3,360	86.3%	0	0
Public	University of Kentucky	29,203	22,223	76.1%	6,980	23.9%	5,144	897
Public	University of Louisville	21,561	15,961	74.0%	5,600	26.0%	2,832	778
Public	University of Maine - Orono	11,286	9,339	82.7%	1,947	17.3%	2,045	414
Public	University of Maryland - Baltimore	6,276	792	12.6%	5,484	87.4%		193
Public	Univ. of Maryland - Baltimore County	13,979	11,379	81.4%	2,600	18.6%	1,616	983
Public	University of Maryland - College Park	37,610	27,056	71.9%	10,554	28.1%	4,148	1,832
Public	Univ. of Massachusetts - Amherst	28,635	22,252	77.7%	6,383	22.3%	4,691	1,198
Public	U. of Mass. Med. Sch. - Worcester	1,103			1,103	100.0%		
Private	University of Miami	16,674	11,175	67.0%	5,499	33.0%	2,052	555
Public	University of Michigan - Ann Arbor	43,625	28,395	65.1%	15,230	34.9%	6,475	906
Public	University of Minnesota - Twin Cities	51,147	34,351	67.2%	16,796	32.8%	5,521	2,241
Public	University of Missouri - Columbia	35,425	27,642	78.0%	7,783	22.0%	6,408	1,035
Public	University of Nebraska - Lincoln	25,006	19,979	79.9%	5,027	20.1%	4,628	895
Public	University of Nebraska Medical Ctr.	3,696	850	23.0%	2,846	77.0%		354
Public	University of Nevada - Reno	19,934	16,839	84.5%	3,095	15.5%	3,332	990
Public	Univ. of New Hampshire - Durham	15,117	12,831	84.9%	2,286	15.1%	3,227	487
Public	Univ. of New Mexico - Albuquerque	27,844	21,792	78.3%	6,052	21.7%	3,089	843
Public	Univ. of North Carolina - Chapel Hill	29,135	18,350	63.0%	10,785	37.0%	3,976	870
Public	University of North Dakota	14,906	11,537	77.4%	3,369	22.6%	1,882	487
Private	University of Notre Dame	12,179	8,448	69.4%	3,731	30.6%	2,012	118
Public	University of Oklahoma - Norman	27,261	21,011	77.1%	6,250	22.9%	3,882	876
Public	University of Oklahoma HSC	3,499	828	23.7%	2,671	76.3%		330
Public	University of Oregon	24,096	20,559	85.3%	3,537	14.7%	3,896	1,181
Private	University of Pennsylvania	24,806	11,548	46.6%	13,258	53.4%	2,350	225
Public	University of Pittsburgh - Pittsburgh	28,617	18,757	65.5%	9,860	34.5%	3,845	791
Public	University of Rhode Island	16,571	13,589	82.0%	2,982	18.0%	3,123	444
Private	University of Rochester	11,060	6,266	56.7%	4,794	43.3%	1,436	112
Public	Univ. of South Carolina - Columbia	32,971	24,866	75.4%	8,105	24.6%	4,943	1,394
Public	University of South Florida - Tampa	41,938	31,067	74.1%	10,871	25.9%	4,071	2,365
Private	University of Southern California	42,453	18,739	44.1%	23,714	55.9%	3,093	1,426
Public	University of Tennessee - Knoxville	30,386	21,664	71.3%	8,722	28.7%	4,689	1,280
Public	University of Tennessee HSC							
Public	University of Texas - Austin	51,313	39,523	77.0%	11,790	23.0%	7,036	2,197
Public	University of Texas HSC - Houston	4,556	657	14.4%	3,899	85.6%		47
Public	Univ. of Texas HSC - San Antonio	3,147	825	26.2%	2,322	73.8%		258
Public	U. of Texas MD Anderson Cancer Ctr.	303	292	96.4%	11	3.6%		102
Public	U. of Texas Med. Branch - Galveston	3,211	708	22.0%	2,503	78.0%		237
Public	U. of Texas SW Med. Center - Dallas	2,341	5	0.2%	2,336	99.8%		
Public	University of Utah	31,515	23,907	75.9%	7,608	24.1%	2,871	1,229
Public	University of Vermont	12,856	10,992	85.5%	1,864	14.5%	2,286	414
Public	University of Virginia	23,732	16,483	69.5%	7,249	30.5%	3,706	579
Public	University of Washington - Seattle	44,784	30,672	68.5%	14,112	31.5%	6,208	1,695
Public	University of Wisconsin - Madison	42,598	30,694	72.1%	11,904	27.9%	6,243	721

Fall 2014 Part-Time Enrollment			2014-2015 Degrees Awarded				
Percentage of Total Students Enrolled Part Time	Percentage of Under-graduates Enrolled Part Time	Percentage of Graduates Enrolled Part Time	Associate's Degrees	Bachelor's Degrees	Master's Degrees	Doctorate Degrees	Professional Degrees
22.1%	16.9%	42.3%	0	2,017	524	80	112
16.8%	7.5%	30.6%	0	3,807	2,204	314	676
8.3%	3.7%	20.6%	0	8,621	3,286	829	305
18.5%	12.6%	36.0%	0	5,419	1,287	453	490
11.9%	10.4%	26.0%	0	3,865	1,279	365	291
31.2%	10.5%	24.6%	0	217	188	25	272
9.4%	6.9%	17.2%	0	4,504	1,260	295	513
23.7%	21.7%	29.2%	25	2,945	1,283	170	395
21.1%	13.0%	60.1%	0	1,651	326	69	0
20.9%	27.9%	19.9%	0	333	845	81	808
22.4%	15.2%	54.3%	0	2,540	694	100	0
12.4%	7.5%	25.0%	0	7,700	2,562	654	39
19.9%	7.0%	64.6%	54	6,069	1,418	268	29
6.8%		6.8%	0	0	53	61	130
7.6%	5.7%	11.3%	0	3,291	1,175	208	678
5.8%	3.5%	10.0%	0	8,097	4,296	882	730
24.5%	15.9%	42.1%	0	8,452	3,308	725	1,036
12.6%	6.5%	34.4%	0	5,995	1,571	435	346
14.6%	6.6%	46.2%	6	4,029	860	325	139
14.2%	18.2%	13.0%	0	434	257	81	287
23.4%	16.9%	59.1%	0	3,178	622	109	70
10.1%	3.5%	46.9%	139	3,204	722	75	4
28.2%	24.5%	41.4%	0	4,068	1,258	222	328
16.7%	4.3%	37.8%	0	5,901	2,141	519	700
27.6%	21.3%	49.3%	0	2,043	747	87	181
1.5%	0.2%	4.5%	0	2,760	991	244	180
22.6%	14.3%	50.7%	0	4,279	1,713	218	148
16.3%	6.5%	19.3%	0	450	334	29	407
10.4%	9.2%	17.7%	0	5,110	897	199	121
13.6%	9.9%	16.8%	1	3,382	4,127	566	682
11.7%	5.7%	23.0%	0	5,232	2,295	438	652
15.4%	10.7%	36.8%	0	3,088	514	93	153
14.7%	5.2%	27.1%	0	1,863	1,340	267	108
12.3%	6.8%	29.4%	4	6,210	1,623	358	393
29.1%	23.4%	45.4%	202	8,166	2,893	321	280
14.1%	3.6%	22.4%	0	5,385	7,710	685	837
12.0%	6.1%	26.7%	0	4,632	1,551	353	219
8.4%	8.1%	9.4%	0	9,503	3,188	899	480
28.3%	18.0%	30.0%	0	421	470	153	335
10.9%	5.5%	12.9%	0	407	175	66	363
17.2%	15.4%	63.6%	0	158	0	0	0
25.7%	17.2%	28.1%	0	419	356	39	328
26.1%		26.2%	0	0	104	88	242
27.0%	28.3%	23.0%	0	5,246	1,948	384	383
13.3%	10.0%	32.7%	0	2,496	362	79	145
8.8%	5.2%	17.0%	0	4,812	1,760	366	525
12.5%	9.5%	19.2%	0	8,343	3,606	687	554
10.4%	7.8%	17.3%	0	8,747	2,153	857	649

Student Characteristics		Fall 2014 Headcount Enrollment						
Institutions with Over $40 Million in Federal Research, Alphabetically		Total Student Enrollment	Total Undergraduate Students	%	Total Graduate Students	%	First-time, Full-time Students	Full-time Transfer Students
Public	Utah State University	27,662	24,271	87.7%	3,391	12.3%	3,696	1,231
Private	Vanderbilt University	12,686	6,851	54.0%	5,835	46.0%	1,604	206
Public	Virginia Commonwealth University	30,848	23,661	76.7%	7,187	23.3%	3,522	1,993
Public	Virginia Polytechnic Inst. and St. Univ.	31,224	24,247	77.7%	6,977	22.3%	5,474	937
Private	Wake Forest University	7,788	4,867	62.5%	2,921	37.5%	1,287	29
Public	Washington State Univ. - Pullman	28,686	23,867	83.2%	4,819	16.8%	4,357	1,936
Private	Washington University in St. Louis	14,348	7,401	51.6%	6,947	48.4%	1,727	117
Public	Wayne State University	27,578	18,347	66.5%	9,231	33.5%	2,101	1,344
Private	Weill Cornell Medical College	1,023			1,023	100.0%		
Public	West Virginia University	29,175	22,563	77.3%	6,612	22.7%	4,850	872
Private	Woods Hole Oceanographic Inst.							
Private	Yale University	12,336	5,477	44.4%	6,859	55.6%	1,360	29
Private	Yeshiva University	6,348	2,814	44.3%	3,534	55.7%	811	16

Fall 2014 Part-Time Enrollment			2014-2015 Degrees Awarded				
Percentage of Total Students Enrolled Part Time	Percentage of Under-graduates Enrolled Part Time	Percentage of Graduates Enrolled Part Time	Associate's Degrees	Bachelor's Degrees	Master's Degrees	Doctorate Degrees	Professional Degrees
38.7%	34.8%	66.7%	1,272	3,551	904	102	6
6.4%	1.1%	12.7%	0	2,116	1,636	340	394
18.9%	15.2%	30.8%	0	5,149	1,557	282	432
8.7%	2.3%	30.9%	49	6,134	1,428	488	105
4.0%	1.3%	8.6%	0	1,350	822	53	249
15.5%	12.7%	29.4%	0	5,513	741	281	183
14.1%	9.7%	18.9%	3	2,155	1,755	292	459
35.3%	34.4%	37.1%	0	3,241	2,053	242	569
			0	0	73	68	96
12.2%	7.5%	28.2%	0	4,437	1,649	183	428
1.5%	0.1%	2.6%	0	1,496	1,730	426	336
15.0%	3.2%	24.4%	263	573	469	96	554

The Center Measures - National Rankings

	Institutions with Over $40 Million in Federal Research, Alphabetically	2016 No. of Measures in Top 25 Nationally	2016 No. of Measures in Top 26-50 Nationally	2015 No. of Measures in Top 25 Nationally	2015 No. of Measures in Top 26-50 Nationally
Public	Arizona State University	2	0	1	0
Public	Auburn University	0	0	0	0
Public	Augusta University	0	0	0	0
Private	Baylor College of Medicine	0	4	0	4
Private	Boston University	0	4	0	4
Private	Brandeis University	0	0	0	0
Private	Brown University	1	3	1	3
Private	California Institute of Technology	2	5	2	4
Private	Carnegie Mellon University	1	2	1	2
Private	Case Western Reserve University	0	3	0	4
Public	Clemson University	0	0	0	0
Public	Cleveland State University	0	0	0	0
Private	Cold Spring Harbor Laboratory	0	0	0	0
Public	Colorado State University - Fort Collins	0	0	0	1
Private	Columbia University	9	0	9	0
Private	Cornell University	4	5	4	5
Private	Dartmouth College	2	1	2	1
Private	Drexel University	0	0	0	0
Private	Duke University	8	1	9	0
Private	Emory University	2	6	3	5
Public	Florida International University	0	1	0	0
Public	Florida State University	0	1	0	1
Public	George Mason University	0	0	0	0
Private	George Washington University	0	2	0	0
Private	Georgetown University	0	2	0	1
Public	Georgia Institute of Technology	2	5	3	5
Private	Harvard University	9	0	9	0
Private	Icahn School of Medicine at Mount Sinai	1	2	0	4
Public	Indiana University - Bloomington	0	3	0	3
Public	Indiana Univ. - Purdue Univ. - Indianapolis	0	0	0	0
Public	Iowa State University	0	0	0	0
Private	Johns Hopkins University	6	3	6	3
Public	Kansas State University	0	0	0	1
Public	Louisiana State University - Baton Rouge	0	0	0	0
Private	Massachusetts Institute of Technology	9	0	9	0
Private	Medical College of Wisconsin	0	0	0	0
Public	Medical University of South Carolina	0	0	0	0
Public	Michigan State University	1	4	1	4
Public	Mississippi State University	0	0	0	0
Public	Montana State University - Bozeman	0	0	0	0
Public	Naval Postgraduate School	0	0	0	0
Public	New Jersey Institute of Technology	0	0	0	0
Public	New Mexico State University - Las Cruces	0	0	0	0
Private	New York University	3	5	3	5
Public	North Carolina State University	0	3	0	4
Private	Northeastern University	0	2	0	1
Private	Northwestern University	6	3	6	3
Public	Ohio State University - Columbus	5	3	6	2
Public	Oregon Health & Science University	0	1	0	1

2014 No. of Measures in Top 25 Nationally	2014 No. of Measures in Top 26-50 Nationally	2013 No. of Measures in Top 25 Nationally	2013 No. of Measures in Top 26-50 Nationally	2012 No. of Measures in Top 25 Nationally	2012 No. of Measures in Top 26-50 Nationally	2011 No. of Measures in Top 25 Nationally	2011 No. of Measures in Top 26-50 Nationally
1	0	1	1	0	1	1	0
0	0	0	0	0	0	0	0
0	0	0	0	0	0	0	0
0	3	0	3	0	3	0	3
1	3	2	2	1	3	0	3
0	0	0	0	0	1	0	1
1	3	0	3	1	3	1	2
3	2	2	4	2	4	3	4
0	2	0	3	0	3	0	2
0	4	0	3	0	4	1	3
0	0	0	0	0	0	0	0
0	0	0	0	0	0	0	0
0	0	0	0	0	0	0	0
0	0	0	0	0	0	0	1
9	0	9	0	9	0	9	0
3	6	4	5	5	4	3	5
2	1	2	1	2	1	2	1
0	0	0	0	0	0	0	0
8	1	8	1	8	0	8	0
3	5	4	4	3	5	2	5
0	0	0	0	0	0	0	0
0	0	0	1	0	1	0	1
0	0	0	0	0	0	0	0
0	0	0	1	0	0	0	1
0	2	0	1	0	2	0	1
2	4	3	4	3	4	1	5
9	0	8	1	8	1	8	1
0	2	0	2	0	2	0	2
0	3	0	3	0	3	0	2
0	1	0	1	0	1	0	1
0	0	0	1	0	1	0	0
8	1	7	2	6	3	7	2
0	0	0	0	0	0	0	0
0	0	0	0	0	0	0	0
9	0	9	0	9	0	9	0
0	0	0	0	0	0	0	0
0	0	0	0	0	0	0	0
0	6	0	6	0	5	1	5
0	0	0	0	0	0	0	0
0	0	0	0	0	0	0	0
0	0	0	0	0	0	0	0
0	0	0	0	0	0	0	0
0	0	0	0	0	0	0	0
4	4	4	5	3	4	3	3
0	4	0	2	0	2	0	2
0	1	0	0	0	0	0	0
6	3	6	3	6	3	5	4
6	2	4	3	5	3	4	4
0	0	0	1	0	1	0	1

The Center Measures - National Rankings

	Institutions with Over $40 Million in Federal Research, Alphabetically	2016 No. of Measures in Top 25 Nationally	2016 No. of Measures in Top 26-50 Nationally	2015 No. of Measures in Top 25 Nationally	2015 No. of Measures in Top 26-50 Nationally
Public	Oregon State University	0	0	0	0
Public	Pennsylvania State Univ. - Hershey Med. Ctr.	0	0	0	0
Public	Pennsylvania State University - Univ. Park	3	5	3	4
Private	Princeton University	4	2	4	3
Public	Purdue University - West Lafayette	1	5	1	5
Private	Rensselaer Polytechnic Institute	0	1	0	1
Private	Rice University	2	1	2	1
Private	Rockefeller University	1	1	1	1
Private	Rush University	0	0	0	0
Public	Rutgers University - New Brunswick	2	3	0	4
Public	San Diego State University	0	0	0	0
Private	Scripps Research Institute	1	2	0	3
Private	Stanford University	9	0	9	0
Public	Stony Brook University	0	0	0	0
Public	Temple University	0	0	0	0
Public	Texas A&M University - College Station	3	5	4	2
Private	Thomas Jefferson University	0	0	0	0
Private	Tufts University	1	0	1	0
Private	Tulane University	0	0	0	1
Public	Uniformed Services Univ. of the HS	0	0	0	0
Public	University at Albany	0	0	0	0
Public	University at Buffalo	0	0	0	0
Public	University of Alabama - Birmingham	0	2	0	2
Public	University of Alabama - Huntsville	0	0	0	0
Public	University of Alaska - Fairbanks	0	0	0	0
Public	University of Arizona	0	6	0	5
Public	University of Arkansas for Medical Sciences	0	0	0	0
Public	University of California - Berkeley	7	2	7	1
Public	University of California - Davis	3	3	2	3
Public	University of California - Irvine	0	3	0	3
Public	University of California - Los Angeles	7	1	7	1
Public	University of California - Riverside	0	0	0	0
Public	University of California - San Diego	5	2	4	3
Public	University of California - San Francisco	6	1	6	1
Public	University of California - Santa Barbara	1	0	1	0
Public	University of California - Santa Cruz	0	0	0	0
Public	University of Central Florida	0	0	0	0
Private	University of Chicago	5	3	5	3
Public	University of Cincinnati - Cincinnati	0	1	0	4
Public	University of Colorado - Boulder	1	4	1	3
Public	University of Colorado - Denver	0	2	0	1
Public	University of Connecticut - Health Center	0	0	0	0
Public	University of Connecticut - Storrs	0	0	0	0
Private	University of Dayton	0	0	0	0
Public	University of Delaware	0	0	0	1
Public	University of Florida	3	4	2	5
Public	University of Georgia	0	1	0	2
Public	University of Hawaii - Manoa	0	0	0	0
Public	University of Houston - University Park	0	0	0	0

2014 No. of Measures in Top 25 Nationally	2014 No. of Measures in Top 26-50 Nationally	2013 No. of Measures in Top 25 Nationally	2013 No. of Measures in Top 26-50 Nationally	2012 No. of Measures in Top 25 Nationally	2012 No. of Measures in Top 26-50 Nationally	2011 No. of Measures in Top 25 Nationally	2011 No. of Measures in Top 26-50 Nationally
0	0	0	1	0	0	0	0
0	0	0	0	0	0	0	0
4	3	3	4	5	2	3	4
4	2	4	2	4	2	4	2
1	4	2	4	2	4	1	6
0	1	0	1	0	1	0	1
2	1	2	1	2	0	2	0
0	2	1	1	1	1	1	1
0	0	0	0	0	0	0	0
1	4	0	4	0	4	0	3
0	0	0	0	0	0	0	0
0	2	0	2	0	3	0	4
9	0	9	0	9	0	9	0
0	0	0	0	0	0	0	0
0	0	0	0	0	0	0	0
4	2	4	3	3	4	4	3
0	0	0	0	0	0	0	0
1	0	1	0	1	0	1	0
0	1	0	0	0	0	0	0
0	0	0	0	0	0	0	0
0	0	0	0	0	0	0	0
0	1	0	0	0	0	0	1
0	2	0	2	0	2	0	2
0	0	0	0	0	0	0	0
0	0	0	0	0	0	0	0
0	5	0	6	0	6	1	4
0	0	0	0	0	0	0	0
7	2	7	2	7	1	7	1
3	3	3	3	3	3	2	4
0	4	0	4	0	4	1	3
7	1	7	1	8	0	7	1
0	0	0	0	0	1	0	0
5	2	6	1	5	2	5	1
6	1	6	1	6	1	6	1
1	1	1	0	1	1	1	1
0	0	0	0	0	0	0	1
0	0	0	0	0	0	0	0
5	4	5	4	5	4	4	5
0	3	0	3	0	2	0	2
1	3	1	3	1	2	0	5
0	2	0	3	0	2	0	2
0	0	0	0	0	0	0	0
0	0	0	0	0	0	0	1
0	0	0	0	0	0	0	0
0	0	0	0	0	0	0	0
2	5	2	5	3	4	3	4
0	1	0	2	0	1	0	1
0	0	0	0	0	0	0	0
0	0	0	1	0	0	0	0

The Center Measures - National Rankings

	Institutions with Over $40 Million in Federal Research, Alphabetically	2016 No. of Measures in Top 25 Nationally	2016 No. of Measures in Top 26-50 Nationally	2015 No. of Measures in Top 25 Nationally	2015 No. of Measures in Top 26-50 Nationally
Public	University of Idaho	0	0	0	0
Public	University of Illinois - Chicago	0	0	0	1
Public	University of Illinois - Urbana-Champaign	3	4	5	2
Public	University of Iowa	0	3	0	4
Public	University of Kansas - Lawrence	0	1	0	1
Public	University of Kansas Medical Center	0	0	0	0
Public	University of Kentucky	0	0	0	0
Public	University of Louisville	0	0	0	0
Public	University of Maine - Orono	0	0	0	0
Public	University of Maryland - Baltimore	0	0	0	2
Public	University of Maryland - Baltimore County	0	0	0	0
Public	University of Maryland - College Park	1	5	1	5
Public	University of Massachusetts - Amherst	0	1	0	0
Public	Univ. of Mass. Med. Sch. - Worcester	0	0	0	1
Private	University of Miami	0	1	0	1
Public	University of Michigan - Ann Arbor	8	1	8	0
Public	University of Minnesota - Twin Cities	6	2	6	2
Public	University of Missouri - Columbia	0	1	0	1
Public	University of Nebraska - Lincoln	0	1	0	0
Public	University of Nebraska Medical Center	0	0	0	0
Public	University of Nevada - Reno	0	0	0	0
Public	University of New Hampshire - Durham	0	0	0	0
Public	University of New Mexico - Albuquerque	0	0	0	0
Public	University of North Carolina - Chapel Hill	4	4	6	2
Public	University of North Dakota	0	0	0	0
Private	University of Notre Dame	3	1	3	1
Public	University of Oklahoma - Norman	0	1	0	0
Public	Univ. of Oklahoma Health Sciences Center	0	0	0	0
Public	University of Oregon	0	0	0	0
Private	University of Pennsylvania	9	0	8	1
Public	University of Pittsburgh - Pittsburgh	4	3	5	2
Public	University of Rhode Island	0	0	0	0
Private	University of Rochester	0	3	0	3
Public	University of South Carolina - Columbia	0	0	0	0
Public	University of South Florida - Tampa	0	2	0	0
Private	University of Southern California	6	3	6	3
Public	University of Tennessee - Knoxville	0	0	0	1
Public	Univ. of Tennessee Health Science Center	0	0	0	0
Public	University of Texas - Austin	4	4	4	4
Public	University of Texas HSC - Houston	0	0	0	0
Public	University of Texas HSC - San Antonio	0	0	0	0
Public	Univ. of Texas MD Anderson Cancer Center	1	2	1	2
Public	Univ. of Texas Medical Branch - Galveston	0	0	0	0
Public	Univ. of Texas SW Medical Center - Dallas	0	4	0	4
Public	University of Utah	0	4	0	5
Public	University of Vermont	0	0	0	0
Public	University of Virginia	1	4	1	4
Public	University of Washington - Seattle	7	1	7	1
Public	University of Wisconsin - Madison	7	1	6	2

2014 No. of Measures in Top 25 Nationally	2014 No. of Measures in Top 26-50 Nationally	2013 No. of Measures in Top 25 Nationally	2013 No. of Measures in Top 26-50 Nationally	2012 No. of Measures in Top 25 Nationally	2012 No. of Measures in Top 26-50 Nationally	2011 No. of Measures in Top 25 Nationally	2011 No. of Measures in Top 26-50 Nationally
0	0	0	0	0	0	0	0
0	0	0	0	0	0	0	0
3	4	3	4	3	4	4	3
1	3	0	5	0	7	0	6
0	1	0	1	0	0	0	0
0	0	0	0	0	0	0	0
0	0	0	0	0	0	0	1
0	0	0	0	0	0	0	0
0	0	0	0	0	0	0	0
0	2	0	0	0	1	0	1
0	0	0	0	0	0	0	0
1	4	1	5	1	5	1	4
0	0	0	0	0	0	0	0
0	1	0	2	0	2	0	2
0	1	0	1	0	1	0	1
8	0	8	1	8	0	8	0
4	4	6	2	6	2	6	2
0	1	0	1	0	1	0	1
0	0	0	0	0	0	0	0
0	0	0	0	0	0	0	0
0	0	0	0	0	0	0	0
0	0	0	0	0	0	0	0
0	0	0	0	0	0	0	1
6	2	5	3	6	2	6	2
0	0	0	0	0	0	0	0
3	1	2	1	2	1	3	0
0	1	0	0	0	1	0	1
0	0	0	0	0	0	0	0
0	1	0	0	0	0	0	1
8	1	9	0	9	0	9	0
4	4	4	4	4	4	4	4
0	0	0	0	0	0	0	0
0	3	0	5	0	5	0	5
0	0	0	0	0	0	0	0
0	0	0	0	0	0	0	0
5	4	6	3	6	3	5	4
0	1	0	2	0	1	0	1
0	0	0	0	0	0	0	0
4	4	5	3	5	2	6	1
0	0	0	0	0	0	0	0
0	0	0	0	0	0	0	0
1	2	1	2	1	2	1	2
0	0	0	0	0	0	0	1
0	4	0	6	0	7	0	6
0	5	1	4	0	3	0	3
0	0	0	0	0	0	0	0
2	4	3	2	1	5	1	5
7	1	7	1	7	1	7	1
7	1	7	1	7	1	7	1

The Center Measures - National Rankings

	Institutions with Over $40 Million in Federal Research, Alphabetically	2016 No. of Measures in Top 25 Nationally	2016 No. of Measures in Top 26-50 Nationally	2015 No. of Measures in Top 25 Nationally	2015 No. of Measures in Top 26-50 Nationally
Public	Utah State University	0	0	0	0
Private	Vanderbilt University	4	3	4	4
Public	Virginia Commonwealth University	0	0	0	0
Public	Virginia Polytechnic Institute and State Univ.	0	2	0	2
Private	Wake Forest University	0	0	0	0
Public	Washington State University - Pullman	0	0	0	0
Private	Washington University in St. Louis	4	4	5	3
Public	Wayne State University	0	0	0	0
Private	Weill Cornell Medical College	0	2	0	2
Public	West Virginia University	0	0	0	0
Private	Woods Hole Oceanographic Institution	0	0	0	0
Private	Yale University	8	1	8	1
Private	Yeshiva University	0	0	0	1

2014 No. of Measures in Top 25 Nationally	2014 No. of Measures in Top 26-50 Nationally	2013 No. of Measures in Top 25 Nationally	2013 No. of Measures in Top 26-50 Nationally	2012 No. of Measures in Top 25 Nationally	2012 No. of Measures in Top 26-50 Nationally	2011 No. of Measures in Top 25 Nationally	2011 No. of Measures in Top 26-50 Nationally
0	0	0	0	0	0	0	0
4	4	4	4	4	4	4	4
0	1	0	0	0	0	0	0
0	2	0	2	0	2	0	2
0	0	0	0	0	0	0	0
0	0	0	0	0	0	0	0
6	2	4	4	5	3	8	0
0	0	0	0	0	0	0	0
0	2	0	0	0	0	0	0
0	0	0	0	0	0	0	0
0	0	0	0	0	0	0	0
8	1	8	1	8	0	7	2
0	0	0	0	0	1	0	1

The Center Measures - Control Rankings

	Institutions with Over $40 Million in Federal Research, Alphabetically	2016 No. of Measures in Top 25 Among Privates/Publics	2016 No. of Measures in Top 26-50 Among Privates/Publics	2015 No. of Measures in Top 25 Among Privates/Publics	2015 No. of Measures in Top 26-50 Among Privates/Publics
Public	Arizona State University	2	5	1	6
Public	Auburn University	0	2	0	2
Public	Augusta University	0	0	0	0
Private	Baylor College of Medicine	4	3	4	1
Private	Boston University	5	3	5	3
Private	Brandeis University	0	7	0	6
Private	Brown University	4	5	4	5
Private	California Institute of Technology	8	1	6	3
Private	Carnegie Mellon University	5	4	6	3
Private	Case Western Reserve University	2	7	2	7
Public	Clemson University	0	2	0	1
Public	Cleveland State University	0	0	0	0
Private	Cold Spring Harbor Laboratory	0	4	0	3
Public	Colorado State University - Fort Collins	0	5	1	5
Private	Columbia University	9	0	9	0
Private	Cornell University	8	1	8	1
Private	Dartmouth College	3	5	3	5
Private	Drexel University	0	7	0	7
Private	Duke University	9	0	9	0
Private	Emory University	8	1	8	1
Public	Florida International University	0	1	0	0
Public	Florida State University	0	4	0	4
Public	George Mason University	0	0	0	0
Private	George Washington University	3	5	2	6
Private	Georgetown University	1	8	1	8
Public	Georgia Institute of Technology	7	1	8	1
Private	Harvard University	9	0	9	0
Private	Icahn School of Medicine at Mount Sinai	3	3	4	2
Public	Indiana University - Bloomington	3	2	2	3
Public	Indiana Univ. - Purdue Univ. - Indianapolis	0	5	0	4
Public	Iowa State University	0	6	0	4
Private	Johns Hopkins University	8	1	8	1
Public	Kansas State University	0	0	1	0
Public	Louisiana State University - Baton Rouge	0	3	0	3
Private	Massachusetts Institute of Technology	9	0	9	0
Private	Medical College of Wisconsin	0	4	0	4
Public	Medical University of South Carolina	0	0	0	0
Public	Michigan State University	4	4	5	3
Public	Mississippi State University	0	0	0	0
Public	Montana State University - Bozeman	0	0	0	0
Public	Naval Postgraduate School	0	0	0	0
Public	New Jersey Institute of Technology	0	0	0	0
Public	New Mexico State University - Las Cruces	0	0	0	0
Private	New York University	8	0	8	0
Public	North Carolina State University	2	7	2	7
Private	Northeastern University	1	7	1	6
Private	Northwestern University	9	0	9	0
Public	Ohio State University - Columbus	9	0	9	0
Public	Oregon Health & Science University	0	5	1	4

2014	2014	2013	2013	2012	2012	2011	2011
No. of Measures in Top 25 Among Privates/Publics	No. of Measures in Top 26-50 Among Privates/Publics	No. of Measures in Top 25 Among Privates/Publics	No. of Measures in Top 26-50 Among Privates/Publics	No. of Measures in Top 25 Among Privates/Publics	No. of Measures in Top 26-50 Among Privates/Publics	No. of Measures in Top 25 Among Privates/Publics	No. of Measures in Top 26-50 Among Privates/Publics
1	5	1	6	1	6	1	5
0	1	0	1	0	1	0	1
0	0	0	0	0	0	0	0
4	2	4	2	4	2	4	2
5	3	5	3	6	2	5	3
1	5	0	6	1	6	0	7
4	5	4	5	5	4	4	5
8	1	8	1	8	1	8	1
4	5	4	5	4	5	4	4
3	6	2	6	4	5	3	5
0	1	0	1	0	1	0	1
0	0	0	0	0	0	0	0
0	3	0	3	0	1	0	1
0	5	0	3	0	3	0	3
9	0	9	0	9	0	9	0
8	1	8	1	8	1	7	2
4	4	3	5	3	5	3	5
0	7	0	7	0	6	0	7
9	0	9	0	9	0	9	0
8	1	8	1	8	1	8	1
0	0	0	0	0	0	0	1
0	3	0	4	0	6	0	6
0	0	0	0	0	0	0	0
2	6	2	6	1	7	2	5
1	8	1	8	1	8	0	9
7	2	7	2	8	1	7	2
9	0	9	0	9	0	9	0
4	2	4	2	3	2	3	3
3	3	2	3	2	3	2	2
0	4	1	4	1	4	1	4
0	3	0	5	0	5	0	5
8	1	8	1	8	1	8	1
0	1	0	0	0	0	0	1
0	3	0	3	0	2	0	3
9	0	9	0	9	0	9	0
0	4	0	4	0	4	0	3
0	1	0	1	0	1	0	0
6	2	4	4	4	4	4	4
0	0	0	0	0	0	0	0
0	0	0	0	0	0	0	0
0	0	0	0	0	0	0	0
0	0	0	0	0	0	0	0
0	0	0	0	0	0	0	0
8	0	8	1	8	0	8	0
3	5	0	8	0	8	1	7
0	7	0	6	0	6	0	5
9	0	9	0	9	0	9	0
9	0	8	1	9	0	9	0
0	5	0	6	0	6	1	5

The Center Measures - Control Rankings

	Institutions with Over $40 Million in Federal Research, Alphabetically	2016 No. of Measures in Top 25 Among Privates/Publics	2016 No. of Measures in Top 26-50 Among Privates/Publics	2015 No. of Measures in Top 25 Among Privates/Publics	2015 No. of Measures in Top 26-50 Among Privates/Publics
Public	Oregon State University	0	1	0	3
Public	Pennsylvania St. Univ. - Hershey Med. Ctr.	0	0	0	0
Public	Pennsylvania State University - Univ. Park	6	2	8	0
Private	Princeton University	7	2	7	2
Public	Purdue University - West Lafayette	6	3	5	4
Private	Rensselaer Polytechnic Institute	0	7	0	7
Private	Rice University	3	6	3	6
Private	Rockefeller University	2	4	2	4
Private	Rush University	0	2	0	2
Public	Rutgers University - New Brunswick	5	4	3	6
Public	San Diego State University	0	0	0	0
Private	Scripps Research Institute	4	1	4	0
Private	Stanford University	9	0	9	0
Public	Stony Brook University	0	5	0	5
Public	Temple University	0	1	0	1
Public	Texas A&M University - College Station	8	0	5	2
Private	Thomas Jefferson University	0	4	0	4
Private	Tufts University	1	8	1	8
Private	Tulane University	0	8	0	7
Public	Uniformed Services University of the HS	0	1	0	0
Public	University at Albany	0	0	0	0
Public	University at Buffalo	0	5	0	4
Public	University of Alabama - Birmingham	1	3	1	3
Public	University of Alabama - Huntsville	0	1	0	0
Public	University of Alaska - Fairbanks	0	0	0	0
Public	University of Arizona	6	2	4	4
Public	University of Arkansas for Medical Sciences	0	0	0	0
Public	University of California - Berkeley	9	0	9	0
Public	University of California - Davis	6	3	5	3
Public	University of California - Irvine	2	4	2	5
Public	University of California - Los Angeles	9	0	9	0
Public	University of California - Riverside	0	1	0	2
Public	University of California - San Diego	8	1	8	1
Public	University of California - San Francisco	7	0	7	0
Public	University of California - Santa Barbara	1	4	1	4
Public	University of California - Santa Cruz	0	1	0	1
Public	University of Central Florida	0	0	0	1
Private	University of Chicago	9	0	9	0
Public	University of Cincinnati - Cincinnati	2	5	2	5
Public	University of Colorado - Boulder	4	4	3	4
Public	University of Colorado - Denver	2	3	1	4
Public	University of Connecticut - Health Center	0	0	0	0
Public	University of Connecticut - Storrs	0	3	0	1
Private	University of Dayton	0	2	0	2
Public	University of Delaware	1	1	1	1
Public	University of Florida	8	1	9	0
Public	University of Georgia	0	6	1	6
Public	University of Hawaii - Manoa	0	4	0	5
Public	University of Houston - University Park	0	4	0	3

2014 No. of Measures in Top 25 Among Privates/Publics	2014 No. of Measures in Top 26-50 Among Privates/Publics	2013 No. of Measures in Top 25 Among Privates/Publics	2013 No. of Measures in Top 26-50 Among Privates/Publics	2012 No. of Measures in Top 25 Among Privates/Publics	2012 No. of Measures in Top 26-50 Among Privates/Publics	2011 No. of Measures in Top 25 Among Privates/Publics	2011 No. of Measures in Top 26-50 Among Privates/Publics
0	2	1	2	0	1	0	1
0	0	0	0	0	0	0	0
8	1	8	0	7	2	7	2
7	2	7	2	7	2	7	2
5	3	6	2	6	2	5	3
0	7	0	7	0	8	0	7
4	5	3	6	4	5	3	6
3	3	3	3	2	4	4	2
0	2	0	3	0	3	0	4
3	6	2	5	1	7	3	5
0	0	0	0	0	0	0	0
4	0	4	0	4	0	4	0
9	0	9	0	9	0	9	0
0	6	0	3	0	4	0	4
0	1	0	0	0	0	0	0
5	4	6	3	6	3	6	3
0	4	0	4	0	4	0	4
1	8	1	8	1	8	1	8
0	7	0	7	0	7	0	7
0	0	0	0	0	0	0	1
0	0	0	0	0	1	0	1
0	6	0	6	0	6	1	5
2	1	2	2	2	2	2	1
0	0	0	0	0	0	0	0
0	0	0	0	0	0	0	0
4	4	5	3	6	2	5	3
0	0	0	0	0	0	0	0
9	0	9	0	9	0	9	0
6	3	5	4	6	3	6	2
3	3	2	4	2	5	3	4
9	0	9	0	9	0	9	0
0	2	0	3	0	2	0	2
7	2	8	1	7	2	7	2
7	0	7	0	7	0	7	0
1	4	1	5	1	4	2	1
0	1	0	1	0	1	0	2
0	0	0	0	0	0	0	0
9	0	9	0	9	0	9	0
3	4	3	4	2	5	1	5
4	2	3	4	3	4	4	4
1	3	2	4	1	4	1	3
0	0	0	0	0	0	0	0
0	2	0	2	0	1	1	2
0	2	0	2	0	2	0	2
1	0	1	3	1	1	1	2
8	1	9	0	9	0	8	1
0	6	1	4	1	2	1	6
0	5	0	4	0	3	0	3
0	3	1	4	0	3	0	3

The Center Measures - Control Rankings

	Institutions with Over $40 Million in Federal Research, Alphabetically	2016 No. of Measures in Top 25 Among Privates/Publics	2016 No. of Measures in Top 26-50 Among Privates/Publics	2015 No. of Measures in Top 25 Among Privates/Publics	2015 No. of Measures in Top 26-50 Among Privates/Publics
Public	University of Idaho	0	0	0	0
Public	University of Illinois - Chicago	0	5	0	5
Public	University of Illinois - Urbana-Champaign	9	0	9	0
Public	University of Iowa	2	6	3	6
Public	University of Kansas - Lawrence	1	3	1	3
Public	University of Kansas Medical Center	0	0	0	0
Public	University of Kentucky	0	6	0	6
Public	University of Louisville	0	1	0	1
Public	University of Maine - Orono	0	0	0	0
Public	University of Maryland - Baltimore	0	4	0	4
Public	University of Maryland - Baltimore County	0	1	0	1
Public	University of Maryland - College Park	6	2	7	0
Public	University of Massachusetts - Amherst	1	1	0	3
Public	University of Mass. Med. Sch. - Worcester	0	3	0	3
Private	University of Miami	3	4	3	4
Public	University of Michigan - Ann Arbor	9	0	9	0
Public	University of Minnesota - Twin Cities	9	0	9	0
Public	University of Missouri - Columbia	0	5	0	5
Public	University of Nebraska - Lincoln	1	2	0	3
Public	University of Nebraska Medical Center	0	0	0	0
Public	University of Nevada - Reno	0	0	0	0
Public	University of New Hampshire - Durham	0	0	0	0
Public	University of New Mexico - Albuquerque	0	2	0	2
Public	University of North Carolina - Chapel Hill	9	0	9	0
Public	University of North Dakota	0	0	0	0
Private	University of Notre Dame	5	4	4	5
Public	University of Oklahoma - Norman	1	2	0	2
Public	Univ. of Oklahoma Health Sciences Center	0	0	0	0
Public	University of Oregon	0	4	0	2
Private	University of Pennsylvania	9	0	9	0
Public	University of Pittsburgh - Pittsburgh	6	3	7	2
Public	University of Rhode Island	0	0	0	0
Private	University of Rochester	5	3	5	2
Public	University of South Carolina - Columbia	0	4	0	2
Public	University of South Florida - Tampa	0	6	0	5
Private	University of Southern California	8	1	8	1
Public	University of Tennessee - Knoxville	0	3	0	5
Public	Univ. of Tennessee Health Science Center	0	0	0	0
Public	University of Texas - Austin	8	1	9	0
Public	University of Texas HSC - Houston	0	0	0	2
Public	University of Texas HSC - San Antonio	0	0	0	0
Public	Univ. of Texas MD Anderson Cancer Center	4	2	4	2
Public	Univ. of Texas Medical Branch - Galveston	0	0	0	0
Public	Univ. of Texas SW Medical Center - Dallas	3	4	4	3
Public	University of Utah	3	5	5	3
Public	University of Vermont	0	0	0	0
Public	University of Virginia	5	4	4	5
Public	University of Washington - Seattle	8	1	8	1
Public	University of Wisconsin - Madison	9	0	9	0

2014 No. of Measures in Top 25 Among Privates/Publics	2014 No. of Measures in Top 26-50 Among Privates/Publics	2013 No. of Measures in Top 25 Among Privates/Publics	2013 No. of Measures in Top 26-50 Among Privates/Publics	2012 No. of Measures in Top 25 Among Privates/Publics	2012 No. of Measures in Top 26-50 Among Privates/Publics	2011 No. of Measures in Top 25 Among Privates/Publics	2011 No. of Measures in Top 26-50 Among Privates/Publics
0	0	0	0	0	0	0	0
0	6	0	6	0	5	0	5
9	0	9	0	9	0	9	0
2	6	4	4	6	2	4	4
1	3	1	3	1	3	1	3
0	0	0	0	0	0	0	0
0	6	0	5	0	6	0	5
0	2	0	2	0	2	0	1
0	0	0	0	0	0	0	0
0	5	0	4	1	4	0	4
0	1	0	1	0	1	0	0
6	1	7	1	7	1	6	2
0	3	0	2	0	2	0	2
0	4	2	2	2	1	2	1
3	4	3	4	3	4	3	4
9	0	9	0	9	0	9	0
9	0	9	0	8	1	8	1
0	4	0	6	0	5	0	4
0	4	0	2	0	3	0	3
0	0	0	0	0	0	0	0
0	0	0	0	0	0	0	0
0	0	0	0	0	0	0	0
0	1	0	1	0	2	1	1
9	0	9	0	9	0	9	0
0	0	0	0	0	0	0	0
4	5	3	6	3	6	4	5
1	1	0	2	1	2	0	3
0	0	0	0	0	0	0	0
1	2	0	3	0	3	1	1
9	0	9	0	9	0	9	0
7	2	8	1	8	1	8	1
0	0	0	0	0	0	0	0
4	4	5	3	6	2	6	2
0	4	0	4	0	3	0	2
0	4	0	4	0	5	0	4
8	1	8	1	8	1	8	1
1	4	2	3	0	5	0	5
0	0	0	0	0	0	0	0
9	0	9	0	7	2	7	2
0	2	0	2	0	1	0	2
0	0	0	0	0	0	0	1
4	2	4	1	4	1	4	1
0	0	0	0	0	0	0	2
4	3	4	3	6	1	5	2
3	5	2	6	2	6	3	5
0	0	0	1	0	0	0	0
5	4	5	3	6	3	5	4
8	1	8	1	8	1	8	1
9	0	9	0	9	0	9	0

The Center Measures - Control Rankings

	Institutions with Over $40 Million in Federal Research, Alphabetically	2016 No. of Measures in Top 25 Among Privates/Publics	2016 No. of Measures in Top 26-50 Among Privates/Publics	2015 No. of Measures in Top 25 Among Privates/Publics	2015 No. of Measures in Top 26-50 Among Privates/Publics
Public	Utah State University	0	0	0	0
Private	Vanderbilt University	8	1	9	0
Public	Virginia Commonwealth University	1	1	1	1
Public	Virginia Polytechnic Institute and State Univ.	2	6	2	6
Private	Wake Forest University	0	6	0	7
Public	Washington State University - Pullman	0	4	0	3
Private	Washington University in St. Louis	9	0	9	0
Public	Wayne State University	0	0	0	1
Private	Weill Cornell Medical College	3	4	4	3
Public	West Virginia University	0	1	0	0
Private	Woods Hole Oceanographic Institution	0	4	0	4
Private	Yale University	9	0	9	0
Private	Yeshiva University	1	5	1	6

2014 No. of Measures in Top 25 Among Privates/Publics	2014 No. of Measures in Top 26-50 Among Privates/Publics	2013 No. of Measures in Top 25 Among Privates/Publics	2013 No. of Measures in Top 26-50 Among Privates/Publics	2012 No. of Measures in Top 25 Among Privates/Publics	2012 No. of Measures in Top 26-50 Among Privates/Publics	2011 No. of Measures in Top 25 Among Privates/Publics	2011 No. of Measures in Top 26-50 Among Privates/Publics
0	0	0	0	0	1	0	0
9	0	9	0	9	0	9	0
1	2	0	4	0	3	0	3
2	5	2	4	0	8	1	7
0	7	0	7	1	6	0	7
0	4	0	5	0	4	0	4
9	0	9	0	9	0	9	0
0	0	0	0	0	1	0	0
3	4	1	6	2	5	3	4
0	2	0	0	0	1	0	0
0	4	0	4	0	4	0	4
9	0	9	0	9	0	9	0
1	7	2	6	2	6	1	7

Federal Research with and without Medical School Research

	Institutions with Over $40 Million in Federal Research excluding Stand-Alone Medical Schools, Alphabetically	AAMC Med School	2014 Federal (x1000)	2014 AAMC Fed (x1000)	2014 Rank Incl AAMC	2014 Rank Excl AAMC	2013 Federal (x1000)	2013 AAMC Fed (x1000)	2013 Rank Incl AAMC	2013 Rank Excl AAMC
Public	Arizona State University		186,126	0	65	38	190,066	0	67	39
Public	Auburn University		49,739	0	149	126	56,809	0	144	121
Public	Augusta University	Yes	47,771	27,219	151	185	47,913	26,605	154	188
Private	Boston University	Yes	254,285	115,773	48	51	265,476	128,285	48	54
Private	Brandeis University		45,800	0	153	130	43,963	0	160	135
Private	Brown University	Yes	125,005	37,446	84	87	120,977	65,748	86	124
Private	California Institute of Technology		276,447	0	42	22	272,223	0	46	23
Private	Carnegie Mellon University		198,247	0	61	34	215,560	0	57	33
Private	Case Western Reserve University	Yes	328,548	265,930	29	112	347,628	283,729	28	111
Public	Clemson University		44,673	0	155	132	47,825	0	155	130
Public	Cleveland State University		44,139	0	156	133	50,002	0	152	129
Private	Cold Spring Harbor Laboratory		41,845	0	158	134	41,002	0	163	137
Public	Colorado State University - Fort Collins		206,958	0	56	33	213,355	0	58	34
Private	Columbia University	Yes	591,523	277,143	8	15	619,557	295,191	7	16
Private	Cornell University		299,320	0	36	20	299,951	0	35	20
Private	Dartmouth College	Yes	145,080	94,250	76	124	154,917	107,186	75	131
Private	Drexel University	Yes	75,557	9,434	122	108	74,047	10,168	125	112
Private	Duke University	Yes	556,847	318,028	10	28	580,416	342,190	10	30
Private	Emory University	Yes	329,254	199,084	27	54	364,136	212,276	26	50
Public	Florida International University	Yes	68,946	1,769	126	106	57,858	2,415	139	123
Public	Florida State University	Yes	140,995	3,413	79	52	132,583	5,177	81	61
Public	George Mason University		53,775	0	143	120	57,154	0	141	119
Private	George Washington University	Yes	139,148	17,636	82	58	119,441	17,357	91	74
Private	Georgetown University	Yes	99,567	82,261	103	204	113,703	96,334	98	203
Public	Georgia Institute of Technology		510,422	0	14	2	520,754	0	14	2
Private	Harvard University	Yes	554,944	170,892	11	8	575,868	186,123	11	9
Public	Indiana University - Bloomington		80,109	0	117	93	82,005	0	120	91
Public	Indiana Univ. - Purdue Univ. - Indianapolis	Yes	142,589	104,971	78	138	151,962	113,888	76	140
Public	Iowa State University		115,285	0	90	62	120,934	0	87	62
Private	Johns Hopkins University	Yes	1,936,953	443,740	1	1	1,881,959	474,194	1	1
Public	Kansas State University		64,565	0	129	109	67,524	0	132	106
Public	Louisiana State University - Baton Rouge		93,584	0	105	79	93,281	0	109	80
Private	Massachusetts Institute of Technology		480,991	0	16	4	487,647	0	19	5
Public	Michigan State University	Yes	247,970	14,634	49	29	246,131	17,935	52	31
Public	Mississippi State University		70,615	0	125	102	73,834	0	126	101
Public	Montana State University - Bozeman		66,770	0	128	107	66,451	0	133	108
Public	Naval Postgraduate School		89,284	0	109	84	86,538	0	115	87
Public	New Jersey Institute of Technology		51,853	0	146	123	55,017	0	147	125
Public	New Mexico State University - Las Cruces		80,247	0	116	92	86,546	0	114	86
Private	New York University	Yes	314,712	204,375	31	67	283,382	194,592	44	84
Public	North Carolina State University		177,722	0	70	41	174,440	0	70	42
Private	Northeastern University		77,401	0	120	97	82,587	0	119	90
Private	Northwestern University	Yes	385,888	224,480	24	46	389,757	234,388	25	48
Public	Ohio State University - Columbus	Yes	416,177	54,055	21	9	425,547	50,560	22	10
Public	Oregon State University		143,815	0	77	50	148,174	0	78	52
Public	Pennsylvania State University - Univ. Park		461,896	0	18	5	500,567	0	16	4
Private	Princeton University		163,805	0	72	44	156,070	0	73	47
Public	Purdue University - West Lafayette		227,857	0	53	30	258,596	0	49	27
Private	Rensselaer Polytechnic Institute		58,940	0	136	115	60,765	0	137	117

2012 Federal (x1000)	2012 AAMC Fed (x1000)	2012 Rank Incl AAMC	2012 Rank Excl AAMC	2011 Federal (x1000)	2011 AAMC Fed (x1000)	2011 Rank Incl AAMC	2011 Rank Excl AAMC	2010 Federal (x1000)	2010 AAMC Fed (x1000)	2010 Rank Incl AAMC	2010 Rank Excl AAMC
182,188	0	68	38	178,153	0	68	40	164,890	0	67	39
55,118	0	149	124	59,061	0	146	119	53,648	0	147	122
55,106	33,213	150	188	54,254	32,147	155	188	51,727	31,335	153	189
273,204	131,422	44	53	300,923	140,561	40	48	298,467	134,153	37	40
44,061	0	162	137	47,793	0	162	133	43,282	0	164	136
127,665	76,219	85	129	123,649	72,951	92	129	120,749	63,118	91	116
322,295	0	34	18	340,131	0	30	12	325,751	0	30	11
209,307	0	60	35	200,878	0	65	35	179,136	0	64	35
358,722	298,298	26	116	352,938	303,849	28	132	333,438	278,053	27	119
48,182	0	157	130	49,365	0	161	131	59,374	0	137	111
46,205	0	159	133	42,292	0	168	141	24,894	0	206	175
43,874	0	163	138	55,450	0	152	124	0	0	737	728
245,573	0	53	29	230,661	0	56	32	205,890	0	59	33
631,961	287,097	6	14	634,973	289,566	7	10	561,531	260,061	8	15
298,596	0	41	21	314,371	0	37	17	290,640	0	40	19
147,218	102,648	79	136	131,518	105,446	87	177	117,909	89,066	95	158
85,584	14,341	119	106	81,424	15,854	123	108	75,339	10,903	122	105
585,636	360,461	10	34	584,161	390,912	9	37	513,469	369,411	13	47
360,934	282,397	25	95	369,945	323,209	25	135	336,948	293,224	26	135
54,204	2,640	153	128	61,687	3,427	139	122	52,784	2,894	149	127
131,998	6,630	84	60	136,332	7,008	81	61	127,571	5,289	84	61
57,504	0	145	119	61,016	0	141	111	59,591	0	136	110
111,068	16,483	96	78	115,463	18,712	99	79	120,844	20,309	90	70
113,229	95,331	94	206	122,802	105,877	93	212	119,509	99,740	94	190
482,349	0	16	3	426,088	0	22	6	370,532	0	23	7
574,346	198,722	11	8	530,908	231,453	14	21	467,237	191,087	15	22
72,501	0	133	104	69,298	0	136	105	67,483	0	131	101
165,374	127,238	73	144	154,966	132,579	77	187	147,375	126,780	76	187
117,144	0	93	63	116,109	0	97	63	108,181	0	99	66
1,845,845	477,549	1	1	1,875,410	500,765	1	1	1,731,818	458,418	1	1
73,247	0	131	103	74,414	0	131	101	66,400	0	133	103
91,238	0	114	85	96,050	0	113	81	94,611	0	110	78
478,955	0	18	4	482,544	0	17	3	451,050	0	17	3
250,416	20,123	52	32	222,937	15,390	60	34	198,735	9,065	60	34
96,132	0	111	77	97,987	0	110	76	105,224	0	102	68
78,409	0	125	96	78,431	0	127	97	84,735	0	114	84
120,209	0	90	61	88,950	0	116	86	86,765	0	113	83
57,513	0	143	118	52,873	0	157	125	47,832	0	158	130
90,338	0	115	86	90,283	0	115	85	98,050	0	105	71
300,271	208,694	40	83	289,172	196,162	45	83	250,006	178,694	48	98
171,464	0	72	41	152,790	0	78	50	137,124	0	78	50
75,733	0	129	100	65,757	0	138	107	56,727	0	142	118
385,377	228,518	24	50	393,449	230,504	24	46	356,193	204,824	24	45
416,304	53,404	23	10	471,331	63,239	18	7	384,633	48,115	21	8
155,667	0	78	51	146,069	0	79	54	135,081	0	79	52
469,597	0	19	5	400,294	0	23	8	410,238	0	19	4
160,985	0	75	46	162,491	0	73	47	149,164	0	75	46
255,691	0	51	27	246,116	0	51	26	221,679	0	54	28
62,063	0	139	114	58,951	0	148	120	54,559	0	145	120

Federal Research with and without Medical School Research

	Institutions with Over $40 Million in Federal Research excluding Stand Alone Medical Schools, Alphabetically	AAMC Med School	2014 Federal (x1000)	2014 AAMC Fed (x1000)	2014 Rank Incl AAMC	2014 Rank Excl AAMC	2013 Federal (x1000)	2013 AAMC Fed (x1000)	2013 Rank Incl AAMC	2013 Rank Excl AAMC
Private	Rice University		73,782	0	124	101	79,742	0	123	94
Private	Rockefeller University		81,820	0	114	89	80,384	0	122	93
Public	Rutgers University - New Brunswick	Yes	355,116	42,392	25	17	288,374	0	40	21
Public	San Diego State University		44,807	0	154	131	45,175	0	157	132
Private	Scripps Research Institute		292,268	0	37	21	308,628	0	33	18
Private	Stanford University	Yes	608,342	366,231	4	27	625,144	361,418	5	26
Public	Stony Brook University	Yes	111,386	51,367	96	114	118,432	54,994	93	113
Public	Temple University	Yes	118,892	43,055	88	99	124,764	43,446	85	92
Public	Texas A&M University - College Station		266,877	0	45	23	270,334	0	47	24
Private	Tufts University	Yes	115,046	35,588	91	94	112,495	36,309	99	99
Private	Tulane University	Yes	94,287	25,285	104	104	97,873	25,465	107	102
Public	University at Albany		104,861	0	99	72	113,736	0	97	66
Public	University at Buffalo	Yes	185,144	28,169	66	48	200,212	28,930	62	43
Public	University of Alabama - Birmingham	Yes	276,112	170,690	44	71	286,873	180,400	41	69
Public	University of Alabama - Huntsville		73,913	0	123	100	83,396	0	118	89
Public	University of Alaska - Fairbanks		83,483	0	113	88	92,602	0	111	83
Public	University of Arizona	Yes	286,595	41,933	38	25	334,680	46,323	31	22
Public	University of California - Berkeley		309,305	0	33	18	305,932	0	34	19
Public	University of California - Davis	Yes	327,697	85,100	30	26	344,632	91,832	29	28
Public	University of California - Irvine	Yes	180,431	53,617	69	55	196,256	58,249	65	53
Public	University of California - Los Angeles	Yes	458,157	268,928	19	36	489,820	283,756	17	35
Public	University of California - Riverside		56,327	2,600	137	121	57,032	0	143	120
Public	University of California - San Diego	Yes	597,270	246,807	7	12	630,009	271,904	4	13
Public	University of California - Santa Barbara		119,816	0	86	60	131,392	0	82	56
Public	University of California - Santa Cruz		89,206	0	110	85	88,600	0	112	85
Public	University of Central Florida	Yes	64,323	7,590	130	117	68,691	7,446	131	116
Private	University of Chicago	Yes	276,237	168,641	43	68	294,862	179,901	38	64
Public	University of Cincinnati - Cincinnati	Yes	243,705	82,031	51	45	256,816	97,383	50	45
Public	University of Colorado - Boulder		302,877	0	34	19	309,072	0	32	17
Public	University of Colorado - Denver	Yes	277,209	156,914	41	59	290,443	160,966	39	59
Public	University of Connecticut - Storrs		80,317	0	115	91	86,471	0	116	88
Private	University of Dayton		63,881	0	131	110	66,396	0	134	109
Public	University of Delaware		111,933	0	95	65	114,048	0	96	65
Public	University of Florida	Yes	279,920	96,651	40	40	285,778	96,537	42	40
Public	University of Georgia		122,145	0	85	57	127,487	0	83	60
Public	University of Hawaii - Manoa	Yes	202,574	18,479	59	39	225,263	21,795	55	36
Public	University of Houston - University Park		55,574	0	138	118	57,569	0	140	118
Public	University of Idaho	Yes	49,423	0	150	127	52,430	0	149	126
Public	University of Illinois - Chicago	Yes	201,646	83,250	60	61	219,473	89,679	56	58
Public	University of Illinois - Urbana-Champaign		336,172	0	26	13	459,791	0	20	6
Public	University of Iowa	Yes	234,122	99,673	52	53	252,161	97,465	51	49
Public	University of Kansas - Lawrence		88,725	0	111	86	99,374	0	105	76
Public	University of Kentucky	Yes	140,450	47,963	80	81	148,758	54,736	77	79
Public	University of Louisville	Yes	63,258	39,871	132	171	72,047	44,043	128	163
Public	University of Maine - Orono		50,338	0	148	125	33,903	0	170	147
Public	University of Maryland - Baltimore County		46,993	0	152	129	44,257	0	158	133
Public	University of Maryland - College Park		328,828	0	28	14	341,942	0	30	15
Public	University of Massachusetts - Amherst		102,682	0	101	74	103,233	0	104	73
Private	University of Miami	Yes	202,818	121,723	58	90	204,315	128,068	61	98

2012 Federal (x1000)	2012 AAMC Fed (x1000)	2012 Rank Incl AAMC	2012 Rank Excl AAMC	2011 Federal (x1000)	2011 AAMC Fed (x1000)	2011 Rank Incl AAMC	2011 Rank Excl AAMC	2010 Federal (x1000)	2010 AAMC Fed (x1000)	2010 Rank Incl AAMC	2010 Rank Excl AAMC
76,431	0	128	99	78,249	0	128	98	69,176	0	129	100
84,616	0	121	90	97,710	0	111	77	88,705	0	112	81
273,498	0	43	23	235,178	0	54	31	218,910	0	56	30
51,690	0	155	127	59,769	0	143	114	53,746	0	146	121
309,471	0	36	20	317,201	0	36	16	313,746	0	33	12
607,578	366,588	8	30	633,287	392,135	8	28	576,553	341,664	7	27
123,198	54,141	89	109	124,938	49,688	89	100	120,090	46,875	92	95
85,062	38,434	120	132	84,581	37,870	119	136	76,170	37,164	121	141
259,506	0	50	26	281,063	0	47	22	276,977	0	44	21
120,042	38,601	92	94	120,864	41,388	95	94	115,159	39,698	97	93
101,130	25,972	108	102	110,222	26,242	103	91	106,021	23,775	100	85
112,161	0	95	65	124,848	0	90	62	123,404	0	86	60
186,747	28,225	67	49	176,923	30,378	69	52	164,477	27,032	68	49
303,677	194,865	39	69	340,342	224,432	29	64	320,704	206,317	32	63
75,715	0	130	101	70,197	0	134	103	71,461	0	128	97
97,472	0	110	76	100,638	0	107	72	97,889	0	106	73
328,369	54,346	33	22	324,751	53,239	35	23	307,038	48,792	34	23
333,179	0	30	16	326,120	0	34	15	303,201	0	35	14
356,540	89,309	27	24	359,704	93,294	27	24	329,041	87,440	29	25
204,062	65,708	62	55	204,134	65,322	63	56	189,343	59,931	63	57
527,899	292,433	14	31	545,882	304,724	13	27	522,423	271,582	11	24
61,304	0	141	115	59,351	0	145	117	58,159	0	139	114
653,549	281,874	5	9	635,223	278,345	6	9	578,889	244,303	6	9
134,984	0	82	57	132,490	0	86	59	127,696	0	83	58
91,409	0	113	84	95,015	0	114	82	81,598	0	116	86
72,620	7,555	132	110	66,736	8,220	137	121	67,795	6,653	130	107
329,119	195,640	31	59	365,824	217,273	26	51	348,537	211,861	25	51
266,507	105,764	48	47	286,003	119,635	46	43	261,982	118,420	47	48
319,019	0	35	19	313,531	0	38	18	282,008	0	42	20
308,023	172,565	37	56	299,230	166,799	41	60	275,573	150,302	45	59
88,834	0	116	87	84,901	0	118	90	73,359	0	124	94
64,369	0	138	112	69,847	0	135	104	72,567	0	125	96
110,760	0	97	66	112,523	0	102	68	102,637	0	103	69
295,745	104,207	42	37	296,950	103,316	42	36	269,765	92,345	46	36
133,525	0	83	58	134,273	0	83	58	116,625	0	96	62
193,722	31,645	66	44	201,700	29,341	64	41	196,275	30,377	62	38
54,657	0	151	125	57,090	0	150	123	50,148	0	156	126
53,765	0	154	126	52,812	0	158	127	45,082	0	161	132
243,622	103,123	54	54	245,323	99,175	52	53	229,131	96,887	51	54
348,536	0	28	12	312,796	0	39	19	294,236	0	38	16
265,780	98,803	49	43	280,989	111,828	48	42	280,089	112,563	43	37
99,034	0	109	75	78,884	0	126	96	81,211	0	117	87
157,813	64,628	77	82	175,801	72,873	70	71	167,192	70,615	66	75
79,252	44,775	124	151	84,557	47,398	120	150	83,593	45,444	115	143
39,428	0	166	141	59,644	0	144	115	48,270	0	157	129
44,669	0	161	135	61,110	0	140	110	58,597	0	138	113
340,180	0	29	15	333,879	0	33	14	293,835	0	39	17
106,470	0	104	71	106,315	0	104	69	97,131	0	107	74
222,535	137,831	58	89	223,870	136,436	59	89	196,435	115,323	61	88

Federal Research with and without Medical School Research

	Institutions with Over $40 Million in Federal Research excluding Stand Alone Medical Schools, Alphabetically	AAMC Med School	2014 Federal (x1000)	2014 AAMC Fed (x1000)	2014 Rank Incl AAMC	2014 Rank Excl AAMC	2013 Federal (x1000)	2013 AAMC Fed (x1000)	2013 Rank Incl AAMC	2013 Rank Excl AAMC
Public	University of Michigan - Ann Arbor	Yes	733,779	297,638	3	6	802,114	351,344	3	7
Public	University of Minnesota - Twin Cities	Yes	483,542	121,874	15	10	489,318	122,906	18	11
Public	University of Missouri - Columbia	Yes	102,784	12,916	100	82	108,305	15,262	100	81
Public	University of Nebraska - Lincoln		93,190	0	106	80	96,177	0	108	78
Public	University of Nevada - Reno	Yes	50,904	18,516	147	144	53,898	16,304	148	144
Public	University of New Hampshire - Durham		89,640	0	107	83	92,778	0	110	82
Public	University of New Mexico - Albuquerque	Yes	151,082	50,456	75	75	155,684	51,883	74	72
Public	University of North Carolina - Chapel Hill	Yes	601,933	248,809	6	11	614,627	251,314	8	12
Public	University of North Dakota	Yes	40,191	7,813	160	145	46,397	8,343	156	141
Private	University of Notre Dame		79,192	0	119	95	79,268	0	124	95
Public	University of Oklahoma - Norman		53,223	0	145	122	68,902	0	130	105
Public	University of Oregon		62,824	0	133	111	61,856	0	136	114
Private	University of Pennsylvania	Yes	606,115	380,930	5	31	623,939	378,442	6	29
Public	University of Pittsburgh - Pittsburgh	Yes	565,409	350,989	9	32	601,358	378,103	9	32
Public	University of Rhode Island		61,836	0	134	113	70,900	0	129	103
Private	University of Rochester	Yes	265,686	153,838	46	66	298,781	161,624	36	55
Public	University of South Carolina - Columbia	Yes	87,844	10,920	112	98	87,562	11,690	113	100
Public	University of South Florida - Tampa	Yes	205,155	59,544	57	49	207,441	58,369	60	51
Private	University of Southern California	Yes	421,887	155,039	20	24	423,708	158,878	23	25
Public	University of Tennessee - Knoxville	No	106,778	0	98	69	104,558	0	103	71
Public	University of Texas - Austin		313,955	0	32	16	352,788	0	27	14
Public	University of Utah	Yes	284,125	95,267	39	37	297,099	97,559	37	37
Public	University of Vermont	Yes	79,727	51,878	118	156	85,028	54,038	117	154
Public	University of Virginia	Yes	192,907	89,693	63	73	212,051	101,570	59	67
Public	University of Washington - Seattle	Yes	849,713	341,694	2	3	869,623	349,868	2	3
Public	University of Wisconsin - Madison	Yes	522,251	129,396	13	7	533,220	129,162	13	8
Public	Utah State University		114,075	0	92	63	106,074	0	102	70
Private	Vanderbilt University	Yes	408,743	310,219	23	76	432,752	325,195	21	68
Public	Virginia Commonwealth University	Yes	119,507	51,909	87	105	119,293	52,514	92	107
Public	Virginia Polytechnic Inst. and State Univ.		198,092	0	62	35	197,462	0	64	38
Private	Wake Forest University	Yes	153,069	145,964	74	266	156,506	149,306	72	275
Public	Washington State University - Pullman		112,568	0	94	64	119,921	0	89	63
Private	Washington University in St. Louis	Yes	410,115	313,053	22	77	402,702	338,572	24	110
Public	Wayne State University	Yes	112,608	65,542	93	128	118,217	66,565	94	128
Public	West Virginia University	Yes	67,450	10,396	127	116	72,677	11,002	127	115
Private	Woods Hole Oceanographic Institution		177,616	0	71	42	158,672	0	71	46
Private	Yale University	Yes	475,585	349,194	17	56	502,439	371,094	15	57
Private	Yeshiva University	Yes	186,885	174,705	64	227	193,831	170,068	66	177

2012 Federal (x1000)	2012 AAMC Fed (x1000)	2012 Rank Incl AAMC	2012 Rank Excl AAMC	2011 Federal (x1000)	2011 AAMC Fed (x1000)	2011 Rank Incl AAMC	2011 Rank Excl AAMC	2010 Federal (x1000)	2010 AAMC Fed (x1000)	2010 Rank Incl AAMC	2010 Rank Excl AAMC
773,766	346,182	3	6	801,194	370,081	3	5	729,779	345,361	3	6
480,531	133,996	17	13	482,639	139,542	16	11	420,102	128,154	18	18
110,446	17,060	99	81	113,072	15,628	100	78	113,362	15,333	98	72
103,294	0	106	72	104,240	0	105	70	95,190	0	109	77
55,150	12,733	148	139	55,374	11,776	153	139	58,115	12,524	140	131
109,728	0	102	68	96,552	0	112	80	76,191	0	120	92
159,302	58,742	76	74	161,950	62,738	74	75	147,003	60,070	77	82
597,629	245,751	9	11	559,620	251,344	12	20	541,910	233,896	9	13
54,411	7,075	152	131	53,913	10,399	156	140	52,381	9,268	151	137
82,244	0	123	93	79,003	0	125	95	61,645	0	134	106
64,427	0	137	111	46,027	0	164	137	52,332	0	152	123
71,157	0	134	107	71,344	0	133	102	66,809	0	132	102
656,425	409,124	4	28	689,571	452,788	4	29	626,816	405,900	4	29
620,070	394,640	7	33	647,060	418,674	5	33	581,148	372,591	5	31
78,194	0	126	97	77,668	0	129	99	60,963	0	135	109
307,390	163,923	38	52	337,312	199,475	31	57	321,258	187,134	31	53
93,237	9,631	112	91	100,045	8,926	108	84	119,890	9,742	93	64
218,772	58,598	59	48	220,931	57,717	61	45	219,634	68,057	55	44
433,136	172,842	20	25	443,458	184,567	20	25	402,372	164,025	20	26
103,147	0	107	73	99,712	0	109	74	96,018	0	108	76
328,560	0	32	17	334,240	0	32	13	331,439	0	28	10
271,629	94,348	46	40	263,623	107,253	50	49	226,489	95,623	52	56
87,843	58,658	117	164	101,465	71,374	106	165	98,588	67,419	104	154
225,558	114,932	57	67	227,937	139,376	58	87	224,607	135,823	53	80
876,941	374,242	2	2	921,399	382,358	2	2	809,433	342,230	2	2
557,688	136,066	13	7	568,389	135,216	11	4	522,473	124,616	10	5
107,054	0	103	70	112,611	0	101	67	89,750	0	111	79
430,445	336,334	22	80	434,213	346,139	21	88	377,185	300,343	22	91
124,836	53,683	88	108	134,431	71,425	82	109	125,713	60,067	85	104
181,371	0	69	39	187,269	0	67	38	161,636	0	70	41
172,779	165,233	70	278	173,004	165,910	71	283	159,084	152,724	71	285
120,146	0	91	62	115,775	0	98	65	105,333	0	101	67
432,434	361,056	21	105	460,282	410,839	19	130	466,993	389,516	16	90
125,965	69,446	86	122	133,925	74,667	85	118	131,418	70,308	81	108
77,981	13,679	127	113	84,061	17,455	121	106	74,465	15,861	123	112
161,115	0	74	45	165,819	0	72	44	153,066	0	73	43
517,072	400,686	15	64	518,195	404,222	15	66	475,010	364,874	14	65
201,397	192,659	64	266	192,241	181,071	66	248	163,399	150,498	69	224

Part III – The Top 200 Institutions

The following tables list the top 200 universities and colleges on each of the nine performance measures, along with National Merit and Achievement Scholars. (The Source Notes section provides detailed information on each of the 10 data elements.) Unlike the previous tables in Parts I and II, this section includes data for all academic institutions regardless of their federal research activity level.

The Center for Measuring University Performance provides each institution's rank nationally among all universities as well as its rank by institutional control (i.e., rank among private or public peers). In cases where several institutions tie for last place, we use a different cutoff point. For National Academy members, we list all institutions with at least one National Academy member among their faculty. Tables in this section include:

- **2014 Total Research Expenditures**
- **2014 Federal Research Expenditures**
- **2015 Endowment Assets**
- **2015 Annual Giving**
- **2015 National Academy Membership**
- **2015 Faculty Awards**
- **2015 Doctorates Awarded**
- **2014 Postdoctoral Appointees**
- **2014 SAT Scores**
- **2015 National Merit and Achievement Scholars**

Data found in these tables may not always match the figures published by the original source. *The Center for Measuring University Performance* makes adjustments, when necessary, to ensure that the data reflect the activity at a single campus rather than that of a multiple-campus institution or state university system. When data are missing from the original source, *The Center for Measuring University Performance* may substitute another figure if available. A full discussion of this subject, and the various adjustments or substitutions made to the original data, is in the Data Notes section of this report.

The Center for Measuring University Performance presents these tables, along with the prior years' top 200, as Microsoft Excel spreadsheets online at [http://mup.asu.edu].

The Top 200 Institutions – Total Research Expenditures (2014)

Top 1-50 Institutions in Total Research Expenditures	Total Research x $1000	National Rank	Control Rank	Institutional Control
Johns Hopkins University	2,227,536	1	1	Private
University of Michigan - Ann Arbor	1,279,603	2	1	Public
University of Washington - Seattle	1,091,135	3	2	Public
University of California - San Francisco	1,084,031	4	3	Public
University of California - San Diego	1,060,207	5	4	Public
Duke University	1,031,404	6	2	Private
University of Wisconsin - Madison	984,830	7	5	Public
University of North Carolina - Chapel Hill	955,601	8	6	Public
University of California - Los Angeles	920,183	9	7	Public
Stanford University	912,244	10	3	Private
Harvard University	875,964	11	4	Private
University of Minnesota - Twin Cities	850,880	12	8	Public
Columbia University	844,766	13	5	Private
University of Pittsburgh - Pittsburgh	835,838	14	9	Public
Massachusetts Institute of Technology	815,008	15	6	Private
University of Texas MD Anderson Cancer Center	794,980	16	10	Public
University of Pennsylvania	792,314	17	7	Private
Yale University	764,002	18	8	Private
Ohio State University - Columbus	752,836	19	11	Public
Texas A&M University - College Station	735,273	20	12	Public
Georgia Institute of Technology	720,248	21	13	Public
University of California - Berkeley	708,485	22	14	Public
Pennsylvania State University - University Park	702,912	23	15	Public
University of California - Davis	699,689	24	16	Public
Vanderbilt University	659,418	25	9	Private
University of Florida	652,341	26	17	Public
University of Southern California	650,506	27	10	Private
Washington University in St. Louis	646,756	28	11	Private
Rutgers University - New Brunswick	627,076	29	18	Public
Northwestern University	621,504	30	12	Private
University of Illinois - Urbana-Champaign	598,531	31	19	Public
Cornell University	580,936	32	13	Private
University of Arizona	575,864	33	20	Public
Emory University	551,556	34	14	Private
University of Texas - Austin	526,173	35	21	Public
Virginia Polytechnic Institute and State University	502,486	36	22	Public
Purdue University - West Lafayette	502,457	37	23	Public
Baylor College of Medicine	496,314	38	15	Private
Michigan State University	492,501	39	24	Public
New York University	490,614	40	16	Private
University of Utah	476,017	41	25	Public
University of Maryland - College Park	472,235	42	26	Public
Icahn School of Medicine at Mount Sinai	463,429	43	17	Private
North Carolina State University	440,392	44	27	Public
University of Iowa	436,852	45	28	Public
University of South Florida - Tampa	436,578	46	29	Public
University of Texas SW Medical Center - Dallas	434,627	47	30	Public
University of Alabama - Birmingham	421,475	48	31	Public
Case Western Reserve University	417,436	49	18	Private
State Univ. of New York - Polytechnic Institute	412,851	50	32	Public

The Top 200 Institutions – Total Research Expenditures (2014)

Top 51-100 Institutions in Total Research Expenditures	Total Research x $1000	National Rank	Control Rank	Institutional Control
University of Colorado - Denver	401,230	51	33	Public
University of Cincinnati - Cincinnati	399,571	52	34	Public
University of Maryland - Baltimore	390,682	53	35	Public
Scripps Research Institute	386,231	54	19	Private
Arizona State University	380,581	55	36	Public
University of Chicago	378,322	56	20	Private
University at Buffalo	370,083	57	37	Public
University of Colorado - Boulder	362,882	58	38	Public
California Institute of Technology	358,137	59	21	Private
Boston University	353,850	60	22	Private
University of Rochester	347,161	61	23	Private
University of Miami	342,852	62	24	Private
University of Illinois - Chicago	339,644	63	39	Public
University of Virginia	337,732	64	40	Public
University of California - Irvine	322,315	65	41	Public
University of Kentucky	322,313	66	42	Public
University of Hawaii - Manoa	319,818	67	43	Public
Indiana University - Purdue University - Indianapolis	316,650	68	44	Public
Rockefeller University	316,368	69	25	Private
University of Georgia	313,445	70	45	Public
Oregon Health & Science University	313,112	71	46	Public
Yeshiva University	306,826	72	26	Private
Colorado State University - Fort Collins	300,572	73	47	Public
Iowa State University	297,293	74	48	Public
Weill Cornell Medical College	293,791	75	27	Private
Brown University	291,917	76	28	Private
Washington State University - Pullman	287,942	77	49	Public
Princeton University	287,730	78	29	Private
Louisiana State University - Baton Rouge	282,462	79	50	Public
Uniformed Services University of the Health Sciences	262,489	80	51	Public
University of Nebraska - Lincoln	254,879	81	52	Public
Carnegie Mellon University	250,497	82	30	Private
Medical University of South Carolina	242,594	83	53	Public
University of Massachusetts Medical Sch. - Worcester	241,869	84	54	Public
University of Texas Health Science Center - Houston	233,737	85	55	Public
University of Missouri - Columbia	233,613	86	56	Public
Florida State University	231,390	87	57	Public
Oregon State University	229,456	88	58	Public
University of California - Santa Barbara	225,614	89	59	Public
University of New Mexico - Albuquerque	221,817	90	60	Public
Woods Hole Oceanographic Institution	220,016	91	31	Private
George Washington University	213,334	92	32	Private
Wayne State University	213,253	93	61	Public
Stony Brook University	210,301	94	62	Public
Temple University	206,556	95	63	Public
Dartmouth College	204,360	96	33	Private
Mississippi State University	200,251	97	64	Public
Medical College of Wisconsin	199,713	98	34	Private
University of Massachusetts - Amherst	183,210	99	65	Public
University of South Carolina - Columbia	181,363	100	66	Public

The Top 200 Institutions – Total Research Expenditures (2014)

Top 101-150 Institutions in Total Research Expenditures	Total Research x $1000	National Rank	Control Rank	Institutional Control
Kansas State University	178,304	101	67	Public
University of Texas Medical Branch - Galveston	178,014	102	68	Public
Virginia Commonwealth University	177,540	103	69	Public
Wake Forest University	176,380	104	35	Private
University of Texas Health Science Ctr. - San Antonio	172,716	105	70	Public
Indiana University - Bloomington	172,380	106	71	Public
University of Tennessee - Knoxville	170,471	107	72	Public
University of Kansas - Lawrence	169,884	108	73	Public
University of Delaware	169,641	109	74	Public
Utah State University	167,256	110	75	Public
University of Louisville	163,199	111	76	Public
Georgetown University	162,983	112	36	Private
University of Notre Dame	160,461	113	37	Private
West Virginia University	156,946	114	77	Public
Tufts University	156,411	115	38	Private
University of Alaska - Fairbanks	152,352	116	78	Public
Tulane University	148,784	117	39	Private
North Dakota State University	148,352	118	79	Public
University of California - Santa Cruz	147,536	119	80	Public
University of Central Florida	143,063	120	81	Public
University of Connecticut - Storrs	142,332	121	82	Public
Auburn University	140,110	122	83	Public
University of Nebraska Medical Center	139,126	123	84	Public
Rice University	136,419	124	40	Private
University of Arkansas for Medical Sciences	131,438	125	85	Public
University of New Hampshire - Durham	130,951	126	86	Public
University at Albany	129,434	127	87	Public
New Mexico State University - Las Cruces	129,124	128	88	Public
University of California - Riverside	128,506	129	89	Public
Oklahoma State University - Stillwater	126,543	130	90	Public
Texas Tech University	125,126	131	91	Public
Drexel University	124,464	132	41	Private
University of Houston - University Park	122,163	133	92	Public
University of Oklahoma - Norman	120,322	134	93	Public
Thomas Jefferson University	118,378	135	42	Private
Clemson University	116,871	136	94	Public
Northeastern University	111,779	137	43	Private
University of Arkansas - Fayetteville	111,703	138	95	Public
University of Vermont	109,343	139	96	Public
Florida International University	107,487	140	97	Public
University of Oklahoma Health Sciences Center	106,782	141	98	Public
University of Connecticut - Health Center	105,047	142	99	Public
Rensselaer Polytechnic Institute	104,844	143	44	Private
Montana State University - Bozeman	104,646	144	100	Public
University of Maine - Orono	100,493	145	101	Public
University of Texas - Dallas	94,961	146	102	Public
New Jersey Institute of Technology	94,371	147	103	Public
University of Idaho	92,512	148	104	Public
Naval Postgraduate School	91,400	149	105	Public
Texas A&M Health Science Center	90,879	150	106	Public

The Top 200 Institutions – Total Research Expenditures (2014)

Top 151-200 Institutions in Total Research Expenditures	Total Research x $1000	National Rank	Control Rank	Institutional Control
University of Alabama - Huntsville	85,994	151	107	Public
George Mason University	85,493	152	108	Public
University of Rhode Island	84,393	153	109	Public
University of Dayton	83,409	154	45	Private
Pennsylvania State University - Hershey Medical Ctr.	82,793	155	110	Public
University of Kansas Medical Center	81,302	156	111	Public
University of Nevada - Reno	81,028	157	112	Public
Georgia State University	80,955	158	113	Public
Rush University	80,551	159	46	Private
University of Oregon	77,655	160	114	Public
San Diego State University	77,474	161	115	Public
Cold Spring Harbor Laboratory	76,733	162	47	Private
University of Texas - Arlington	74,261	163	116	Public
University of Texas - El Paso	70,475	164	117	Public
University of Tennessee Health Science Center	67,841	165	118	Public
University of North Dakota	67,199	166	119	Public
University of Tennessee - Institute of Agriculture	67,171	167	120	Public
Brandeis University	67,048	168	48	Private
Southern Illinois University - Carbondale	65,256	169	121	Public
Michigan Technological University	64,791	170	122	Public
University of Maryland - Baltimore County	64,329	171	123	Public
University of Akron - Akron	64,270	172	124	Public
Augusta University	64,116	173	125	Public
Binghamton University	63,960	174	126	Public
Cleveland State University	61,291	175	127	Public
University of Louisiana - Lafayette	59,068	176	128	Public
Colorado School of Mines	58,498	177	129	Public
Ohio University - Athens	58,238	178	130	Public
South Dakota State University	58,199	179	131	Public
University of Toledo	56,710	180	132	Public
University of Montana - Missoula	54,808	181	133	Public
Wright State University - Dayton	54,456	182	134	Public
Wichita State University	53,614	183	135	Public
University of Mississippi - Oxford	53,208	184	136	Public
Old Dominion University	52,832	185	137	Public
University of Massachusetts - Lowell	52,595	186	138	Public
City University of NY - City College	52,072	187	139	Public
University of Wisconsin - Milwaukee	51,316	188	140	Public
Univ. of Maryland Center for Environmental Science	50,814	189	141	Public
University of California System Admin Central Office	50,103	190	142	Public
College of William and Mary	49,428	191	143	Public
Loyola University Chicago	48,996	192	49	Private
University of Wyoming	48,736	193	144	Public
New Mexico Institute of Mining and Technology	48,260	194	145	Public
Syracuse University	48,034	195	50	Private
University of Alabama - Tuscaloosa	47,920	196	146	Public
University of North Texas Health Science Center	47,002	197	147	Public
Louisiana State University HSC - New Orleans	45,486	198	148	Public
University of Southern Mississippi	45,127	199	149	Public
University of Memphis	44,351	200	150	Public

The Top 200 Institutions – Federal Research Expenditures (2014)

Top 1-50 Institutions in Federal Research Expenditures	Federal Research x $1000	National Rank	Control Rank	Institutional Control
Johns Hopkins University	1,936,953	1	1	Private
University of Washington - Seattle	849,713	2	1	Public
University of Michigan - Ann Arbor	733,779	3	2	Public
Stanford University	608,342	4	2	Private
University of Pennsylvania	606,115	5	3	Private
University of North Carolina - Chapel Hill	601,933	6	3	Public
University of California - San Diego	597,270	7	4	Public
Columbia University	591,523	8	4	Private
University of Pittsburgh - Pittsburgh	565,409	9	5	Public
Duke University	556,847	10	5	Private
Harvard University	554,944	11	6	Private
University of California - San Francisco	544,697	12	6	Public
University of Wisconsin - Madison	522,251	13	7	Public
Georgia Institute of Technology	510,422	14	8	Public
University of Minnesota - Twin Cities	483,542	15	9	Public
Massachusetts Institute of Technology	480,991	16	7	Private
Yale University	475,585	17	8	Private
Pennsylvania State University - University Park	461,896	18	10	Public
University of California - Los Angeles	458,157	19	11	Public
University of Southern California	421,887	20	9	Private
Ohio State University - Columbus	416,177	21	12	Public
Washington University in St. Louis	410,115	22	10	Private
Vanderbilt University	408,743	23	11	Private
Northwestern University	385,888	24	12	Private
Rutgers University - New Brunswick	355,116	25	13	Public
University of Illinois - Urbana-Champaign	336,172	26	14	Public
Emory University	329,254	27	13	Private
University of Maryland - College Park	328,828	28	15	Public
Case Western Reserve University	328,548	29	14	Private
University of California - Davis	327,697	30	16	Public
New York University	314,712	31	15	Private
University of Texas - Austin	313,955	32	17	Public
University of California - Berkeley	309,305	33	18	Public
University of Colorado - Boulder	302,877	34	19	Public
Icahn School of Medicine at Mount Sinai	300,667	35	16	Private
Cornell University	299,320	36	17	Private
Scripps Research Institute	292,268	37	18	Private
University of Arizona	286,595	38	20	Public
University of Utah	284,125	39	21	Public
University of Florida	279,920	40	22	Public
University of Colorado - Denver	277,209	41	23	Public
California Institute of Technology	276,447	42	19	Private
University of Chicago	276,237	43	20	Private
University of Alabama - Birmingham	276,112	44	24	Public
Texas A&M University - College Station	266,877	45	25	Public
University of Rochester	265,686	46	21	Private
Baylor College of Medicine	264,641	47	22	Private
Boston University	254,285	48	23	Private
Michigan State University	247,970	49	26	Public
Oregon Health & Science University	246,050	50	27	Public

The Top 200 Institutions – Federal Research Expenditures (2014)

Top 51-100 Institutions in Federal Research Expenditures	Federal Research x $1000	National Rank	Control Rank	Institutional Control
University of Cincinnati - Cincinnati	243,705	51	28	Public
University of Iowa	234,122	52	29	Public
Purdue University - West Lafayette	227,857	53	30	Public
University of Maryland - Baltimore	220,700	54	31	Public
Uniformed Services University of the Health Sciences	213,389	55	32	Public
Colorado State University - Fort Collins	206,958	56	33	Public
University of South Florida - Tampa	205,155	57	34	Public
University of Miami	202,818	58	24	Private
University of Hawaii - Manoa	202,574	59	35	Public
University of Illinois - Chicago	201,646	60	36	Public
Carnegie Mellon University	198,247	61	25	Private
Virginia Polytechnic Institute and State University	198,092	62	37	Public
University of Virginia	192,907	63	38	Public
Yeshiva University	186,885	64	26	Private
Arizona State University	186,126	65	39	Public
University at Buffalo	185,144	66	40	Public
University of Texas SW Medical Center - Dallas	185,137	67	41	Public
University of Massachusetts Med. Sch. - Worcester	183,582	68	42	Public
University of California - Irvine	180,431	69	43	Public
North Carolina State University	177,722	70	44	Public
Woods Hole Oceanographic Institution	177,616	71	27	Private
Princeton University	163,805	72	28	Private
University of Texas MD Anderson Cancer Center	158,986	73	45	Public
Wake Forest University	153,069	74	29	Private
University of New Mexico - Albuquerque	151,082	75	46	Public
Dartmouth College	145,080	76	30	Private
Oregon State University	143,815	77	47	Public
Indiana University-Purdue University - Indianapolis	142,589	78	48	Public
Florida State University	140,995	79	49	Public
University of Kentucky	140,450	80	50	Public
Weill Cornell Medical College	139,514	81	31	Private
George Washington University	139,148	82	32	Private
University of Texas Health Science Center - Houston	136,145	83	51	Public
Brown University	125,005	84	33	Private
University of Georgia	122,145	85	52	Public
University of California - Santa Barbara	119,816	86	53	Public
Virginia Commonwealth University	119,507	87	54	Public
Temple University	118,892	88	55	Public
Medical University of South Carolina	118,649	89	56	Public
Iowa State University	115,285	90	57	Public
Tufts University	115,046	91	34	Private
Utah State University	114,075	92	58	Public
Wayne State University	112,608	93	59	Public
Washington State University - Pullman	112,568	94	60	Public
University of Delaware	111,933	95	61	Public
Stony Brook University	111,386	96	62	Public
Medical College of Wisconsin	111,241	97	35	Private
University of Tennessee - Knoxville	106,778	98	63	Public
University at Albany	104,861	99	64	Public
University of Missouri - Columbia	102,784	100	65	Public

The Top 200 Institutions – Federal Research Expenditures (2014)

Top 101-150 Institutions in Federal Research Expenditures	Federal Research x $1000	National Rank	Control Rank	Institutional Control
University of Massachusetts - Amherst	102,682	101	66	Public
University of Texas Medical Branch - Galveston	101,761	102	67	Public
Georgetown University	99,567	103	36	Private
Tulane University	94,287	104	37	Private
Louisiana State University - Baton Rouge	93,584	105	68	Public
University of Nebraska - Lincoln	93,190	106	69	Public
University of New Hampshire - Durham	89,640	107	70	Public
University of Texas Health Science Ctr - San Antonio	89,303	108	71	Public
Naval Postgraduate School	89,284	109	72	Public
University of California - Santa Cruz	89,206	110	73	Public
University of Kansas - Lawrence	88,725	111	74	Public
University of South Carolina - Columbia	87,844	112	75	Public
University of Alaska - Fairbanks	83,483	113	76	Public
Rockefeller University	81,820	114	38	Private
University of Connecticut - Storrs	80,317	115	77	Public
New Mexico State University - Las Cruces	80,247	116	78	Public
Indiana University - Bloomington	80,109	117	79	Public
University of Vermont	79,727	118	80	Public
University of Notre Dame	79,192	119	39	Private
Northeastern University	77,401	120	40	Private
University of Nebraska Medical Center	76,195	121	81	Public
Drexel University	75,557	122	41	Private
University of Alabama - Huntsville	73,913	123	82	Public
Rice University	73,782	124	42	Private
Mississippi State University	70,615	125	83	Public
Florida International University	68,946	126	84	Public
West Virginia University	67,450	127	85	Public
Montana State University - Bozeman	66,770	128	86	Public
Kansas State University	64,565	129	87	Public
University of Central Florida	64,323	130	88	Public
University of Dayton	63,881	131	43	Private
University of Louisville	63,258	132	89	Public
University of Oregon	62,824	133	90	Public
University of Rhode Island	61,836	134	91	Public
University of Connecticut - Health Center	59,277	135	92	Public
Rensselaer Polytechnic Institute	58,940	136	44	Private
University of California - Riverside	56,327	137	93	Public
University of Houston - University Park	55,574	138	94	Public
University of Arkansas for Medical Sciences	55,556	139	95	Public
University of Oklahoma Health Sciences Center	55,133	140	96	Public
Thomas Jefferson University	54,676	141	45	Private
Pennsylvania State University - Hershey Medical Ctr.	54,404	142	97	Public
George Mason University	53,775	143	98	Public
Rush University	53,501	144	46	Private
University of Oklahoma - Norman	53,223	145	99	Public
New Jersey Institute of Technology	51,853	146	100	Public
University of Nevada - Reno	50,904	147	101	Public
University of Maine - Orono	50,338	148	102	Public
Auburn University	49,739	149	103	Public
University of Idaho	49,423	150	104	Public

The Top 200 Institutions – Federal Research Expenditures (2014)

Top 151-200 Institutions in Federal Research Expenditures	Federal Research x $1000	National Rank	Control Rank	Institutional Control
Augusta University	47,771	151	105	Public
University of Maryland - Baltimore County	46,993	152	106	Public
Brandeis University	45,800	153	47	Private
San Diego State University	44,807	154	107	Public
Clemson University	44,673	155	108	Public
Cleveland State University	44,139	156	109	Public
University of Kansas Medical Center	42,461	157	110	Public
Cold Spring Harbor Laboratory	41,845	158	48	Private
University of Tennessee Health Science Center	41,830	159	111	Public
University of North Dakota	40,191	160	112	Public
City University of NY - City College	39,860	161	113	Public
University of Wyoming	39,778	162	114	Public
Oklahoma State University - Stillwater	36,687	163	115	Public
North Dakota State University	35,308	164	116	Public
Louisiana State University HSC - New Orleans	34,637	165	117	Public
University of Texas - El Paso	34,528	166	118	Public
Colorado School of Mines	33,908	167	119	Public
University of Mississippi Medical Center	33,272	168	120	Public
New Mexico Institute of Mining and Technology	33,168	169	121	Public
Morehouse School of Medicine	33,020	170	49	Private
U.S. Air Force Academy	32,284	171	122	Public
University of Texas - Dallas	32,096	172	123	Public
Howard University	32,052	173	50	Private
University of Toledo	31,648	174	124	Public
Texas A&M Health Science Center	31,612	175	125	Public
Old Dominion University	30,568	176	126	Public
Michigan Technological University	30,214	177	127	Public
University of Puerto Rico - Medical Sciences	30,197	178	128	Public
University of Montana - Missoula	30,164	179	129	Public
Loyola University Chicago	29,989	180	51	Private
University of Mississippi - Oxford	29,798	181	130	Public
Georgia State University	29,470	182	131	Public
South Dakota State University	29,454	183	132	Public
Saint Louis University - St. Louis	29,396	184	52	Private
Eastern Virginia Medical School	28,532	185	133	Public
San Jose State University	28,475	186	134	Public
Wright State University - Dayton	27,523	187	135	Public
College of William and Mary	27,232	188	136	Public
University of Nevada - Las Vegas	26,585	189	137	Public
Texas Tech University	26,161	190	138	Public
Portland State University	26,147	191	139	Public
University of Arkansas - Fayetteville	26,014	192	140	Public
University of Southern Mississippi	25,956	193	141	Public
University of Massachusetts - Lowell	25,874	194	142	Public
State Univ. of New York - Downstate Medical Center	25,802	195	143	Public
Illinois Institute of Technology	25,506	196	53	Private
University of Alabama - Tuscaloosa	25,477	197	144	Public
Florida A&M University	25,313	198	145	Public
Syracuse University	24,163	199	54	Private
University of Texas - Arlington	24,079	200	146	Public

The Top 200 Institutions – Endowment Assets (2015)

Top 1-50 Institutions in Endowment Assets	Endowment Assets x $1000	National Rank	Control Rank	Institutional Control
Harvard University	36,448,817	1	1	Private
Yale University	25,572,100	2	2	Private
Princeton University	22,723,473	3	3	Private
Stanford University	22,222,957	4	4	Private
Massachusetts Institute of Technology	13,474,743	5	5	Private
University of Texas - Austin	10,507,795	6	1	Public
Northwestern University	10,193,037	7	6	Private
University of Pennsylvania	10,133,569	8	7	Private
University of Michigan - Ann Arbor	9,952,113	9	2	Public
Texas A&M University - College Station	9,856,983	10	3	Public
Columbia University	9,639,065	11	8	Private
University of Notre Dame	8,566,952	12	9	Private
University of Chicago	7,549,710	13	10	Private
Duke University	7,296,545	14	11	Private
Washington University in St. Louis	6,818,748	15	12	Private
Emory University	6,684,305	16	13	Private
University of Virginia	6,180,515	17	4	Public
Rice University	5,557,479	18	14	Private
Cornell University	4,760,560	19	15	Private
University of Southern California	4,709,511	20	16	Private
Dartmouth College	4,663,491	21	17	Private
Vanderbilt University	4,133,542	22	18	Private
University of California - Berkeley	4,045,451	23	5	Public
Ohio State University - Columbus	3,633,887	24	6	Public
University of Pittsburgh - Pittsburgh	3,588,775	25	7	Public
New York University	3,576,180	26	19	Private
University of California - Los Angeles	3,493,903	27	8	Public
Johns Hopkins University	3,412,617	28	20	Private
University of Minnesota - Twin Cities	3,297,460	29	9	Public
University of Washington - Seattle	3,076,226	30	10	Public
Brown University	3,073,349	31	21	Private
University of North Carolina - Chapel Hill	2,988,806	32	11	Public
University of Wisconsin - Madison	2,792,622	33	12	Public
Michigan State University	2,673,652	34	13	Public
Purdue University - West Lafayette	2,397,902	35	14	Public
Williams College	2,395,100	36	22	Private
University of Richmond	2,371,810	37	23	Private
Boston College	2,219,600	38	24	Private
California Institute of Technology	2,198,887	39	25	Private
Amherst College	2,193,511	40	26	Private
University of California - San Francisco	2,124,970	41	15	Public
Pomona College	2,098,704	42	27	Private
University of Rochester	2,050,199	43	28	Private
Rockefeller University	1,987,027	44	29	Private
Georgia Institute of Technology	1,858,977	45	16	Public
Pennsylvania State University - University Park	1,854,222	46	17	Public
Wellesley College	1,853,503	47	30	Private
Swarthmore College	1,845,799	48	31	Private
Grinnell College	1,787,775	49	32	Private
Smith College	1,781,763	50	33	Private

The Top 200 Institutions – Endowment Assets (2015)

Top 51-100 Institutions in Endowment Assets	Endowment Assets x $1000	National Rank	Control Rank	Institutional Control
Case Western Reserve University	1,775,999	51	34	Private
Carnegie Mellon University	1,739,474	52	35	Private
Boston University	1,644,117	53	36	Private
Virginia Commonwealth University	1,638,147	54	18	Public
University of Texas SW Medical Center - Dallas	1,620,501	55	19	Public
George Washington University	1,616,357	56	37	Private
Tufts University	1,593,019	57	38	Private
University of Florida	1,555,703	58	20	Public
University of Illinois - Urbana-Champaign	1,530,658	59	21	Public
Georgetown University	1,528,869	60	39	Private
Texas Christian University	1,514,296	61	40	Private
Southern Methodist University	1,505,296	62	41	Private
Washington and Lee University	1,471,274	63	42	Private
Bowdoin College	1,392,760	64	43	Private
University of Delaware	1,341,373	65	22	Public
Weill Cornell Medical College	1,276,986	66	44	Private
University of Iowa	1,263,043	67	23	Public
Tulane University	1,220,464	68	45	Private
Lehigh University	1,213,207	69	46	Private
University of Texas MD Anderson Cancer Center	1,200,742	70	24	Public
University of Cincinnati - Cincinnati	1,195,899	71	25	Public
Trinity University	1,185,370	72	47	Private
University of Kansas - Lawrence	1,170,313	73	26	Public
Baylor University	1,168,242	74	48	Private
Wake Forest University	1,167,400	75	49	Private
Syracuse University	1,166,109	76	50	Private
University of Kentucky	1,142,722	77	27	Public
Berea College	1,101,476	78	51	Private
Middlebury College	1,101,054	79	52	Private
Baylor College of Medicine	1,095,326	80	53	Private
Saint Louis University - St. Louis	1,093,348	81	54	Private
University of Oklahoma - Norman	1,066,117	82	28	Public
Princeton Theological Seminary	1,065,784	83	55	Private
Yeshiva University	1,061,440	84	56	Private
University of Tulsa	1,037,169	85	57	Private
University of Utah	1,023,004	86	29	Public
University of California - Davis	1,013,936	87	30	Public
University of Georgia	1,004,987	88	31	Public
North Carolina State University	983,979	89	32	Public
Vassar College	982,974	90	58	Private
Indiana University - Bloomington	960,625	91	33	Public
University of California - San Diego	951,367	92	34	Public
University of Arkansas - Fayetteville	948,679	93	35	Public
Brandeis University	915,087	94	59	Private
University of Nebraska - Lincoln	906,156	95	36	Public
Colgate University	892,231	96	60	Private
University of Miami	887,329	97	61	Private
Washington State University - Pullman	885,777	98	37	Public
Santa Clara University	884,746	99	62	Private
Berry College	879,501	100	63	Private

The Top 200 Institutions – Endowment Assets (2015)

Top 101-150 Institutions in Endowment Assets	Endowment Assets x $1000	National Rank	Control Rank	Institutional Control
University of Missouri - Columbia	857,471	101	38	Public
Hamilton College (NY)	856,067	102	64	Private
Bryn Mawr College	852,985	103	65	Private
University of Louisville	844,288	104	39	Public
Oberlin College	832,382	105	66	Private
Indiana University-Purdue University - Indianapolis	825,184	106	40	Public
Virginia Polytechnic Institute and State University	817,759	107	41	Public
College of William and Mary	811,217	108	42	Public
Wesleyan University	810,018	109	67	Private
Pepperdine University	805,154	110	68	Private
Denison University	797,101	111	69	Private
Bucknell University	789,354	112	70	Private
Loma Linda University	787,454	113	71	Private
Iowa State University	786,205	114	43	Public
Carleton College	783,456	115	72	Private
Medical College of Wisconsin	778,315	116	73	Private
Lafayette College	777,553	117	74	Private
University of Arizona	767,940	118	44	Public
Macalester College	762,018	119	75	Private
University of Alabama - Tuscaloosa	761,691	120	45	Public
Rochester Institute of Technology	758,606	121	76	Private
Colby College	745,957	122	77	Private
Cooper Union for the Advancement of Science & Art	738,415	123	78	Private
Claremont McKenna College	733,871	124	79	Private
Northeastern University	729,400	125	80	Private
College of the Holy Cross	721,310	126	81	Private
Colorado College	720,085	127	82	Private
University of Oregon	719,111	128	46	Public
Icahn School of Medicine at Mount Sinai	717,372	129	83	Private
Rutgers University - New Brunswick	710,802	130	47	Public
University of Houston - University Park	707,437	131	48	Public
Mount Holyoke College	700,304	132	84	Private
Principia College	686,425	133	85	Private
St. John's University (NY)	685,942	134	86	Private
Davidson College	682,500	135	87	Private
Rensselaer Polytechnic Institute	676,546	136	88	Private
Drexel University	668,386	137	89	Private
Fordham University	665,532	138	90	Private
Texas Tech University	661,235	139	49	Public
Howard University	659,630	140	91	Private
Clemson University	648,611	141	50	Public
DePauw University	643,787	142	92	Private
Arizona State University	643,188	143	51	Public
Auburn University	641,993	144	52	Public
University of Denver	632,761	145	93	Private
Furman University	631,397	146	94	Private
University of South Carolina - Columbia	625,186	147	53	Public
University at Buffalo	619,296	148	54	Public
University of Tennessee - Knoxville	608,873	149	55	Public
Florida State University	605,275	150	56	Public

The Top 200 Institutions – Endowment Assets (2015)

Top 151-200 Institutions in Endowment Assets	Endowment Assets x $1000	National Rank	Control Rank	Institutional Control
American University	600,336	151	95	Private
University of Colorado - Boulder	598,355	152	57	Public
Oregon Health & Science University	571,341	153	58	Public
Trinity College (CT)	562,182	154	96	Private
National University	558,978	155	97	Private
Rush University	555,610	156	98	Private
Villanova University	553,859	157	99	Private
Marquette University	551,558	158	100	Private
Reed College	545,159	159	101	Private
Loyola University Chicago	542,909	160	102	Private
University of Mississippi - Oxford	540,291	161	59	Public
West Virginia University	533,599	162	60	Public
University of Texas Medical Branch - Galveston	531,562	163	61	Public
University of South Alabama - Mobile	529,718	164	62	Public
Whitman College	514,676	165	103	Private
University of California - Irvine	512,904	166	63	Public
Ohio University - Athens	506,989	167	64	Public
Oregon State University	505,369	168	65	Public
University of Dayton	500,407	169	104	Private
Haverford College	495,044	170	105	Private
University of Colorado - Denver	491,942	171	66	Public
Kansas State University	488,936	172	67	Public
University of Maryland - College Park	482,628	173	68	Public
University of Wyoming	481,469	174	69	Public
University of Texas Health Science Ctr - San Antonio	476,632	175	70	Public
Hillsdale College	470,554	176	106	Private
University of San Diego	469,984	177	107	Private
Miami University - Oxford	460,280	178	71	Public
University of Oklahoma Health Sciences Center	456,907	179	72	Public
University of St. Thomas (MN)	456,494	180	108	Private
University of Vermont	453,653	181	73	Public
Creighton University	449,443	182	109	Private
Mississippi State University	449,106	183	74	Public
St. Olaf College	448,489	184	110	Private
College of the Ozarks	442,272	185	111	Private
DePaul University	438,193	186	112	Private
Loyola Marymount University	437,792	187	113	Private
Thomas Jefferson University	437,750	188	114	Private
Union College (NY)	436,317	189	115	Private
Pennsylvania State University - Hershey Medical Ctr.	436,288	190	75	Public
Worcester Polytechnic Institute	435,867	191	116	Private
Miami Dade College	434,555	192	76	Public
Virginia Military Institute	430,742	193	77	Public
Louisiana State University - Baton Rouge	427,852	194	78	Public
University of Toledo	422,249	195	79	Public
University of South Florida - Tampa	417,415	196	80	Public
Dickinson College	415,079	197	117	Private
Hofstra University	413,872	198	118	Private
Wheaton College (IL)	409,613	199	119	Private
Earlham College	405,520	200	120	Private

The Top 200 Institutions – Annual Giving (2015)

Top 1-50 Institutions in Annual Giving	Annual Giving x $1000	National Rank	Control Rank	Institutional Control
Stanford University	1,625,036	1	1	Private
Harvard University	1,045,872	2	2	Private
University of Southern California	653,025	3	3	Private
University of California - San Francisco	608,580	4	1	Public
Johns Hopkins University	582,675	5	4	Private
Columbia University	552,682	6	5	Private
Princeton University	549,840	7	6	Private
Northwestern University	536,831	8	7	Private
University of Pennsylvania	517,198	9	8	Private
University of California - Los Angeles	473,205	10	2	Public
Duke University	472,008	11	9	Private
University of Washington - Seattle	447,021	12	3	Public
University of Chicago	443,792	13	10	Private
Yale University	440,807	14	11	Private
New York University	439,662	15	12	Private
Massachusetts Institute of Technology	439,404	16	13	Private
Cornell University	434,465	17	14	Private
University of Michigan - Ann Arbor	394,310	18	4	Public
University of Notre Dame	379,869	19	15	Private
University of California - Berkeley	366,116	20	5	Public
Ohio State University - Columbus	359,798	21	6	Public
University of Minnesota - Twin Cities	344,303	22	7	Public
University of Wisconsin - Madison	330,454	23	8	Public
University of Texas - Austin	310,212	24	9	Public
University of North Carolina - Chapel Hill	301,177	25	10	Public
Texas A&M University - College Station	255,179	26	11	Public
University of Oklahoma - Norman	252,475	27	12	Public
George Washington University	248,030	28	16	Private
Washington University in St. Louis	246,714	29	17	Private
University of Virginia	233,218	30	13	Public
Emory University	228,034	31	18	Private
Dartmouth College	218,832	32	19	Private
University of Florida	215,580	33	14	Public
Indiana University - Bloomington	211,471	34	15	Public
University of Miami	193,809	35	20	Private
University of Arizona	190,184	36	16	Public
Brown University	187,754	37	21	Private
University of California - Davis	185,840	38	17	Public
University of Nebraska - Lincoln	177,321	39	18	Public
University of Illinois - Urbana-Champaign	177,235	40	19	Public
University of Texas MD Anderson Cancer Center	176,908	41	20	Public
University of Kansas - Lawrence	176,704	42	21	Public
Georgetown University	172,452	43	22	Private
Purdue University - West Lafayette	172,219	44	22	Public
University of Colorado - Denver	171,102	45	23	Public
University of California - San Diego	171,059	46	24	Public
California Institute of Technology	161,929	47	23	Private
University of Iowa	159,532	48	25	Public
Weill Cornell Medical College	156,176	49	24	Private
Pennsylvania State University - University Park	155,658	50	26	Public

The Top 200 Institutions – Annual Giving (2015)

Top 51-100 Institutions in Annual Giving	Annual Giving x $1000	National Rank	Control Rank	Institutional Control
Boston College	152,210	51	25	Private
University of Colorado - Boulder	151,553	52	27	Public
University of Texas SW Medical Center - Dallas	149,243	53	28	Public
University of Oregon	145,109	54	29	Public
Oregon Health & Science University	141,018	55	30	Public
Boston University	140,393	56	26	Private
Carnegie Mellon University	139,563	57	27	Private
Case Western Reserve University	132,826	58	28	Private
Hillsdale College	131,730	59	29	Private
Michigan State University	131,499	60	31	Public
Arizona State University	130,775	61	32	Public
Louisiana State University - Baton Rouge	130,763	62	33	Public
Rutgers University - New Brunswick	127,846	63	34	Public
University of Utah	126,244	64	35	Public
University of Pittsburgh - Pittsburgh	124,602	65	36	Public
University of Maryland - College Park	122,694	66	37	Public
Rice University	122,186	67	30	Private
Indiana University - Purdue University - Indianapolis	121,989	68	38	Public
Vanderbilt University	121,909	69	31	Private
University of Tennessee - Knoxville	119,749	70	39	Public
University of Cincinnati - Cincinnati	119,700	71	40	Public
North Carolina State University	119,150	72	41	Public
Georgia Institute of Technology	119,118	73	42	Public
University of Kentucky	118,190	74	43	Public
Southern Methodist University	115,447	75	32	Private
University of South Carolina - Columbia	113,506	76	44	Public
West Virginia University	110,384	77	45	Public
Icahn School of Medicine at Mount Sinai	109,733	78	33	Private
University of Missouri - Columbia	108,689	79	46	Public
University of Rochester	108,217	80	34	Private
Washington State University - Pullman	106,370	81	47	Public
Auburn University	106,353	82	48	Public
Iowa State University	105,512	83	49	Public
University of Georgia	104,108	84	50	Public
University of Nevada - Reno	100,048	85	51	Public
Wake Forest University	99,763	86	35	Private
Oregon State University	99,318	87	52	Public
Kansas State University	98,094	88	53	Public
Baylor University	97,974	89	36	Private
University of Arkansas - Fayetteville	97,619	90	54	Public
University of Houston - University Park	95,602	91	55	Public
Villanova University	92,933	92	37	Private
University of Hawaii - Manoa	90,650	93	56	Public
University of Nebraska Medical Center	89,054	94	57	Public
Drexel University	88,916	95	38	Private
Tulane University	88,422	96	39	Private
University of Alabama - Tuscaloosa	87,742	97	58	Public
Stony Brook University	86,687	98	59	Public
Virginia Polytechnic Institute and State University	86,391	99	60	Public
University of Louisville	86,309	100	61	Public

The Top 200 Institutions – Annual Giving (2015)

Top 101-150 Institutions in Annual Giving	Annual Giving x $1000	National Rank	Control Rank	Institutional Control
Syracuse University	84,216	101	40	Private
University of Mississippi - Oxford	83,112	102	62	Public
Clemson University	81,861	103	63	Public
Oklahoma State University - Stillwater	77,009	104	64	Public
Marquette University	76,932	105	41	Private
University of Alabama - Birmingham	76,612	106	65	Public
San Diego State University	76,036	107	66	Public
Texas Christian University	70,428	108	42	Private
University of Maryland - Baltimore	69,153	109	67	Public
University of New Mexico - Albuquerque	68,992	110	68	Public
Texas Tech University	68,832	111	69	Public
Florida State University	68,634	112	70	Public
Virginia Commonwealth University	67,256	113	71	Public
University of California - Irvine	66,617	114	72	Public
University of Oklahoma Health Sciences Center	64,872	115	73	Public
University of California - Santa Barbara	63,413	116	74	Public
University of Illinois - Chicago	62,590	117	75	Public
Tufts University	62,131	118	43	Private
Baylor College of Medicine	61,656	119	44	Private
Brandeis University	60,196	120	45	Private
University of South Florida - Tampa	59,903	121	76	Public
Northeastern University	59,857	122	46	Private
Yeshiva University	59,420	123	47	Private
Temple University	58,792	124	77	Public
Mississippi State University	56,857	125	78	Public
College of William and Mary	56,200	126	79	Public
Williams College	53,287	127	48	Private
George Mason University	53,164	128	80	Public
Davidson College	52,783	129	49	Private
Utah State University	52,076	130	81	Public
Smith College	51,830	131	50	Private
Wellesley College	51,486	132	51	Private
University of Tulsa	50,908	133	52	Private
U.S. Military Academy	50,847	134	82	Public
Lehigh University	50,188	135	53	Private
Pomona College	49,997	136	54	Private
Bowdoin College	49,381	137	55	Private
Washington and Lee University	48,512	138	56	Private
University of Denver	48,473	139	57	Private
University of Wyoming	48,390	140	83	Public
Wayne State University	47,983	141	84	Public
California Polytechnic State Univ - San Luis Obispo	47,050	142	85	Public
University of Akron - Akron	46,528	143	86	Public
University of Texas Health Science Center - Houston	46,346	144	87	Public
Claremont McKenna College	46,093	145	58	Private
Western Michigan University	44,943	146	88	Public
University of Delaware	44,896	147	89	Public
University of Kansas Medical Center	44,176	148	90	Public
Fordham University	43,203	149	59	Private
Creighton University	43,116	150	60	Private

The Top 200 Institutions – Annual Giving (2015)

Top 151-200 Institutions in Annual Giving	Annual Giving x $1000	National Rank	Control Rank	Institutional Control
University of Texas Health Science Ctr. - San Antonio	42,764	151	91	Public
Oberlin College	41,829	152	61	Private
Middlebury College	41,451	153	62	Private
Colorado State University - Fort Collins	41,342	154	92	Public
University of Texas Medical Branch - Galveston	41,039	155	93	Public
University of Connecticut - Storrs	40,751	156	94	Public
University of Vermont	40,458	157	95	Public
Wesleyan University	39,845	158	63	Private
College of the Holy Cross	39,831	159	64	Private
Biola University	39,629	160	65	Private
Amherst College	39,203	161	66	Private
Thomas Jefferson University	38,809	162	67	Private
Colorado School of Mines	38,623	163	96	Public
Rensselaer Polytechnic Institute	38,364	164	68	Private
University of Nevada - Las Vegas	37,961	165	97	Public
Santa Clara University	37,835	166	69	Private
Miami University - Oxford	37,633	167	98	Public
Colgate University	36,083	168	70	Private
Vassar College	35,867	169	71	Private
University of Massachusetts - Amherst	35,327	170	99	Public
Pennsylvania State University - Hershey Medical Ctr.	35,023	171	100	Public
Bryn Mawr College	34,829	172	72	Private
Berea College	34,702	173	73	Private
City University of NY - Hunter College	34,356	174	101	Public
Lawrence University	34,332	175	74	Private
University of Central Florida	32,779	176	102	Public
Chapman University	31,551	177	75	Private
Medical University of South Carolina	31,498	178	103	Public
University of Montana - Missoula	31,417	179	104	Public
Haverford College	31,284	180	76	Private
Drake University	31,217	181	77	Private
Loyola University Chicago	30,900	182	78	Private
American University	30,686	183	79	Private
University at Buffalo	30,565	184	105	Public
Carleton College	29,863	185	80	Private
Seattle University	29,786	186	81	Private
Bucknell University	29,010	187	82	Private
University of St. Thomas (MN)	28,960	188	83	Private
University of Dayton	28,219	189	84	Private
University of Alaska - Fairbanks	27,865	190	106	Public
Gonzaga University	27,572	191	85	Private
Trinity College (CT)	27,428	192	86	Private
Rochester Institute of Technology	27,320	193	87	Private
Wheaton College (IL)	27,279	194	88	Private
University of Missouri - Kansas City	27,245	195	107	Public
Portland State University	26,748	196	108	Public
Ohio Wesleyan University	26,047	197	89	Private
Kenyon College	25,985	198	90	Private
Mount Holyoke College	25,878	199	91	Private
Baldwin Wallace University	25,610	200	92	Private

The Top 200 Institutions – National Academy Membership (2015)

Top 1-48 Institutions in National Academy Membership	Number of Members	National Rank	Control Rank	Institutional Control
Harvard University	371	1	1	Private
Stanford University	320	2	2	Private
Massachusetts Institute of Technology	268	3	3	Private
University of California - Berkeley	230	4	1	Public
University of California - San Francisco	135	5	2	Public
Columbia University	134	6	4	Private
Princeton University	120	7	5	Private
University of California - San Diego	117	8	3	Public
University of Pennsylvania	117	8	6	Private
University of Washington - Seattle	115	10	4	Public
Yale University	114	11	7	Private
California Institute of Technology	112	12	8	Private
University of Michigan - Ann Arbor	108	13	5	Public
University of California - Los Angeles	101	14	6	Public
Johns Hopkins University	97	15	9	Private
University of Wisconsin - Madison	77	16	7	Public
University of Chicago	69	17	10	Private
University of Texas - Austin	69	17	8	Public
Duke University	66	19	11	Private
Cornell University	62	20	12	Private
New York University	59	21	13	Private
University of California - Santa Barbara	56	22	9	Public
University of Illinois - Urbana-Champaign	56	22	9	Public
Rockefeller University	51	24	14	Private
University of Southern California	50	25	15	Private
Washington University in St. Louis	46	26	16	Private
University of California - Davis	45	27	11	Public
Northwestern University	43	28	17	Private
University of Minnesota - Twin Cities	41	29	12	Public
University of Texas SW Medical Center - Dallas	40	30	13	Public
Carnegie Mellon University	39	31	18	Private
Rutgers University - New Brunswick	39	31	14	Public
University of North Carolina - Chapel Hill	38	33	15	Public
Vanderbilt University	36	34	19	Private
Emory University	32	35	20	Private
Ohio State University - Columbus	32	35	16	Public
University of Pittsburgh - Pittsburgh	32	35	16	Public
Georgia Institute of Technology	31	38	18	Public
University of Arizona	31	38	18	Public
University of California - Irvine	31	38	18	Public
University of Colorado - Boulder	30	41	21	Public
Weill Cornell Medical College	28	42	21	Private
Pennsylvania State University - University Park	27	43	22	Public
Purdue University - West Lafayette	27	43	22	Public
Texas A&M University - College Station	27	43	22	Public
Scripps Research Institute	26	46	22	Private
University of Maryland - College Park	26	46	25	Public
Rice University	25	48	23	Private
University of Florida	25	48	26	Public

The Top 200 Institutions – National Academy Membership (2015)

Top 50-92 Institutions in National Academy Membership	Number of Members	National Rank	Control Rank	Institutional Control
Baylor College of Medicine	24	50	24	Private
Gerstner Sloan-Kettering Grad. Sch. of Biomed Sci.	24	50	24	Private
University of Rochester	24	50	24	Private
University of Virginia	24	50	27	Public
University of Utah	23	54	28	Public
Arizona State University	22	55	29	Public
Brown University	22	55	27	Private
University of Iowa	22	55	29	Public
Boston University	20	58	28	Private
Case Western Reserve University	20	58	28	Private
North Carolina State University	20	58	31	Public
Icahn School of Medicine at Mount Sinai	17	61	30	Private
Dartmouth College	15	62	31	Private
Stony Brook University	14	63	32	Public
University of Colorado - Denver	14	63	32	Public
Michigan State University	13	65	34	Public
Virginia Polytechnic Institute and State University	13	65	34	Public
Yeshiva University	13	65	32	Private
George Washington University	12	68	33	Private
University of Texas MD Anderson Cancer Center	12	68	36	Public
Brandeis University	11	70	34	Private
Tufts University	11	70	34	Private
University of Miami	11	70	34	Private
City University of NY - City College	10	73	37	Public
Oregon Health & Science University	10	73	37	Public
University of California - Santa Cruz	10	73	37	Public
University of Hawaii - Manoa	10	73	37	Public
Colorado State University - Fort Collins	9	77	41	Public
Georgetown University	9	77	37	Private
University of Houston - University Park	9	77	41	Public
University of Maryland - Baltimore	9	77	41	Public
University of Missouri - Columbia	9	77	41	Public
University of Oregon	9	77	41	Public
Washington State University - Pullman	9	77	41	Public
Howard University	8	84	38	Private
Indiana University - Bloomington	8	84	47	Public
Iowa State University	8	84	47	Public
University at Buffalo	8	84	47	Public
University of Alabama - Birmingham	8	84	47	Public
University of California - Riverside	8	84	47	Public
University of Cincinnati - Cincinnati	8	84	47	Public
University of South Florida - Tampa	8	84	47	Public
Drexel University	7	92	39	Private
Florida State University	7	92	54	Public
Rensselaer Polytechnic Institute	7	92	39	Private
University of Delaware	7	92	54	Public
University of Massachusetts - Amherst	7	92	54	Public
University of Massachusetts Med. Sch. - Worcester	7	92	54	Public
Wake Forest University	7	92	39	Private

The Top 200 Institutions – National Academy Membership (2015)

Top 99-119 Institutions in National Academy Membership	Number of Members	National Rank	Control Rank	Institutional Control
Indiana University - Purdue University - Indianapolis	6	99	58	Public
Lehigh University	6	99	42	Private
University of Georgia	6	99	58	Public
University of Illinois - Chicago	6	99	58	Public
Virginia Commonwealth University	6	99	58	Public
Cold Spring Harbor Laboratory	5	104	43	Private
Oregon State University	5	104	62	Public
University of Kansas - Lawrence	5	104	62	Public
University of New Mexico - Albuquerque	5	104	62	Public
University of Tennessee - Knoxville	5	104	62	Public
University of Texas - Dallas	5	104	62	Public
University of Texas HSC - San Antonio	5	104	62	Public
Colorado School of Mines	4	111	68	Public
Morehouse School of Medicine	4	111	44	Private
Temple University	4	111	68	Public
Texas Tech University	4	111	68	Public
Thomas Jefferson University	4	111	44	Private
Uniformed Services University of the Health Sciences	4	111	68	Public
University of Connecticut - Health Center	4	111	68	Public
University of Notre Dame	4	111	44	Private
Boston College	3	119	47	Private
Clark University (MA)	3	119	47	Private
Illinois Institute of Technology	3	119	47	Private
Louisiana State University - Baton Rouge	3	119	73	Public
Medical College of Wisconsin	3	119	47	Private
Medical University of South Carolina	3	119	73	Public
Meharry Medical College	3	119	47	Private
Naval Postgraduate School	3	119	73	Public
Northeastern University	3	119	47	Private
Oklahoma State University - Stillwater	3	119	73	Public
Rutgers University - Newark	3	119	73	Public
Southern Methodist University	3	119	47	Private
Syracuse University	3	119	47	Private
Texas A&M Health Science Center	3	119	73	Public
University of Arkansas - Fayetteville	3	119	73	Public
University of Kansas Medical Center	3	119	73	Public
University of Kentucky	3	119	73	Public
University of Nebraska - Lincoln	3	119	73	Public
University of Texas - Arlington	3	119	73	Public
University of Texas Health Science Center - Houston	3	119	73	Public
University of Texas Medical Branch - Galveston	3	119	73	Public
Wayne State University	3	119	73	Public
Woods Hole Oceanographic Institution	3	119	47	Private

The Top 200 Institutions – National Academy Membership (2015)

Institutions with at Least 2 National Academy Members	Number of Members	National Rank	Control Rank	Institutional Control
Brigham Young University - Provo	2	142	56	Private
Chapman University	2	142	56	Private
Clemson University	2	142	87	Public
Drew University	2	142	56	Private
Florida Atlantic University	2	142	87	Public
Florida Institute of Technology	2	142	56	Private
George Mason University	2	142	87	Public
Mayo Medical School	2	142	56	Private
Pardee RAND Graduate School	2	142	56	Private
Pennsylvania State University - Hershey Medical Ctr.	2	142	87	Public
Rowan University	2	142	87	Public
Rush University	2	142	56	Private
Stevens Institute of Technology	2	142	56	Private
University at Albany	2	142	87	Public
University of Alaska - Fairbanks	2	142	87	Public
University of Louisville	2	142	87	Public
University of Nevada - Reno	2	142	87	Public
University of Rhode Island	2	142	87	Public
University of Vermont	2	142	87	Public
University of Wyoming	2	142	87	Public
West Virginia University	2	142	87	Public

The Top 200 Institutions – Faculty Awards (2015)

Top 1-45 Institutions in Faculty Awards	Number of Awards	National Rank	Control Rank	Institutional Control
Harvard University	84	1	1	Private
Stanford University	56	2	2	Private
University of California - Berkeley	45	3	1	Public
University of Michigan - Ann Arbor	42	4	2	Public
Massachusetts Institute of Technology	41	5	3	Private
University of Washington - Seattle	39	6	3	Public
University of Minnesota - Twin Cities	35	7	4	Public
Columbia University	34	8	4	Private
Johns Hopkins University	33	9	5	Private
Northwestern University	33	9	5	Private
University of California - San Francisco	31	11	5	Public
Cornell University	30	12	7	Private
Duke University	30	12	7	Private
University of Illinois - Urbana-Champaign	30	12	6	Public
University of Pennsylvania	30	12	7	Private
University of Southern California	30	12	7	Private
University of Wisconsin - Madison	30	12	6	Public
Yale University	30	12	7	Private
University of California - Los Angeles	29	19	8	Public
University of California - San Diego	29	19	8	Public
Washington University in St. Louis	29	19	12	Private
New York University	27	22	13	Private
University of Chicago	25	23	14	Private
Arizona State University	23	24	10	Public
University of Florida	23	24	10	Public
Princeton University	22	26	15	Private
Georgia Institute of Technology	21	27	12	Public
University of Colorado - Boulder	21	27	12	Public
Brown University	20	29	16	Private
Rutgers University - New Brunswick	20	29	14	Public
University of California - Irvine	20	29	14	Public
University of Maryland - College Park	20	29	14	Public
Emory University	19	33	17	Private
Pennsylvania State University - University Park	19	33	17	Public
Purdue University - West Lafayette	19	33	17	Public
University of North Carolina - Chapel Hill	19	33	17	Public
University of Texas - Austin	19	33	17	Public
Ohio State University - Columbus	17	38	21	Public
University of Massachusetts - Amherst	17	38	21	Public
Boston University	16	40	18	Private
California Institute of Technology	16	40	18	Private
Indiana University - Bloomington	15	42	23	Public
University of Virginia	15	42	23	Public
Vanderbilt University	15	42	20	Private
George Washington University	14	45	21	Private
Northeastern University	14	45	21	Private
Texas A&M University - College Station	14	45	25	Public
University of Notre Dame	14	45	21	Private

The Top 200 Institutions – Faculty Awards (2015)

Top 49-90 Institutions in Faculty Awards	Number of Awards	National Rank	Control Rank	Institutional Control
Carnegie Mellon University	13	49	24	Private
Florida International University	13	49	26	Public
University of Pittsburgh - Pittsburgh	13	49	26	Public
University of South Florida - Tampa	13	49	26	Public
University of Texas SW Medical Center - Dallas	13	49	26	Public
University of California - Davis	12	54	30	Public
University of California - Santa Barbara	12	54	30	Public
University of Massachusetts Med. Sch. - Worcester	12	54	30	Public
University of Rochester	12	54	25	Private
Case Western Reserve University	11	58	26	Private
Colorado State University - Fort Collins	11	58	33	Public
Michigan State University	11	58	33	Public
North Carolina State University	11	58	33	Public
Rutgers University - Newark	11	58	33	Public
Syracuse University	11	58	26	Private
University of Illinois - Chicago	11	58	33	Public
University of Kansas - Lawrence	11	58	33	Public
University of Oregon	11	58	33	Public
Stony Brook University	10	67	40	Public
Temple University	10	67	40	Public
University of Cincinnati - Cincinnati	10	67	40	Public
University of Iowa	10	67	40	Public
University of Kentucky	10	67	40	Public
University of New Mexico - Albuquerque	10	67	40	Public
University of Utah	10	67	40	Public
Virginia Polytechnic Institute and State University	10	67	40	Public
Weill Cornell Medical College	10	67	28	Private
Brandeis University	9	76	29	Private
Florida State University	9	76	48	Public
University of Arizona	9	76	48	Public
University of Connecticut - Storrs	9	76	48	Public
University of Delaware	9	76	48	Public
University of Missouri - Columbia	9	76	48	Public
University of Oklahoma - Norman	9	76	48	Public
University of South Carolina - Columbia	9	76	48	Public
University of Texas - Dallas	9	76	48	Public
Oregon Health & Science University	8	85	56	Public
Scripps Research Institute	8	85	30	Private
University of California - Santa Cruz	8	85	56	Public
University of Tennessee - Knoxville	8	85	56	Public
West Virginia University	8	85	56	Public
Portland State University	7	90	60	Public
Rockefeller University	7	90	31	Private
Texas Tech University	7	90	60	Public
University of California - Riverside	7	90	60	Public
University of Central Florida	7	90	60	Public
University of Miami	7	90	31	Private
University of Texas - San Antonio	7	90	60	Public
Washington State University - Pullman	7	90	60	Public

The Top 200 Institutions – Faculty Awards (2015)

Top 98-127 Institutions in Faculty Awards	Number of Awards	National Rank	Control Rank	Institutional Control
Baylor College of Medicine	6	98	33	Private
Boston College	6	98	33	Private
College of William and Mary	6	98	66	Public
Dartmouth College	6	98	33	Private
Icahn School of Medicine at Mount Sinai	6	98	33	Private
Iowa State University	6	98	66	Public
New Mexico State University - Las Cruces	6	98	66	Public
Rice University	6	98	33	Private
Tufts University	6	98	33	Private
University at Buffalo	6	98	66	Public
University of Georgia	6	98	66	Public
Virginia Commonwealth University	6	98	66	Public
Binghamton University	5	110	72	Public
Boise State University	5	110	72	Public
Bucknell University	5	110	39	Private
Drexel University	5	110	39	Private
George Mason University	5	110	72	Public
Louisiana State University - Baton Rouge	5	110	72	Public
Michigan Technological University	5	110	72	Public
Oregon State University	5	110	72	Public
Rensselaer Polytechnic Institute	5	110	39	Private
Seton Hall University	5	110	39	Private
Southern Methodist University	5	110	39	Private
University of Colorado - Denver	5	110	72	Public
University of Louisville	5	110	72	Public
University of North Carolina - Charlotte	5	110	72	Public
University of Vermont	5	110	72	Public
Wayne State University	5	110	72	Public
Yeshiva University	5	110	39	Private
American University	4	127	45	Private
California State University - Long Beach	4	127	83	Public
Eastern Michigan University	4	127	83	Public
Fordham University	4	127	45	Private
Georgetown University	4	127	45	Private
Lehigh University	4	127	45	Private
Marquette University	4	127	45	Private
Mississippi State University	4	127	83	Public
North Dakota State University	4	127	83	Public
Saint Louis University - St. Louis	4	127	45	Private
Tulane University	4	127	45	Private
University at Albany	4	127	83	Public
University of Arkansas - Fayetteville	4	127	83	Public
University of California - Merced	4	127	83	Public
University of Hawaii - Manoa	4	127	83	Public
University of Houston - University Park	4	127	83	Public
University of Portland	4	127	45	Private

The Top 200 Institutions – Faculty Awards (2015)

Institutions with at Least 3 Faculty Awards	Number of Awards	National Rank	Control Rank	Institutional Control
Appalachian State University	3	144	92	Public
Auburn University	3	144	92	Public
California State University - Fresno	3	144	92	Public
Carleton College	3	144	53	Private
Catholic University of America	3	144	53	Private
Chapman University	3	144	53	Private
City University of NY - Bernard M. Baruch College	3	144	92	Public
City University of NY - City College	3	144	92	Public
Clemson University	3	144	92	Public
College of Charleston	3	144	92	Public
Colorado School of Mines	3	144	92	Public
DePaul University	3	144	53	Private
Elon University	3	144	53	Private
Haverford College	3	144	53	Private
Howard University	3	144	53	Private
Indiana University-Purdue University - Indianapolis	3	144	92	Public
Macalester College	3	144	53	Private
Mayo Graduate School	3	144	53	Private
Northern Illinois University	3	144	92	Public
Oklahoma State University - Stillwater	3	144	92	Public
Rochester Institute of Technology	3	144	53	Private
San Diego State University	3	144	92	Public
State Univ. of New York - Buffalo State	3	144	92	Public
University of Connecticut - Health Center	3	144	92	Public
University of Maryland - Baltimore	3	144	92	Public
University of Massachusetts - Boston	3	144	92	Public
University of Massachusetts - Lowell	3	144	92	Public
University of Nebraska - Lincoln	3	144	92	Public
University of New Hampshire - Durham	3	144	92	Public
University of North Carolina - Wilmington	3	144	92	Public
University of Texas MD Anderson Cancer Center	3	144	92	Public
University of Wyoming	3	144	92	Public
Utah State University	3	144	92	Public
Wake Forest University	3	144	53	Private

The Top 200 Institutions – Doctorates Awarded (2015)

Top 1-50 Institutions in Doctorates Awarded	Number of Degrees	National Rank	Control Rank	Institutional Control
University of Texas - Austin	899	1	1	Public
University of Michigan - Ann Arbor	882	2	2	Public
University of Wisconsin - Madison	857	3	3	Public
Ohio State University - Columbus	832	4	4	Public
University of Illinois - Urbana-Champaign	829	5	5	Public
University of California - Berkeley	826	6	6	Public
University of California - Los Angeles	774	7	7	Public
University of Florida	754	8	8	Public
Harvard University	745	9	1	Private
Texas A&M University - College Station	740	10	9	Public
University of Minnesota - Twin Cities	725	11	10	Public
Purdue University - West Lafayette	717	12	11	Public
Stanford University	688	13	2	Private
Arizona State University	687	14	12	Public
University of Washington - Seattle	687	14	12	Public
University of Southern California	685	16	3	Private
Pennsylvania State University - University Park	673	17	14	Public
University of Maryland - College Park	654	18	15	Public
Nova Southeastern University	627	19	4	Private
Massachusetts Institute of Technology	606	20	5	Private
Rutgers University - New Brunswick	597	21	16	Public
Michigan State University	577	22	17	Public
University of Pennsylvania	566	23	6	Private
Columbia University	564	24	7	Private
University of California - Davis	553	25	18	Public
Indiana University - Bloomington	538	26	19	Public
Johns Hopkins University	535	27	8	Private
University of Arizona	528	28	20	Public
Georgia Institute of Technology	526	29	21	Public
University of North Carolina - Chapel Hill	519	30	22	Public
North Carolina State University	512	31	23	Public
University of California - San Diego	505	32	24	Public
Virginia Polytechnic Institute and State University	488	33	25	Public
Cornell University	487	34	9	Private
Duke University	485	35	10	Private
Boston University	484	36	11	Private
University of Georgia	467	37	26	Public
University of Iowa	453	38	27	Public
New York University	438	39	12	Private
Northwestern University	438	39	12	Private
University of Pittsburgh - Pittsburgh	438	39	28	Public
University of Missouri - Columbia	435	42	29	Public
University of Colorado - Boulder	434	43	30	Public
Alliant International University	430	44	14	Private
Yale University	426	45	15	Private
Florida State University	424	46	31	Public
City University of NY - Grad. Sch. and University Ctr.	411	47	32	Public
University of Chicago	392	48	16	Private
University of California - Irvine	390	49	33	Public
University of Utah	384	50	34	Public

The Top 200 Institutions – Doctorates Awarded (2015)

Top 51-100 Institutions in Doctorates Awarded	Number of Degrees	National Rank	Control Rank	Institutional Control
Princeton University	371	51	17	Private
University of Virginia	366	52	35	Public
University of Kansas - Lawrence	365	53	36	Public
University of South Carolina - Columbia	358	54	37	Public
University of Tennessee - Knoxville	353	55	38	Public
University of California - Santa Barbara	349	56	39	Public
Stony Brook University	347	57	40	Public
University at Buffalo	342	58	41	Public
Vanderbilt University	340	59	18	Private
Iowa State University	336	60	42	Public
Texas Tech University	336	60	42	Public
Carnegie Mellon University	333	62	19	Private
Louisiana State University - Baton Rouge	331	63	44	Public
University of Houston - University Park	326	64	45	Public
University of Nebraska - Lincoln	325	65	46	Public
University of Connecticut - Storrs	323	66	47	Public
University of South Florida - Tampa	321	67	48	Public
University of Illinois - Chicago	314	68	49	Public
University of Kentucky	295	69	50	Public
Washington University in St. Louis	292	70	20	Private
University of North Texas	287	71	51	Public
University of Central Florida	286	72	52	Public
Virginia Commonwealth University	282	73	53	Public
Washington State University - Pullman	281	74	54	Public
University of California - Riverside	272	75	55	Public
University of Massachusetts - Amherst	268	76	56	Public
University of Rochester	267	77	21	Private
Emory University	264	78	22	Private
University of Alabama - Tuscaloosa	264	78	57	Public
Auburn University	257	80	58	Public
Colorado State University - Fort Collins	251	81	59	Public
George Mason University	249	82	60	Public
University of Notre Dame	244	83	23	Private
Oklahoma State University - Stillwater	242	84	61	Public
Saint Louis University - St. Louis	242	84	24	Private
Wayne State University	242	84	61	Public
University of Hawaii - Manoa	239	87	63	Public
Clemson University	237	88	64	Public
University of Delaware	237	88	64	Public
Georgia State University	231	90	66	Public
George Washington University	222	91	25	Private
University of New Mexico - Albuquerque	222	91	67	Public
University of Oklahoma - Norman	218	93	68	Public
Brown University	215	94	26	Private
Oregon State University	215	94	69	Public
Drexel University	213	96	27	Private
University of Cincinnati - Cincinnati	213	96	70	Public
University of Miami	208	98	28	Private
Teachers College at Columbia University	202	99	29	Private
University of Oregon	199	100	71	Public

The Top 200 Institutions – Doctorates Awarded (2015)

Top 101-150 Institutions in Doctorates Awarded	Number of Degrees	National Rank	Control Rank	Institutional Control
Case Western Reserve University	197	101	30	Private
Temple University	197	101	72	Public
University of Texas - Dallas	195	103	73	Public
Liberty University	194	104	31	Private
University of Texas - Arlington	193	105	74	Public
Medical University of South Carolina	191	106	75	Public
Kansas State University	190	107	76	Public
Florida International University	189	108	77	Public
West Virginia University	183	109	78	Public
California Institute of Technology	182	110	32	Private
Old Dominion University	179	111	79	Public
Southern Illinois University - Carbondale	179	111	79	Public
Rice University	176	113	33	Private
University of Arkansas - Fayetteville	173	114	81	Public
University of Alabama - Birmingham	170	115	82	Public
University of Louisville	170	115	82	Public
University of Wisconsin - Milwaukee	168	117	84	Public
Kent State University - Kent	165	118	85	Public
Rensselaer Polytechnic Institute	164	119	34	Private
University at Albany	164	119	86	Public
Northeastern University	157	121	35	Private
Syracuse University	155	122	36	Private
University of Texas Health Science Center - Houston	153	123	87	Public
University of California - Santa Cruz	151	124	88	Public
University of Nevada - Las Vegas	149	125	89	Public
University of Southern Mississippi	149	125	89	Public
Boston College	146	127	37	Private
Mississippi State University	146	127	91	Public
San Diego State University	140	129	92	Public
Claremont Graduate University	138	130	38	Private
Ohio University - Athens	138	130	93	Public
University of Memphis	138	130	93	Public
University of Toledo	138	130	93	Public
Loyola University Chicago	137	134	39	Private
Regent University	136	135	40	Private
Fielding Graduate University	133	136	41	Private
Binghamton University	132	137	96	Public
New Mexico State University - Las Cruces	131	138	97	Public
University of California - San Francisco	130	139	98	Public
Maryville University of Saint Louis	129	140	42	Private
University of North Carolina - Greensboro	129	140	99	Public
St. John's University (NY)	127	142	43	Private
Fordham University	126	143	44	Private
Colorado School of Mines	124	144	100	Public
University of North Carolina - Charlotte	124	144	100	Public
University of Texas - El Paso	124	144	100	Public
Tulane University	123	147	45	Private
East Tennessee State University	122	148	103	Public
University of Akron - Akron	121	149	104	Public
Howard University	119	150	46	Private

The Top 200 Institutions – Doctorates Awarded (2015)

Top 151-199 Institutions in Doctorates Awarded	Number of Degrees	National Rank	Control Rank	Institutional Control
University of Mississippi - Oxford	118	151	105	Public
Indiana University of Pennsylvania	117	152	106	Public
Tufts University	116	153	47	Private
Georgetown University	114	154	48	Private
University of Denver	112	155	49	Private
Western Michigan University	112	155	107	Public
Baylor College of Medicine	111	157	50	Private
Northern Illinois University	109	158	108	Public
University of Nevada - Reno	109	158	108	Public
University of Texas - San Antonio	109	158	108	Public
Lehigh University	108	161	51	Private
Shenandoah University	107	162	52	Private
University of the Cumberlands	107	162	52	Private
Catholic University of America	106	164	54	Private
North Dakota State University	106	164	111	Public
Florida Atlantic University	104	166	112	Public
University of Puerto Rico - Rio Piedras	104	166	112	Public
University of Colorado - Denver	103	168	114	Public
Utah State University	102	169	115	Public
Brandeis University	100	170	55	Private
University of Maryland - Baltimore County	100	170	116	Public
Baylor University	99	172	56	Private
Duquesne University	98	173	57	Private
University of Missouri - Kansas City	98	173	117	Public
Brigham Young University - Provo	97	175	58	Private
Rutgers University - Newark	97	175	118	Public
East Carolina University	96	177	119	Public
Yeshiva University	96	177	59	Private
Missouri University of Science and Technology	95	179	120	Public
Texas Woman's University	94	180	121	Public
University of Rhode Island	93	181	122	Public
University of Wyoming	93	181	122	Public
Loma Linda University	92	183	60	Private
Carlos Albizu University - San Juan	91	184	61	Private
Wilmington University (DE)	90	185	62	Private
University of Texas SW Medical Center - Dallas	88	186	124	Public
University of Massachusetts - Lowell	87	187	125	Public
University of North Dakota	87	187	125	Public
Illinois Institute of Technology	86	189	63	Private
Lamar University	86	189	127	Public
Southern Methodist University	86	189	63	Private
Dartmouth College	85	192	65	Private
Indiana State University	85	192	128	Public
Pepperdine University	84	194	66	Private
University of Missouri - St. Louis	84	194	129	Public
Bowling Green State University - Bowling Green	82	196	130	Public
Seton Hall University	82	196	67	Private
University of Northern Colorado	82	196	130	Public
University of Maryland - Baltimore	81	199	132	Public
University of Nebraska Medical Center	81	199	132	Public

The Top 200 Institutions – Postdoctoral Appointees (2014)

Top 1-50 Institutions in Postdoctoral Appointees	Number of Postdocs	National Rank	Control Rank	Institutional Control
Harvard University	5,761	1	1	Private
Stanford University	2,048	2	2	Private
Johns Hopkins University	1,715	3	3	Private
Massachusetts Institute of Technology	1,516	4	4	Private
University of California - San Diego	1,338	5	1	Public
Columbia University	1,274	6	5	Private
University of Michigan - Ann Arbor	1,238	7	2	Public
Yale University	1,201	8	6	Private
University of Washington - Seattle	1,184	9	3	Public
University of California - Berkeley	1,148	10	4	Public
University of California - Los Angeles	1,088	11	5	Public
University of California - San Francisco	1,051	12	6	Public
University of Pennsylvania	919	13	7	Private
University of Colorado - Boulder	879	14	7	Public
University of North Carolina - Chapel Hill	802	15	8	Public
University of Wisconsin - Madison	767	16	9	Public
University of California - Davis	765	17	10	Public
Northwestern University	708	18	8	Private
University of Minnesota - Twin Cities	679	19	11	Public
Emory University	674	20	9	Private
Icahn School of Medicine at Mount Sinai	670	21	10	Private
University of Pittsburgh - Pittsburgh	659	22	12	Public
Duke University	656	23	11	Private
Scripps Research Institute	648	24	12	Private
University of Florida	644	25	13	Public
University of Texas MD Anderson Cancer Center	640	26	14	Public
Vanderbilt University	634	27	13	Private
Ohio State University - Columbus	629	28	15	Public
Washington University in St. Louis	625	29	14	Private
New York University	596	30	15	Private
Baylor College of Medicine	594	31	16	Private
University of Chicago	583	32	17	Private
University of Texas SW Medical Center - Dallas	571	33	16	Public
California Institute of Technology	552	34	18	Private
University of Illinois - Urbana-Champaign	525	35	17	Public
Mayo Graduate School	523	36	19	Private
University of Southern California	480	37	20	Private
North Carolina State University	473	38	18	Public
Cornell University	466	39	21	Private
University of Cincinnati - Cincinnati	466	39	19	Public
Princeton University	464	41	22	Private
University of Arizona	451	42	20	Public
Michigan State University	450	43	21	Public
University of Virginia	447	44	22	Public
Boston University	444	45	23	Private
University of Maryland - College Park	437	46	23	Public
University of Utah	429	47	24	Public
Texas A&M University - College Station	386	48	25	Public
University of Texas - Austin	370	49	26	Public
Pennsylvania State University - University Park	365	50	27	Public

The Top 200 Institutions – Postdoctoral Appointees (2014)

Top 51-100 Institutions in Postdoctoral Appointees	Number of Postdocs	National Rank	Control Rank	Institutional Control
Purdue University - West Lafayette	358	51	28	Public
University of Maryland - Baltimore	358	51	28	Public
University of Iowa	355	53	30	Public
Rutgers University - New Brunswick	345	54	31	Public
Iowa State University	331	55	32	Public
Weill Cornell Medical College	322	56	24	Private
University of California - Irvine	315	57	33	Public
University of Massachusetts Medical School - Worcester	315	57	33	Public
Yeshiva University	303	59	25	Private
University at Buffalo	301	60	35	Public
University of South Florida - Tampa	300	61	36	Public
Rockefeller University	298	62	26	Private
Colorado State University - Fort Collins	297	63	37	Public
University of California - Santa Barbara	285	64	38	Public
Oregon Health & Science University	270	65	39	Public
University of Colorado - Denver	267	66	40	Public
University of Houston - University Park	258	67	41	Public
Arizona State University	253	68	42	Public
Indiana University - Purdue University - Indianapolis	249	69	43	Public
Virginia Commonwealth University	249	69	43	Public
Brown University	244	71	27	Private
University of Hawaii - Manoa	243	72	45	Public
University of Illinois - Chicago	238	73	46	Public
University of Georgia	231	74	47	Public
University of Alabama - Birmingham	228	75	48	Public
Virginia Polytechnic Institute and State University	226	76	49	Public
Stony Brook University	224	77	50	Public
Dartmouth College	222	78	28	Private
University of Rochester	222	78	28	Private
Georgia Institute of Technology	217	80	51	Public
Carnegie Mellon University	215	81	30	Private
University of Texas Health Science Center - Houston	212	82	52	Public
Florida State University	211	83	53	Public
Rice University	206	84	31	Private
Oregon State University	201	85	54	Public
University of Nebraska - Lincoln	201	85	54	Public
University of Miami	198	87	32	Private
Tufts University	194	88	33	Private
Temple University	192	89	56	Public
Case Western Reserve University	190	90	34	Private
Augusta University	188	91	57	Public
Wayne State University	185	92	58	Public
University of Missouri - Columbia	184	93	59	Public
Medical College of Wisconsin	175	94	35	Private
Medical University of South Carolina	173	95	60	Public
University of Notre Dame	171	96	36	Private
Washington State University - Pullman	169	97	61	Public
Sanford-Burnham Medical Research Institute	167	98	37	Private
Texas Tech University	167	98	62	Public
University of Delaware	166	100	63	Public

The Top 200 Institutions – Postdoctoral Appointees (2014)

Top 101-149 Institutions in Postdoctoral Appointees	Number of Postdocs	National Rank	Control Rank	Institutional Control
University of Texas Health Science Ctr - San Antonio	165	101	64	Public
University of Kentucky	155	102	65	Public
University of Kansas - Lawrence	154	103	66	Public
Cold Spring Harbor Laboratory	153	104	38	Private
University of Massachusetts - Amherst	153	104	67	Public
Wake Forest University	152	106	39	Private
University of Oklahoma - Norman	145	107	68	Public
Indiana University - Bloomington	144	108	69	Public
University of South Carolina - Columbia	144	108	69	Public
University of Tennessee - Knoxville	143	110	71	Public
Kansas State University	142	111	72	Public
Louisiana State University - Baton Rouge	141	112	73	Public
University of California - Riverside	141	112	73	Public
University of New Mexico - Albuquerque	139	114	75	Public
University of Texas Medical Branch - Galveston	131	115	76	Public
Georgetown University	127	116	40	Private
Tulane University	124	117	41	Private
Texas A&M Health Science Center	122	118	77	Public
University of Connecticut - Storrs	121	119	78	Public
University of California - Santa Cruz	120	120	79	Public
Thomas Jefferson University	119	121	42	Private
Irell and Manella Graduate School of Biological Sciences	117	122	43	Private
Northeastern University	117	122	43	Private
University of Tennessee Health Science Center	113	124	80	Public
University of Kansas Medical Center	111	125	81	Public
University of Nebraska Medical Center	110	126	82	Public
University of Connecticut - Health Center	104	127	83	Public
Brandeis University	102	128	45	Private
University of Wisconsin - Milwaukee	100	129	84	Public
University of Louisville	97	130	85	Public
Woods Hole Oceanographic Institution	97	130	46	Private
University of Vermont	95	132	86	Public
George Washington University	94	133	47	Private
Pennsylvania State University - Hershey Medical Center	91	134	87	Public
University of Oklahoma Health Sciences Center	89	135	88	Public
University of Oregon	85	136	89	Public
Rensselaer Polytechnic Institute	82	137	48	Private
University of Texas - Dallas	78	138	90	Public
Georgia State University	76	139	91	Public
Drexel University	74	140	49	Private
Northern Illinois University	69	141	92	Public
University at Albany	69	141	92	Public
West Virginia University	67	143	94	Public
Clemson University	65	144	95	Public
University of Nevada - Reno	65	144	95	Public
Florida International University	64	146	97	Public
University of Maryland - Baltimore County	63	147	98	Public
University of Arkansas - Fayetteville	62	148	99	Public
Syracuse University	61	149	50	Private

The Top 200 Institutions – Postdoctoral Appointees (2014)

Top 150-200 Institutions in Postdoctoral Appointees	Number of Postdocs	National Rank	Control Rank	Institutional Control
City University of NY - City College	57	150	100	Public
Loyola University Chicago	57	150	51	Private
Oklahoma State University - Stillwater	57	150	100	Public
University of Arkansas for Medical Sciences	57	150	100	Public
University of Idaho	56	154	103	Public
Louisiana State University HSC - New Orleans	55	155	104	Public
University of Wyoming	55	155	104	Public
Loma Linda University	53	157	52	Private
University of Texas - San Antonio	52	158	106	Public
Colorado School of Mines	49	159	107	Public
University of Texas - Arlington	49	159	107	Public
North Dakota State University	48	161	109	Public
University of Alabama - Tuscaloosa	48	161	109	Public
University of Alaska - Fairbanks	47	163	111	Public
University of Central Florida	47	163	111	Public
Utah State University	47	163	111	Public
Boston College	46	166	53	Private
Mississippi State University	46	166	114	Public
University of New Hampshire - Durham	45	168	115	Public
University of Mississippi - Oxford	44	169	116	Public
Rutgers University - Newark	43	170	117	Public
University of Mississippi Medical Center	43	170	117	Public
East Carolina University	42	172	119	Public
University of Akron - Akron	42	172	119	Public
Saint Louis University - St. Louis	41	174	54	Private
Auburn University	40	175	121	Public
University of North Texas	40	175	121	Public
University of South Alabama - Mobile	40	175	121	Public
Kent State University - Kent	38	178	124	Public
Montana State University - Bozeman	38	178	124	Public
University of Michigan - Dearborn	38	178	124	Public
Albany Medical College	36	181	55	Private
Uniformed Services University of the Health Sciences	36	181	127	Public
University of California - Merced	36	181	127	Public
University of Montana - Missoula	36	181	127	Public
Lehigh University	34	185	56	Private
George Mason University	33	186	130	Public
Rush University	33	186	57	Private
San Diego State University	32	188	131	Public
University of Nevada - Las Vegas	32	188	131	Public
Old Dominion University	30	190	133	Public
Richard Gilder Grad. School at the Am Mus of Nat History	30	190	58	Private
Louisiana State University - Shreveport	29	192	134	Public
Northern Arizona University	29	192	134	Public
Ohio University - Athens	29	192	134	Public
New Mexico State University - Las Cruces	28	195	137	Public
University of Toledo	28	195	137	Public
University of Massachusetts - Lowell	27	197	139	Public
University of Rhode Island	27	197	139	Public
University of North Texas Health Science Center	26	199	141	Public
Rosalind Franklin University of Medicine and Science	25	200	59	Private
Southern Methodist University	25	200	59	Private

The Top 200 Institutions – SAT Scores (2014)

Top 1-50 Institutions in Median SAT Scores	Median SAT Score	National Rank	Control Rank	Institutional Control
California Institute of Technology	1550	1	1	Private
University of Chicago	1518	2	2	Private
Harvard University	1505	3	3	Private
Yale University	1505	3	3	Private
Princeton University	1500	5	5	Private
Massachusetts Institute of Technology	1495	6	6	Private
Harvey Mudd College	1494	7	7	Private
Columbia University	1480	8	8	Private
Franklin W. Olin College of Engineering	1480	8	8	Private
Northwestern University	1475	10	10	Private
Stanford University	1475	10	10	Private
Rice University	1470	12	12	Private
Duke University	1460	13	13	Private
Pomona College	1460	13	13	Private
University of Notre Dame	1460	13	13	Private
Vanderbilt University	1460	13	13	Private
Washington University in St. Louis	1460	13	13	Private
Dartmouth College	1455	18	18	Private
University of Pennsylvania	1455	18	18	Private
Williams College	1455	18	18	Private
Swarthmore College	1450	21	21	Private
Amherst College	1449	22	22	Private
Brown University	1440	23	23	Private
Carnegie Mellon University	1440	23	23	Private
Tufts University	1440	23	23	Private
Claremont McKenna College	1435	26	26	Private
Johns Hopkins University	1435	26	26	Private
Cornell University	1420	28	28	Private
Georgetown University	1420	28	28	Private
Northeastern University	1420	28	28	Private
Webb Institute	1420	28	28	Private
Carleton College	1415	32	32	Private
Haverford College	1410	33	33	Private
Vassar College	1405	34	34	Private
Georgia Institute of Technology	1400	35	1	Public
Grinnell College	1400	35	35	Private
Rensselaer Polytechnic Institute	1395	37	36	Private
Hamilton College (NY)	1390	38	37	Private
University of Michigan - Ann Arbor	1390	38	2	Public
Washington and Lee University	1390	38	37	Private
Reed College	1385	41	39	Private
Wellesley College	1385	41	39	Private
University of Southern California	1380	43	41	Private
Colgate University	1375	44	42	Private
Cooper Union for the Advancement of Science & Art	1375	44	42	Private
Case Western Reserve University	1370	46	44	Private
College of William and Mary	1370	46	3	Public
Emory University	1370	46	44	Private
University of California - Berkeley	1370	46	3	Public
Macalester College	1368	50	46	Private

The Top 200 Institutions – SAT Scores (2014)

Top 51-103 Institutions in Median SAT Scores	Median SAT Score	National Rank	Control Rank	Institutional Control
Boston College	1365	51	47	Private
Brandeis University	1365	51	47	Private
Middlebury College	1365	51	47	Private
Scripps College	1360	54	50	Private
Tulane University	1360	54	50	Private
Oberlin College	1355	56	52	Private
University of Virginia	1355	56	5	Public
Jewish Theological Seminary of America	1350	58	53	Private
Barnard College	1345	59	54	Private
New York University	1345	59	54	Private
Colorado School of Mines	1340	61	6	Public
Stevens Institute of Technology	1340	61	56	Private
U.S. Air Force Academy	1340	61	6	Public
Davidson College	1335	64	57	Private
Colby College	1330	65	58	Private
Kenyon College	1325	66	59	Private
St. John's College (MD)	1325	66	59	Private
University of California - Los Angeles	1325	66	8	Public
University of Richmond	1325	66	59	Private
Bryn Mawr College	1320	70	62	Private
Lehigh University	1320	70	62	Private
Rose-Hulman Institute of Technology	1320	70	62	Private
Southern Methodist University	1320	70	62	Private
University of Miami	1320	70	62	Private
University of North Carolina - Chapel Hill	1320	70	9	Public
Wheaton College (IL)	1320	70	62	Private
University of Maryland - College Park	1315	77	10	Public
Whitman College	1315	77	68	Private
University of California - San Diego	1310	79	11	Public
Villanova University	1310	79	69	Private
Bucknell University	1305	81	70	Private
Boston University	1300	82	71	Private
Brigham Young University - Provo	1300	82	71	Private
Lafayette College	1300	82	71	Private
Occidental College	1300	82	71	Private
Ohio State University - Columbus	1300	82	12	Public
Rhodes College (TN)	1300	82	71	Private
Santa Clara University	1300	82	71	Private
St. Olaf College	1300	82	71	Private
University of Illinois - Urbana-Champaign	1300	82	12	Public
University of Tulsa	1300	82	71	Private
Pontifical College Josephinum	1298	92	79	Private
George Washington University	1295	93	80	Private
Binghamton University	1290	94	14	Public
University of Texas - Austin	1290	94	14	Public
U.S. Naval Academy	1285	96	16	Public
Centre College	1280	97	81	Private
Missouri University of Science and Technology	1280	97	17	Public
New College of Florida	1280	97	17	Public
University of Wisconsin - Madison	1280	97	17	Public
Babson College	1275	101	82	Private
U.S. Military Academy	1275	101	20	Public
University of Pittsburgh - Pittsburgh	1270	103	21	Public

The Top 200 Institutions – SAT Scores (2014)

Top 104-143 Institutions in Median SAT Scores	Median SAT Score	National Rank	Control Rank	Institutional Control
Thomas Aquinas College	1265	104	83	Private
Trinity University	1265	104	83	Private
University of Florida	1265	104	22	Public
Hendrix College	1260	107	85	Private
Illinois Institute of Technology	1260	107	85	Private
University of Minnesota - Twin Cities	1260	107	23	Public
U.S. Coast Guard Academy	1255	110	24	Public
University of Texas - Dallas	1255	110	24	Public
Fordham University	1250	112	87	Private
Stony Brook University	1250	112	26	Public
American University	1245	114	88	Private
Clemson University	1245	114	27	Public
North Carolina State University	1245	114	27	Public
Rhode Island School of Design	1245	114	88	Private
Bentley University	1240	118	90	Private
College of Wooster	1240	118	90	Private
Drake University	1240	118	90	Private
Florida State University	1240	118	29	Public
Illinois Wesleyan University	1240	118	90	Private
Kalamazoo College	1240	118	90	Private
Miami University - Oxford	1240	118	29	Public
Michigan Technological University	1240	118	29	Public
Milwaukee School of Engineering	1240	118	90	Private
Saint Louis University - St. Louis	1240	118	90	Private
Skidmore College	1240	118	90	Private
Transylvania University	1240	118	90	Private
University of Connecticut - Storrs	1240	118	29	Public
University of Denver	1240	118	90	Private
Yeshiva University	1240	118	90	Private
City University of NY - Bernard M. Baruch College	1235	133	33	Public
Emerson College	1235	133	101	Private
University of California - Santa Barbara	1235	133	33	Public
University of Georgia	1235	133	33	Public
Soka University of America	1230	137	102	Private
University of Washington - Seattle	1230	137	36	Public
California Polytechnic State Univ. - San Luis Obispo	1225	139	37	Public
Elon University	1225	139	103	Private
Pepperdine University	1225	139	103	Private
University of San Diego	1225	139	103	Private
Auburn University	1220	143	38	Public
Baylor University	1220	143	106	Private
Butler University	1220	143	106	Private
DePauw University	1220	143	106	Private
Kettering University	1220	143	106	Private
Loyola University Chicago	1220	143	106	Private
Marquette University	1220	143	106	Private
State Univ. of New York - College at Geneseo	1220	143	38	Public
Taylor University	1220	143	106	Private
Texas Christian University	1220	143	106	Private
Truman State University	1220	143	38	Public
University of Alabama - Huntsville	1220	143	38	Public
University of Colorado - Boulder	1220	143	38	Public
University of Puget Sound	1220	143	106	Private

The Top 200 Institutions – SAT Scores (2014)

Top 157-184 Institutions in Median SAT Scores	Median SAT Score	National Rank	Control Rank	Institutional Control
College of New Jersey	1215	157	43	Public
Rochester Institute of Technology	1215	157	115	Private
Rutgers University - New Brunswick	1215	157	43	Public
University of Massachusetts - Amherst	1215	157	43	Public
Virginia Polytechnic Institute and State University	1215	157	43	Public
University of Maryland - Baltimore County	1210	162	47	Public
University of South Carolina - Columbia	1210	162	47	Public
Birmingham-Southern College	1205	164	116	Private
Cornell College	1205	164	116	Private
Creighton University	1205	164	116	Private
Purdue University - West Lafayette	1205	164	49	Public
University of Alabama - Tuscaloosa	1205	164	49	Public
University of California - Davis	1205	164	49	Public
University of Dayton	1205	164	116	Private
University of St. Thomas (MN)	1205	164	116	Private
University of Tennessee - Knoxville	1205	164	49	Public
Grove City College	1202	173	121	Private
Chapman University	1200	174	122	Private
Drexel University	1200	174	122	Private
Loyola Marymount University	1200	174	122	Private
University of Dallas	1200	174	122	Private
Willamette University	1200	174	122	Private
Gonzaga University	1195	179	127	Private
Texas A&M University - College Station	1195	179	53	Public
University of North Carolina - Asheville	1195	179	53	Public
University of Portland	1195	179	127	Private
St. Mary's College of Maryland	1194	183	55	Public
Belmont University	1190	184	129	Private
Calvin College	1190	184	129	Private
Cedarville University	1190	184	129	Private
Clarkson University	1190	184	129	Private
College of Saint Benedict	1190	184	129	Private
Covenant College	1190	184	129	Private
Drury University	1190	184	129	Private
Franciscan University of Steubenville	1190	184	129	Private
Hope College	1190	184	129	Private
Lipscomb University	1190	184	129	Private
Mercer University	1190	184	129	Private
Millsaps College	1190	184	129	Private
New Mexico Institute of Mining and Technology	1190	184	56	Public
North Greenville University	1190	184	129	Private
Ohio Northern University	1190	184	129	Private
Oklahoma Baptist University	1190	184	129	Private
Pennsylvania State University - University Park	1190	184	56	Public
Samford University	1190	184	129	Private
South Dakota School of Mines and Technology	1190	184	56	Public
St. Louis College of Pharmacy	1190	184	129	Private
University of Delaware	1190	184	56	Public
University of Jamestown	1190	184	129	Private
University of Oklahoma - Norman	1190	184	56	Public
Valparaiso University	1190	184	129	Private

The Top 200 Institutions – National Merit Scholars (2015)

Top 1-49 Institutions in National Merit Scholars	Number of Scholars	National Rank	Control Rank	Institutional Control
University of Chicago	294	1	1	Private
University of Oklahoma - Norman	288	2	1	Public
University of Southern California	226	3	2	Private
Harvard University	209	4	3	Private
Northwestern University	206	5	4	Private
Vanderbilt University	206	5	4	Private
Stanford University	176	7	6	Private
Yale University	166	8	7	Private
University of Alabama - Tuscaloosa	148	9	2	Public
University of Minnesota - Twin Cities	147	10	3	Public
Princeton University	146	11	8	Private
University of Florida	146	11	4	Public
Texas A&M University - College Station	142	13	5	Public
Massachusetts Institute of Technology	139	14	9	Private
University of Pennsylvania	139	14	9	Private
University of California - Berkeley	129	16	6	Public
Arizona State University	112	17	7	Public
University of Kentucky	111	18	8	Public
Duke University	108	19	11	Private
University of Texas - Dallas	101	20	9	Public
Purdue University - West Lafayette	94	21	10	Public
Northeastern University	85	22	12	Private
Columbia University	78	23	13	Private
Brown University	76	24	14	Private
Baylor University	75	25	15	Private
Cornell University	72	26	16	Private
University of Central Florida	69	27	11	Public
Indiana University - Bloomington	68	28	12	Public
University of Arizona	65	29	13	Public
Auburn University	64	30	14	Public
Dartmouth College	64	30	17	Private
Brigham Young University - Provo	63	32	18	Private
University of Maryland - College Park	61	33	15	Public
Case Western Reserve University	60	34	19	Private
University of Texas - Austin	60	34	16	Public
Georgia Institute of Technology	59	36	17	Public
Rice University	59	36	20	Private
Emory University	58	38	21	Private
University of Notre Dame	57	39	22	Private
University of Michigan - Ann Arbor	56	40	18	Public
Clemson University	55	41	19	Public
Tufts University	55	41	23	Private
Carleton College	52	43	24	Private
Carnegie Mellon University	51	44	25	Private
Johns Hopkins University	47	45	26	Private
University of Nebraska - Lincoln	47	45	20	Public
University of South Carolina - Columbia	46	47	21	Public
California Institute of Technology	45	48	27	Private
Fordham University	44	49	28	Private
University of Cincinnati - Cincinnati	44	49	22	Public

The Top 200 Institutions – National Merit Scholars (2015)

Top 51-98 Institutions in National Merit Scholars	Number of Scholars	National Rank	Control Rank	Institutional Control
Harvey Mudd College	43	51	29	Private
Michigan State University	43	51	23	Public
University of California - Los Angeles	43	51	23	Public
University of Georgia	42	54	25	Public
University of Mississippi - Oxford	40	55	26	Public
Mississippi State University	37	56	27	Public
University of Arkansas - Fayetteville	37	56	27	Public
University of Rochester	37	56	30	Private
University of Virginia	36	59	29	Public
Boston University	35	60	31	Private
Rutgers University - New Brunswick	35	60	30	Public
University of Miami	35	60	31	Private
University of Tulsa	35	60	31	Private
Bowdoin College	33	64	34	Private
Iowa State University	33	64	31	Public
Tulane University	33	64	34	Private
University of Utah	33	64	31	Public
Georgetown University	32	68	36	Private
Washington University in St. Louis	32	68	36	Private
Oberlin College	31	70	38	Private
Macalester College	30	71	39	Private
University of Houston - University Park	29	72	33	Public
Wheaton College (IL)	28	73	40	Private
Louisiana State University - Baton Rouge	27	74	34	Public
University of Illinois - Urbana-Champaign	26	75	35	Public
University of Kansas - Lawrence	26	75	35	Public
Kenyon College	25	77	41	Private
Stony Brook University	25	77	37	Public
University of Alabama - Birmingham	24	79	38	Public
Grinnell College	23	80	42	Private
Liberty University	23	80	42	Private
University of Idaho	23	80	39	Public
University of Tennessee - Knoxville	23	80	39	Public
Florida State University	22	84	41	Public
Pennsylvania State University - University Park	21	85	42	Public
Williams College	21	85	44	Private
Southern Methodist University	20	87	45	Private
University of Iowa	20	87	43	Public
University of North Carolina - Chapel Hill	20	87	43	Public
Rensselaer Polytechnic Institute	19	90	46	Private
St. Olaf College	19	90	46	Private
University of Louisville	19	90	45	Public
Ohio State University - Columbus	18	93	46	Public
University of California - San Diego	18	93	46	Public
University of Missouri - Columbia	18	93	46	Public
George Washington University	17	96	48	Private
Oklahoma State University - Stillwater	17	96	49	Public
Pomona College	16	98	49	Private
Truman State University	16	98	50	Public
University of Nevada - Reno	16	98	50	Public
University of Pittsburgh - Pittsburgh	16	98	50	Public

The Top 200 Institutions – National Merit Scholars (2015)

Top 102-143 Institutions in National Merit Scholars	Number of Scholars	National Rank	Control Rank	Institutional Control
Claremont McKenna College	15	102	50	Private
University of Dallas	15	102	50	Private
University of North Texas	15	102	53	Public
University of Wisconsin - Madison	15	102	53	Public
Calvin College	14	106	52	Private
Franklin W. Olin College of Engineering	14	106	52	Private
Rochester Institute of Technology	14	106	52	Private
University of New Mexico - Albuquerque	14	106	55	Public
Rose-Hulman Institute of Technology	13	110	55	Private
Swarthmore College	13	110	55	Private
Washington and Lee University	13	110	55	Private
Worcester Polytechnic Institute	13	110	55	Private
Brandeis University	12	114	59	Private
Lawrence University	12	114	59	Private
New York University	12	114	59	Private
University of Washington - Seattle	12	114	56	Public
Hendrix College	11	118	62	Private
Lehigh University	11	118	62	Private
American University	10	120	64	Private
Amherst College	10	120	64	Private
Furman University	10	120	64	Private
Hillsdale College	10	120	64	Private
Louisiana Tech University	10	120	57	Public
Rhodes College (TN)	10	120	64	Private
University of Vermont	10	120	57	Public
West Virginia University	10	120	57	Public
Kansas State University	9	128	60	Public
Loyola University Chicago	9	128	69	Private
Miami University - Oxford	9	128	60	Public
North Dakota State University	9	128	60	Public
University of Nevada - Las Vegas	9	128	60	Public
University of South Florida - Tampa	9	128	60	Public
Whitman College	9	128	69	Private
Boston College	8	135	71	Private
Colorado College	8	135	71	Private
Davidson College	8	135	71	Private
Harding University	8	135	71	Private
New College of Florida	8	135	65	Public
Texas Tech University	8	135	65	Public
Transylvania University	8	135	71	Private
Villanova University	8	135	71	Private
Dickinson College	7	143	77	Private
Drexel University	7	143	77	Private
Luther College	7	143	77	Private
Montana State University - Bozeman	7	143	67	Public
Oklahoma Christian University	7	143	77	Private
Saint Louis University - St. Louis	7	143	77	Private
Texas Christian University	7	143	77	Private
University of Evansville	7	143	77	Private
Wayne State University	7	143	67	Public

The Top 200 Institutions – National Merit Scholars (2015)

Top 152-173 Institutions in National Merit Scholars	Number of Scholars	National Rank	Control Rank	Institutional Control
Colorado School of Mines	6	152	69	Public
Marquette University	6	152	84	Private
Missouri University of Science and Technology	6	152	69	Public
Santa Clara University	6	152	84	Private
University of Oregon	6	152	69	Public
University of Southern Mississippi	6	152	69	Public
Abilene Christian University	5	158	86	Private
Bucknell University	5	158	86	Private
Colby College	5	158	86	Private
College of William and Mary	5	158	73	Public
Drake University	5	158	86	Private
Haverford College	5	158	86	Private
North Carolina State University	5	158	73	Public
Scripps College	5	158	86	Private
Trinity University	5	158	86	Private
University of Colorado - Boulder	5	158	73	Public
University of Missouri - Kansas City	5	158	73	Public
University of Wisconsin - Eau Claire	5	158	73	Public
University of Wyoming	5	158	73	Public
Washington State University - Pullman	5	158	73	Public
Willamette University	5	158	86	Private
Bethel University (MN)	4	173	94	Private
College of Charleston	4	173	80	Public
College of Wooster	4	173	94	Private
Colorado State University - Fort Collins	4	173	80	Public
Concordia College at Moorhead	4	173	94	Private
Creighton University	4	173	94	Private
Hope College	4	173	94	Private
Kalamazoo College	4	173	94	Private
Michigan Technological University	4	173	80	Public
Middlebury College	4	173	94	Private
Oregon State University	4	173	80	Public
Ouachita Baptist University	4	173	94	Private
Pepperdine University	4	173	94	Private
Samford University	4	173	94	Private
Sewanee-The University of the South	4	173	94	Private
University of California - Santa Barbara	4	173	80	Public
University of Dayton	4	173	94	Private
University of Richmond	4	173	94	Private
Virginia Polytechnic Institute and State University	4	173	80	Public
Wichita State University	4	173	80	Public

Source Notes

Total Research Expenditures
Federal Research Expenditures
Source: Higher Education Research and Development (HERD) Survey, FY 2014

Each year, the National Science Foundation (NSF) collects data from hundreds of academic institutions on expenditures for research and development in science and engineering fields and classifies them by source of funds (e.g., federal government, state and local government, industry, etc.). These data are the primary source of information on academic research and development (R&D) expenditures in the United States. Included in this survey are all activities specifically organized to produce research outcomes that are separately budgeted and accounted for. This "organized research" may be funded by an external agency or organization ("sponsored research") or by a separately budgeted organizational unit within the institution ("university research"). This report excludes activities sponsored by external agencies that involve instruction, training (except training in research techniques, which is considered organized research), and health service, community service or extension service projects.

All Federally Funded Research Labs (FFRLs) are excluded from these academic expenditures data, including the following: Jet Propulsion Laboratory (California Institute of Technology); Los Alamos National Lab, Lawrence Livermore Lab, Lawrence Berkeley Lab (University of California); Software Engineering Institute (Carnegie Mellon); Argonne National Laboratory (University of Chicago); National Astronomy and Ionospheric Center (Cornell); Ames Laboratory (Iowa State University); Lincoln Laboratory (MIT); Plasma Physics Lab (Princeton); and SLAC National Accelerator Laboratory (Stanford). The NSF data no longer classify the Applied Physics Lab (APL) at Johns Hopkins as an FFRL, but federal funds support the vast majority of research conducted there. The APL makes up more than one-half of Johns Hopkins' total federal R&D expenditures.

While inconsistencies in reporting (known and unknown) do exist here, as in any survey of this type, problems arise mostly when one breaks out the data by source of funds. NSF expects institutions to use year-end accounting records to complete this report, and there are nationally recognized accounting guidelines for higher education institutions. However, there are also countless variations in institutional policy that determine whether the university reports a particular expenditure as coming from one source or another, or possibly not counted at all. Take federal formula funds for agriculture (e.g., Hatch-McIntire, Smith-Lever) as an example. We conducted an informal survey of the appropriate institutions in the Association of American Universities (AAU) and found that two out of eleven land grants did not include any of these federal funds in their 1997 NSF data, while others included all or some of these monies. Because these funds make up a very small percentage of the total research expenditures in

any given year, the impact on our total research rankings is slight. The agriculture formula funds will have a somewhat greater, but still small, impact on the federal research rankings. NSF notes, "An increasing number of institutions have linkages with industry and foundations via subcontracts, thus complicating the identification of funding source. In addition, institutional policy may determine whether unrestricted state support is reported as state or as institutional funds." [1]

We believe that the reporting inconsistencies in the data are relatively minor when using the total research expenditures and the federal research expenditures component. Federal and state government audits of institutional accounting make deceptive practices highly unlikely, even though these entities do not audit the NSF data directly. NSF goes to great lengths to verify the accuracy of the data, especially federal expenditure data—checking them against several other federal agencies that collect the same or similar information. In fact, all major federal agencies and their subdivisions submit data to NSF identifying research obligations to universities each year. Historically, the NSF data have tracked very closely the data reported by universities. Further, for their National Patterns of R&D Resources series, NSF prefers to use the figures reported by the performers of the work (that is, academic institutions, industry, nonprofits) because they believe that the performers are in the best position to accurately report these expenditures.

In some sections of this report, these expenditure data are deflated to constant 1983 dollars to show real change over time. While NSF uses the Gross Domestic Price (GDP) implicit price deflator in its reports on federal trends in research, we use the Higher Education Price Index (HEPI) because of its narrower focus. Originally developed by Research Associates of Washington and currently managed by Commonfund Institute, the HEPI illustrates the effect of inflation on college and university operations. [2] In contrast, the GDP implicit price deflator is based on change in the entire U.S. economy and, as noted by NSF itself, "[its] use more accurately reflects an 'opportunity cost' criterion [i.e., the value of R&D in terms of the amount of other goods and services that could have been spent with the same amount of money], rather than a measure of cost changes of doing research." [3]

Endowment Assets

Source: NACUBO-Commonfund Study of Endowment, endowment market value as of June 30, 2015.

Institutions report the market value of their endowment assets as of June 30 to three different sources, and they quite often use three different values. For this project, we use the NACUBO-Commonfund Study of Endowment because of NACUBO's long history of reporting endowments of higher education institutions, their emphasis on using audited financial statements, and their focus on net assets (i.e., includes returns on investments and excludes investment fees and other withdrawals). NACUBO conducts its study annually and reports the results each February in the Chronicle of Higher Education.

Another source for endowment assets is the Council for Aid to Education's (CAE) annual Voluntary Support of Education (VSE) survey, cosponsored by the Council for Advancement and Support of Education (CASE) and the National Association of Independent Schools. The VSE survey is useful as a secondary resource because it provides more single-campus data than the other two sources. For those institutions that report a system-wide total to NACUBO, we often use the VSE data to calculate a campus' percentage contribution to the entire system, applying that factor to the NACUBO figure. In other cases, we may substitute the VSE figure when the institution indicates that this is a good data source.

The National Center for Education Statistics (NCES) Integrated Postsecondary Education Data System (IPEDS) Finance Survey also collects information on endowment assets. IPEDS data are released later than other two sources and are used when NACUBO nor VSE figures are unavailable.

In our inaugural report of *The Top American Research Universities* in 2000, we noted the wide variation in the reporting of endowment market value between all three sources. An examination of the 1997 endowment figures showed only one university (University of North Carolina at Chapel Hill) had submitted the same figure to each of the three organizations. In a more recent study of major research universities, we found about one-third of the all institutions report identical figures but just seven universities in our over $40 million federal research group. In the earlier study, we found that endowment assets reported to IPEDS tended to be lower than NACUBO or VSE data, but this is no longer true. In general, the greater the endowment the likelihood that the figures reported to the three sources will vary. Both studies found no consistent pattern to explain reporting variations among the institutions.

Annual Giving

Source: Council for Aid to Education's Voluntary Support of Education (VSE) Survey, FY 2015.

The Council for Aid to Education (CAE), formerly an independent subsidiary of RAND, has produced the Voluntary Support of Education (VSE) Survey since 1957. The annual giving data include all contributions actually received during the institution's fiscal year in the form of cash, securities, company products, and other property from alumni, non-alumni individuals, corporations, foundations, religious organizations, and other

groups. Not included in the totals are public funds, earnings on investments held by the institution, and unfulfilled pledges.

CAE's VSE Data Miner service, available online, provides 11 years of data for all participating institutions. Although this is a subscription-based service and requires a user ID and password, limited access is available online at [http://www.cae.org/vse].

National Academy Members

Source: National Academy of Sciences, National Academy of Engineering, and National Academy of Medicine membership directories for 2015.

One of the highest honors that academic faculty can receive is membership in the National Academy of Sciences (NAS), the National Academy of Engineering (NAE), or the National Academy of Medicine (NAM), formerly known as the Institute of Medicine. All three are private, nonprofit organizations and serve as advisors to the federal government on science, technology, and medicine. Nominated and voted on by active members, newly elected members of these organizations receive life terms. Individuals elected to membership come from all sectors—academia, industry, government, and not-for-profit agencies or organizations. Member election dates are in February (NAE), April (NAS), and October (NAM).

The data collected for these rankings use active or emeritus members at their affiliated work institution, as reported in the online membership directories. In all cases, we were able to determine the specific campus for individual members. We re-check institutional affiliation annually to account for established members who have changed employers or whose membership is no longer active.

Faculty Awards in the Arts, Humanities, Science, Engineering, and Health

Source: Directories or web-based listings for multiple agencies or organizations.

For this category, we collect data from several prominent grant and fellowship programs in the arts, humanities, science, engineering, and health fields. Included in this measure are:

- American Council of Learned Societies (ACLS) Fellows, 2014-15

- Beckman Young Investigators, 2015

- Burroughs Wellcome Fund Career Awards, 2015

- Cottrell Scholars, 2015

- Fulbright American Scholars, 2015-16

- Getty Scholars in Residence, 2015-16

- Guggenheim Fellows, 2015

- Howard Hughes Medical Institute Investigators, 2015

- Lasker Medical Research Awards, 2015

- MacArthur Foundation Fellows, 2015

- National Endowment for the Humanities (NEH) Fellows, 2016

- National Humanities Center Fellows, 2015-16

- National Institutes of Health (NIH) MERIT (R37), FY 2015

- National Medal of Science and National Medal of Technology, 2014

- NSF CAREER awards, 2015

- Newberry Library Long-term Fellows, 2015-16

- Pew Scholars in Biomedicine, 2015

- Presidential Early Career Awards for Scientists and Engineers (PECASE), 2014

- Robert Wood Johnson Policy Fellows, 2015-16

- Searle Scholars, 2015

- Sloan Research Fellows, 2015

- Woodrow Wilson Fellows, 2015-16

While the vast majority of these programs clearly identify a particular campus, in a few instances we used the institution's web-based phone directory to determine the correct campus.

Doctorates Awarded

Source: NCES IPEDS Completions Survey, doctoral degrees awarded between July 1, 2014, and June 30, 2015.

Each year, universities report their degrees awarded to the NCES in the IPEDS Completions Survey. IPEDS provides straightforward instructions for reporting doctoral degrees awarded, and we do not find any inconsistencies in reporting among the universities included in our rankings. IPEDS asks each institution to identify the number of Doctor of Education, Doctor of Juridical Science, Doctor of Public Health, and Doctor of Philosophy degrees awarded between July 1 and June 30.

Most institutions in our study submit degree data by campus or offer doctoral degrees solely or primarily at the main campus.

In addition to doctorate degrees, we present degrees awarded at other levels—associate's, bachelor's, master's, and professional degrees—in the Student Characteristics table.

Postdoctoral Appointees

Source: NSF/Division of Science Resource Statistics (SRS) Survey of Graduate Students and Postdoctorates in Science and Engineering, Fall 2014.

Each year, NSF and NIH collect data from all institutions offering graduate programs in any science, engineering, or health field. The Survey of Graduate Students and Postdoctorates in Science and Engineering (also called the Graduate Student Survey or GSS) reflects graduate enrollment and postdoctoral employment at the beginning of the academic year. Postdoctorates are defined in the GSS as "individuals with science and engineering PhD's, MD's, DDS's or DVM's and foreign degrees equivalent to U.S. doctorates who devote their primary effort to their own research training through research activities or study in the department under temporary appointments carrying no academic rank." The definition excludes clinical fellows and those in medical residency training programs unless the primary purpose of their appointment is for research training under a senior mentor.

In the methodological notes for this survey,[4] NSF indicates that it verifies the data with the institutional coordinator when dramatic year-to-year fluctuations are noted. In addition, in this data set, it is unclear whether an institution has actually reported zero postdocs or NSF has simply assigned a zero for non-response (rather than imputing by using prior-year or peer data, as described in NSF methodological notes). This year, in cases where we suspect it is not a true zero, we left the field blank.

Although each doctorate-granting campus submits data separately, NSF often aggregates them in its published reports. In all cases, we obtain the single-campus data for these schools directly from NSF.

SAT Scores

Source: NCES IPEDS Survey, SAT and ACT scores for Fall 2014.

IPEDS reports the 25th and 75th percentiles for verbal and quantitative SAT I scores for most institutions in our study. For our measure, we calculated the median of that range. Some institutions report the ACT instead of the SAT to IPEDS and some report both. We selected the test which has the greatest percentage of students reporting. To convert ACT scores, we use a conversion table provided by The College Board[5] to generate a comparable SAT equivalent score. When an institution submits neither an SAT nor ACT score, we substitute data from other national data sources.

Other Measures of Undergraduate Quality

National Merit and Achievement Scholars

Source: The 2014-15 National Merit Scholarship Corporation Annual Report, which reflects the 2015 freshman class.

The National Merit Scholarship Corporation (NMSC) is an independent, nonprofit organization that awards scholarships to the nation's outstanding high school seniors based on their academic achievement, qualifying test scores, high school principal and counselor recommendations, and their activities, interests, and goals. The NMSC names approximately 15,000 National Merit Finalists each February. Of these, about 8,000 will receive a National Merit $2,500 Scholarship, a corporate-sponsored scholarship, or a college-sponsored scholarship.

Until it was discontinued in 2015, National Achievement Scholars were selected and funded in a similar fashion and represented the nation's outstanding African-American students. Ideally, the National Hispanic Scholars Program should also be included in this category, but it does not track the enrollment of its scholarship winners. Should it do so in the future, we will include these students in our data. In this study, Merit and Achievement scholarships are credited to the main campus if the NMSC Annual Report does not indicate a branch campus.

While the number of National Merit and National Achievement award winners in the entering class provides an indication of the attractiveness of a university's undergraduate program to outstanding students, it is also an indicator that is sensitive to institutional policies on financial aid. Because the number of Merit Scholars is small, relatively small changes in institutional aid policies can have a significant impact on the number of National Merit Scholars enrolling in institutions. The average SAT score provides a broader-based and more reliable measure of overall undergraduate quality; for those reasons, we prefer the SAT scores to the number of National Merit and Achievement Scholars as an indicator of undergraduate quality.

Institutional Characteristics

Medical Schools

Source: NCES IPEDS Completions Survey, MD degrees awarded between July 1, 2014, and June 30, 2015.

Although the IPEDS Institutional Characteristics Survey does have a "medical" field that indicates whether an institution grants a medical degree, we choose not to use its data because it includes medical degrees in Veterinary Medicine, Dentistry, and other professional health-related fields. For our measure, we determined whether a particular campus awarded any MD degrees during the academic year. If the institution did not submit any data to IPEDS for that year, we then looked at whether it was accredited by the American Medical Association to determine whether the institution has a medical school.

Land Grant Institutions

Source: National Association of State Universities and Land Grant Colleges.

The first Morrill Act in 1862 appropriated federal funds for universities to provide agricultural and technical education to their citizens. A second Morrill Act in 1890 expanded eligibility to include several historically black colleges and universities, and in 1994 several Native American tribal colleges were recognized as land grant institutions. Today, there is at least one land grant institution in each state and U.S. territory and in the District of Columbia. Of the 105 institutions, most are public universities. Federal land grant institutions receive both federal and state dollars in support of their agricultural and extension activities.

While land grant status technically applies to some university systems, such as the University of California and the University of Nebraska, for our study we designate as land grant institutions only those schools that actually perform that function (e.g., UC-Berkeley, UC-Davis, UC-Riverside, Nebraska-Lincoln). In these cases, the land grant field will identify whether an institution is part of a system-wide land grant and whether the vast majority of the activity occurs on that campus. For example, UC-Davis is coded as "Yes-System" while UCLA is coded as "No-System." We consider the 1890 institutions as land grant institutions, but we identify them separately because they do not perform extension activities.

Research Focus

NSF/SRS Survey of R&D Expenditures at Universities and Colleges, FY 2014.

In addition to reporting expenditure data by source of funds, NSF identifies in what major disciplines the money is expended. In the Research by Discipline table we provide the proportion of total and federal expenditures in each discipline for those institutions with more than $40 million in federal research. These data are useful for developing groups of similar institutions for peer analysis.

The Institutional Characteristics table provides a summary measure of an institution's research strength and concentration based on these discipline-level expenditures. Universities with 95-100% of their federal research dollars spent in one particular discipline are coded as "all." We identify institutions with 75-94% in one area as "heavy" and label those with 50-74% of their expenditures concentrated as "strong." Other universities with 25-49% in one or more disciplines we describe as "moderate." A few institutions (but none in the more than $40 million group) have expenditures distributed fairly evenly across the disciplines; those we code as "mixed."

In some cases, where an institution reports as a multi-campus entity, we made adjustments to break out the discipline-level expenditure data by single campus. Typically, this involved moving all or a portion of the life sciences expenditures to the health or medical center campus. IPEDS fall enrollment and graduate degrees by discipline data also were used to help in this effort.

While these data offer some insight as to the research structure of a university, their usefulness is limited. For example, we may be tempted to use the life sciences as a surrogate for medical research, but we must remember that they also include agricultural and biological sciences. Further, the growing trend toward multidisciplinary and interdisciplinary projects may make it more difficult for universities to accurately reflect expenditures by discipline or sub-discipline. We choose not to break out these sub-disciplines because the data are increasingly prone to error as further adjustments are made.

Student Characteristics

Fall Enrollment

Source: NCES IPEDS Fall Enrollment Survey, 2014.

Each November, institutions report their current fall headcount enrollment to the IPEDS Fall Enrollment Survey. Enrollment figures include both degree seeking and non-degree seeking students. We provide the headcount enrollment by level as presented by IPEDS, along with the percentage of those attending part-time. Graduate students include those seeking specialist degrees in engineering and education. First professional students include those seeking degrees in medical fields, such as Chiropractic, Dentistry, Medicine, Optometry, Osteopathic Medicine, Pharmacy, Podiatry, and Veterinary Medicine, as well as those seeking degrees in Law and Theology.

Each campus in our study submits enrollment data by campus, except for the few institutions identified in our Data Notes section. Because this is an informational item and not one of our nine quality measures, we did not attempt to adjust these figures.

Federal Research with and without Medical School Research

AAMC Federal Research

Source: Association of American Medical Colleges

The Association of American Medical Colleges collects data on federally sponsored research at medical colleges through on the Liaison Committee on Medical Education (LCME) Part I-A, Annual Financial Questionnaire. We calculate each medical school's federal R&D by summing the recorded dollars and a portion of the relative administrative costs. We exclude the not-recorded dollars.

Footnotes

1 Academic R&D Expenditures, FY 2009: Technical Notes (Online: http://www.nsf.gov/statistics/nsf11313/)

2 About HEPI, Commonfund Institute (Online: http://www.commonfund.org/CommonfundInstitute/HEPI)

3 National Patterns of R&D Resources, 2003: Technical Notes (Online: http://www.nsf.gov/statistics/nsf05308/appa.htm)

4 Survey Methodology: Survey of Graduate Students and Postdoctorates in Science and Engineering (Online: http://www.nsf.gov/statistics/srvygradpostdoc/)

5 ACT and SAT Concordance Tables, November 6, 2009 (Online: http://www.research.collegeboard.org/publications)

Data Notes

The raw data used for *The Top American Research Universities* project—obtained from federal agencies and national organizations—often contain information on single-campus institutions, multiple-campus institutions, and state university systems, without clearly identifying the distinctions. This makes national comparisons difficult and unreliable.

To increase the validity and usefulness of these data, we adjusted the original reported figures, when necessary, to ensure that all data represent the strength of a single-campus institution. MUP bases its adjustments on information gathered from the reporting agency or from the university itself. In cases where the published data represent a single campus, we do not adjust the data. When the data represent more than one campus, we first attempt to obtain a figure directly from the National Science Foundation (NSF) (for research expenditures and post-doctorates), from the institution itself, or from the university system office that submitted the data. If unavailable from those primary sources, we use an estimated or substitute figure derived from information found on the institution's website.

If the institution provides an estimate representing at least 97% of the originally published figure, we credit the full amount to the main campus. Otherwise, we use the estimate provided by the institution.

MUP does not adjust the private university data because of multi-campus or system-wide reporting. We treat all private universities in this study as single-campus institutions because, while some may have multiple campuses, they are generally in or around a single city and considered an integral part of the main campus. Furthermore, private institutions generally do not break out their data by regional, branch, or affiliated campus as often happens with public institutions.

The following tables outline the various adjustments or substitutions that we made to the original data. The tables list institutions alphabetically and include both private and public universities. For the purpose of this report, we provide notes for institutions with more than $40 million in fiscal year 2014 federal research.

Data Notes for Universities with Over $40 Million in Federal Research

University / Statistics	Original Data (dollars in thousands)	MUP Data (dollars in thousands)	Comments
Arizona State University			
2015 Doctorates		687	Combined IPEDS reported data.
Auburn University			
2015 Endowment	641,993	641,993	Estimate at least 97% is main campus.
2015 Giving	106,353	106,353	Estimate at least 97% is main campus.
Augusta University			
2014 Postdocs	188	188	Reported under Georgia Regents University
Baylor College of Medicine			
2015 Giving	Not Reported	61,656	Substituted IPEDS.
Carnegie Mellon University			
2014 Endowment	1,599,990	1,599,900	Revised 2014 NACUBO data.
Cleveland State University			
2015 Endowment	Not Reported	74,900	Substituted 2015 VSE.
Cold Spring Harbor Laboratory			
2015 Endowment	Not Reported		Did not report to NACUBO nor VSE in 2015.
2015 Giving	Not Reported		No substitute data available.
Colorado State University - Fort Collins			
2015 Giving	Not Reported	41,342	Substituted IPEDS.
Cornell University			
2014 Federal R&D	438,834	299,320	Estimate 68.2% based on university documents.
2014 Total R&D	874,727	580,936	Estimate 66.4% based on university documents.
2015 Endowment	6,037,546	4,760,560	Substituted IPEDS.
2015 Giving	590,641	434,465	Estimate 73.6% based on 2015 IPEDS.
Harvard University			
2014 Endowment	35,883,691	35,883,891	Revised 2014 NACUBO data.
Icahn School of Medicine at Mount Sinai			
2015 Endowment	Not Reported	717,372	Substituted IPEDS. Did not report to NACUBO nor VSE in 2015.
2015 Giving	Not Reported	109,733	Substituted IPEDS.
Indiana University - Bloomington			
2015 Endowment	1,974,215	960,625	Substituted IPEDS.
2015 Giving	359,319	211,471	Estimate based on IPEDS and university documents.
Indiana University - Purdue University - Indianapolis			
2015 Endowment	1,974,215	825,184	Substituted IPEDS.
2015 Giving	359,319	121,989	Estimate based on IPEDS and university documents.

Data Notes for Universities with Over $40 Million in Federal Research

University / Statistics	Original Data (dollars in thousands)	MUP Data (dollars in thousands)	Comments
Kansas State University			
2014 SAT	Not Reported		Does not require SAT/ACT.
Louisiana State University - Baton Rouge			
2015 Endowment	851,833	427,852	Substituted 2015 VSE.
Medical College of Wisconsin			
2015 Giving	Not Reported	20,907	Substituted IPEDS.
Michigan State University			
2015 Endowment		2,673,652	Combined university and foundation.
Montana State University - Bozeman			
2015 Giving	Not Reported	13,299	Substituted IPEDS.
Naval Postgraduate School			
2015 Giving	Not Reported		No substitute data available.
New Mexico State University - Las Cruces			
2015 Endowment	221,005	221,005	Estimate at least 97% is main campus.
New York University			
2014 Endowment	3,424,000	3,422,227	Revised 2014 NACUBO data.
2015 Doctorates		438	Includes NYU and former Polytechnic Institute of NYU.
Ohio State University - Columbus			
2015 Endowment	3,633,887	3,633,887	Estimate at least 97% is main campus.
2015 Giving	359,798	359,798	Estimate at least 97% is main campus.
Pennsylvania State University - Hershey Medical Center			
2014 Federal R&D	516,300	54,404	Estimate 10.5% based on university documents.
2014 Postdocs	456	91	Estimate 20% based on university documents.
2014 Total R&D	785,705	82,793	Estimate 10.5% based on university documents.
2015 Endowment	3,635,730	436,288	Substituted data from published documents.
2015 Giving	194,572	35,023	Estimate 18% based on university documents.
Pennsylvania State University - University Park			
2014 Federal R&D	516,300	461,896	Estimate 89.5% based on university documents.
2014 Postdocs	456	365	Estimate 80% based on university documents.
2014 Total R&D	785,705	702,912	Estimate 89.5% based on university documents.
2015 Endowment	3,635,730	1,854,222	Substituted data from published documents.
2015 Giving	194,572	155,658	Estimate 80% based on university documents.
Purdue University - West Lafayette			
2015 Endowment	2,397,902	2,397,902	Estimate at least 97% is main campus.
2015 Giving	172,219	172,219	Estimate at least 97% is main campus.

Data Notes for Universities with Over $40 Million in Federal Research

University / Statistics	Original Data (dollars in thousands)	MUP Data (dollars in thousands)	Comments
Rockefeller University			
2015 Giving	Not Reported	18,562	Substituted IPEDS.
Rush University			
2014 Endowment	551,489	554,269	Revised 2014 NACUBO data.
2015 Giving	Not Reported	3,689	Substituted IPEDS.
Rutgers University - New Brunswick			
2014 Postdocs		345	Includes NB campus and former UMDNJ.
2015 Doctorates		597	Includes NB campus and former UMDNJ.
2015 Endowment	1,001,969	710,802	Substituted IPEDS.
2015 Giving	150,407	127,846	Estimate 85% based on university documents.
2015 National Academy		24	Includes NB campus and former UMDNJ.
Scripps Research Institute			
2015 Endowment	Not Reported		Did not report to NACUBO nor VSE in 2015.
2015 Giving	Not Reported		No substitute data available.
Texas A&M University - College Station			
2014 Federal R&D	298,489	266,877	Estimate 89.4% based on university documents.
2014 Postdocs	508	386	Estimate 76% based on last year's main campus proportion.
2014 Total R&D	826,152	735,273	Estimate 89% based on university documents.
2015 Doctorates	758	740	Substituted data from university factbook.
2015 Endowment	10,477,102	9,856,983	Substituted 2015 VSE.
Thomas Jefferson University			
2015 Endowment	Not Reported	437,750	Substituted 2015 VSE.
Uniformed Services University of the Health Sciences			
2015 Endowment	Not Reported		Did not report to NACUBO nor VSE in 2015.
2015 Giving	Not Reported		No substitute data available.
University of Alabama - Birmingham			
2015 Endowment	1,238,954	388,405	Substituted 2015 VSE.
University of Alabama - Huntsville			
2015 Endowment	1,238,954	65,978	Substituted 2015 VSE.
University of Alaska - Fairbanks			
2014 SAT	Not Reported		Did not report SAT/ACT.
2015 Endowment	310,616	189,476	Estimate 61% based on IPEDS.
2015 Giving	Not Reported	27,865	Estimate based on university documents.
University of Arizona			
2014 SAT	Not Reported		Does not require SAT/ACT.

Data Notes for Universities with Over $40 Million in Federal Research

University / Statistics	Original Data (dollars in thousands)	MUP Data (dollars in thousands)	Comments
University of Arkansas for Medical Sciences			
2015 Endowment	Not Reported	32,632	Substituted IPEDS. Did not report to NACUBO nor VSE in 2015.
2015 Giving	Not Reported	16,815	Substituted IPEDS.
University of California - Berkeley			
2015 Endowment	7,997,099	4,045,451	Substituted 2015 VSE.
University of California - Davis			
2015 Endowment	335,632	1,013,936	Substituted 2015 VSE.
University of California - Los Angeles			
2015 Endowment	1,864,605	3,493,903	Substituted 2015 VSE.
University of California - Riverside			
2015 Endowment	132,635	185,335	Substituted 2015 VSE.
University of California - San Diego			
2015 Endowment	548,317	951,367	Substituted 2015 VSE.
University of California - San Francisco			
2015 Endowment	1,160,627	2,124,970	Substituted 2015 VSE.
University of California - Santa Cruz			
2015 Endowment	7,997,099	164,331	Substituted 2015 VSE.
University of Cincinnati - Cincinnati			
2015 Endowment	1,195,899	1,195,899	Estimate at least 97% is main campus.
University of Colorado - Boulder			
2015 Endowment	1,090,297	598,355	Substituted data from published documents.
2015 Giving	Not Reported	151,553	Estimate based on IPEDS and university documents.
University of Colorado - Denver			
2015 Endowment	1,090,297	491,942	Substituted data from published documents.
2015 Giving	Not Reported	171,102	Estimate based on IPEDS and university documents.
University of Connecticut - Health Center			
2014 Endowment	103,644	103,885	Revised 2014 NACUBO data.
2014 Federal R&D	139,594	59,277	Estimate 42.5% based on university documents.
2014 Total R&D	247,379	105,047	Estimate 42.5% based on university documents.
2015 Doctorates	339	16	Estimate based on university factbook.
2015 Endowment	383,149	103,450	Estimate 27% based on published documents.
2015 Giving	49,226	8,475	Estimate 17.2% based on university documents.

Data Notes for Universities with Over $40 Million in Federal Research

University / Statistics	Original Data (dollars in thousands)	MUP Data (dollars in thousands)	Comments
University of Connecticut - Storrs			
2014 Endowment	280,222	280,876	Revised 2014 NACUBO data.
2014 Federal R&D	139,594	80,317	Estimate 57.5% based on university documents.
2014 Total R&D	247,379	142,332	Estimate 57.5% based on university documents.
2015 Doctorates	339	323	Estimate based on university factbook.
2015 Endowment	383,149	279,699	Estimate 73% based on published documents.
2015 Giving	49,226	40,751	Estimate 82.8% based on university documents.
University of Georgia			
2014 Endowment	939,024	975,890	Revised 2014 NACUBO data.
University of Hawaii - Manoa			
2015 Endowment	280,210	280,210	Estimate at least 97% is main campus.
University of Houston - University Park			
2015 Endowment	794,556	707,437	Substituted 2015 VSE.
University of Illinois - Chicago			
2015 Endowment	2,388,469	302,121	Substituted 2015 VSE.
University of Illinois - Urbana-Champaign			
2015 Endowment	2,388,469	1,530,658	Substituted 2015 VSE.
University of Kansas - Lawrence			
2014 Federal R&D	131,186	88,725	Estimate 67.6% based on university documents.
2014 Postdocs	265	154	Estimate 58% based on university documents.
2014 Total R&D	251,186	169,884	Estimate 67.6% based on university documents.
2015 Doctorates	390	365	Estimate based on KS Board of Regents data book and IPEDS Completions.
2015 Endowment	1,500,402	1,170,313	Estimate 78% based on published documents.
2015 Giving	220,880	176,704	Estimate 80% based on university documents.
University of Kansas Medical Center			
2014 Federal R&D	131,186	42,461	Estimate 32.4% based on university documents.
2014 Postdocs	265	111	Estimate 42% based on university documents.
2014 Total R&D	251,186	81,302	Estimate 32.4% based on university documents.
2015 Doctorates	390	25	Estimate based on KS Board of Regents data book and IPEDS Completions.
2015 Endowment	1,500,402	330,089	Estimate 22% based on published documents.
2015 Giving	220,880	44,176	Estimate 20% based on university documents.
University of Maine - Orono			
2015 Endowment	185,613	280,878	Substituted 2015 VSE.

Data Notes for Universities with Over $40 Million in Federal Research

University / Statistics	Original Data (dollars in thousands)	MUP Data (dollars in thousands)	Comments
University of Maryland - Baltimore			
2015 Endowment	986,248	256,008	Substituted 2015 VSE.
University of Maryland - Baltimore County			
2015 Endowment	986,248	75,752	Substituted 2015 VSE.
University of Maryland - College Park			
2015 Endowment	283,123	482,628	Substituted 2015 VSE.
University of Massachusetts - Amherst			
2015 Endowment	770,222	303,984	Substituted 2015 VSE.
University of Massachusetts Medical School - Worcester			
2015 Endowment	770,222	194,251	Estimate 25.2% based on IPEDS. Did not report to VSE.
2015 Giving	Not Reported	8,328	Substituted IPEDS.
University of Michigan - Ann Arbor			
2015 Endowment	9,952,113	9,952,113	Estimate at least 97% is main campus.
2015 Giving	394,310	394,310	Estimate at least 97% is main campus.
University of Minnesota - Twin Cities			
2014 Endowment	3,164,792	3,176,456	Revised 2014 NACUBO data.
2015 Endowment	3,297,460	3,297,460	Estimate at least 97% is main campus.
2015 Giving	357,861	344,303	Estimate based on IPEDS and university documents.
University of Missouri - Columbia			
2015 Endowment	1,476,959	857,471	Substituted 2015 VSE.
University of Nebraska - Lincoln			
2015 Endowment	1,538,071	906,156	Substituted IPEDS.
2015 Giving	266,375	177,321	Estimate 66.6% based on 2014 IPEDS.
University of Nebraska Medical Center			
2015 Endowment	1,538,071	226,077	Substituted IPEDS.
2015 Giving	266,375	89,054	Estimate 33.4% based on 2014 IPEDS.
University of New Hampshire - Durham			
2015 Endowment	676,268	346,926	Substituted IPEDS.
2015 Giving	Not Reported	9,605	Substituted IPEDS.
University of New Mexico - Albuquerque			
2014 Endowment	422,934	412,772	Revised 2014 NACUBO data.
University of North Dakota			
2014 Endowment	198,476	226,800	Revised 2014 NACUBO data.
2015 Giving	Not Reported	9,284	Substituted IPEDS.

Data Notes for Universities with Over $40 Million in Federal Research

University / Statistics	Original Data (dollars in thousands)	MUP Data (dollars in thousands)	Comments
University of Oklahoma - Norman			
2014 Federal R&D	108,356	53,223	Estimate 49.1% based on university documents.
2014 Total R&D	227,104	120,322	Estimate 53% based on university documents.
2015 Endowment	1,523,024	1,066,117	Estimate 70% based on published documents.
2015 Giving	317,347	252,475	Estimate 79.6% based on 2014 IPEDS.
University of Oklahoma Health Sciences Center			
2014 Federal R&D	108,356	55,133	Estimate 50.9% based on university documents.
2014 Total R&D	227,104	106,782	Estimate 47% based on university documents.
2015 Endowment	1,523,024	456,907	Estimate 30% based on published documents.
2015 Giving	317,347	64,872	Estimate 20.4% based on 2014 IPEDS.
University of Rhode Island			
2014 Endowment	118,850	132,234	Revised 2014 NACUBO data.
University of Rochester			
2014 SAT	Not Reported		Did not report SAT/ACT.
University of Tennessee - Knoxville			
2015 Endowment	1,106,924	608,873	Substituted 2015 VSE.
University of Tennessee Health Science Center			
2015 Endowment	Not Reported		Did not report to NACUBO nor VSE in 2015.
University of Texas - Austin			
2015 Endowment	24,083,150	10,507,795	Substituted 2015 VSE.
University of Texas Health Science Center - Houston			
2015 Endowment	24,083,150	306,094	Substituted 2015 VSE.
University of Texas Health Science Center - San Antonio			
2015 Endowment	24,083,150	476,632	Substituted 2015 VSE.
University of Texas MD Anderson Cancer Center			
2015 Endowment	24,083,150	1,200,742	Substituted 2015 VSE.
University of Texas Medical Branch - Galveston			
2015 Endowment	24,083,150	531,562	Substituted 2015 VSE.
University of Texas SW Medical Center - Dallas			
2015 Endowment	24,083,150	1,620,501	Substituted 2015 VSE.
University of Vermont			
2015 Endowment	Not Reported	453,653	Substituted 2015 VSE.
University of Washington - Seattle			
2015 Endowment	3,076,226	3,076,226	Estimate at least 97% is main campus.
2015 Giving	447,021	447,021	Estimate at least 97% is main campus.

Data Notes for Universities with Over $40 Million in Federal Research

University / Statistics	Original Data (dollars in thousands)	MUP Data (dollars in thousands)	Comments
University of Wisconsin - Madison			
2015 Endowment	2,465,051	2,792,622	Substituted 2015 VSE.
Wake Forest University			
2014 SAT	Not Reported		Does not require SAT/ACT.
Washington State University - Pullman			
2015 Endowment	885,777	885,777	Estimate at least 97% is main campus.
2015 Giving	106,370	106,370	Estimate at least 97% is main campus.
Weill Cornell Medical College			
2014 Federal R&D	438,834	139,514	Estimate 31.8% based on university documents.
2014 Total R&D	874,727	293,791	Estimate 33.6% based on university documents.
2015 Endowment	6,037,546	1,276,986	Substituted IPEDS.
2015 Giving	590,641	156,176	Estimate 26.4% based on 2015 IPEDS.
Woods Hole Oceanographic Institution			
2015 Endowment	Not Reported		Did not report to NACUBO nor VSE in 2015.
2015 Giving	Not Reported		No substitute data available.
Yale University			
2014 Endowment	23,900,000	23,894,800	Revised 2014 NACUBO data.
Yeshiva University			
2014 Endowment	1,093,136	1,094,558	Revised 2014 NACUBO data.
Yeshiva University			
2014 Endowment	1,093,136	1,094,558	Revised 2014 NACUBO data.

The Center for Measuring University Performance Publications

The Top American Research Universities. (MUP Center Reports, 2000-2015). [http://mup.asu.edu/publications]

What's in a Name? The Classification of Research Universities, 2015.

Tracking Academic Research Funding: The Competitive Context for the Last Ten Years, 2014.

The Best American Research Universities Ranking: Four Perspectives, 2013.

Measuring Research Performance: National and International Perspectives, 2012.

Moving Up: The Marketplace for Federal Research in America, 2011.

In Pursuit of Number One, 2010.

Research University Competition and Financial Challenges, 2009.

Competition and Restructuring the American Research University, 2008.

Rankings, Competition, and the Evolving American University, 2007.

Deconstructing University Rankings: Medicine and Engineering, and Single Campus Research Competitiveness, 2005.

Measuring and Improving Research Universities: TheCenter at Five Years, 2004.

The Sports Imperative in America's Research Universities, 2003.

University Organization, Governance, and Competitiveness, 2002.

Quality Engines: The Competitive Context for Research Universities, 2001.

The Myth of Number One: Indicators of Research University Performance, 2000.

Improving student success using technology-based analytics. *Diversity & Democracy*, Volume 17, Number 1 (2014) by Elizabeth D. Capaldi. [http://aacu.org/diversitydemocracy/2014/winter/phillips]

Rainer and Julie Martens Invited Lecture: Research Universities—the Next Five Years, *Kinesiology Review*, Volume 3, Issue 1 (2014), 4-12 by John V. Lombardi. [http://journals.humankinetics.com/kr-back-issues/kr-volume-3-issue-1-february]

Leading the University: The Roles of Trustees, Presidents, and Faculty, *Change*, 45:1 (2013), 24-32 by Richard Legon, John V. Lombardi, and Gary Rhoades. [http://www.changemag.org/Archives/Back%20Issues/ 2013/January-February%202013/leading-the-university-abstract.html]

Improving Advising Using Technology and Data Analytics, *Change*, 45:1 (2013), 48-55 by Elizabeth D. Phillips. [http://www.changemag.org/Archives/Back Issues/2013/January-February 2013/improving-advising-full.html]

How Universities Work, Baltimore: Johns Hopkins (2013) by John V. Lombardi.

Performance and Costs in Higher Education: A Proposal for Better Data. *Change*, April, 23, 8-15 (2011) by Elizabeth D. Capaldi and Craig. W. Abbey. [http://www.changemag.org/Archives/Back%20Issues/2011/March-April%202011/better-data-full.html]

Intellectual Transformation and Budgetary Savings through Academic Reorganization. *Change*, July/August, 19-27. (2009) by Elizabeth D. Capaldi. [http://www.changemag.org/Archives/Back%20Issues/July-August%202009/full-intellectual-budgetary.html]

Improving Graduation Rates: A Simple Method That Works, *Change*, 38:4 (2006), 44-58 by Elizabeth D. Capaldi, John Lombardi, and Victor Yellen. [http://jvlone.com/A%20Simple%20Method_Change2006.pdf]

Using National Data in University Rankings and Comparisons (*TheCenter Reports*, June 2003) by Denise S.Gater. [http://mup.asu.edu/gaternatldata.pdf]

A Review of Measures Used in U.S. News & World Report's "America's Best Colleges" (*TheCenter* Occasional Paper) by Denise S. Gater. [http://mup.asu.edu/Gater0702.pdf]

TheCenter Top American Research Universities: An Overview (*TheCenter Reports*, 2002) by Diane D. Craig. [http://mup.asu.edu/TARUChina.pdf]

The Competition for Top Undergraduates by America's Colleges and Universities (*TheCenter Reports*, 2001) by Denise S. Gater. [http://mup.asu.edu/gaterUG1.pdf]

The Use of IPEDS/AAUP Faculty Data in Institutional Peer Comparisons (*TheCenter Reports*, 2001) by Denise S. Gater and John V. Lombardi [http://mup.asu.edu/gaterFaculty1.pdf]

Toward Determining Societal Value Added Criteria for Research and Comprehensive Universities (*TheCenter Reports*, 2001) by Roger Kaufman. [http://mup.asu.edu/kaufman1.pdf]

U.S. News & World Report's Methodology (*TheCenter Reports*, 2001, Revised) by Denise S. Gater. [http://mup.asu.edu/usnews.html]

A Decade of Performance at the University of Florida (1990-1999) (University of Florida, 1999) by John V. Lombardi and Elizabeth D. Capaldi [http://mup.asu.edu/10yrPerformance.html]

The Center for Measuring University Performance Advisory Board

Chaouki T. Abdallah
Interim President
University of New Mexico

Arthur M. Cohen
Professor Emeritus
Division of Higher Education
Graduate School of Education and Information Studies
University of California, Los Angeles

Larry Goldstein
President, Campus Strategies, LLC

Gerardo M. Gonzalez
Dean Emeritus
Professor, Educational Leadership and Policy Studies
School of Education
Indiana University

Roger Kaufman
Professor Emeritus, Educational Psychology and Learning
Florida State University
Director, Roger Kaufman & Associates
Distinguished Research Professor
Sonora Institute of Technology

Richard H. Stanley
Senior Vice President and University Planner
Arizona State University

The Center for Measuring University Performance Staff

John V. Lombardi
MUP Director
Professor of History, University of Massachusetts Amherst
President Emeritus, University of Florida

Elizabeth D. Capaldi Phillips (d. 2017)
MUP Director
Provost Emerita, University Professor
Arizona State University

Craig W. Abbey
Research Director, MUP Center
Associate Vice Provost and
Director of Institutional Research
University at Buffalo

Diane D. Craig
Research Associate, MUP Center
University of Florida

Lynne N. Collis
Administrative Services, MUP Center

Notes

Notes

Notes